Trek East Africa

David Else

Trekking in East Africa

1st edition

Published by
   Lonely Planet Publications
   Head Office: PO Box 617, Hawthorn, Vic 3122, Australia
   Branches: PO Box 2001A, Berkeley, CA 94702, USA
               12 Barley Mow Passage, Chiswick, London W4 4PH, UK

Printed by
   Colorcraft Ltd, Hong Kong

Photographs by
   Jill Bitten (JB)
   Corinne Else (CE)
   David Else (DE)
   Jeff Williams (JW)

   Front Cover: Kilimanjaro from Little Meru (DE)
   Title Page: Mt Kenya from Mackinder's Camp
   Back Cover: Sunrise over Kilimanjaro from Mt Meru (DE)

First Published
   August 1993

Although the authors and publisher have tried to make the information as accurate as possible, they accept no responsibility for any loss, injury or inconvenience sustained by any person using this book.

National Library of Australia Cataloguing in Publication Data

Else, David
   Trekking in East Africa.

   1st ed.
   Includes index.
   ISBN 0 86442 186 9.

   1. Hiking – Africa, East – Guidebooks. 2. Africa, East – Guidebooks.
   I. Title.

916.7604

text © David Else 1993
maps © Lonely Planet 1993
photos © photographers as indicated 1993
climate charts compiled from information supplied by Patrick J Tyson, © Patrick J Tyson, 1993

All rights reserved. No part of this publication may be reproduced, stored in a retrieval system or transmitted in any form by any means, electronic, mechanical, photocopying, recording or otherwise, except brief extracts for the purpose of review, without the written permission of the publisher and copyright owner.

David Else

After hitchhiking through Europe for a couple of years, David Else kept heading south and finally reached Africa in 1983. Since then, he has travelled and trekked all over the continent, reaching most of the major mountain ranges, and several of the more obscure ones as well. He writes for a living, and also works as a tour leader in East Africa for a specialist trekking company. When he's not in Nairobi, or halfway up Kilimanjaro, David lives in Sheffield, where he walks to the shops, polishes his mountain bike and occasionally talks about rock climbing.

Dedication

To my parents, for letting me get on with it.

From the Author

Several words of thanks must go to all the people who helped me research and write this book.

Firstly, a special thankyou to my wife Corinne, who was with me a lot of the way; on the road, up the mountains, and looking over my shoulder as I tried to get the words in the right order. In her professional capacity as Dr Corinne Else MB BCh DA, she wrote the Health chapter in this book.

Thanks also to the other people who checked the route descriptions, contributed large sections of information about the places I have not been, or provided details on recent changes. To Robin Saxby and Helen Long, who valiantly trekked across Mt Elgon and Mt Kenya on some of the more unusual routes, contending with rain, mud, bamboo and charging buffalo; to Geoffrey Simpson, Mike Brydon and Graeme Watson (Crater Highlands); to Jill Bitten, Aidan Leheup, Robin Saxby (again), Nicci Haynes (for extra Kilimanjaro details); and to Michael Neumann and Jutta Musgen (Rwenzoris), Mark Kippax (Mulanje and Nyika), and Andy Black of Natural Action (Kilimanjaro and Rwenzoris).

Special thanks should also go to our various guides, who showed us the way and were good company on the mountains: Moran Idi Lewarani, Moran Charles Lenaimalda and Mzee Lele (Loroghi Hills); Kimani (Suguta Valley), Loyford Kibaara, Ambrose Karimi, John Abbas, Edwin Mwalimu (Mt Kenya); Guides Minja and Balthazar (Kilimanjaro); Daniel Masereka and Simon Bwambale (Rwenzoris); Ignus Gara (Mt Meru); Bula Sabali (Usambaras); Manfred Kmwenda and Felix Gondwe (Nyika); Austin Pindan, Raphael Maglas, Thomas Walusa (Mulanje). Extra thanks should go to Sammy Kariuki, without doubt one of the most experienced guides on Mt Kenya, and probably in the whole of East Africa.

For ground support, proofreading, advice, information and help in many other ways, thanks also to the following people. In the UK: Andy Black, Jim Grey, Rachel Toft, David Gray, Alan Morgan, Henry Osmaston, Rob Beckley, Chris Morris. Special thanks and gratitude to Guy Yeoman for detailed proofreading and constructive criticism. In the USA: Chalotte Melville, Tom and Tommy Hoskins. In Tanzania: Gratian Luhikula (Tanzanian Tourist Corporation), Benjamin Kanza (Tanzania National Parks), Geoffrey Simpson, Mike and Ishbel Brydon, Mbwa Bran, Robert M'mari, Abdi, Wesley Krause, Roman Chewa, Eric Christin, Harshit Shah. In Kenya: Connie Maina

(Kenya Wildlife Services), Paul Clarke and Graeme Watson (Mountain Club of Kenya), Bongo Woodley (Mount Kenya National Park), Jackson Mwangi, Edwin and Gail Sadd, Ken Bacia, Alan Dixson, Stewart Vetch, Mo Hussein, Clive Ward, Iain Allan, Joyce Chianda and Halewijn Scheuerman, John and Jane Bisley, David Chianda, Malcolm Gascoigne, Susan and Sara at Yare's office, Aussie Walker, James Mbugua, Patrick Wanjohi, Craig Oulton, Jane Sparrow, Karen Twining, Liz Slinn, Terry and Judy MacDowell. In Uganda: Alfred Labongo (Rwenzori Mountains National Park), Amy and Craig Ellis, Said Famao, Paul and Nathalie Vare, Jan Betlem (Mount Elgon Project), Tom Lucas, Colin Stuart. In Malawi: Mark Kippax (Mountain Club of Malawi), Carl Bruessow (Wildlife Society of Malawi), Hector Banda and Elias Jijide (Nyika National Park), Pam and Chris Badger, Mark and Angie Sprong, Blair Quick, Rosemary and Nigel Hinde, James Hinde.

From the Publisher

This edition of Trekking in East Africa was edited at the Lonely Planet office in Australia by Kay Waters. Rachel Black was responsible for design, layout, mapping, map corrections and illustrations. Margaret Jung designed the cover. Climate charts were adapted by Dan Levin. Indexing was done by Sharon Wertheim. Thanks to Margaret Jung, Matthew King, Sally Woodward and Valerie Tellini for additional illustrations. Proofing was done by Jeff Williams, who also assisted with editing and production. Thanks to James Lyon and Vicki Beale for editorial and design assistance.

Disclaimer

Although the author and publisher have done their utmost to ensure the accuracy of all information in this guide, they cannot accept any responsibility for any loss, injury or inconvenience sustained by people using this book. They cannot guarantee that the tracks and routes described have not become impassable for any reason in the interval between research and publication. The fact that a trip or area is described in this guidebook does not necessarily mean that it is a safe one for you and your walking party. You are ultimately responsible for judging your own capabilities in light of the conditions that you encounter.

Warning & Request

Things change – prices go up, schedules change, good places go bad and bad places go bankrupt – nothing stays the same. So if you find things better or worse, recently opened or long since closed, please write and tell us and help make the next edition better.

Your letters will be used to help update future editions and, where possible, important changes will also be included in a Stop Press section in reprints.

We greatly appreciate all information that is sent to us by travellers. Back at Lonely Planet we employ a hard-working readers' letters team to sort through the many letters we receive. The best ones will be rewarded with a free copy of the next edition, or another Lonely Planet guide if you prefer. We give away lots of books but, unfortunately, not every letter/postcard receives one.

Contents

MAP LEGEND

–·–·–·–	International Boundaries	—750—	Contour, Contour Interval
··········	National Park Boundaries		Volcanic Crater
–··–··–	Forest Reserve		Escarpment or Cliff
--------	The Equator	⌂	Hut with Facilities
————	Major Tarred Roads	⌂	Hut without Facilities
————	Graded Roads (unsealed)	■	Other Buildings/Hotels
--------	Ungraded Roads/Tracks	⚐	Campsite (Offical)
··············	Paths	⚐	Camping Place (Wild)
··············	Indistinct Paths	▲	Mountain, Peak
+++++++++	Railways	)(	Pass, Saddle
～⤳	Rivers, Creeks	—⫸—	Bridge
▱	Lakes	☀	Viewpoint
𝇈 𝇈 𝇈	Swamp	✈	Airport
～#～	Waterfall		Cave
▨	Glacier		

Map Legend

Preface

Eastern Africa is largely a flat, dry, bush-covered plain, but often in the distance rises a blue mountain, or perhaps a modest range of snow and ice. These visions stir the minds of imaginative travellers and make them wonder what it must be like to leave behind the hot and dusty lowland world and make their way to the ethereal heights above the clouds.

To walk upon these East African mountains can be a delight, leading to something like an earthly paradise. With every upward step the traveller experiences a thrilling transition, from the tropics, through temperate climes, to sup-alpine conditions, and even alpine conditions in the case of the three great snow-covered peaks. The high mountains are the last secret places of the continent, forever blessed with rain. A wonderful succession of nature is revealed: the flowers and birds are ever new, the streamlets fresh, and the air cool, pure and intoxicating. These experiences, though hard-won, are truly uplifting and provide the motivation for trekking in East Africa.

But before you set out, as an individual or as a member of a group, reflect on two things. First, these upland environments, whether forest, moorland or alpine, are amongst the most delicate in the world. Alas, some routes already call to mind the line that '... every prospect pleases, and only man is vile'. Treat the environment with respect – do nothing to damage it, leave behind no trace of your visit, and have the moral courage to call to task those who transgress. Second, these hills and mountains are the age-old domain of indigenous people who are poor beyond the imagination of even the most impecunious Western visitor. You do not have to come, but if you do, grant these people their dignity, behave generously with heart and hand, and let good manners, patience and integrity be your guides.

Guy Yeoman

Guy Yeoman is a mountaineer who has worked and travelled in East Africa for over 50 years, and made many expeditions into the high mountain areas, always in close companionship with local Africans. He is active in calling world attention to the continuing destruction of these unique ecosystems. In 1984 he undertook the case for the protection of the Rwenzori range by the creation of a national park, and this was successfully brought about in 1991. His book *Africa's Mountains of the Moon* was written as part of that campaign.

Introduction

Trekking on the high mountains of East Africa is like going from the tropics to the tundra and back again, often in less than a week. Here you can walk through deserts, grassy hills, dense bush, rainforest, Afro-alpine moorland and wide areas of bare rock and ice. It's all completely different to the flat savanna grasslands usually seen by visitors.

East Africa is most famous for its wildlife safaris but, in contrast to the sometimes crowded 'game parks', the mountain wilderness areas are rarely visited. Of course, it takes some physical effort but trekking here means you can leave the vehicles and the hotels behind and experience the wilderness of Africa at first hand.

This book describes a selection of treks in Tanzania, Kenya, Uganda and Malawi. All the main peaks and ranges are covered, and several smaller mountains and lesser-known trekking areas are also included. Some areas are personal favourites, based on my experience of trekking in many different parts of the region. Most of the trekking areas described can be reached by public transport with a minimum of hassle.

Most of the treks are between four and ten days in length, and some can be extended. There's a wide range to choose from: a tough traverse of Kilimanjaro, via the summit glaciers, will certainly appeal to hardy hikers looking to work up a bit of a sweat, while other people will prefer less demanding walks across the wooded Loroghi Hills or the rolling grasslands of the Nyika Plateau.

There are different types of trekking in East Africa. You may prefer to carry all your own gear and be completely self-contained for a week in the wilderness, or you might be happier with the help of local guides and porters. If time is limited, or you're new to trekking, you can join an organised trek, arranged either locally or in your home country, where everything is taken care of and all you have to do is enjoy the walk.

The costs involved can differ too. If money (or lack of it) is a consideration, you can be at one with the wilderness for few dollars a day, while at the other end of the scale you can join a top-quality organised trek for a few hundred dollars a day. And, of course, there's a whole range of choices in between these two extremes.

Generally, the treks keep to tracks or paths, although paths in the more remote areas are often very faint, or non-existent. Some treks include sections through dense bush or across open moorland, where map-reading skills or the services of a local guide may be required. This book also covers opportunities for wandering away from the more usual routes.

Trekking is not climbing. Although there are rock and ice mountaineering routes on several of the peaks covered in this book, none of the treks involve any technical ascents and (with one possible exception) you will not need ropes, crampons or other hardware. Some treks include optional sections of scrambling, or some fairly exposed sections of walking, but generally it's 'hands in pockets' all the way.

Even though there's no technical climbing, it is still possible to reach the summit of many of the mountains. As well as the pleasures of unspoilt wilderness walking, there's the added satisfaction of getting all the way to the top – an extra attraction for 'peak-baggers'.

Most of the treks described are through national parks. By visiting these mountain wilderness areas we can help to increase their chances of survival, provided we do not destroy them in the process.

Although most of the treks are in wilderness areas, several sections also pass through local villages and cultivated land, or cross areas of grazing land used by nomadic pastoral people. On foot, you will have time to stop and meet the local people, and see them as real human beings rather than as colourful extras in the landscape.

The mountains of East Africa rise as solitary peaks and ranges above the surrounding plains. Most treks take about a week, so trekkers usually include two or more mountains in their visit (presuming they are staying for three weeks or more – and allowing time for travel in between). Combinations might be Mt Kenya and Kilimanjaro, Mt Elgon and the Rwenzoris, or Kilimanjaro and Nyika or Mulanje, plus some of the shorter treks on the region's smaller peaks. This involves travel by local transport between mountains, and often across national borders. This book gives enough information to cover the direct routes from one trekking area to the next.

For further travel in other parts of the region (eg the coast, the lakes and the lowland national parks) you should use a more general guidebook.

Trekking in East Africa is rewarding and enlightening. I have been addicted to the mountains and wilderness areas here for many years, and I am sure you will enjoy them also. Beyond the mountains described here, experienced trekkers will find plenty of other areas for further exploration. I wish you the best of luck and hope you'll report back so your information can be used for the next edition.

Go well, and *safiri salama*.

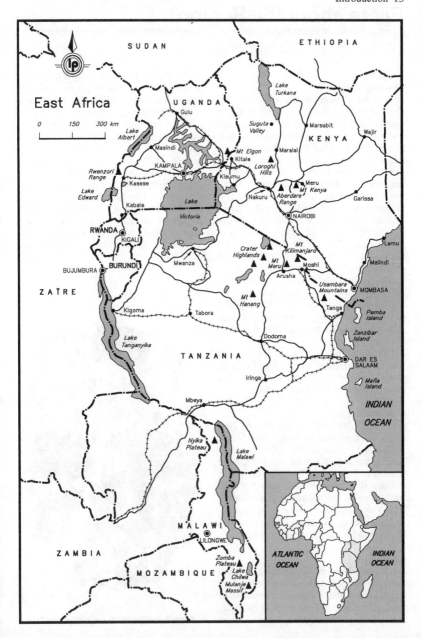

Facts about the Region

HISTORY
The Beginning

In *On the Origin of Species...*, Charles Darwin stated that humans and the 'higher apes' probably had a common ancestor, and because these apes were found in East Africa, he concluded that humankind originated there. This was based on a fair bit of guess-work, but Darwin's theory was later supported by the discovery of ancient hominoid (human-like) skulls at the Olduvai Gorge in Tanzania, on the shores of Lake Turkana in Kenya, and along the Kagera River in Uganda. Some of these skulls have been dated at 2½ million years old, and it seems there were at least three different species of hominid wandering around on the plains of Africa at that time. Archaeologists believe that two of these early human species declined and vanished, while the third evolved into *Homo sapiens*, giving East Africa a strong claim to the title 'Cradle of Humanity'.

Of course, many of these theories are based on conjecture, as is much of African history, usually deduced from oral tradition and sketchy archaeological evidence.

The Stone Ages

Around 50,000 BC, *Homo sapiens* first began to experiment with stone tools, but it wasn't until after 10,000 BC that stone-making techniques and the use of fire were mastered. At this time, early humans also developed a basic language and began to form hunting and gathering communities. This period is called the New Stone Age and, in some areas, this pattern of life remained unchanged for many thousands of years.

Migrations

During the New Stone Age, while some groups continued as hunter-gatherers, others began to learn about agriculture. Evidence of food production and the tending of cattle, dating from about 1000 BC, has been found in the highland and Rift Valley regions of southern Kenya and northern Tanzania. These were apparently introduced by people from the highlands of what is now Ethiopia.

This was the first of the 'great migrations' that are an important feature of East Africa's history. In the last 3000 years, waves of peoples have crossed and re-crossed the region, some groups searching for new territory as their populations grew, others forced to move by climatic changes. The movements inevitably had a knock-on effect too, as groups being invaded from one side expanded in the other direction. Most migrations took place over hundreds of years, and were made up of many short moves (from

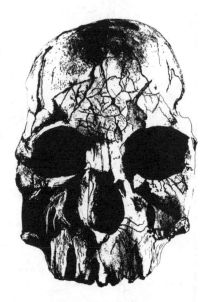

Ancient skull, possibly 2½ million years old

14

valley to valley, or from one cultivation area to the next), with dominant peoples slowly absorbing and assimilating other groups in the process.

The most significant migration was that of the Bantu people. Armed with iron tools to clear forest and cultivate more effectively, the Bantu migrated from the area that is now Cameroon, through the Zaire basin and onto the East African plateau, arriving in the region around 100 BC. Over the next thousand years they spread across present-day Uganda, Kenya, Tanzania, Malawi and several other areas.

Across East Africa the various Bantu peoples generally lived in small farming communities, but around 1300 AD a large kingdom called Chwezi was established in the west of the region. In the 16th century, Nilotic people (originally from the southern Nile Valley) migrated into the area and intermixed with the Bantu. At this time, the Chwezi kingdom split and the Buganda kingdom was founded, which remained in place until the arrival of the British at the end of the 19th century. (For more details on the terms Bantu, Nilotic and Cushitic, see the People section.)

Meanwhile, in northern Kenya, it is thought that another Bantu kingdom called Shungwaya existed until an invasion of Cushitic people from the north around 1600 forced the Bantu (including the Kikuyu and Kamba groups) south to their present territories to the west and east of Mt Kenya.

At around the same period, in Malawi, the Tumbuka and Phoka people (also Bantu) migrated into the north of the country (their tradition does not agree on where from) between the 14th and 16th centuries AD. Meanwhile, in the south, the Maravi people (of whom the Chewa became the dominant group) came in from present-day Zaire and established a large and powerful kingdom that spread all over southern Malawi and parts of present-day Mozambique and Zambia.

In the 18th century, another wave of Nilotic people, the warlike Maasai, spread into northern Kenya and then down the Rift Valley into Tanzania. Smaller Bantu groups, such as the Chagga in the Kilimanjaro area, retreated to high ground for safety, while the Kikuyu remained in the forested highlands on Mt Kenya and the Aberdare Range.

In the early 19th century, the Ngoni people, who were related to the Zulu and just as warlike, migrated to Malawi from the south and settled in the middle of the country, conquering the Chewa, while another group of Ngoni pushed further north into Tanzania. It is thought that their northern expansion was stopped by the Maasai heading south through the same area. Around the same time, the Yao arrived from northern Mozambique, settling around the Shire Highlands and the southern end of Lake Malawi, and forcing the Maravi inhabitants into slavery, and selling them to slave traders from the coast.

The Coast

In the early part of the first millennium AD, Arabs from the area now called Yemen sailed around the Horn of Africa and began exploring the east coast. They traded with the local inhabitants, buying mainly ivory, gold and slaves to take back to Arabia.

Pillar tomb in Gedi, a ruined 15th-century Arab-African town, Kenya

Trade was brisk. The merchants brought glass and metal spearheads from Arabia and, later, spices from India and porcelain from China. They also introduced new crops such as bananas and yams. By 700 AD the Arabs had founded several trading settlements on the coast from Mogadishu (in present-day Somalia) down to Kilwa (in southern Tanzania). By this time, the Bantu people had arrived on the coast from the interior, and the Arabs intermarried with them, gradually creating a mixed language and culture, called Swahili.

Islam had been founded by the prophet Mohammed in Arabia around 600 AD and the Arab traders brought the new faith with them to east Africa; by 1100 AD Islam was practised widely all along the coast.

The Swahili civilisation continued to flourish and the towns became wealthy independent city-states ruled by sultans, although they maintained a close link with Arabia. The wealth was based on trade goods from the African hinterland but no attempt was made to conquer land or create settlements in the interior. The coast and the interior existed as completely separate worlds.

Coral relief from the ruined 600 year-old village of Jumba La Mtwana, Kenya

Arabs, Europeans & Slavery

Things started to change when the first Europeans arrived on the scene. Since the early 1400s, Portuguese navigators had been pushing further round the West African coast, searching for a route to China. The breakthrough came in 1498 when a ship under the command of Vasco de Gama rounded the Cape of Good Hope and sailed up the East African coast from the south.

De Gama was not welcomed by the sultan at Mombasa, although the sultan of Malindi (a great rival of Mombasa) was friendly towards the new arrivals. But diplomacy was not a Portuguese strong point – over the next few years they bombarded and looted several Swahili cities.

The Portuguese remained on the East African coast for 200 years, trading gold from the interior and exporting slaves to work on the plantations in the Americas and East Indies.

But the Arabs did not forget their East African outposts – throughout the 17th century, Omani ships continually threatened the Portuguese trading stations. By the early 1700s the Portuguese had been routed completely and the east African coast was back in the hands of the Arabs.

Throughout the 18th century the Omani Arabs rebuilt their trade links and their cities, and in 1832 the Sultan of Oman, Seyyid Said, moved his capital and entire court to Zanzibar, an island about halfway down the East African coast, and part of present-day Tanzania.

During the first half of the 19th century, Arab slavers pushed into the interior and established several trading centres, including Tabora, in present-day Tanzania, and Karonga on Lake Malawi. The Arabs exploited rivalries between local tribes, encouraging powerful groups to conquer their neighbours and sell them into slavery. The slaves were then forced to the coast, from where they were taken to Zanzibar, which was fast becoming the centre of a very lucrative trade in slaves and ivory from the interior, and spices (particularly cloves) from the island itself.

Exploration & Empire

By the mid-19th century, the interest of the powerful countries in northern Europe – particularly Britain – centred on two things: the abolition of the slave trade, and the quest to discover the source of the Nile. This period, from around 1840 to 1880, is often called (by Europeans) the Golden Age of Exploration, when great names such as Livingstone, Stanley, Burton and Speke, confident, brave and certain of their racial superiority, mapped and recorded the interior of Africa.

For the first time Europeans saw the great lakes of Tanganyika, Victoria and Malawi, the sources of the Nile, the Rift Valley and the snow-capped mountains of Mt Kenya, Kilimanjaro and the Rwenzoris. (See the section on Exploration in East Africa.)

The explorers returned home with the reports of their discoveries, but at first the governments of Britain and the other European powers saw the interior of Africa as hostile and unproductive. At this stage there was no incentive to occupy these lands.

This attitude changed towards the end of the 19th century. Germany, the rising power in Europe, had seen French activity in West Africa, and watched Britain's interests begin to grow in East Africa. Bismarck, the German leader, also wanted 'a place in the sun'. The reaction was sudden: in a very short period, the European powers all laid claim to territories, mainly to keep the opposing nations out rather than for any other reason. This period became known as the 'Scramble for Africa'.

The various claims of the European powers were settled at the Berlin Conference of 1884-85, when most of the continent of Africa was split neatly into colonies. France got most of West Africa, Germany got some territory in the east (now Tanzania), King Leopold of Belgium got the Congo (now Zaire), Portugal kept Mozambique and Angola, and Britain got more or less everything else. The European powers were happy with the results of the conference. What the Africans thought of it remains unrecorded – they weren't invited to attend.

EXPLORATION IN EAST AFRICA

The history of exploration in East Africa is of special interest to trekkers, as much of the early speculation and 'discovery' was based around the region's great snow-covered mountains. And, of course, the early explorers trekked everywhere themselves, across the great plains and up into the highlands around the mountains. When you're on the train from Mombasa to Nairobi, or strolling through the beautiful forest on the slopes of Mt Kenya, or even getting near the summit of Kilimanjaro, remember those early pioneers, and their porters (who had to carry loads as well), who foot-slogged and trail-blazed the whole way.

The Source of the Nile

Exploration in East Africa has always been linked to the search for the source of the Nile. As long ago as 400 BC the Greek geographer Herodotus travelled through Egypt, and south beyond Aswan, hoping to reach the source of the great river that had maintained the empires of Egypt for thousands of years.

A few hundred years later the Roman emperor Nero sent a military expedition on the same mission. His soldiers got as far as The Sudd, a massive swamp in present-day Sudan. On their way south they probably passed the junction of the Blue and White Niles, near present-day Khartoum.

It was also realised by the early geographers that the source of the Nile could be reached from the coast of East Africa. Legend has it that a Greek merchant-traveller called Diogenes went inland from a point somewhere on the north coast of present-day Tanzania, reached two great lakes and saw a snow-covered range of mountains which, he said, were the source of the Nile. The legend was recorded by the Greek Marinus of Tyre, who wrote a guide for shipping on the Indian Ocean in the second half of the 1st century AD.

From that description, in the 2nd century the geographer Ptolemy produced a map of Africa showing the River 'Nilus', the two lakes, called 'Nili Paludes', and the range of mountains which he called 'Lune Montes' –

the Mountains of the Moon. The name is evocative, but it is not known where the term 'moon' derived from. Maybe it implied 'beyond the world'; on his map Ptolemy annotated the region south of the range as *Terra Incognita* (unknown territory).

It has also been proposed that Ptolemy was referring to the mountains of Ethiopia and Lake Tana, the source of the Blue Nile. This is unlikely, and not suggested by the map, although much of this was based on conjecture and ancient, second-hand story-telling.

Explorers

The legendary Mountains of the Moon and the source of the White Nile inspired and intrigued European story-tellers and geographers for centuries afterwards, but no new information was received about the mysterious snow-covered mountains of Africa until the mid-19th century, when the first British and German missionary-explorers arrived on the east coast and started to push inland. Often their travels lasted for several months, or even years, and the explorers, along with their followers, suffered considerable deprivation and hardship.

Rebmann & Krapf Kilimanjaro was the first of the great East African mountains to be seen by a European. It was sighted in 1848 by a Swiss missionary called Johannes Rebmann, a member of the London-based Church Missionary Society. With his colleague Ludwig Krapf, he travelled inland from Mombasa, following a route similar to the one probably taken by Diogenes and at that time used by Arab slave traders. Krapf recorded that the local Chagga people called the mountain 'Kibo', which he understood to mean 'snow', but the Swahili people of the coast called it 'Kilima Njaro', meaning either 'Mountain of Greatness' or 'Mountain of Caravans'.

Rebmann and Krapf also travelled south from Mombasa and reached the Usambara Mountains. This was a fertile area, with a cool climate, much more pleasant than the coast. They found the local people agreeable

too and recommended that a mission be built in the area. Krapf also went north-west, to the region around Kitui. From here, in late 1849, he became the first European to see Mt Kenya. He called it 'Kimaji Kegnia', which he said meant 'Mountain of Whiteness' in the local language, and described the snow on the higher peaks and the 'two large horns' of the twin summits.

Rebmann and Krapf's descriptions of the huge snow-covered peak of Kilimanjaro were published in London in 1849, but they were refuted by W D Cooley, the most influential geographer of the time, and several other members of the Royal Geographical Society (RGS). This was not because they thought snow couldn't exist on the equator, as is often supposed (snow was already known on the equatorial Andes), but because the sighting lent weight to the theory that Kilimanjaro's snows were the source of the Nile. At the time, geographers were divided into two camps, some holding that the source of the Nile was in East Africa, others believing that it arose in Central Africa. Cooley and his followers were in the latter camp. It took until 1861, when the sightings were confirmed by Baron Karl von der Decken, an aristocratic German explorer, for Rebmann and Krapf's account to be accepted.

Burton & Speke After the snow-capped peaks, the source of the Nile still obsessed most geographers. In 1857 the British explorers Richard Burton and John Hanning Speke were sent by the RGS to East Africa, to find the source of the Nile and settle the disputes. They followed the old slave routes for six months to reach the settlement of Ujiji on the east shore of Lake Tanganyika. On their return journey Burton became ill and Speke travelled northwards alone. He reached Lake Victoria, near present-day Mwanza, in August 1858, the first European to see this huge inland sea.

Speke & Grant In 1862 Speke returned to East Africa with another British explorer, James Grant. They retraced Speke and Burton's original route, then travelled to the north side of Lake Victoria, eventually reaching a large river that flowed northwards out of the lake. To prove that it was the Nile, they followed the river downstream to reach Gondokoro, near Juba in southern Sudan, which then was the limit of exploration from the north. This filled the gap, and finally solved the riddle of the source of the Nile.

Livingstone Meanwhile, further south, another British explorer was also busy. Between 1842 and 1856, David Livingstone explored the Kalahari Desert and the Upper Zambezi, and crossed the continent from the east to the west coast. On his return to Britain, he spoke at several public meetings about the 'undiscovered' interior of Africa. A speech at Cambridge University in 1857 led to the founding of the Universities Mission in Central Africa (UMCA), whose aim was to establish missions and promote the spread of Christianity.

When Livingstone returned to Africa in 1858 to explore the Zambezi region, he was accompanied by seven UMCA missionaries. On a small steamboat, Livingstone and his party travelled up the Zambezi River, and then the Shire River. They reached Lake Malawi in September 1859 and explored much of its western shore. By 1861 the first UMCA mission had been built, although it suffered many problems, including the deaths of several missionaries and conflict with the local people. The surviving missionaries withdrew to Zanzibar and abandoned the mission for several years.

Livingstone returned to the region around Lake Malawi in 1868, then travelled north to reach the southern end of Lake Tanganyika. He knew of Ujiji from Speke and Burton's accounts, and reached there in early 1869. In July of that year he pushed even further north, intending to be gone for a few months (a short jaunt by his standards) but he was not seen or heard of for over two years. Livingstone was found by Henry Stanley (a Welsh-American journalist) on the banks of Lake Tanganyika in late 1871, when Stanley uttered the immortal words: 'Dr Livingstone, I presume'.

Stanley Stanley returned to Africa in 1874 and the following year he became probably the first European to see the Rwenzori Mountains, although at the time he didn't realise it. Somewhere to the west of Lake Victoria he recorded a faint sighting of a distant mountain range, but made no attempt at that time to find out more.

Stanley returned to Africa again in 1887. This time, his aim was to rescue Emin Pasha, a German who had settled in Africa, taken an Islamic name and become governor of the Anglo-Egyptian province of Equatoria. Emin Pasha had been trapped by the forces of the Mahdi, who two years before had defeated the army of General Gordon. Stanley sailed round Africa to the mouth of the Congo (Zaire) River, and headed inland from there.

Of all the early European pioneering journeys through Africa, this one was the worst. Conditions were appalling: heat, rain, disease, hunger, and attacks from local people, through 3000 km of near-impenetrable forest. Stanley was ruthless. He solved most problems by beating or shooting his hapless load-bearers. After a few months of slow progress he became impatient, named half his company the 'rear column' and simply abandoned them in the middle of the forest. It took him another 14 months to reach Lake Albert, where Emin Pasha had a camp.

Stanley was annoyed to find Emin and his troops in good condition, with plenty of supplies. In fact, Emin gave a lot of his stuff to Stanley's party. As one of his men later wrote, 'the rescuers were rescued'

In his accounts of this expedition, Stanley recorded a sighting of a vast mountain covered with snow but he did not seem to connect this with the range he had seen on his second expedition in 1875. He refers to the range as 'Ruwenzori', a corruption of the local name meaning 'Hill of Rain', and presumed them to be the Mountains of the Moon described by the early geographers. But even here, although Stanley claimed discovery of the range, some of his officers had already spotted it at least a month earlier – Stanley had ignored their reports, and subsequently got the glory.

The First Ascents

By now, the explorers were not just looking at the mountains from far off, but actually going up them. In 1871, another British missionary called Charles New walked for several days up Kilimanjaro to reach the snow line at an altitude above 4000 metres. He started his expedition up the mountain in the small settlement of Moshi, today the base for trekking on Kilimanjaro, and was helped by the local chief, called Mandara, after whom one of the huts on the mountain is named.

Mandara was still around in 1883, when the Scottish explorer Joseph Thomson passed through the foothills of Kilimanjaro on his way to explore northern Kenya. Thomson also skirted the edge of the Nyandarua Mountains, renaming them the Aberdare Range, and got to the forest on the western slopes of Mt Kenya. He then crossed the Rift Valley and continued east to reach Lake Victoria, catching an unexpected glimpse of Mt Elgon on the way.

The next explorer to get high on Kilimanjaro was Count Samuel Teleki, an Austro-Hungarian aristocrat who mounted a large private expedition across East Africa in 1887. But Teleki was not just a rich man playing games. With his colleague Ludwig Von Hohnel, Teleki travelled to the far north of present-day Kenya, through the Suguta Valley, one of the hottest parts of Africa, to reach Lake Turkana, the legendary Jade Sea. On their route from the coast, Teleki and Von Hohnel reached The Saddle of Kilimanjaro between the main peaks of Kibo and Mawenzi. They also passed the Aberdare Mountains (Nyandarua), which they called the Sattima Range, and reached an altitude of around 4000 metres on Mt Kenya, as far as the base of the main peaks.

The Rwenzori Range was the last of the major mountains to be climbed to any significant height by the European explorers. In 1889, after their earlier sightings, Stanley and Emin Pasha explored the area, and a member of their team, a Lieutenant Stairs, reached a point at about 3000 metres on the north-west side of the range.

After more than 2000 years of legend and conjecture, and half a century of frantic exploration, the major mountains of East Africa had been seen by Europeans; by the first years of the 20th century, the summits had also been conquered: Hans Mayer reached the summit of Kilimanjaro in 1889; Halford Mackinder finally climbed Batian, the highest point on Mt Kenya, 10 years later; and in 1906, the Duke of Abruzzi polished off the period of achievement by climbing most of the major peaks in the Rwenzoris.

Gregory

Mention should be made of John Gregory, a Scottish geologist who explored parts of the Rift Valley in Kenya during the 1890s. From his studies of the huge escarpments near Mt Longonot and Lake Bogoria in Kenya he deduced that the Rift Valley was created by sinking between parallel fault lines, rather than more normal erosion by water and ice (see the Geography section in this chapter for more details). He coined the term 'Rift Valley' and the eastern section of the valley is sometimes called the Gregory Rift after him. Away from the Rift Valley, Gregory was the first explorer to study the geology of Mt Kenya in great detail. He also noticed and recorded with similar attention to detail the effects of altitude sickness.

GEOGRAPHY

Africa is the largest continent in the world but, geographically, it is not a land of great contrasts. It can be divided into two main geographical regions, called simply High and Low Africa, on either side of the line that runs diagonally across the continent from the mouth of the Zaire River to the Red Sea coast in northern Ethiopia.

High Africa consists of the eastern and southern areas of the continent, which are made up mainly of plateau between 1000 and 2000 metres above sea level. Low Africa consists of the western and northern areas of the continent, which lie mainly between 200 and 1000 metres. The region covered by this book is in High Africa.

The high plateau of East Africa is dissected by the Afro-Arab Rift System, more commonly known as the Great Rift Valley, a 6500-km fissure in the earth's crust that stretches from Turkey to Mozambique. In the region north of Lake Turkana, the valley splits in two. The eastern branch, where it cuts a deep gash through Kenya and Tanzania, is often called the Great Rift Valley, where features include sheer escarpments, a chain of lakes (including some of the largest in Africa), hot springs, steaming fissures and volcanic cones.

The western branch of the Rift is on the other side of Lake Victoria, stretching from the Uganda-Zaire border, down Lake Tanganyika and into southern Tanzania. Here the lakes are even larger, and Tanganyika is the deepest lake in Africa. The two branches meet in northern Malawi. The Rift Valley continues down Lake Malawi and into Mozambique to finally fizzle out near the mouth of the Zambezi River.

Geologists say that the Great Rift Valley is where the continent of Africa is literally breaking apart. In the last few million years, huge chunks of land have sunk between giant cracks in the earth's surface. Beyond the valley wall, mountains were formed when gargantuan amounts of magma (molten rock) erupted upwards through these huge cracks.

Most of East Africa's major mountains were created in this way. Kilimanjaro, Mt Meru and the Crater Highlands in Tanzania, Mt Kenya and the Aberdare Range in Kenya, and Mt Elgon on the Kenya-Uganda border are all old volcanoes formed by the movements of the Great Rift Valley. Of the major mountains described in this book, only the Rwenzori and the plateaus of Malawi are not volcanic, but even they are the result of the uplifting associated with the formation of the Rift.

It's fair to say that without the Great Rift Valley there'd certainly be far fewer mountains in East Africa, and certainly a lot less trekking to be done.

CLIMATE

The main feature of East Africa's climate is the band of rain that moves across the region between northern Uganda and the south of Malawi. This band is called the inter-tropical convergence zone and is created when warm air rising in the tropical regions cools over the equator. As the air cools, the moisture in it condenses to form rain. The band of rain follows the apparent movement of the sun as the earth tilts on its axis. It is at its most northerly point in July and at its most southerly in January. Because it crosses East Africa twice each year, most areas get two rainy seasons and two dry seasons.

In Kenya and Uganda the dry seasons are generally from December to February and from June to September. In northern Tanzania the dry seasons are at more or less the same time as Kenya's, although they tend to start and end slightly later. In southern Tanzania and Malawi there is only one dry season, from April to September or October. (More details about each country's climate are given in the individual country chapters.)

During the rainy season, most mornings are clear, getting hotter towards midday, and then rain falls as a shower or a deluge in the afternoon.

Away from the highlands of the interior, weather patterns on the low coastal strip are hot and humid, and are influenced by ocean currents and monsoonal winds. Here it can rain at any time, but the heaviest falls come between March and June.

In recent years, the climate of East Africa – and, indeed, the whole world – has become harder to predict. Rainfall levels are lower than they were 10 years ago; the rainy seasons seem to start later and end earlier. Droughts in marginal areas all over East Africa have become increasingly common, and even in areas such as Malawi, where once the seasons were as reliable as clockwork, the rains now come late, if at all.

East Africa is cooler than other equatorial regions of the world – its climate is more temperate than equatorial – because of the strong influence of altitude. And as altitude increases, so does its effect on the climate.

Even though they lie virtually on the equator, the isolated mountain massifs of Eastern Africa, such as Mt Kenya and Kilimanjaro, have a complete range of climatic conditions. A trek on one of these mountains is like going from the tropics to the tundra and back again, usually in less than a week! Starting from dry savanna plains, you pass through dense rainforest, and zones of temperate heath and moorland, before reaching the bare rock and ice of the high peaks.

Protea flower

FLORA

As altitude influences the climate of the East African mountains, so it also has a great effect on the vegetation. The major mountains stand as isolated peaks or ranges above the plains, and the various types of flora are classified very broadly into concentric zones according to altitude. Generally, the lower slopes are wet and warm, with luxurious growth and many different species. Higher up the mountain, the climate becomes drier but colder (except in the Rwenzoris where it becomes colder and wetter), with increasingly extreme variations between day and night temperatures, and the vegetation becomes less diverse and more specialised.

These zones of vegetation occur in a similar pattern on all the major mountains of East Africa, although their width and density,

and the range of species they contain, varies considerably between mountains and even between areas on the same mountain. For example, species more normally found on the lower slopes can grow higher up the mountain in sheltered valleys, while highland plants may be found on exposed ridges further down.

The flora of the East African mountains is very rich, and many species are unique to the region. In this section, only the common species, which you're more likely to see and easily recognise, are described. The common English names have been used for the plants, with their genus name in italics (sometimes this is the same).

Mount Kenya contains characteristics of all the major mountains, so its pattern of vegetation is described in detail here. Differences between Mt Kenya and the other mountains are also outlined. (Throughout this section, altitudes are approximate.)

Mt Kenya

Lower Montane Forest Much of the land around the lower slopes of the mountains has been cleared and farmed, but where the natural vegetation remains, above 2000 metres, it is usually dense montane forest, containing many large trees including the *Octea* or East African camphor, a tall species, often buttressed and with a dark red fluted trunk. Lower montane forest grows particularly on the wet southern and eastern slopes of Mt Kenya, where it forms a dense barrier; there are no regularly used trekking routes on this side of the mountain.

Upper Montane Forest On the drier northern slopes the trees are still large, although their canopy is less dense. This zone is called upper montane forest. The main trees here are the East African yellow wood or 'podo' *(Podocarpus)*, and the juniper, or African pencil cedar *(Juniperus)*. Both these trees are very tall, with straight trunks, although the bark on the juniper is pale brown and the branches grow much lower down the main trunk. The bark on the podo is pale grey and very rough. To further help identification, juniper leaves are triangular, whereas podo leaves are long and narrow.

Also in this zone you may see shorter trees, such as the East African olive *(Olea)*, with smooth pale-grey bark and a dense canopy of olive-green leaves, and pillar wood *(Cassipourea)*, about the same size as the olive, but with a straighter trunk, lined bark and darker leaves.

In high or low montane forests, you may also see the *Nuxia* tree, with stumpy trunk, crooked branches and a bushy canopy of green leaves and white flowers, or the many-tentacled strangler fig *(Ficus)* growing round one of the other trees.

Another feature of the upper montane forest is the great range of lichens, mosses and ferns that grow on the trees. The most obvious is *Usnea*, known more appropriately as 'old man's beard'.

Bamboo At around 2500 metres, the forest gives way to the bamboo zone, which is also much denser on the wet southern slopes, and almost nonexistent on the north. Some bamboo trunks are very thick; the plants can grow to heights of over 15 metres. Bamboo grows very quickly and can colonise areas where the original vegetation has been destroyed. It is also very hard (or impossible) to walk through, unless you're on a cut path.

Hagenia-Hypericum Beyond the bamboo, at about 2900 metres, is a small zone of East African rosewood *(Hagenia)*, trees about 12 metres high with red bark, crooked branches and huge clusters of leaves, and Giant St John's Wort *(Hypericum)*, a large bush around 10 metres high, with long, thin stalks and leaves, and bright orange flowers. These plants are usually well-spaced, with grass in between, creating open 'glades'.

Heath & Moorland Above 3200 metres, trees can no longer grow, and the main plants are the giant heathers *(Erica* and *Philippia)*, which are similar in appearance to the heather in temperate countries, except that some species grow over 10 metres high. In the lower part of this zone, you'll also see

protea bushes, about two metres high with large red flowers. If you are particularly lucky you will see the red Mackinder's lily.

In the upper moorland, grass is the dominant vegetation, growing in humps or tussocks about half a metre high, which can make moorland walking very tiring! Also in this zone are the dry, delicate 'everlasting' flowers *(Helichrysum)*, of which there are several species, varying in size and colour.

The plants that dominate the upper moorland zone are the giant groundsel *(Senecio)* and the giant lobelia *(Lobelia),* growing between the tussock grass above 3500 metres. These are the classic symbols of

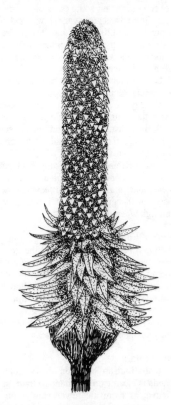

Giant lobelia

African mountain vegetation, and unique to this region. These plants have relatives in temperate countries which are usually only a few centimetres across, but on the mountains of East Africa they grow to massive dimensions. Biologists believe that this phenomenon of 'gigantism' helps the plants survive the severe cold and extremes of temperature that occur each day. Basically, big things take up more heat and lose the heat more slowly, and the inside of the plant is better insulated. There are various species: the largest are tree-groundsels, which look like shaggy cabbages on gnarled poles, can grow well over five metres tall and in dense concentrations on some parts of the mountain. Groundsels grow very slowly and up to a great age (120 years) and flower irregularly, once every decade or more, when large stalks of yellow flowers grow from the centre of the 'cabbage'.

Lobelias have narrower, firmer leaves, in a circular clump which opens and closes every day to catch sunlight and moisture. From the centre of this circle grows a single stalk of delicate flowers and leaves, sometimes called the 'ostrich plume', which can grow to around two metres tall.

Also in this zone you may find lady's mantle *(Alchemila)*, a low plant with narrow stems and small pale green leaves, gowing between the groundsels, and hard to walk through when there's no path.

High Altitude Desert As you gain height, the grass becomes thinner, and the groundsels become smaller, until about 4300 metres, where you get above most of the vegetation and reach the zone called high altitude desert, or 'nival'. The only thing that grows here is bright orange lichen, or maybe a 'lost' groundsel or everlasting in the more sheltered spots between the rocks.

Kilimanjaro

The distinction between the vegetation bands is clearer on Kilimanjaro than on Mt Kenya, as there are fewer valleys on the upper slopes of the mountain, so intermixing is limited. There are also fewer bands, as Kili has no significant bamboo forest, and no *Hagenia-Hypericum* zone.

Kilimanjaro receives less rain than Mt Kenya and the ground is also drier, as the lava rock is very porous. Consequently, the montane forest contains many of the trees found on the dry slopes on Mt Kenya, and the treeline is lower, with the forest giving way abruptly to heath at about 3000 metres.

The very extensive zone of giant heathers and moorland spreads up to about 3800 metres. Giant groundsels and lobelias occur in this zone, although not in such large numbers as on Mt Kenya.

The vegetation thins out almost completely above 4000 metres, apart from a few deep valleys. Above this level is Kilimanjaro's high altitude desert zone, which is similar to Mt Kenya's but much larger.

The Rwenzori Range

The major feature of the Rwenzoris is the very wet climate. Even when it's not raining, the mountains are continually covered in mist and cloud. But this cloud acts like a blanket and the temperature variations between day and night are less pronounced on the Rwenzoris than on Mt Kenya or on Kilimanjaro.

Also, the range's many deep valleys provide shelter. Consequently, growth is very luxuriant and the vegetation zones generally extend to higher altitudes, although the valleys create a lot of intermixing.

The montane forest and bamboo extends up to 3500 metres. There is no distinct *Hagenia-Hypericum* zone, although both species occur. Beyond the forest, the heath and moorland zone extends to about 4200 metres, and the giant heather, giant groundsels and giant lobelias here are even bigger than on the other mountains. There are small nival zones above 4200 metres on the range's several peaks.

Other Mountains

The other large mountains of East Africa generally share the characteristic zonal vegetation pattern of the major mountains. On

Mt Elgon and the Aberdare Range, the montane forest and bamboo extend to about 3000 metres, with small areas of *Hagenia*, and zones of heath and moorland continue to the summits. These mountains are too wet and low to have nival zones.

Several unique species occur on these mountains: Mt Elgon has particularly tall podo and olive trees in the forest zone, and its own species of lobelia in the moorland. The Aberdare Range has a subspecies of lobelia *(L. deckenii satimae)*, which is even more localised, being found only on the slopes below Satima, the summit peak.

Mount Meru is of similar height, but much drier. The montane forest contains similar species to those of Kilimanjaro and the northern slopes of Mt Kenya up to about 2800 metres, plus areas of giant St John's wort and *Hagenia* up to 3000 metres. The heath zone extends to 3500 metres and there are a few groundsels in the very small moorland, but beyond 3600 metres, the mountain consists of bare rock.

FAUNA
Animals

The vast range of vegetation types on the East African mountains creates a similarly vast range of wildlife habitats. Most species occur in the forests, as animals depend on plants for food. As the vegetation decreases with altitude, and conditions become increasingly harsh, so animals become more scarce. Even though East Africa is famous for its wildlife, generally you won't see much in the way of large animals while trekking on the mountains. Large mammal populations are small, and most things will run away long before you even know they were there.

The forested lower slopes of most of the major mountains are inhabited by elephant and buffalo, but these are unlikely to be seen. (Mount Meru is an exception, as you will almost certainly see buffalo, plus giraffe and zebra, here.) There may still be a few rhino hiding deep in the forests, but sightings are extremely rare. You're more likely to see waterbuck, bushbuck, duiker (all members of the antelope family) or giant forest hog, bush pig, or forest warthog, but you'll still have to be lucky.

The mammals you've got most chance of seeing are monkeys. The distinctive black and white colobus monkey, with shaggy coat and brush-like tail, occurs in many of the mountains. You may also see vervet monkey, mainly grey, with a black face and distinctive blue genitalia) in the forest and bamboo of Mt Kenya, or blue monkey (mainly dark, with short fur and a long thin tail) on Kilimanjaro. Mount Meru and Kilimanjaro also have groups of baboon which are often seen, and the Rwenzoris have chimpanzees, which are very rarely sighted. Most forests also have squirrel populations.

(On the Nyika Plateau in Malawi you have a very good chance of seeing several types of large mammal including roan antelope, reedbuck, warthog and zebra, and the possibility of seeing jackal and even leopard. This is an excellent area for walking safely among wildlife. See the Malawi chapter for more details.)

Higher up, on the moorland zones of most of the major mountains, and particularly on the Aberdare (Nyandarua) Range, there are

leopard and hyaena, and even lion, but these are very rarely seen, although you might notice footprints and droppings. On rocky outcrops you're more likely to see the small klipspringer, with its distinctive 'tip-toe' hoofs.

The most common animal on the upper forests and moorland is the hyrax, a rodent-like animal about the size of a rabbit, a close relative of the rock hyrax (dassie) found at lower altitudes. There are also several different kinds of rat and shrew in this zone.

Above the vegetation line, no mammals of any kind are usually found. However, Kilimanjaro has at least one herd of eland (large, spiral-horned antelope), seen on The Saddle and the Shira Plateau, and Leopard Point on Kibo is named after a leopard that was found frozen in a block of ice here. There's a pile of rhino bones above the moorland on Mt Meru, and there used to be the skeleton of an elephant, nicknamed Icy Mike, just below the peaks of Terere and Sendeo on Mt Kenya. No doubt you'll hear other stories about legendary non-human mountain ascents, from guides and porters during your trek.

Birds

You are much more likely to see birds than other animals during your trek. There are several common, easily recognisable species.

The eastern mountains (Kilimanjaro, Mt Kenya, Mt Meru and the Aberdare Range) share many common species and there is considerable overlap with the birds of Mt Elgon and the Rwenzoris, although here there are several western African species not found elsewhere. Similarly, on the mountains of Malawi there are several southern African species particular to that region. (These are covered in the Malawi chapter.)

Each mountain has its own local species, and keen birdwatchers should invest in a good field guide which covers all the areas in detail; bring binoculars.

Birds regularly seen in the eastern mountain forests include the common bulbul (mainly brown with a broad tail and yellow rump), the white-browed robin-chat (grey

upper body, orange chest, and black and white head) and the speckled mousebird (short bill and tuft on its head, and a long tail, giving it a mouse-like appearance).

Higher up, you may also see the silvery cheeked hornbill (a large black bird with a ridge across the top of its bill) and possibly a Hartlaub's turaco (mainly green with red underwings and a cry very similar to the colobus monkey's). Different species of turaco are seen on various mountains. Olive doves (small pigeons) are very common.

Malachite sunbird

In the moorland you might see the hill chat (short, brown with white stripes on the tail) or the scaly francolin (a brown, grouse-like bird). A beautiful bird often seen on the high moorland is the malachite sunbird (vivid green, small and slender with a fairly long tail and long curving bill) often seen feeding on lobelias. Lower down you'll see the regal sunbird, similar in shape with a shorter tail and red and yellow chest.

Around huts and campsites you'll see the white-necked raven (like a large crow) usually scavenging in the rubbish pit. On the bare rocky areas of the high mountains, birds of prey are seen. The most common is the augur buzzard (usually grey, with a fairly short reddish tail) and the Verreaux's eagle (larger and mainly black, with a white back and rump).

PEOPLE

The modern states of East Africa are all less than a century old and the concept of 'nation' is still fairly new. For many African people, 'nation' is less important than 'tribe'.

The word 'tribe' opens a real can of worms. It is commonly used when discussing different groups of people in Africa, but it is vague, and some Europeans are embarrassed to use it, especially as, for them, it can have slightly negative implications: 'tribalism', for example, is always regarded as a bad thing. Anthropologists favour the term 'ethnic group', but this is equally vague, and is used by different writers to categorise people in confusingly broad or narrow bands. Other words that are sometimes used are 'race', 'clan' and even 'caste', all correct in some contexts but all adding to the general confusion. The word 'people', used in its singular context – for example, 'the Maasai people', is 'safe' but sometimes clumsy. It is interesting to note that most Africans use the word 'tribe' without any embarrassment. The best thing is to use whatever term seems suitable, but just be aware of the differences and implications.

You might notice groups of people being referred to as, for example, Wakikuyu and Washambala instead of Kikuyu and Shambala. The Wa-prefix implies 'people' in some African languages. Similarly, the prefix for language is Ki-, hence Kiswahili, the language of the Swahili people. When writing in English, these prefixes are usually dropped and, generally, they have not been used in this book.

The peoples of Africa are usually classified according to their main language group, of which there are four in East Africa. These are Bantu, Nilotic, Cushitic and Khoisan. (You'll also find terms like Semitic, Hamitic or even Nilo-hamitic, although these aren't used much these days.) In Kenya there are people of all four groups, mainly Bantu, with large groups of Nilotic and Cushitic origin. In Tanzania, Uganda and Malawi, Bantu groups are even more predominant.

Meeting People

Most of the treks described in this book are through wilderness areas, which are either uninhabited or sparsely populated, but several routes pass villages and farmland on the mountains' lower slopes, and others go through populated areas for the whole trek.

One of the rewards of trekking in East Africa is having the chance to meet the locals face to face, and having time to stop and talk (or nod and smile across the language barrier), and see them as real people rather than as colourful extras in a movie-set backdrop.

If you're trekking with a local guide through a populated area, you will often feel less of a stranger. Your guide can also help with introductions and translations, and this is a much more interesting way to learn about other peoples' culture and way of life than ploughing through a stodgy textbook.

Avoiding Offence

Have respect for the people you meet. In some areas, very short trousers, particularly on women, will raise a few eyebrows. It's like walking down your own main street in your underwear. There's no need for full body cover, but just be aware of local sensitivities. In this way, local people will find it much easier to accept and talk to you. Open displays of affection are also usually frowned upon, although you're unlikely to start necking with your partner halfway up a mountain path!

Before you take someone's photo, ask them. It's a simple matter of manners. Think how you would feel if complete strangers constantly invaded your personal privacy in this way. Some people might ask you for money before posing.

LANGUAGE

Within the four main groups of people are several hundred subgroups, all with their own distinct language or dialect. Difficulties with classification can arise here too, as some groups have adopted completely different languages during their history, as they conquered or were absorbed by others.

Of course, theories are constantly changing as fresh evidence comes to light, so you might find conflicting information in different books if you want to read up on this fascinating subject.

The common language used throughout the region is Swahili (or *Kiswahili* when you're speaking the language), originally used as a *lingua franca* by traders on the coast. Over the centuries, in the coastal region, it developed into a rich language, lending itself particularly to poetry. Zanzibar is today regarded as the home of Swahili, where the language is purest. Although it is derived from Arabic and various Bantu languages, Swahili also has many words of Indian, Portuguese and English origin.

Swahili is widely spoken in Kenya and Tanzania, but as you get further away from the coast the language becomes more basic (particularly in western Kenya, eastern Uganda and northern Malawi), with a lot more English words. (While stuck on a broken-down bus once, I heard the driver describe the problem as 'Breaki pipi faili'.)

English is also widely spoken throughout East Africa, especially in towns and tourist areas, and by educated people. English is taught in all schools in Uganda, Tanzania, Kenya and Malawi. In Kenya there are more books and newspapers available in English than there are in Swahili.

In Uganda and Malawi, Swahili is not used much; English is the common language. The national papers of both these countries are printed in English, and very little published work is available in local languages.

SWAHILI FOR TREKKERS

A small grasp of Swahili is particularly useful when you're trekking in fairly remote areas, or if you want to do more than just nod at your porters on Kilimanjaro and the other high mountains. The best way to learn more is to start talking. Most people will always be happy to teach you more words or explain their proper uses.

Generally, Swahili is a straightforward language with regular rules and pronunciation. It can be slightly confusing for beginners as most words have prefixes, as well as suffixes, which change according to context. Fortunately, you can often ignore these rules and still be understood, especially in 'upcountry' areas where the local people use Swahili as a second or third language and probably speak it almost as badly as you. The most common word suffixes are included in this section.

The words listed here will help you survive in the hills. If you want to do more than just get by, there are several phrasebooks available. The one by Lonely Planet is probably the most accessible and the easiest to carry in your rucksack.

Greetings & Civilities

Hello
Jambo
Hello (Can I come in?)
Hodi
Welcome (inside)
Karibu
Thank you (very much)
Asante (sana)
How are things?
Habari?
(Very) fine
Mzuri (sana)
Completely fine
Mzuri kabisa
OK
Sawa, Sawa sawa
Not bad
Si mbaya
Greetings
Salama salama
Good night
Lala salama
Yes
Ndiyo
No
Hapana
Sorry
Pole
No problem
Hakuna matata
Please
Tefadhali (not used much)

Goodbye
  Kwaheri
Have a good journey
  Safiri salama

Features
mountain
  mulima
hill
  mulima kidogo
col, pass, small valley
  bonde
summit, top
  kilele
lake
  nyanza, ziwa
pond, tarn
  nyanza/ziwa kidogo
river
  mto
stream
  kijito
stone, rock
  jiwe
road, street
  barabara
dirt road
  barabara ya mchanga
path, track
  njia
track for cars
  njia ya ghari
track for walking
  njia ya miguu
short-cut
  njia ya mkato, shortikuti
village
  kijiji (or 'centre')
field, farm
  shamba
hut
  chuba
house
  nyumba
compound
  boma (*manyatta* in Samburu and Maasai
  areas)
shop
  duka

lodging
  nyumba ya kulala
toilet
  choo
water
  maji
food
  chakula
donkey
  punda
firewood
  kuni
white person/white people
  mzungu/wazungu
journey
  safari
traveller/s
  msafiri/wasafiri
guest/s, visitors/s
  mgeni/wageni

Directions
let's go
  twende
now
  sasa
early
  mapema
late
  chelewa
stop
  simama
wait
  ngoja
wait a bit
  ngoja kidogo
quickly
  haraka
slowly
  pole pole
straight on
  tawali, moja kwa moja
here
  hapa
there
  hapo
there isn't
  hakuna
left
  kushoto

right
kulia

middle
kati

between
kati kati

up, high
juu

down, low
chini

more, again, another
ingine

north
kaskazini, si kasini

south
kusini

west
magaribi

east
mashariki

(The last four terms can cause confusion, so use as a general direction, not for precise compass bearings.)

Weather

rain
mvua

snow
theruji

hail, ice
barafu

cloud
mawingu

mist, fog
ukunga

wind
upepo

storm
kipunga

hot sun, or outdoors
jua kali

Adjectives

cold
baridi

warm
moto

hot
moto sana

good
mzuri

bad
mbaya

big
kubwa

small
kidogo

easy
rahisi

hard
ngumu

strong
dhabiti

tired
choka

heavy
nzito

happy
furaha

unhappy
kihoro, huzuni

expensive
ghali

cheap
rahisi

hungry
njaa

thirsty
kiu

many
mingi

Pronouns

me
mimi

you
wewe

him/her
yeye

us
sisi

you
nyinyi

them
wao

Questions

how much/many?
ngapi?

where?
wapi?
is there?
iko?
what?
nini?
when?
lini?
why?
kwa-nini?

Dangers & Difficulties

hatari
danger
help
usaidizi
help!
saidia!
(very) ill/sick
mgonjwa (sana)
medicine
dawa
chemist
duka ya dawa
doctor
daktari
problem
matata
police
polisi
buffalo
nyati
lion
simba
crocodile
mamba
snake
nyoka
insect
dudu

Numbers

½	*nusu*
1	*moja*
2	*mbili*
3	*tatu*
4	*nne*
5	*tano*
6	*sita*
7	*saba*
8	*nane*
9	*tisa*
10	*kumi*
11	*kumi na moja*
12	*kumi na mbili*
20	*shirini*
21	*shirini na moja*
30	*thalethini*
40	*arobaini*
50	*hamsini*
60	*sitini*
70	*sabini*
80	*themanini*
90	*tisini*
100	*mia moja*
101	*mia na moja*
200	*mia mbili*
1000	*alfu moja*

Time

Swahili time, sensibly, starts at dawn (6 am), so 7 am is *saa moja* (literally hour one), even though it's usually written 7 am, but it can lead to all sorts of confusion when finding out what time buses leave, or arranging to meet porters. Double check everything.

one o'clock (hour seven)
saa saba
two o'clock (hour eight)
saa nane
six o'clock (hour twelve)
saa kumi na mbili
daytime
mchana
night-time
usiku
dawn
alfajiri
morning
asubuhi
afternoon
alasiri
evening
jioni
today
leo
tomorrow
kesho

yesterday
  jana
this, last, next
  hii, lijayo, lililopita
week
  juma, wiki
Monday
  Jumatatu
Tuesday
  Jumanne
Wednesday
  Jumatano
Thursday
  Alhamisi
Friday
  Ijumaa
Saturday
  Jumamosi
Sunday
  Jumapili

Useful Phrases

Where are you going?
  Unakwenda wapi?
I am going to Namanga
  Ninakwenda/Nenda Namanga
I came from Nairobi today
  Nina toka Nairobi leo
Where are you from?
  Unatoka wapi?
I come from England/America
  Nina toka England/America (countries have proper Swahili forms but this will be understood)
What is your name?
  Jina lako nani?
My name is...
  Jina langu ni..., Mimi ninaitwa...
I don't speak/understand Swahili
  Sijui Kiswahili
I only speak a little Swahili
  Nazungumza Kiswahili kidogo tu
I am lost
  Nimepotea
Please help me
  Tafadhali nisaidie
Can I find/hire a guide?
  Naweza kupata msaidizi?
Can you show me the way to... ?
  Unaweza kunionyesha njia ya kenda...?

I will pay you
  Nita kulipa
How much?
  Pesa ngapi bei gani? or *Shilling ngapi bei gani?*
What time is it?
  Saa ngapi?
How many hours to...?
  Masaa mangapi...?
Can I pass this way?
  Naweza kupita njia hii?
Can I sleep here?
  Naweza kulala hapa?
Is the water good to drink?
  Maji haya nisafi ya kunyua?
Is there a shop in the village?
  Kuna duka hapa kijijini?
Can I buy food?
  Naweza kununua chakula?
Is there food here/there?
  Iko chakula hapa/hapo?
I want to walk to...
  Nataka kutembea hadi...
Where does this path go to?
  Njia hii inaenda wapi? or *Njia nenda wapi?*
I will come back tomorrow/ on Friday/ next year
  Nitarudi kesho/ ijumaa/ mwaka ujao

In Kenya and Tanzania, the following Swahili/African words are commonly used and generally not translated:

askari
  security guard
banda
  cabin, bungalow
boma
  compound
drift
  dry river bed
duka
  small shop
fundi
  expert, repairer, mechanic
lugga
  dry river bed (northern Kenya)
manyatta
  compound (Samburu/Maasai)

Top: Everlastings on high moorland below Kilimanjaro's Kibo dome (DE)
Left: Giant lobelia on the high moorland in the Aberdare Range (DE)
Right: Groundsels at Hut Tarn on Mt Kenya (DE)

Top: Giant groundsel on Kilimanjaro's Shira Plateau (DE)
Bottom: Aloes growing on exposed rock outcrop (DE)

matatu
  minibus
moran
  warrior (Samburu/Maasai)
mzee
  old man
panga
  machete
shamba
  field/small farm
soda
  any bottled fizzy drink
hoteli
  small teashop (a small hotel is usually called a lodging *(nyumba ya kulala)*, or boarding & lodging, or simply B&L)

The following Alpine/English mountain terms are also commonly used:

cairn
  pile of stones for waymarking

col
  pass, low point between hills
gendarme
  pinnacle
tarn
  small mountain lake or pool
scree
  loose stones
snout
  lower end of a glacier
crevasse
  deep fissure in a glacier
kop/inselberg
  isolated rocky hill rising from a plain

You will also hear the term 'game' being used for large wildlife, even though in the walking areas animals are not hunted for sport any more. The term 'soda', as in soda lake, means saline. A murram road is a graded dirt road.

Facts for the Trekker

VISAS & DOCUMENTS

A full passport is essential for entering or travelling between Tanzania, Kenya, Uganda and Malawi. Change your passport if it has stamps from anywhere that might be considered suspect (South Africa, Israel or Libya, for example).

You can get all your visas before you go, or get them in neighbouring countries as you travel. This will probably be determined by the length of your trip. Most visas are only valid for a certain period, so don't get them all in advance if your plans are likely to change.

Other entry requirements may include a return ticket, to prove you're going to leave the country eventually and not settle down and build a hut somewhere. You may also need 'sufficient funds' to support yourself during your stay, especially if you don't have a return ticket. This tends to be flexible, so that customs officials can prevent 'undesirables' from entering, but a few hundred dollars for a short visit (or a credit card) is usually enough. It also helps if you don't look like an undesirable. International vaccination certificates are also often required (see the Health & First Aid chapter).

Entry regulations differ between countries and also depend on your nationality and where you've flown in from, so it's best to contact the nearest embassy or high commission of the countries you plan to visit and check the latest regulations with them.

Other useful documents include an international driving licence (if you're going to hire or drive a car), a youth hostel membership card, an international student card (if you're eligible, or can get one anyway), and a list of your travellers' cheque and credit card numbers (in case of loss). Also useful is a set of passport photos; they're often needed for visa application forms.

Travel Insurance

An insurance policy that covers you for medical expenses, and an emergency flight home, is highly recommended. Hospitals in East Africa are not free, and the good ones are not cheap. Air ambulances and emergency international flights are frighteningly expensive. Most travel insurance also covers your baggage in case of loss, and several other items such as cancellation or hijack. (Reading the small print is enough to put you off flying!)

Some companies are jumpy about the word 'trekking'. They seem to equate a trek up Kilimanjaro with storming the south face of Everest and quote an extra premium to match. Others are much more sensible and only raise the premium if you trek above a certain altitude, or get into technical mountaineering with ropes, crampons, ice-axes and all the rest.

If your travel agent can't help you, try a student travel service or your national walking/climbing organisation for advice.

MONEY

You should carry the money you need in a mixture of travellers' cheques and cash. The currency should be freely convertible ('hard') and well known. In East Africa the best currencies are US dollars and, to a lesser extent, UK pounds. In main banks, French francs, Swiss or German marks and Japanese yen are also recognised.

Travellers' cheques are safe because they can be replaced if lost or stolen (although this can sometimes take a long time), but they can be exchanged for local currency only in banks or change bureaus. Cash cannot be replaced if lost but can be exchanged more easily in other places (hotels, shops or travel companies), which is useful when the banks are closed or far away.

Cash is also useful in countries where there's a an unofficial ('black') market for hard currency (although sometimes travellers' cheques can be used). If you change money on the black market you'll usually get a higher rate than the bank but you'll also be breaking the law and standing on pretty slippery moral ground as well.

If you're going to be away for a long time, or don't want to carry too much money around, in Kenya and Malawi you can use credit or charge cards to draw local cash or travellers' cheques in hard currency, or have money transferred from your home bank account.

Additional details about currency rates and regulations are given in the individual country chapters.

Costs

A daily rate of expenditure for trekking is very hard to work out. Trekking itself costs nothing more than food and boot leather. It's all the other things that add up – like getting there, park charges, hut and camping fees, guide and porter wages, and so on. Reading the individual trek descriptions, which contain details on all these things, should give you a better idea.

When you're not trekking, how you travel between the mountains also affects costs. If you're on a tight budget, as a very rough rule of thumb you should allow about US$10 per day for food, accommodation and local transport, although I've met travellers who hitch and camp everywhere and buy local food from the markets, and only get through a few dollars a day. If you want to travel in a bit more style, allow US$20 to US$30. Other costs can include organised treks and safaris, internal flights, rental cars and visas.

Full details about all these aspects of trekking and travelling are given in the relevant country and mountain sections.

WHEN TO GO

The main feature of East Africa's weather is the pattern of wet and dry seasons. There are two of each per year (see the Climate section in the Facts about the Region chapter). Walking in the rain can be a bit of a downer after a while, so the best time for trekking is during the dry seasons. In Uganda, Kenya and northern Tanzania, broadly speaking, these are from December to February, when it's dry and warm, and from May to September, when it's dry and cool. In Malawi the dry season is April to September – cool in the early months, getting hotter in August and September.

However, the climate of East Africa is becoming increasingly unpredictable – it seems that the amount of rain falling during the wet seasons is decreasing, making trekking at this time less unattractive. Usually, the rain falls in the afternoon which means you can walk in the morning and get to your hut, or put your tent up not long after midday, and avoid the worst of the weather. On the high mountains, like Mt Kenya, Kilimanjaro and the Rwenzoris, snow usually falls in the rainy season and routes can be more difficult or blocked completely.

But even in the dry seasons, rain on the mountains is never unlikely. You should be prepared for bad weather at *all* times.

A country's public holidays won't stop you trekking, but they might sometimes make travelling or buying supplies difficult, and could involve a small alteration to your plans. They could also mean some trekking areas having more visitors than usual. Public holidays are listed in the individual country chapters.

WHAT TO BRING

If you are doing an independent or supported trek (see the Types of Trekking section in this chapter) you'll need all your own equipment including tent, sleeping bag and cooking kit. On an organised trek you normally just need a sleeping bag. And on any kind of trek you're also going to need a rucksack to carry your gear, and a set of appropriate clothes.

Although you're in Africa, and near the equator, don't be fooled into thinking it's always going to be dry and warm. You probably will get some days of blistering heat, but rain can fall at any time of year, and many of the treks in this book go above 4000 metres, where night temperatures often drop below freezing. The higher you go, the colder it gets. At dawn on the summit of Kilimanjaro, wind-chill can force the apparent temperature down to near -30°C. That's cold enough for you to lose all feeling in your fingers if you take your gloves off for more than a couple of seconds.

So the most important thing about trekking in East Africa is the huge range of temperatures and weather conditions you will encounter, even on a fairly short trek. Your clothing and equipment must be flexible and versatile. And if you're carrying it yourself, it also needs to be light.

Good-quality, lightweight clothing and equipment for camping and trekking is difficult to buy in East Africa. Most trekkers bring everything they need with them.

If you are already a regular walker or backpacker, you'll probably have most of the clothing and equipment required, and also have your own ideas about what sort is best for you, so you may want to skip some parts of this section. But make sure all your gear is in good condition before you leave. It's no good finding out you've got a split flysheet or worn boots halfway up the Rwenzoris.

If you are fairly new to trekking, and you're kitting yourself out from scratch, you should also read a few outdoor magazines or equipment manuals, and discuss your trek with a good outdoor gear shop where the staff have trekked themselves and can offer suggestions.

Choosing suitable mountain equipment is either complicated or very simple, depending on who you talk to. There's a lot of specialised, highly technical gear around these days. The effectiveness of some of it is exaggerated, but other stuff is very good and worth having if you can afford it. Some trekkers make do with very simple equipment. This is fine if there's no other choice, as long as the gear does the job it's supposed to. Not having high-tech gear shouldn't stop you going, but whatever you have must provide adequate levels of safety and comfort. If it doesn't, there's no point going on a trek.

The following list is based on the presumption that you'll be trekking on at least one of the high mountains of East Africa, where the weather conditions are more severe (Kilimanjaro, Mt Kenya, the Rwenzoris). If you're only going to the lower mountain areas you won't need quite so much. (See the individual mountain sections for details on weather and climate.)

Equipment List

Footwear
    walking boots
    training shoes
    sandals
    socks
    gaiters

Clothing
    jacket/s
    shell jacket
    shirts
    trousers
    skirt
    shorts
    underwear

Personal Equipment
    sunglasses
    snow goggles
    walking pole
    water bottle/s
    water purification kit
    torch/flashlight
    emergency foil blanket

Trekking Equipment
    rucksack
    tent
    sleeping bag
    sleeping mat
    cooking & eating kit

Miscellaneous Items
    sun cream/block & lip salve
    washing kit
    sewing kit
    first-aid kit
    compass
    map case
    whistle
    penknife
    toilet paper

Footwear

If you buy new boots and socks, check that they're completely comfortable before leaving home.

Boots & Shoes For lower treks, walking shoes or training shoes with good support are suitable. For the higher mountains, medium-weight boots – leather or synthetic – are required. Kilimanjaro, and possibly Mt

Kenya, are the only mountains where you'll be on snow for a short period, but even here you won't need stiff plastic mountaineering boots. Unless you're really keeping the weight down, a pair of light training shoes for the evenings in camp are a very good idea. Sandals let your feet breath on warm evenings and reduce the chance of blisters or other skin problems.

Socks Good socks are as important as good boots. Wool dries slowly, but there are several synthetic fabrics available which are more suitable. Some people prefer to wear two pairs, but there's no reason for this if your boots are good. Extra layers can chafe as much as cushion; it's a personal choice. Take several pairs, so you always have a dry set to put on. Wet socks in the morning can ruin a trek!

Gaiters These are very useful, as you'll almost certainly be crossing snow, scree or swamp (or all three!) during your trek. Unless you're doing a Rwenzori trek, gaiters do not need to be the heavy-duty Yeti-type. (See the special note on footwear in the Rwenzori section of the Uganda chapter.)

Clothing

To give you more flexibility, it's better to take several thin layers of clothing, rather than a few thick layers. The range of fabrics and styles available is mindboggling, but important buzzwords when you're looking round the gear shops are 'wicking' and 'breathability'. Basically, clothes which wick moisture away from your skin keep you dry and warm on the inside, and clothes which breath allow the moisture to escape.

Jackets This includes anoraks, parkas, cagouls, coats and so on. This is the outside layer of clothing you wear most of the time for trekking when temperatures are cool. A jacket should be reasonably wind-proof and shower-proof. There are many different fabric types, including close-weave nylon or cotton and acrylic pile, but the most usual is

fleece, usually available in a range of thicknesses, and sometimes with a wind-proof or shower-proof membrane attached.

On the high mountains, carrying another jacket is highly recommended for when you need an extra layer of warmth around camp in the evening, for pre-dawn summit approaches, or for using inside your sleeping bag on very cold nights. This can be any sort, but many trekkers favour a padded sleeveless 'body warmer' or 'duvet jacket', as these are light and pack down fairly small, which is important as you'll probably be carrying it more than wearing it.

A shell jacket is useful when conditions get more serious. It should be capable of coping with heavy rain and high winds. A hood and elasticised cuffs and waistband are also essential. Several types of shell jacket are available, some lined or padded for extra warmth, but remember that when it rains on African mountains, it doesn't always get colder, so putting on a waterproof jacket warms you up, which just makes you sweat more and get wet anyway.

To get round this problem some jackets are made in waterproof breathable fabrics such as Gore-Tex. Alternatively, clothes made from a combination of pile fabric and close-weave nylon such as Pertex are ideal for trekking in African mountains: one layer is fine for the warm, wet conditions on the lower slopes, and two or three layers can cope with the snow and high winds on the summits. The main manufacturer of this type of clothing is called Buffalo (an appropriate name for trekking in Africa!).

Shirt This is another catch-all term for the middle layer between your jacket and your underwear. You can choose from all sorts of technical synthetic fabrics or use a traditional wool sweater, or you may just use another thin jacket of fleece, pile, or whatever. Cotton sweatshirts are not really suitable; they get wet when you perspire and take ages to dry. Fleece sweatshirts are available, which are basically a thin fleece jacket without a zip.

Trousers Shorts are ideal for warm conditions. Many women trekkers find skirts comfortable. For when it gets cooler, lightweight, breeze-proof trousers are available. These are usually called 'trekking trousers', and you pay extra for pockets with zips and a nice badge, but nevertheless they're ideal. For more freedom of movement, you may prefer stretch-nylon tracksuit trousers (not cotton sweat-pants).

As conditions get colder you can build up the layers by using these under your trekking trousers or over long underwear. (Almost as much heat is lost through your legs as through your upper body.) You may also find a pair of padded trousers useful for evenings in camp and for sleeping in, in the same way as the 'duvet jacket' already mentioned. This is a real luxury, but well worth it on the high mountains.

Underwear Cotton T-shirts and undies are OK for warm conditions, but for higher, colder areas an insulating, wicking fabric (usually called 'thermal') that keeps moisture away from your skin is much better. The best method is to carry two sets of thermal undies. Use one set for walking every day and change into a dry set as soon as you reach camp in the evening. Thermal T-shirts and undershorts are good for walking, while long-sleeved vests and long johns are better for cold evenings. The walking set can be dried overnight inside your sleeping bag.

Hats & Gloves The sun is strong at high altitudes, so a sun hat that also covers the back of your neck is essential. A scarf can also be used. For the cold days, you need a warm hat. Balaclavas that can be rolled up are ideal. Again, wool takes a long time to dry, so synthetic materials are better. Used with the hood on your jacket you should be able to withstand that chill wind screaming across the summit of Kili!

Even with gloves a layer system is best: use light silk or thermal gloves for cool days, with overmitts to cope with strong winds and rain.

Personal Equipment

Sunglasses & Snow Goggles Sunglasses are recommended to cut the intense glare you often get on the high mountains. Snow goggles with side flaps are only essential for the summit stage on Kili, but also useful on the lower slopes below the glaciers, and on Mt Kenya.

Walking Pole One or two telescopic walking poles are very useful for taking some of the stress off your knees going up or down hills, particularly on the steep approaches to the summits of the major mountains. They're also good for providing extra balance on scree, snow and tussock grass.

Water Bottle You should carry at least a one-litre bottle for days on trek. Flexible water bags, holding between four and 10 litres, are ideal for extra water on long or hot days, and very good for camping as they help avoid pollution and will save several trips between your tent and the nearest river.

Water Purification Kit This consists of a water filter and/or a supply of purification tablets or solution (see the Health & First Aid chapter).

Torch/Flashlight A head-mounted torch is more useful than hand-held models, as it leaves your hands free for eating and cooking or for putting in your pockets when it's cold. Bring spare bulbs and plenty of batteries, as they fade quickly in cold conditions. Locally made batteries do not last long.

Emergency Foil Blanket A foil blanket is small and light to carry in the bottom of your day-pack, but can occasionally be useful if you get unexpectedly delayed in cold, wet conditions.

Trekking Equipment

Rucksack If you're trekking independently, your rucksack obviously needs to be large enough to carry all your gear and food. Many trekkers in East Africa visit more than one mountain, which means travelling between different areas on public transport, when this large rucksack can be half-full and unwieldy.

To overcome this, some makes of 'alpine' rucksacks have zips or straps to change the size of the sack, which is very useful for this kind of situation. Most alpine sacks do not have side pockets, which also makes things easier on public transport, although less handy for trekking. Some rucksacks come with detachable pockets, or you can buy separate pockets to fit on. Karrimor, Berghaus and Lowe are leading rucksack manufacturers, producing several different models of the types described here.

If you're going on a completely supported or organised trek, a porter will carry your main bag while you carry only a day-pack with your camera, spare clothing, lunch and so on. Several rucksacks are available which have a small day-pack attached by zips or straps, and these are ideal for this purpose.

Some manufacturers produce rucksacks that convert into travel bags, which are good if you're combining trekking with some general travelling, or if you want to appear respectable when you spend a night in a smart hotel to celebrate a successful trek. These convertible bags are OK if you're on a supported trek, but they should not be overloaded for long independent treks, as they tend to sag and be uncomfortable.

No matter what rucksack makers claim about waterproofing, your spare clothing and sleeping bag should be wrapped inside tough plastic bags to keep them dry – heavy-duty garbage bags are ideal. This also helps to keep out dust when you're travelling.

On any flight, tie all your rucksack straps so none can get snagged by trolleys and conveyer belts. I've seen several rucksacks come down the carousel at Nairobi airport with half the harness torn off. (If this does happen, rucksacks can be repaired by the shoe *fundis* (menders) in Nairobi and other towns, but it's best to avoid it happening in the first place.)

Tent There's an amazing range of designs and fabrics available, but there are few point-

ers to look for. If you're carrying everything yourself, your tent needs to be small and light, but even on supported treks you need to keep the weight fairly low. For trekking and travelling in East Africa one of the most important features is mosquito netting across all openings. Free-standing tents are also useful, as many campsites are on areas of very thin soil, and even on bare rock in the higher mountains.

Weather conditions do not usually reach Himalayan storm standards, so your tent will not need to have several hoops or poles and a whole web of guy-ropes. Heavy falls of snow are also very unlikely during the trekking seasons, so a steep-sided 'four-season' tent is not necessary.

A good tent for tropical trekking is the Tadpole made by North Face. It was designed for Californian campers who are up the mountains one weekend and on the beach a few days later, but it's also ideal for the range of conditions in East Africa. The inner has large panels of netting and can be used alone in warm conditions. I've even used it in hotel bedrooms to keep the bugs out!

Some light tents must be erected with care. If you're on a supported trek, it's usually a good idea not to let porters put them up, as they could be damaged.

Sleeping Bag There are endless variations and, once again, flexibility and layering are important features when choosing a bag for treks in East Africa, so that you can cope with the range of temperatures and conditions. The two main types of bag are those filled with natural down or feathers and those with synthetic filling. Basically, the difference is this: down bags are lighter, smaller when compacted and last longer; synthetic bags are cheaper and lose less of their warmth if they get wet.

For the high camps on the major mountains you need a good 'four-season' bag. So that you can also use it in lower, warmer conditions a long zip allows ventilation. Alternatively, as with the clothing, you can build up a series of layers from two or more lighter sleeping bags used together. Sleeping bag liners made from Pertex (a close-weave nylon) can add a lot of warmth to your system for very little extra weight. For high camps on Kili and Mt Kenya I use two sleeping bags, plus one liner inside the bags and a big one outside which envelopes the whole lot. As the trek gets lower down the mountain, fewer layers are required. You can put together your own layers, or buy a complete set. A company called Sung-Pak produce a layered system of three sleeping bags in one, called the Kwart, which is very versatile, and good for trekking on most East African mountains.

For the high camps on the major mountains, some trekkers carry an extra lightweight sleeping bag, to use as a middle layer in the same way as the 'duvet jacket' mentioned in the clothing section. A lightweight bag can then be used on its own in the warm areas. This can be synthetic or down: one of the smallest synthetic bags is the Kestrel, made by Snug-Pak; for even more warmth and weight-saving, the smallest down sleeping bag is the Micro, made by Rab, which packs to about the same size as a pair of trekking socks. When I'm trekking with a group, even when porters have the main rucksacks, I always carry one of these small lightweight sleeping bags in my own rucksack in case of emergency.

If you don't want to carry an extra sleeping bag just for a few nights, you could hire one. Details on equipment hire are given in the various trekking sections.

Sleeping Mat A sleeping mat is very important to insulate your body from the cold ground at night. The traditional Karrimat is robust and light, but beware of cheap copies which compress easily and soon become useless. Thermarests are a more recent innovation; they are very comfortable and only slightly heavier, but they provide more insulation, which means if you're really counting the grams, you can save weight by using a lighter sleeping bag.

Cooking & Eating Kit Relying on open fires is not recommended and is ecologically unsound, so a stove is essential. Camping stoves can be classified according to fuel type and are really a matter of personal preference. Cartridges for butane gas (eg Gaz) stoves are available in Nairobi (see the Buying & Hiring Locally section in this chapter) but in very few other places. For petrol stoves, fuel is cheap and readily available all over East Africa, although often dirty, which can cause stoves to block. Methylated sprits can also be bought in hardware shops and chemists in large towns. Meths (eg Trangia) stoves are perhaps the best as they have no moving parts and nothing to break.

To go with your stove, you need a windshield, fuel bottle, cooking pots (those with a non-stick coating make washing up easier and require less soap), a pan grip, wooden spoon for cooking, plastic mug and bowls, plus aluminium knife, fork and spoon. You also need a lighter, a spare lighter and a box of waterproof matches for emergencies, plus a foam pad for washing up and some detergent (preferably biodegradable). A foldable bowl is useful and helps avoid polluting streams with dirty water (see the Responsible Trekking section later in this chapter), although a large plastic bag in a ring of stones will do the job.

Miscellaneous Items

The sun can be strong at high altitude, so protect arms and legs with sun cream. For nose and ears use a complete sun block. Also vital is lip salve.

Your washing kit should be small. Take only the essentials. (I've seen people up Mt Kenya with beach towels!)

Likewise for the sewing kit and first-aid kit (see the Health & First Aid chapter). Medicated hand-wipes are useful for cuts and grazes, and for a final clean just before eating.

A compass is essential if you're going off the main routes. Make sure you know how to use it. Note also that good compasses are calibrated differently for various parts of the world. For the treks in this book, you need one for equatorial regions. If your compass is set for another region you'll need to keep changing the angle of the base plate to make it work. Silva make a range of compasses for all regions.

A transparent map case, or a strong clear plastic bag, will protect maps (or this book) from rain.

A whistle can be very useful if you get lost or separated from companions in mist or darkness (although it's better not to get into this situation), and for scaring off animals in bush areas. A penknife is also useful but it doesn't need 97 blades and gadgets. The essentials are sharp knife, bottle opener and tin opener. Nail scissors are useful for mid-trek pedicures.

Toilet paper can be bought in even quite small shops all over East Africa, although it tends to be a bit on the coarse side. Keep it dry. Wet loo roll is even worse than wet socks! (Bring matches to burn it after use, or a plastic bag – see the Responsible Trekking section.) Tampons and sanitary towels are available from chemists in Nairobi, Dar, Lilongwe, Blantyre and some other large towns.

Buying & Hiring Locally

There is nothing you need for trekking in East Africa which cannot be brought from home, but if you forget or lose something, or need a few extra items of trekking gear, Nairobi is the best place to be, as it has the only specialised climbing and trekking equipment shop on the whole continent of Africa (outside South Africa). The Natural Action Mountain Centre is in the Museum Hill Shopping Mall, opposite the National Museum. The stuff they've got – rucksacks, sleeping bags, tents, clothing, and so on – is new and good quality, but it's imported, and so a bit on the expensive side if you want to buy. But everything is for hire, at reasonable rates. The guys who run the shop are professional mountain guides and can help you with advice and information.

Gear is also available for hire from a few other shops and trekking companies in Nairobi (details in the Kenya Equipment Hire & Supply section) and from various places at the base of Mt Kenya and Kilimanjaro (details in the mountain sections).

For camping stoves, the most popular sizes of butane gas canisters (size C206) are available in Nairobi. Methylated spirits for meths burners can be bought from hardware shops or supermarkets in any large town, or from chemists, but tends to be more expensive. For petrol stoves, the low-grade petrol in Kenya, Tanzania and Uganda is OK, but tends to be very dirty. In Malawi, petrol is blended with ethanol, which is ideal for stoves.

Basic items, such as aluminium cooking pots, plastic plates, kerosene stoves and blankets, even pullovers, hats and gloves, can be bought cheaply in the shops or market of any large town.

TOURIST OFFICES

National tourist offices, both local and overseas, generally only provide very limited information (if any) on trekking routes and conditions. They might be able to provide you with the names of some of the trekking companies, but mostly they only send out details of mainstream travel agencies and tour operators.

USEFUL ORGANISATIONS

Each country covered in this book has a national mountain club for local walkers and climbers. These clubs are mainly for citizens and expatriate residents and they do not usually cater for casual visitors. Generally, they are not able to reply to individual requests for advice and information unless you are a member of a mountain club in your own country which has reciprocal arrangements with the clubs overseas. Some of the mountain clubs in East Africa produce guidebooks to local mountains and climbing areas which are for sale to the general public. (More details are given in each country chapter.)

POST

Post in and out of all the countries covered in this book is cheap and generally reliable. All cities and large towns have a post office, and letters from any East African capital usually take about a week to reach Europe, and slightly longer to reach North America or Australasia.

You can have letters sent to you by using the Poste Restante service. Letters should be addressed:

Your NAME
Poste Restante
Main Post Office
Nairobi (or Arusha, or wherever)
Kenya.

To collect your mail, go to the main post office in that town and show your passport. Letters sometimes take a few weeks to work through the system, so have them sent to a place where you're going to be for a while, or will be passing through more than once. Most poste restantes are reliable, although Nairobi's is a bit chaotic, as so many letters are sent to it. American Express customers can have mail sent to Amex offices.

Letters are filed alphabetically by family name. If you can't find letters you're expecting, see if they've been filed under one of your other names. Mail can get lost, but it's usually due to bad writing or an unclear address. Ask people writing to you to use just one name, and use capitals. If your family name is common, it should be underlined and your given name written in lower case.

TELEPHONE

Most cities and large towns have public telephone offices where you can make international calls, or send messages by fax and telex. You can also make calls from large hotels but these tend to charge a high commission. Cost and reliability varies. Calls from Nairobi and Lilongwe are fairly cheap and easy, from Kampala it takes time, and calls from anywhere in Tanzania are very expensive.

BOOKS
Travel Guides & Manuals

General guidebooks on East Africa include Lonely Planet's *East Africa – a travel sur-*vival kit and *Africa on a shoestring*, and IC Publications' *Traveller's Guide to East Africa*. For general guidebooks on specific countries, Kenya is particularly well-covered, although there's less to choose from on the other countries included in this book. These are detailed in the individual country chapters.

Among the more specialised guidebooks, the *East Africa International Mountain Guide* (West Col, UK) is mainly for technical climbers and mountaineers, covering rock and ice routes on Mt Kenya, Kilimanjaro and the Rwenzoris plus several more obscure crags in the region, although it does contain some information on trekking.

The *Camping Guide to Kenya* (Bradt, UK/Hunter, USA) and *Cycling Kenya* (Bicycle Books, USA) both contain sections of general information, useful wherever you go in East Africa with a tent or a bike.

Another useful book to read before you go is *Backpacking & Camping in the Developing World*, by Scott Graham (Wilderness Press, USA, 1988). The title is self-explanatory and the book is full of useful information which will help you plan your trip and enjoy your trekking. More specialised is *Desert Hiking* by Dave Ganci (Wilderness Press, USA, 1979), mainly about American deserts but with useful tips if you're planning any treks in northern Kenya or the low parts of Tanzania's Rift Valley.

For general travel advice read the large and very comprehensive *Travellers Handbook* (Wexas, UK) which covers all aspects of international travel, or the more concise *A to Z Guide for Lightweight Travellers* by Clive Tully (Writer's Block, UK) which contains good information and advice for independent travellers and trekkers. If you want to know more about travelling and trekking without destroying the country and the mountains you've come to enjoy, have a look at *Holidays that Don't cost the Earth*, by John Elkington and Julia Hailes (Gollancz, UK).

For staying healthy while you're away from home try *Traveller's Health – How to*

Stay Healthy Abroad by Dr Richard Dawood (Oxford University Press, UK), or *The Tropical Traveller* by John Hatt (Pan UK). For more specifics read *Mountaineering Medicine* by Fred Darvill (Wilderness Press), USA).

Background Reading

The books listed here can provide background information and inspiration before you go, or make good souvenirs after your trek.

The following are hardback, large-format books, combining full-colour pictures with descriptions and travelogues:

Snowcaps on the Equator (The Bodley Head, UK, 1988), with photos by Clive Ward, and writing by Iain Allan and Gordon Boy, beautifully portrays many of East Africa's mountains, including all the major snowcapped peaks, plus some of the smaller ranges in Tanzania, Kenya and Uganda.

Anthony Smith's *The Great Rift: Africa's Changing Valley* (BBC Books, London, 1988) has interesting chapters on the explorer JW Gregory, the geology of the Rift, and anthropology.

Kilimanjaro, by John Reader (Elm Tree Books, UK, 1982) is a highly readable account of the trek to the top of Africa's highest peak, with plenty of historical asides. The author is a professional photo-journalist and the book is lavishly illustrated with excellent colour pictures. *Mount Kenya*, by the same author and publisher, is written and produced to the same high standards.

On God's Mountain, by Mohamed Amin, Duncan Willetts and Brian Tetley (Camerapix, Kenya/Moorland, UK, 1991) covers Mt Kenya and is another from the huge list of photo-essay books produced by this team. The pictures are what you'd expect from two of Africa's leading photographers, and the accompanying text covers all aspects of the landscape and history of the mountain.

Two other more general books by this team are *Journey Through Kenya* and *Journey Through Tanzania* (Camerapix, Kenya/Moorland, UK), which provide good information and excellent photos. Mohamed

Amin has also produced *Cradle of Mankind* (Camerapix, Kenya, 1989) about northern Kenya, which includes a section on the Suguta Valley and Lake Turkana.

Africa's Mountains of the Moon, by Guy Yeoman (Elm Tree Books, UK, 1989) covers the Rwenzori Range, and has stories of the author's several epic journeys through the area, good photos, and exquisite hand-drawn pictures of the mountains' unique vegetation, as well as thoughts and positive suggestions on the future of Africa's people and wilderness areas.

Malawi, Wildlife, Parks & Reserves by Judy Carter (Macmillan, UK, 1989) is a combination of 'coffee-table' book and field guide on the wilderness areas of Malawi, and succeeds in both aspects with good-quality wildlife and landscape shots, plus comprehensive background information. Includes sections on the Mulanje Massif and the Nyika Plateau.

Smaller, more portable, books include:

No Picnic on Mount Kenya by Felice Benuzzi (Kimber, UK, 1952; reprinted by Patrick Stevens, UK, 1989) is a ripping yarn of three Italian Prisoners of War who escaped from a camp in Nanyuki during the WW II, and climbed halfway up Batian and all the way to Lenana on Mt Kenya, using homemade equipment and a meat tin label for a route map. Classic adventure, recently reprinted.

Journey to the Jade Sea by John Hillaby (Paladin, UK, 1964, several reprints) is another adventurous story of one man's walk through northern Kenya to Lake Turkana. *In Teleki's Footsteps* by Tom Heaton (Macmillan, UK, 1990) covers similar ground, plus Mt Kenya, Kilimanjaro and the Rift Valley, as the author follows the great explorer's route through Kenya and Tanzania on foot and by bike.

Venture to the Interior by Laurens Van Der Post (Hogarth Press, UK). The grand philosopher of travel writing describes his ill-fated journey to the then virtually unknown mountains of Mulanje and Nyika in Malawi.

The Tree Where Man Was Born by Peter Matthiessen (Collins/Picador, UK, 1984) is a fascinating book – part travelogue, part anthropology, part idle musings – based on the author's travels through northern Kenya and the Crater Highlands of Tanzania, and on his fascination with the last remnants of the original 'Old People' of East Africa.

Other Books

If you're looking for something which covers your own special interest, such as history, geology, politics, womens' issues, African literature, art or natural history, contact your library or a good quality specialist bookshop. Several of the general guidebooks mentioned in this book have comprehensive bibliographies. Alternatively, you can find almost everything that has been written about the region (including most of the titles listed here) in Nairobi, which has some very good bookshops. To point you further in the right direction, you could refer to *The Sub-Saharan African Travel Resource Guide* (Bowker Saur, UK, 1993), which critically annotates some 1500 books and maps on the region, and covers various other aspects such as travel bookshops, magazines and publishers.

MAPS OF THE REGION

General maps of the East African region are Bartholomews' *Africa, Central & Southern* at a scale of 1:5,000,000 and *Africa, East* at 1:2,500,000. Both cover the countries included in this book. The maps have altitude tinting, but the information on roads and settlements is not so good.

The Michelin map *Africa, Central & South* at 1:4,000,000 (sheet 955) does not indicate high ground so clearly, but it has more detail and is a much easier map to use for general travel.

Locally produced maps showing Kenya, Tanzania and Uganda are available from bookshops in Nairobi. Details of maps covering single countries in more detail are given in the individual country chapters.

For most of the areas covered in this book, particularly the smaller mountain ranges, the maps included in each section will be sufficient. If you want more detail, or intend to trek in areas not covered in this book, large-scale government survey maps are produced in each country. These are usually based on surveys made during colonial times, and the British Directorate of Overseas Surveys (DOS) continues to assist with the production of maps. These are sometimes corrected, but many are considerably out of date. New roads and villages are not shown, although most of the topographical information is reasonably correct. You should be able to buy DOS/government survey maps at the Government Map Office in each country's capital city. Maps of popular areas are often out of stock, and you might not be able to buy maps which are considered 'strategic'. For some of the most popular mountain areas, commercially produced large-scale maps are also available. More details about specific maps and where to buy them are given in the individual country and mountain sections.

FILM & PHOTOGRAPHY
Before You Go

If you're buying a new camera for your trekking trip, go to a good camera shop and tell them what you're doing, and they can advise you on the most suitable models, and suitable film. For trekking you don't necessarily need anything fancy with a long lens, as most of your shots will be of landscapes.

If you're also visiting a wildlife area, a camera with a zoom lens is almost essential for good shots. The best combination for a trekking and wildlife holiday is a camera with a long zoom for close-ups, say 70 to 210 mm (if you go up to 300 or 400 mm you'll need a tripod and that's a whole different ball game), and a short zoom which can go down to a wide angle for landscapes, say 35 to 70 mm. Some models are available with one lens covering the whole range.

If you're not fully conversant with your camera, buy a book (there are several which specialise in mountain and landscape photography), and practice techniques by shooting a few rolls of film before you go. It's worth getting it right – there are no second chances if your shots on the summit don't come out!

While You're Away

The only places in East Africa with a good selection of quality film are Nairobi and Blantyre/Lilongwe. Elsewhere it is possible to find film (for example, in Kampala, Dar es Salaam ('Dar') and Arusha, where it's imported from Nairobi) but supplies are not always reliable, so it's best to bring what you need.

You can get prints developed in several large towns, but slides can only be done in Nairobi. There's a choice of places doing developing, some better than others. Camera spares and repairs are also a problem. Batteries for sale are often of poor quality, and camera fundis may attack your precious Nikon with nothing more than a blunt knife. Bring batteries and have your camera serviced before you leave home.

If your camera does develop problems, or you just need some more film, the place where everybody goes is the Expo Camera Centre in Nairobi (on Mama Ngina St, a block up from the Hilton). Mo, the bloke who runs the shop, is a genius and will do his best to fix any problem for you. He sells film, does overnight print processing, and also does specialist developing. Some of the best wildlife photographers bring their stuff to him from all over East Africa, so he must be good.

Use your camera sensitively when outside the national parks and wilderness areas. Do not take photos of anything that may be considered 'strategic', such as army camps, police stations, bridges, railways, etc. You may get arrested as a spy. At best you could have your film confiscated. At worst you could be imprisoned.

DANGERS & ANNOYANCES
Animals

Most of the treks described in this book are in highland areas, where you are unlikely to meet large unfriendly animals. On mountains where there is a chance of meeting dangerous wildlife (Mt Meru, the Aberdare Range and the Nyika Plateau), national park rangers usually accompany trekkers, although close encounters are very unlikely.

You might also see elephant droppings on the forested slopes of Mt Kenya, and even leopard prints on Mulanje, but you'll be very lucky (or unlucky) to even catch a glimpse of the animals themselves.

If you are walking in an area where there might be dangerous wildlife about, the best thing to do is make a noise as you walk. Most animals will move out of your way long before you even know they were there. One trekker I know ties a couple of bells to his rucksack when walking through the bush, which seems to have worked well to date.

Unfortunately, some old buffalo are deaf! In the very unlikely situation of you suddenly coming face to face with a buffalo, it will probably be as surprised as you and almost certainly run off. If it doesn't move, you should back away slowly to show no sign of threat. If there's a tree nearby, drop your pack and climb it. Fast. If there are no trees, lie down or 'run like a rat', crawling through the bush so the buffalo's horns can't reach you.

In reality, the biggest problem you're likely to have with animals is mice in the mountain huts, or hyrax wandering around the campsite, nibbling your food. Mosquitoes can be problematic too (see the Health & First Aid chapter).

Hyrax

Humans

In rural areas there is very little chance of robbery or theft. On mountains and in wilderness areas, there is even less chance, as the areas are usually uninhabited. Porters, guides and bunkhouse caretakers are generally trustworthy. Even on the most popular routes on Mt Kenya and Kilimanjaro, where the porters and guides have a reputation for being somewhat mercenary, actual theft is uncommon.

Even so, if you do use porters, you should carry valuables in your day-sack, and it's better not to leave money or items like cameras and penknives lying around unattended at huts or campsites. This is not necessarily because they will be stolen, although it's certainly going to tempt some people (including other trekkers), but because such action might be seen as a casual display of wealth and only go to increase the already large financial gap that exists between visitors and locals.

In small towns and villages, security is not usually a problem. You are usually quite safe walking around, and your hotel room is very unlikely to be broken into. In the larger towns and cities, such as Nairobi, Mombasa, Kampala, Dar, Moshi and Arusha, pickpockets operate in the bus stations and markets, but hotels are generally safe. Unfortunately, violent robberies do occur in Nairobi and Dar, and Western tourists are often the victims (because they've got more money), but such cases still happen far less often than they do in, say, London or New York.

When wandering around any large town try not to look too lost. Pretend you know where you are going, even if you don't. Avoid standing on busy street corners with the guidebook open at the city map page. It's best to keep your camera out of sight, and hang on tightly to your day-sack. Use your commonsense and be careful, but there's no need to be paranoid. Nairobi (or sometimes Nai-robbery) is particularly bad, and a bit of paranoia doesn't hurt in this town – some travellers say it's the only way to survive! Bag-snatching is not uncommon, and you should be on your guard for groups of thieves operating on crowded buses and matatus.

THE NATURE OF TREKKING IN EAST AFRICA

The trekking routes of East Africa are generally through mountains or wilderness areas.

Most of the treks described in this book keep to paths or tracks, but they are not always clear. There are few, if any, signposts. Most of the areas are uninhabited or have only a sparse, scattered population, so usually there'll be nobody around to show you the way.

This means you should be reasonably competent with a map and compass – at least enough to know whether you're going in the right direction. This is particularly important if you want to follow a seldom-used route. As on any mountain, mist or fog can completely block your view and make good navigation essential. If you are not sure about your ability, you should not even consider trekking without somebody more competent. Even if you are using a local guide, it still helps to have a basic knowledge. (See the Guides & Porters section.)

The lack of population in the wilderness areas also means that supplies will not be available on most of the treks described in this book, so you will need to be self-sufficient in food, usually for several days.

Generally, you will also need to be self-contained, with a tent and full set of camping gear, although some routes have huts and bunkhouses where you can sleep. In nearly all areas, at each hut or campsite there will be a supply of water (either tap, borehole or stream) but you should carry everything else.

Access

The beauty of trekking in East Africa is that all the major mountains can be easily reached by car, bus or hitching. This is an extra bonus for trekkers relying on public transport, who are so often excluded from wilderness areas. In this book, approach routes to the mountain area, and access routes to the start of each trek, are all fully described. Only two trekking areas described are difficult to reach without a vehicle. To get to these areas, you can hire a car (if your budget allows) or join an organised trek.

Types of Trekking

There are various types of trekking in East Africa. The three main ones are independent trekking, supported trekking and organised trekking. There are some sub-classifications and overlaps, but the following outlines will give you a general idea.

Independent Trekking In this book, 'independent' means completely self-sufficient and self-contained. Independent trekkers will have a full set of camping gear, and carry all their equipment and food for the duration of the trek. Independent, in this sense, does not necessarily mean a single person trekking alone, although this is possible (albeit not always recommended) in several of the areas.

Independent trekking allows you to be completely flexible. The end of your day's walking is determined only by where you can find water and a flat space to pitch your tent. With enough food for an extra couple of days (which you should always carry anyway, in case of emergency) you can extend your trek, or sidetrack off the main route, as the fancy takes you.

Where huts and bunkhouses exist on the routes, independent trekkers can use these, or combine camping and 'hutting', while still remaining self-sufficient in every other way.

Supported Trekking A supported trek means you are self-contained and self-sufficient in equipment, food and supplies, but you use the services of local porters to carry all or some of your gear. On a few of the treks described in this book, you may be supported by donkeys or a vehicle instead of human porters.

On a trek of this nature you might also employ a local guide, to organise the porters and to take the worry out of route-finding, especially if you're inexperienced or trekking alone. It is also possible to hire only a guide, if you prefer to carry your own gear or want to keep the size of your party to a minimum.

With porters carrying your gear, you can usually go further each day or keep going for longer (if you want to). It also makes your trek much easier on the legs and back, and generally adds to the overall enjoyment. Using porters can give you more freedom (diverting off the main route to bag an extra peak or sidetrack up an interesting valley is a lot more inviting if you haven't got a week's worth of food on your back!). But porters can also restrict you, as they generally do not have their own tents, and you must plan to stay each night near a hut or cave, so that they have somewhere to sleep.

It's also possible to hire porters just for the first half of your trek, or even for the first day, until you've limbered up or your rucksack becomes a bit lighter. At the halfway point, or first night's camp, you can pay the porter his wages, and he'll go back down, leaving you to carry on.

Guides and porters can be arranged through local trekking companies and agencies in the main towns, and at local porter-guide cooperatives near the mountains. Employing people in this way obviously costs more than doing a trek independently, but wages are not expensive and it's a good way to put some of your money directly into the local economy.

Some guides will also cook, and you can arrange to hire tents and equipment from the trekking companies, but if you get this far, you might as well do an organised trek.

For more information, see the Guides & Porters section in this chapter.

Organised Trekking It is possible to have your whole trek organised by a specialist trekking company. This can be arranged in advance with a locally based company, or even done after you've arrived in East Africa. Alternatively, you can arrange one trek, or even a series of treks, with a trekking company in your own country.

Many trekking companies in Europe, North America and Australasia can also arrange a complete deal including international flights, local transport and accommodation, as well as the trek itself, and many also provide a trek leader to oversee the running of the whole trip and to act as intermediary between the trekkers and the local guides and porters (see the Organised

Treks section in the Getting There & Away chapter).

On an organised trek, you either join a group and fit in with a pre-set schedule and itinerary, or you can request that the company arrange something to suit your own specifications.

Whether your trek is organised locally or in advance from your home country, the main advantage is that all the pre-trek preparation is taken care of, including transport to the start of the trek, buying food, arranging supplies and hiring equipment and porters. When trekking, you have guides and cooks to handle route-finding and cooking, while you relax and enjoy the trek. If your holiday time is limited, an organised trek can save you several precious days.

On the other hand, an organised trek means you have to follow a fairly rigid itinerary, with less opportunity for alterations and diversions, although good companies will always build in a bit of flexibility. Also, you'll probably be trekking with people you have not met before, which may add extra interest to your trip, or may not...

Costs vary considerably and depend on many factors. These include the number of days included in the trip as a whole, the number of days spent actually trekking, the standard of accommodation before and after the trek, the quality of bunkhouses or tents in the mountains, and the knowledge and experience of the guide or trek leader. When making comparisons, note that companies which camp on trek tend to use the more unusual routes or visit remote areas, and are often more expensive than those using bunkhouses on the main routes.

The number of porters and guides used is also important. Check that the company employs enough to carry everything. Most outfits also provide a cook. The better companies will often provide an assistant guide (or even two) to back up the main guide in case the group splits into slower and faster factions, or in case anybody has to return due to illness or altitude sickness. Many of the treks are in national parks where entrance fees have to be paid. When comparing costs

it's very important to check whether the price includes park entrance fees, or whether these are extra. Also check the number of days on offer: a five-day trek usually means four nights' accommodation, a six-day trek means five nights, and so on.

Wherever you arrange your trek, it's usually better to deal with the companies that actually organise the treks (the 'operators'), rather than the agents who simply sell them. Operators can usually give you much more practical help and advice, and the treks are often cheaper too.

Organised treks arranged locally start at about US$70 per day (all inclusive), and the better companies charge considerably more than this. If you organise a complete deal in your own country, the price will of course be much higher, as it will also include international air fares, local transport, trek-leader costs, accommodation, administration and so on.

Obviously, you can do things much more cheaply than on an organised trek if you arrange your own supported trek or go independently. But if you wanted to cover the same route in the same time, and with the same provisions and facilities, normally it would be very difficult to do it more cheaply yourself.

Confusion can be caused by travel companies offering 'walking safaris' or 'foot safaris'. Check these very carefully. Some walking safaris are fully organised treks in the mountains or through lowland regions, but others are vehicle-based with some sections of walking (long or short) included. Nevertheless, vehicle-based walking safaris can be very good, and ideal if you want to see some wildlife without being cooped up in a car all day.

You may also see the term 'climbing safari', which probably means a trek, and 'mountain climbing' which almost certainly means a trek, rather than technical rock climbing or mountaineering (see the Trekking is not Climbing section).

Note Of all the treks described in this book, only on Kilimanjaro is it essential to use the services of a trekking company (see the Kilimanjaro section in the Tanzania chapter).

Organised Trek Itinerary If you arrange an all-inclusive trek with a company, it will probably follow a basic itinerary that has become well established over the years, originally based on the Himalayan style of trekking.

The trek begins when the company's vehicle drops you off at the roadhead or a national park entrance gate. Here you meet your porters and guide (unless he's travelled with you). If this hasn't already been done, some time might be spent sorting out porter loads, although normally the guide will oversee this. Park fees may need to be paid.

Then you start trekking. Your guide will stay with your group, which may spread out over a long distance as people walk at different speeds. (This is why it's better to go with a company that also provides assistant guides.) Stronger porters will go ahead, while others lag behind. Even with organised treks, it's important to give the right bags to the right porters, otherwise you might arrive at your campsite to find a week's worth of food already there, while dry clothes and the tents are still three hours back down the mountain. Explain to your guide what you need and he will arrange the porters.

Normally, you carry a packed lunch for the midday break. While you're resting, more porters will come by. Loads seem to become particularly heavy at this stage!

You continue walking to reach your bunkhouse or campsite for the night. You might have to help put up the tents, depending on whether you're on a fully serviced trek or one where you're expected to lend a hand. Tea and biscuits will be provided while you rest for a while and change into dry clothes, and relax while the evening meal is prepared. Again, depending on your trek, you may be expected to lend a hand with cooking or washing up.

Next day, any small problems will have been ironed out and you can get into the rhythm of the trek proper. The day is based on best use of natural light. Sunrise is

between 6 and 6.30 am, and sunset is always 12 hours later. You normally get up at first light, to make the most of the clear weather, as afternoon mist sometimes occurs. Breakfast will be served in your hut or mess tent, or outside on the grass of your campsite. You pack your main rucksack ready for the porters to carry, and leave the cook to pack up the group food and equipment. You may help with taking tents down before starting the day's trek at around 8 am.

You walk until noon for lunch, and arrive at the next hut or campsite in the middle of the afternoon. Tea and biscuits are served while you rest. If the weather is good, there's often time for a short walk in the area around the camp, or you may prefer to just relax while the cook prepares the evening meal. After the meal, and the effects of a hard day's trekking, most trekkers hit the sack a few hours after sunset.

Trekking is not Climbing

On several of the treks in this book you often reach peaks and passes at heights between 4000 and 5000 metres, and the summit of Kilimanjaro tops the lot, at almost 6000 metres. Although you can go very high, this book describes trekking routes only. This means walking, with no technical climbing or mountaineering, and no specialised equipment required, such as ropes, crampons and ice-axes.

There are technical rock and ice routes on the mountains of East Africa, including Kilimanjaro, Mt Kenya and the Rwenzoris, plus shorter climbs on several smaller crags and outcrops, but these are not included in this book.

Be Physically Prepared

Although the trekking is non-technical, this doesn't mean that routes may not be demanding or strenuous. Some treks involve days where you might be walking for more than 10 hours, or covering distances of more than 30 km, although many are much shorter. The spectacular landscape can often make things harder too, whether you're walking through bamboo forest, tussock grass or desert sand.

And you may be surprised to learn that some of these mountains have steep sides; going up or down can put considerable strain on your lungs and legs. Add to that the effects of lack of oxygen when you're at high altitude – trekking is not to be taken lightly.

Some treks include very airy sections on narrow ridges, exposed peaks or fairly steep snow slopes. There are also a few optional sidetracks which may involve a bit of easy scrambling (using your hands).

Of course, if you're a regular walker in your own country, or have trekked in other parts of the world, you will be used to (and relish) these situations. But you should not think of doing a serious trek in East Africa as a way of 'getting in shape'. If you're not properly prepared, 'doing' Kilimanjaro or Mt Kenya, just as you'd tick off Serengeti or the Maasai Mara, is not recommended.

Pre-trek Formalities

For countries that are often bogged down by their bureaucracies, the paperwork involved when trekking in East Africa is remarkably straightforward. For treks in national parks, you have to pay park fees, but these can be settled on your way into the park at each entrance gate. For areas outside the national parks, there are generally no formalities, apart from maybe 'checking in' at a police station or local government office in some remote areas (details are given in the individual trek sections).

Bunkhouses and huts can be reserved in advance, but this is not always essential, and booking procedures are sometimes a bit slack, so you end up taking your chances anyway.

The only place where some advance planning might be necessary is Kilimanjaro, where the number of trekkers on some of the routes could be restricted. If this does happen, bookings will have to be made for the national park, but as all Kili treks have to be organised, this will be taken care of by your trekking company anyway.

If you want to take an organised trek on any other area during the 'high' season (see each mountain section for details), you might

need to contact the various trekking companies well in advance to be sure of a place. Having said that, whatever the season, it seems you can always find something.

Guides & Porters

For treks in East Africa, local guides and porters (always men) are sometimes available. Using the services of guides and porters is generally optional, and depends on the type of trekking you want to do (see the Types of Trekking section).

One of the main distinctions between guides and porters on the major mountains is that all guides speak English, whereas not all porters do. In fact, one of the ways a porter can improve his position is to learn to speak English.

More specific information about guides and porters in each area is provided in the individual mountain sections.

Guides Guides are highly recommended in some areas, especially if you're inexperienced or trekking alone, or where routes do not follow clear paths (or any path at all), and maps do not show enough detail for accurate navigation.

Guides are either part-time freelancers or work directly for the trekking companies. Generally, you shouldn't expect too much. Guides will usually be able to show you the way, and that's it. They do not have any qualifications or formal training. Even on the popular mountains, many guides only know the straightforward routes, and are not much use if you want to do something slightly unusual.

For the less-frequented routes and mountains, even if you take a guide, it is very important to familiarise yourself as much as possible with route conditions, water points, the likelihood of wild animals and so on. How you perceive factors such as 'near', 'far', 'easy', 'good to drink' and so on may be very different from how your guide sees them.

Of course, there are exceptions. In some areas, you may be able to arrange a knowledgeable and experienced guide through a reputable trekking company. A few companies have very experienced professional guides with knowledge of local vegetation and wildlife, first aid, map and compass work, rescue techniques and so on.

Only on Kilimanjaro, where all treks have to be organised through a trekking company, are guides obligatory. Unfortunately, this doesn't necessarily mean they are any better (see the Kilimanjaro section in the Tanzania chapter).

Several of the trekking areas described in this book are also wildlife reserves inhabited by animals such as buffalo, elephant and lion. An armed park ranger is obligatory here to protect you in case of close encounters. If required, these rangers will also act as guides. They are normally very knowledgeable and reliable.

Porters Porters are nearly always freelancers, doing some part-time carrying between working on their farms in the foothills of the mountains. In the major mountain areas, they have formed unions or clubs to standardise wages and improve conditions. If you want to do a supported trek, go to the club headquarters at the foot of the mountain and make arrangements there. The porters will usually be ready within a few hours, or next day at the longest.

Deals vary – usually you pay a daily rate plus a small extra fee to cover their food. Porters rarely have any equipment of their own, so you have to provide rucksacks for them. The usual way of doing things is for a porter to carry your main bag while you walk with just a day-pack containing camera, waterproofs, lunch and so on. There's normally a weight limit of around 16 kg, so if you're on a long trek, with camping gear and food for a week, you'll probably need two or even three porters per trekker. If you haven't got a spare rucksack, these can sometimes be hired, or you can make something up out of sacks and ropes from a market. A large foldable kitbag is a useful thing to have for this.

If you're hiring more than one porter, it's usual to appoint a 'chief porter' who will arrange the others. If you have hired a guide as well, he will often organise porters for you.

Anything in your rucksack that's likely to be damaged should be well packed, as bags are not always handled with reverence. Make sure the porter who's carrying the tomatoes or bottle of oil know's what he's got in his bag, and ask him to take care.

Even though you pay wages to your guide and porters, it is customary to tip them after your trek, if the service has been satisfactory. Rates vary in different areas, and are covered in more detail in the individual sections.

Emergency & Rescue

On the main mountains, it is very important to realise that if you have a serious accident it may be several days before you reach a hospital. In the more remote ranges it may take even longer. That's why trekking alone is never recommended.

Because you'll be trekking rather than climbing, an incapacitating accident is quite unlikely. In mountain national parks, rangers at the park entrance gates are usually in radio contact with their headquarters, so if you are involved in an emergency situation, help can be arranged. On the high mountains there are ranger posts on the mountain itself, at the bunkhouses on the main routes (the Marangu Route on Kilimanjaro and the Naro Moru Route on Mt Kenya). On these mountains, the park rangers have stretchers and operate a mountain rescue service.

Obviously, you should try to avoid leaving an injured person alone, but if there is no other option you should put them in a tent and sleeping bag and leave them plenty of food and water. If you send a local porter or guide to get help, it is better to write down all the details of the accident, in order to avoid confusion. A promise of a large bonus payment for speedy work is usually appropriate.

Responsible Trekking

Most of the treks in this book pass through mountain wilderness areas where the natural environment is protected. It's usually protected because it's in danger, and the danger comes from many sources, including the presence of trekkers.

To trek in the mountains of East Africa is a privilege, but with this privilege comes responsibility. There are several things you can do to lessen your own impact upon this fragile environment.

Fires Try to avoid using wood fires, or keep them as small as possible, in all areas where wood is scarce. This includes the high moorlands above the forests on the main mountains. Encourage porters to do the same. Even burning dead heather and groundsels is harmful, as this rotting vegetation supports various insects which are a vital link in the food chain; it also protects the thin covering of soil which would otherwise be washed away by rain.

Wood can be saved if you treat your drinking water with purification solutions instead of boiling it (this is usually more effective anyway – see the Health & First Aid chapter). If possible, you should support trekking companies who use stoves rather than wood fires for cooking.

A complete ban on wood fires may soon be introduced on several of the major mountains in East Africa. As the number of trekkers continues to increase this is to be welcomed and encouraged.

Water Do not pollute water supplies. For washing, take water from streams or tarns in a bowl or mug – do not wash or rinse cooking pans in the stream itself. Encourage porters to do the same. Wherever possible, use biodegradable soap and detergent. These are available from good outdoor equipment shops. Again, support trekking companies who follow these methods.

Toilets Wherever a toilet is provided at a hut or campsite, always use it, even if it's close to overflowing. If your hut or campsite does not have a toilet, bury your crap and toilet paper well away from paths and water supplies. Some trekking companies provide groups with a small spade specifically for this purpose. If toilet paper cannot be buried, burn it (if you've stopped using a fire, use matches, although this is very hard on wet windy days) or keep it in a strong plastic bag until you can dispose of it properly.

Rubbish Some huts and campsites have rubbish pits, but these are ugly and can injure scavenging wildlife, so it's better to bring down everything you take up, especially silver foil, plastics and tins. (I've seen trekkers, who *appeared* completely rational, dispose of tins and foil packets by throwing them on the fire.) Take strong plastic bags for carrying rubbish down and instruct your porters to do the same (it's got to be lighter than when it came up). A promise of a slightly larger tip for their trouble will make the matter easier. Once again, you can support trekking companies who instruct their porters to carry rubbish down.

NATIONAL PARKS
Entrance Fees

Most of the mountain wilderness areas described in this book are national parks, and this normally means you have to pay fees to trek and camp within them. Fees vary between park and between country (see the individual mountain sections for details). In some areas the fees are very low, but in other parks they can certainly bump up the cost of trekking.

For example, park fees for a six-day trek (five nights) on Mt Kenya come to about US$100, while fees for six days on Kilimanjaro's Marangu Route are almost US$200. For seven days on one of Kili's other routes, the fees total US$345.

Many trekkers complain about the high prices, but there is no reason why rich visitors from the West should come to a developing country and expect everything to be cheap. If national parks can produce revenue rather than be a drain on those countries' limited resources, this should be welcomed. It's only fair that part of your money should contribute to this process.

Some of the revenue can be channelled back into the management of the parks, and some of it can be directed to local people who live in the surrounding areas. Unfortunately, in many places the revenue does not go to back into the parks or to the local people, but to government treasuries, where it gets swallowed up by other schemes, or simply 'disappears'.

Benefits

It is generally agreed that the conservation of forests has many benefits, on a local and global level, and many of the mountain national parks and reserves in East Africa protect large areas of forest. It is important to remember, however, that national parks are a luxury in Africa, where populations continue to expand and the demand for cultivation land is high. When local people are prevented from clearing the forests and cultivating the land, this naturally leads to resentment. Even if the forest on the mountain protects the land lower down and ensures water supplies, and may have several other benefits, this is not always understood or appreciated. (Put more simply, for a family with 10 hungry kids, the long-term benefits of national parks are less important than the immediate task of finding somewhere to grow food for next year.)

It may be possible to overcome this clash of interests if some of the money earnt by the national parks goes to local people in the surrounding areas. In this way the land is seen to have a tangible value, and the park itself (and everything it contains) is more likely to survive intact.

The local people could benefit in many ways. In the most direct (although rather unproductive) way, the park revenue could be passed on in the form of cash hand-outs, or go towards providing food to replace the crops that couldn't be grown. More farsighted uses for the revenue could include putting it into schemes to improve farming techniques or the development of clean water supplies. Other uses might be the provision of health centres or family planning clinics, or education schemes where the benefits of the national parks, and the forests they contain, are clearly explained. In this way, eventually, the demand for more land might be reduced and the revenue earnt by the park would have gone towards ensuring its own survival, as well as benefiting the local people in the process. (These arguments are necessarily simplified and most are not original, but they are still very important.)

Park management and conservation schemes employing some of these proposals already exist in several parks in East Africa, but they are noticeably lacking in others. But generally, things are changing, and as they do, the local people will benefit and the parks themselves will become increasingly secure. Trekkers should bare all this in mind when complaining about entrance fees.

TREKKING ROUTES

This book covers a selection of trekking routes in all the major mountains and ranges of East Africa, plus several other routes through some areas of plain, plateau or rolling hill country, and in lesser-known areas. Generally, the treks are through wilderness areas, although some sections may pass through farms and villages on the foothills of mountains, and some routes pass through lightly populated areas.

The emphasis of this book is firmly on treks, meaning long walks of several days' duration, so areas where shorter walks are possible have been covered only briefly. Because this book is written mainly for visitors who may have limited time, treks which would involve difficult access or complex logistics have not been included.

Most of the mountains in East Africa are isolated peaks or massifs surrounded by plains. They are not extended ranges like the Alps, the Andes or the Himalaya. Therefore, most of the treks described in this book are between four days and one week long, although on the major mountains this can be extended by splitting some days in two and adding rest days and long sidetracks.

It is common for trekkers visiting East Africa to include two or more mountains, which usually means travelling overland (or by air) between the trekking areas. Consequently, the chapters contain enough travel information to help you get between the different mountains.

If this is your first visit to East Africa, you'll almost certainly want to include a major trek on one of the region's main attractions, Kilimanjaro and Mt Kenya, where there's a choice of several different trekking routes of varying lengths and standards. Including another large mountain during your visit will help you acclimatize for the major trek, and also show you that East Africa has a lot more to offer the trekker than just these two giants. Some of the trekking areas described in this book are much lower, and include a variety of landscapes, from fertile farmland to baking desert, which contrasts sharply with the mountain wilderness of the high peaks; again, this will give you a wider perspective on what East Africa has to offer.

In the major mountain areas, between one and four different trekking routes are described in detail, and a number of other trekking possibilities for more adventurous or experienced trekkers are outlined. Some of the routes are established 'classics' while others are more unusual.

In some mountain areas there are no properly defined trekking routes, so I've 'created' them by joining up a series of existing paths and tracks, or made suggestions on where you can do this yourself.

The table shows the trekking routes that are described in detail.

Trek Standards and Times

Country	Trekking Area	Name of Trek	Days	Standard	Access
Tanzania	Mt Kilimanjaro	Marangu Route	5-6	Mod	OT
		Machame-Mweka Route	6-7	Mod-Diff	OT
	Mt Meru	Momella Route	3-4	Mod	Bus
	Crater Highlands	Traverse	5-7	Easy-Mod	OT
Kenya	Mt Kenya	Naro Moru Route	3-4	Easy-Mod	Bus
		Burguret Route	4-5	Diff	Bus
		Sirimon-Chogoria Traverse	5-8	Mod	Bus
		Timau Route	4-5	Diff	Bus
	Aberdare Range	Aberdare Contrasts	4	Easy	Car/OT
	Loroghi Hills	Loroghi Hills Circuit	3-5	Easy	Bus
	Suguta Valley	Long Route	8-9	Mod-Diff	Bus/OT
		Short Route	5-7	Mod-Diff	Bus/OT
Uganda	Rwenzoris	Bujuku-Mubuku Circuit	6-7	Mod-Diff	Bus
	Mt Elgon	Sasa Route	4-6	Easy-Mod	Bus
Malawi	Mulanje Massif	Traverse	5-6	Easy-Mod	Bus
		Lichenya Loop	3	Easy	Bus
	Nyika Plateau	Nyika Highlights	4-5	Easy-Mod	Bus
		Livingstonia	3-4	Easy-Mod	Bus

Abbreviations: OT – Organised Trek   Mod – Moderate   Diff – Difficult

Route Standard

Routes are classified in this book as 'easy', 'moderate' or 'difficult'. Classifying a route is difficult and often tends to be subjective. It can also depend very much on the weather at that time of year, or even that day. Each route description outlines the condition of the route (eg clear or hard to follow, boggy or easy underfoot) and how strenuous it is (eg long or short days, generally flat or several steep gradients).

Obviously, some people will find the routes easier than others. The classifications are based on the assumption that you're a fairly regular walker or backpacker (or reasonably fit from another sport) who would have no trouble covering 15 to 20 km in a day on reasonable paths.

Days Required

The trekking routes have all been divided into stages, each corresponding to a day's walk.

The end of each stage is either a bunkhouse, a hut or a place for camping. Most of these overnight sites have water, but there are a few 'dry sites' where water has to be carried in. It's not always possible to stop for the night just anywhere. Even if you're not using mountain huts (where they exist) you'll still be restricted to places that can provide a good campsite.

Some stages are short, while others are very long. It's sometimes possible to divide a long stage in half or combine two shorter stages.

Most treks also include 'sidetracks', which branch off the main route for a few minutes, a few hours, or even for an extra couple of days. For many stages, alternatives are suggested which are either harder or easier.

Distance, Time & Altitude

Each stage or sidetrack heading includes details on the number of km, hours and metres of ascent, where these figures are useful or relevant.

Kilometres are approximate. They are measured off the maps, which cannot take account of winding paths, steep gradients, or route conditions such as snow, scree or thick mud. Read on their own, the number of km covered by each stage is virtually meaningless. It is essential to read the km figure alongside the number of hours required to cover the stage. The hours given are based on average minimum and maximum walking times, and are intended as a guideline only.

On the higher stages they presume you are reasonably well-acclimatized. You may find yourself doing the stages in more or less time than the amounts shown, but you will still be able to see if the stage is long or short, hard or easy. Note that times are walking times only, and do not include long stops. You should allow extra time for photo and lunch breaks, especially if you're a keen to take photographs (or have a hearty appetite).

The km-to-hours ratio also gives you an indication of the difficulty of the stage. For example, on the way to the summit of Kilimanjaro, it takes at least six hours to cover only three km. By this you know the going is steep and hard!

Where metres of ascent are given, this is the overall altitude gain (or loss) between one night's camp and the next. It is not the total metres of ascent you actually have to cover on that stage. On major mountains, due to the nature of the landscape, most stages are either mainly up (or mainly down) anyway. Crossing several large ridges and valleys in Himalayan style, although it does occur, is not usual.

The overall metres gained is most useful for calculating your rate of ascent, as keeping below a certain amount each day helps you to avoid altitude sickness (see the Health & First Aid chapter).

Altitudes are rounded to the nearest 10 metres (except for major features). Some figures are also given in feet (for all you imperialists out there). There's a conversion table at the back of the book.

Asking for Directions

When asking local guides or porters how far it is to the next camp or wherever, you should always ask in terms of hours, as most have a fairly hazy idea about distance and, as already indicated, this is often meaningless anyway. In practice, many guides have a fairly hazy idea about time too, so never take anything too literally.

Outside the wilderness areas, if asking local people for directions, time and distance often become very difficult to tie down. 'Short' and long', 'near' and far' take on completely different meanings. Most people in Africa don't have our obsession with time. If they walk a route it may not matter whether it takes three or eight hours. They just know they'll get there some time that day, and can't see why you should want it any more precise than that.

Asking directions can also be problematic. At a fork in the path, never say 'Is this the way to...?', as you'll almost certainly be told 'Yes' whichever way you point. Asking 'Where is...?' gives you a much better chance of getting shown the right direction.

Terms Used in This Book

The treks in this book generally keep to 'paths', which are normally clear to follow, and are for walking only, or 'tracks', which are drivable, even though they're unsurfaced and most are very rarely used by vehicles. A trek generally would not follow 'trails', because in Africa these are routes created by animals, which may not go anywhere useful, if they go anywhere at all. Some treks follow routes where paths are very faint or non-existent; here you make your own way through bush or open moorland.

Rivers have 'true' left and right banks. I have avoided the confusion this sometimes causes by saying 'Keep the river to your right', or referring to the river's north or south bank.

I have distinguished between 'bunkhouses' (usually with facilities and a caretaker) and 'huts' (usually without) in the accommodation sections. I have also distinguished between official 'campsites', which may have facilities for which a fee is usually charged, and 'camping places' which are unofficial and have no facilities (you just put up your tent).

Place Names

During your trek, you are likely to find different books and maps using various spellings for certain place names. Variations are usually slight and shouldn't cause too much confusion. Some are due to 'old' colonial spellings being Africanised, others are due to plain old error and inconsistency. The emphasis put by some writers on the 'correct' spelling of places, where traditionally names were never written down, is sometimes just a tad too obsessive. In this book, where mountains or features have been completely renamed I include old and new names, and if the change is slight I have generally used the latest version. But if you come across inconsistencies between this book and the real world don't worry about it too much.

Similarly, you may also come across slight inconsistencies where various maps give different heights for mountains and other features. Usually, the differences are slight and unlikely to cause any problems.

Maps

The maps in this book provide enough information if you keep to the routes described. Unless you're a real stickler for detail, you probably won't need any other map. But it's impossible to show every single feature. Small streams, for example, have been omitted unless they are an important reference point. Faint paths have also been omitted, unless they form part of the route. On some treks there is no path at all and you must make your own way – this is shown on the map as a dotted line.

Trek Profiles

The trek profile diagrams indicate daily altitude gains and losses for major treks. The stage numbers shown on the horizontal line relate to the stages in the text. Metres of altitude gained or lost are shown on the vertical line.

Route Changes

Most of the treks in this book are in mountain wilderness areas which are unlikely to be affected by major projects such as road-building schemes or logging concessions. Most natural features are unlikely to change, although fragile soil and vegetation covers are slowly disappearing on some routes, and glaciers are receding at an alarming rate on the major peaks.

In some managed areas, the authorities make alterations to trekking routes. This can involve opening up new paths to take the pressure off existing routes, or closing old ones to allow the damaged land to recover.

On some mountains, the routes are being 'improved' by the addition of facilities such as bridges and signposts. In some areas, huts are being constructed, while in other places old huts are being removed and new campsites established.

New regulations concerning fires, rubbish disposal, campsites and so on are frequently introduced. The most likely changes are outlined in the individual route descriptions. In Africa, 'a plan is an alternative to what actually happens', as the old saying goes, but by trekking through this region you will normally have more than the usual amount of control over your own destiny. If you are ready and prepared for the changes you can usually take them (often quite literally) in your stride.

ACCOMMODATION
On the Mountains

Most of the treks described in this book are through wilderness areas where there are no settlements, and nothing in the way of fully serviced Alpine hotels or Himalayan teashops. On some of the more popular routes there are bunkhouses and huts, which means you can do the trek without a tent. To trek in the more remote areas you need a tent and a full set of camping gear. Even on the routes where basic accommodation is available, many trekkers still camp anyway.

Bunkhouses are generally large, fairly well maintained, with separate sleeping and dining rooms, and a permanent caretaker. The bunkhouses on Kilimanjaro's Marangu Route even have electric lights. Huts are usually smaller and a lot more basic, with little more than a roof and four walls (if you're lucky), such as the tin sheds found on some parts on Mt Kenya and the Rwenzoris. The word 'hut' is often used to describe any kind of building on a mountain, so if you're planning to rely on them, make sure you know what facilities are available. Just to confuse matters, other words such as 'lodge', 'camp' and 'cottage' are used in different countries. Wherever you stay, you always need a sleeping bag. If you're not on an organised trek, you need cooking gear too.

Carrying a tent (and a good set of camping equipment) means you can be completely self-contained and self-sufficient, allowing you to trek on unusual routes and through more remote mountain areas, and giving you a lot more freedom and independence wherever you go. Although some routes on the main mountains have huts, a tent is either essential or highly recommended for most of the treks described in this book.

If you are using local guides and porters, they usually sleep in the huts or in their own section of the bunkhouses, even if you are camping (see the Guides & Porters section earlier in this chapter).

Bunkhouses, huts and campsites, and the facilities available at each are described in detail in the individual mountain sections.

In Between Mountains

When travelling in East Africa, getting to and from the mountain areas, you'll inevitably need accommodation in some of the towns and cities you pass through. Each country chapter mentions a few hotels in the towns nearest the trekking areas, and in the capital city (as you'll arrive there first, or pass through between mountains).

In all the countries covered in this book, you can find a wide range of places to stay, from international-class Hiltons and Sheratons in the cities, through reasonably priced, comfortable, mid-range hotels, down to the most basic lodging houses out in the sticks or the rough end of town. In Malawi most towns have a Council Resthouse which provides cheap accommodation. Some towns in Kenya and Tanzania have youth hostels and YMCAs, with dormitories or private rooms.

All over East Africa you can also find public campsites, although most of these tend to be on the coast or in the national parks rather than in the towns.

Standards vary between countries but quality generally reflects price. Hotels at the top end of the range have clean, air-conditioned, self-contained rooms with hot showers and toilets that work all the time. In the mid range, rooms are self-contained, but there may not always be hot water, and probably fans instead of air-conditioning. Near the bottom end, hotel rooms are not always clean (they are sometimes downright filthy), bathrooms are usually shared and often in an appalling state, and a hole in the window may provide some fresh air.

Some hotels charge for a bed only, with all meals extra. Others offer bed & breakfast (B&B). If breakfast is provided it's usually on a par with the standard of accommodation: a full buffet in more expensive places; tea, toast and eggs further down the scale.

FOOD
Where to Buy Food
Wherever you go in East Africa you can always find enough food in the cities and large towns to provide for a trek in the wilderness. Freeze-dried lightweight food used by mountaineers is not usually necessary. If you need to save every gram, you can buy food at the Natural Action Mountain Centre in Nairobi (see the Buying & Hiring Locally section).

For treks in Kenya, the best place to buy food and supplies is Nairobi. Here you can get just about anything in the many large shops and supermarkets. Some items are imported and expensive, but you can usually find a locally made, cheaper version. Food suitable for trekking, and easy to find in Nairobi, includes: rice, several sorts of pasta, lentils, packet soups, bread, porridge oats, cornflakes, sweet biscuits, crackers, margarine and jam (in tins), peanut butter, honey, cheese, eggs, fresh meat, packets of bacon, sausage and cooked meats, tins of cooked mince and steak, corned beef, luncheon meat and sardines, tins of beans, tomatoes and

other vegetables, dried fruit, nuts, chocolate, coffee, tea, drinking chocolate, and dried or UHT milk in cartons. There are sometimes shortages of flour and loose sugar, although you can usually find sugar cubes. You can also buy vegetable or meat stock cubes, curry powder and all sorts of herbs and spices to liven up your meals.

Most of the stuff listed above can also be found in other large towns in Kenya, so you won't need to go back to Nairobi in between treks. A lot of food from Kenya is shipped to Tanzania and Uganda, so you also can find most of the things on this list in Arusha, Moshi and Kampala (although not always with the same range or choice).

In the cities and large towns of Malawi, there's even more choice than Nairobi. Most of the stuff is imported from South Africa and the choice in the supermarkets is the same as in any developed country, although prices are about the same too. If you've been in the bush for a while, it's fairly mind-blowing to come into the hypermarket in Lilongwe and see a whole aisle of different breakfast cereals, and at least six sorts of mustard.

Fruit and vegetables can be bought in markets all over East Africa. Depending on the seasons, you can usually find potatoes, carrots, cabbage, onions, tomatoes, courgettes, zuchinis, aubergines (eggplants), avocados, green beans, spinach, peas and all sorts of dried beans. In the fruit line there's bananas, pineapples, oranges and mangoes.

(For full details of where to buy food before a trek, see Supplies, in each trekking section.)

Cooking Tips
When you're on trek, it's always worth trying to carry as much fresh stuff as you can, to cut down on tins and packets. This saves weight and also reduces the amount of rubbish you need to bring down. Vegetables are also cheap, easy to find, nutritious, quick-cooking (if you chop them up small) and long-lasting.

Remember that water boils at a lower temperature as you get higher in the mountains, so food takes longer to cook. When you're above 4000 metres, lentils and rice are bad news for the fuel supply and the digestion. Pasta is better at this height. Dried beans always take a long time to cook and are not really suitable as trekking food. If you're a bean fiend, you can buy them in tins, or wait until you get off the mountain and then go to a restaurant!

Places to Eat

In the cities and large towns there's usually a good choice, ranging from quality restaurants serving international or speciality foods, through a broad spectrum of mid-range cafes, down to basic snack-bars with only three things on the menu.

In villages and rural areas the choice is also limited. The eating houses cater for the locals and serve straightforward, cheap, filling meals, usually a meat stew with some stodge – rice, plantain bananas, or the ubiquitous maize meal *(ugali* in Kenya, Uganda and Tanzania, *nsima* in Malawi).

Vegetarians don't have an easy time. The smarter places usually have fish; otherwise it's egg and chips in the mid-range places and bean stew in the cheapies. Many large towns have at least one Indian restaurant, and some of these do good vegetarian meals.

Snacks are available everywhere, at roadside stalls or in snack-bars with a cup of tea. These include *mandazis/ndazi*, a deep-fried dough ball, not unlike a doughnut when fresh, plus chapattis, samosas (usually called *sambusas)* and cake.

If your tongue craves a break, Nairobi has an amazing selection of junk-food joints, which are great to come back to after a few weeks of trekking in the wilds. You can also get pizzas in Blantyre, Ethiopian food in Kampala, and Chinese takeaway in Arusha.

Health & First Aid

The health and first-aid information in this chapter was prepared by Dr Corinne Hunter, MB BCh DA.

PRE-DEPARTURE PREPARATIONS
General Health & Fitness
Before leaving for a trek in East Africa consider carefully your physical health and general fitness, and don't leave it all until the last minute! Trekking in Africa, particularly in the hotter areas, can be very strenuous and should not be underestimated, so it is sensible to be reasonably fit before you start. If you have any known medical problems or are concerned about your health, have a full check-up. It is far better to have any problems recognised and treated at home than to find out about them halfway up a mountain. Get your teeth checked as well; dental fillings are more likely to come loose at high altitude.

First-aid Training
In the unlikely event of a medical emergency, a good understanding of resuscitation techniques (CPR), and control of bleeding could save a life. If your first-aid skills and knowledge are not up-to-date, it would be a good idea to do an appropriate course before you leave home.

Vaccinations
Give yourself plenty of time to get your vaccinations. There may be a gap of several weeks between the administration of different vaccines, or of two boosters of the same vaccine.

Yellow Fever This vaccine is compulsory for travel in East Africa, and a valid International Certificate of Vaccination is required at most borders and airports in the East African region. The vaccination is safe for healthy individuals, confers almost 100% immunity and is valid for at least 10 years.

Typhoid There are three different typhoid vaccines: two are given by injection and the third is oral. All seem to be about 70 to 80% effective in preventing typhoid fever. Side effects are usually pain and inflammation around the area of injection, but the vaccine may cause a mild systemic illness lasting one or two days.

Meningococcus Vaccination against meningococcal meningitis is now highly recommended for travel in East Africa. Immunisation against this potentially lethal disease is up to 90% effective and lasts for about three years.

Polio Poliomyelitis is rare in the West but endemic in some developing countries. The vaccination is recommended for travel in East Africa. If you were immunised as a child, a single booster will confer immunity for ten years; if not, then the full course of three doses, four weeks apart, will be required.

Tetanus This is required if you have not had a tetanus vaccine booster during the past 10 years. Most people have had a primary course in childhood; if you missed out, you will need the full course of three injections, each a month apart.

Tuberculosis You may have received the BCG vaccination against TB during childhood. If you are unsure, consult your doctor, who can check your immunity and advise you accordingly.

Hepatitis A This is usually a mild disease but can, very rarely, be fatal. It is therefore highly recommended that you be vaccinated against it. Until recently, gamma globulin injections were used, but there is now a specific anti-Hepatitis A preparation which confers immunity for several years.

Cholera This vaccine is of very limited use, conferring about 50% protection at best. The World Health Organization no longer recommends the cholera vaccination for travel to or from endemic areas, but on some of the more sleepy border crossings in East Africa this message has not got through to immigration officials, so you may still be asked for a certificate of cholera vaccination.

Rabies This vaccination is not routinely recommended for travellers to East Africa, unless you are likely to be a long way from medical help, or working with animals.

Antimalarial Prophylaxis

Antimalarial prophylaxis regimens vary between countries, so follow the advice of your doctor, who should be able to obtain up-to-date recommendations. Remember that no antimalarial medication gives you full protection – it is equally, if not more, important to avoid mosquito bites in the first place. Cover your skin as much as possible, particularly during the evenings, use insect repellents and sleep under a mosquito net (see the Malaria section).

First-Aid Kit

This can be as small or as big as you wish, but remember that you have to carry it! You cannot possibly cover every eventuality, but you should equip yourself with enough to cope with minor accidents and illnesses. The type and extent of medication that you carry with you will probably depend on how many days from help you are likely to be. You can obtain practically any type of medicine in Nairobi, and most of the larger towns throughout East Africa have a pharmacy or local hospital where you can buy some of the frequently used medicines, including a variety of antibiotics. Cities and most large towns have private doctors' surgeries, where you can obtain advice or have tests done. As at home, you may well be required to obtain a doctor's prescription before buying any medicines.

Your first-aid kit should include most of the following items:

Supplies
- bandages
- gauze swabs
- adhesive tape
- non-adhesive dressings (eg Melonin)
- elasticated support bandage (for knees and ankles)
- sterile alcohol wipes
- steri-strips (paper stitches)
- safety pins
- small pair of scissors
- thermometer
- tweezers
- syringes
- sutures, surgical needles

Medication
- antiseptic cream
- antihistamine cream
- antibiotic cream – for infected wounds
- anti-sickness tablets
- anti-diarrhoeal tablets
- antihistamine tablets
- oral rehydration tablets or powder
- pain killers, aspirin or paracetamol (acetamenophen)
- codeine
- chloramphenicol eye drops or ointment
- Diamox
- metronidazole or tinidazole – seven-day course
- other antibiotics
- Mefloquin

If you are on regular medication at home, take enough supplies for your trip if there is any doubt of its availability abroad.

Antibiotics The use of metronidazole or tinidazole is discussed in the section on giardiasis and amoebiasis. Which other antibiotics (if any) are worth carrying is debatable. No single antibiotic works for all types of infection, and there is frequent resistance of bacteria to antibiotics because of their widespread use. The treks described in this book are not as remote as in some other parts of the world (eg the Himalaya), and you will rarely be more than a few days from medical help. It could be argued that if you are ill enough to require antibiotic treatment you ought to be seeking medical advice rather than self-administering these drugs.

Having said that, it is probably worth carrying a course of antibiotics such as cotrimoxazole to treat a persistent bacterial diarrhoea (see the Bacterial Diarrhoea section). In addition, if you know that you are prone to certain infections – for example, of the ear or the urinary tract – then it is worth carrying one or two courses of the appropriate antibiotic to treat the symptoms.

In summary, try to keep things simple, and discuss with your doctor all the medication you intend to take with you.

AIDS Prevention There is no guarantee of availability of sterile, contamination-free medical equipment in parts of East Africa. It is worth buying a pre-packed kit or at least carrying a small supply of hypodermic needles and syringes, venous cannulae and sutures (stitches).

BASIC RULES
Hygiene

To reduce the chances of contracting any illness, you should wash your hands frequently, particularly before handling or eating food. If you are on an organised trek, make sure your cooks, and any other people handling your food, also wash their hands. (Take an extra bar of soap to give to the cook.)

Food

Whether on trek or travelling between the mountains, be careful about eating fresh fruit or uncooked vegetables, as these may have been contaminated through handling, or soaked in contaminated water. Salads are notorious for harbouring all sorts of disease organisms. Fruit such as bananas, or anything that you peel or prepare yourself (presuming your own hands are clean) should be safe. Try to avoid food which has not been freshly cooked or has been not been fully reheated. Avoid raw meat and raw seafood.

Water

Many diseases are carried in water in the form of insect eggs, worms, protozoa, bacteria, viruses and so on. You can avoid these illnesses if your drinking water is purified.

This can be done by boiling, but this is a waste of fuel, and not always effective when you're on trek, as water boils at a lower temperature at altitude. For example, at the high camps on Mt Kenya, which are around 4200 metres, water boils at 86°C. This does not purify the water, and is also the reason why your tea is never really hot.

To purify water, use a filter to clear out the larger substances (anything you can see). For the smaller things, use a chemical agent. Chlorine and iodine are normally used, as tablets, powder or liquid, which you can buy from outdoor equipment suppliers. Both are effective if you keep to the recommended dosages, and allow the water to stand for the correct length of time. Silver-based tablets are also available, but these are not effective against some protozoa when they are in their 'cyst' stage, in which case a filter is essential. Even if the large substances in the water are not harmful (silt or vegetation), the purifying agents work better if you filter them out first.

Silver-based tablets are tasteless, whereas chlorine and iodine leave a taste which some people find unpleasant. Iodine can also have side effects if used on a very long-term basis, although it should be fine for a few weeks (or even a few months) on trek.

Water filters range from a simple canvas bag to some high-tech pumps with ceramic inserts. A cheap filter bag is fine if you're also using a chemical agent. Some filter systems also contain chemical agents, so you don't need to treat the water afterwards. When buying a water filter, make sure you know exactly what it does. A good supplier will be able to advise you. In the UK, a handy booklet on water treatment is produced by a company called SafariQuip (13a Waterloo Park, Stockport SK1 3BP (☎ (061) 429 8700). They also supply water filters and chemical agents, and other equipment for treks and safaris in Africa.

Dehydration This is a potentially dangerous and generally preventable condition. It is caused by excessive fluid loss through sweating, diarrhoea, vomiting or high fever, or inadequate fluid intake. The first obvious symptoms of dehydration are weakness, thirst, and passing small amounts of very concentrated urine. In extreme cases this may progress to drowsiness, inability to stand upright without fainting, and, finally, coma.

It is easy to forget how much fluid you are losing via perspiration whilst you are trekking, particularly if a strong breeze is drying your skin quickly; a good fluid intake should be maintained. A minimum of three litres a day is recommended, although up to five is better.

It is particularly important to maintain a reasonable fluid intake if you are suffering from diarrhoea or vomiting. Drink as much clear fluid as possible to replace what you are losing. If fluid loss is severe, use an oral rehydration solution as well. In the unlikely event that you cannot keep down any fluids and the vomiting and diarrhoea continue, you should not be trekking at all, and should seek medical attention.

Climatic Extremes

Trekking in East Africa may expose you to some of the most extreme temperatures you are ever likely to encounter.

If you are walking in the sun, always protect yourself. Ultraviolet light is stronger at high altitude. Beware of sunburn and use plenty of high-factor sunscreen. Always wear a sun hat, and drink plenty of fluid to avoid dehydration. Be especially careful on breezy days – even a light wind can cool your skin and make you less aware of potential sunburn. It can also cause rapid evaporation of sweat, making you unaware of the amount of body fluid that you are losing through perspiration.

It can become very cold on the higher slopes of East African mountains, but as long as you are adequately equipped there should be few problems. Make sure that you always carry enough extra clothing or a sleeping bag to ensure that you can keep yourself (or a companion) warm in case of injury. A reflective foil blanket for emergencies is compact and light. (See the What to Bring section in the Facts for the Trekker chapter.)

MEDICAL PROBLEMS & TREATMENT

This section outlines the symptoms and treatment of some of the illnesses more frequently encountered in East Africa. It also touches on certain conditions which are much less common, but which could have serious implications if left unrecognised. It certainly is not intended to put you off travelling in East Africa. Don't forget: the vast majority of travellers and trekkers go home having at worst suffered from a couple of bouts of diarrhoea.

Diarrhoea

Most travellers' diarrhoea is caused by infectious agents which are transmitted by faecal contamination of food or water, by contaminated utensils, or directly from one person's hands to another. When trekking it can usually be avoided by maintaining good personal hygiene, by ensuring your water is safe to drink, and by taking care with what you eat, as discussed earlier in this chapter.

Bacterial Diarrhoea This is by far the most common type of diarrhoea for trekkers and travellers. It may be associated with nausea, vomiting, fever, abdominal cramps and bloating. A small number of sufferers have bloody stools. Generally it is self-limiting and lasts about three to four days. Its main distinguishing feature is its sudden onset, whereas giardiasis and amoebiasis tend to have a more gradual onset over a period of days. Treatment is not usually required apart from ensuring that you take enough oral fluids. If the diarrhoea is severe you may want to replace the lost fluid with some reconstituted oral rehydration preparations. If you have none of these you can make your own, mixing one level teaspoon of salt and eight of sugar with one litre of (purified!) water. If the diarrhoea does not stop after a few days if may be worth taking a course of an appropriate antibiotic such as cotrimoxazole (Septrin or Bactrim) or amoxycillin, which should bring about a rapid improvement. If it does not, seek medical advice.

Giardiasis Giardiasis is caused by *Giardia*, an organism which inhabits the upper small intestine of humans. It leaves the intestine as a strong cyst, which is excreted in the faeces. It can then survive for three or more months in water before re-entering another human. It is most often transmitted through infected water, but can also be transmitted via food or directly from person to person. The cysts can be filtered out of water, or killed by boiling or chemical treatment (see the Water section).

The incubation period of giardiasis is normally about seven to 10 days. It has a gradual onset, and the stools tend to be loose, greasy and sometimes watery. The diarrhoea is often intermittent. Other symptoms are upper abdominal discomfort, churning intestines, and offensive-smelling belches and farts.

The symptoms may disappear without treatment after a few days, but normally will come and go for weeks or months. If you think that you have got giardiasis, and are unable to get to a doctor, it is reasonable to treat yourself with a course of either metronidazole (Flagyl) or tinidazole. The dose of metronidazole is two grams once a day for three days. That of tinidazole is two grams once only, repeated if necessary. If your diagnosis was right you will be rapidly cured.

Amoebic Dysentery Amoebiasis is transmitted in contaminated food and water, and is similar to giardiasis in that the amoeba can form a cyst which passes out of the human body in the faeces. It can then survive for weeks in the soil. Any cysts in water can be destroyed by boiling, or by treatment with iodine or chlorine preparations. The incubation period of the disease is two to four weeks. Most carriers are asymptomatic, but in those who are not, the symptoms are usually mild colicky abdominal pain with moderate diarrhoea, which often stops and then starts again just when you thought you were getting better. Occasionally, symptoms may progress to dysentery with fever and profuse diarrhoea.

If these latter symptoms appear, you should treat yourself immediately with either metronidazole (400 mg three times a day for five days), or tinidazole (two grams once a day for two or three days). The amoebae can occasionally pass via the bloodstream to the liver, giving rise to a liver abscess. The symptoms of this serious complication are fever, and pain in the liver below the ribcage on the right side of the abdomen.

Bacillic Dysentery This is a severe form of bacterial diarrhoea, most commonly caused by a bacterium called shigella. The symptoms are rapid onset of high fever, feeling unwell, and profuse, watery, bloody diarrhoea a few days later. Vomiting and severe abdominal cramps are common. Again, the fundamental treatment is rest and adequate hydration, preferably using oral rehydration solutions. Take small amounts of fluid at frequent intervals – about two to four times an hour. You may well need at least five litres of fluid per day, if not more. The symptoms will abate after about five days to a week, usually without antibiotic treatment, and will not recur.

Cholera For every severe case of cholera there are ten very mild cases. If you are unlucky enough to get the classic severe form, the symptoms are sudden onset of profuse, painless diarrhoea, which looks like water with white flecks in it. Vomiting is common but fever is not. The disease is self-limiting, lasting about a week. Fluid loss due to the diarrhoea can be massive, and rehydration is essential, with the sufferer requiring up to 20 litres of fluid per day to keep up with losses. This can be a medical emergency and help should be sought.

Fever

Fever is generally a reaction by the body to an ongoing infection. The fever itself can, and should, be brought down by sponging the sufferer with tepid water, and by giving paracetamol or aspirin. The cause may be obvious, such as in a bad case of food poisoning. It may be due to a viral illness which resolves after a few days without treatment.

Top: View of Kilimanjaro from Kenya's Amboseli National Park (DE)
Bottom: Marangu Route: The Saddle, the desert zone between Kibo & Mawenzi,
Kilimanjaro (DE)

Top: Kibo crater rim, eastern icefields in background, Kilimanjaro (DE)
Left: Umbwe Route: Barranco Hut and campsite, with Kibo behind, Kilimanjaro (DE)
Right: Trekker and guide at Kilimanjaro's summit flag (DE)

The cause may be a localised problem, such as a wound infection. If this is the case, with infection being severe enough to cause fever, a course of antibiotics is indicated.

Occasionally, a fever may be due to something more serious. It will rarely be an isolated symptom, and the descriptions listed here aim to give some guide as to what the illness may be. If there is any doubt, it is far safer to seek medical advice.

Hepatitis A Hepatitis A virus (HAV) is transmitted by ingestion of food contaminated with faeces from an infected person. The incubation period is about 15 to 40 days, and symptoms include fever, abdominal discomfort or pain, loss of appetite, nausea and headache. After a few days the stools become light-coloured, the urine turns dark, and the sufferer becomes jaundiced, with the skin and the whites of the eyes turning yellow. When the jaundice starts the fever will stop, but the nausea, headache and anorexia will continue for a week to a month. There is no specific treatment apart from rest, but it is important to drink a lot, particularly during the jaundice phase. Avoid alcohol completely. Normally a full recovery will take place but very rarely HAV can cause a devastating 'fulminant' hepatitis which is fatal within a few days. So it is always worth immunising yourself against it.

Typhoid & Paratyphoid Fever These two illnesses are very similar, and can be referred to collectively as enteric fever. They are caused by *Salmonella typhi* and *S. paratyphi*, bacteria, which are transmitted by faecal contamination of food and water. Most types of salmonella cause only local infection of the gut – gastroenteritis or 'food poisoning'. *Salmonella typhi* and *paratyphi* may invade the bloodstream, producing a serious illness with a gradual onset of high fever, headache, loss of appetite, abdominal pain and pink 'rose' spots on the skin. Constipation may occur, with diarrhoea starting later. The heart rate may be slow (particularly relative to the high fever, which would normally be expected to cause a fast heart rate).

If typhoid fever is left untreated it will cause serious complications in the gut, lungs and blood. Treat with rest and plenty of fluids, and keep the temperature down with tepid sponging and paracetamol or aspirin. Antibiotic treatment will be needed, and medical help should be sought rapidly if this disease is suspected.

Meningococcal Meningitis This is best avoided by getting immunised. Spread of the disease is person to person. The incubation period is two to three days, and the onset of the disease may be gradual or very rapidly progressive. Symptoms include headache, sensitivity to light, vomiting, high fever, neck stiffness and a skin rash. Urgent antibiotic treatment is required, as this disease can be rapidly fatal.

Schistosomiasis (Bilharzia) This is caused by blood flukes, which are tiny worms that invade the blood vessels and tissues of the intestine, liver and bladder. They are carried and multiply in certain types of freshwater snails, from which they are released in their thousands. The young schistozomes can survive in fresh non-chlorinated water and are able to directly penetrate human skin. Having entered the body they make their way to the liver where they develop and mate; the adult schistozomes then travel to the veins of the intestine or bladder. From here the eggs can be excreted via the faeces or urine.

Various types of disease can result from schistozome infection. It may cause local skin inflammation and a rash where the flukes have penetrated the skin. It can cause an acute illness about three to eight weeks later with a high fever, sweats, headache, cough and inflammation of the glands. Or schistosomiasis may result in chronic liver (or, less commonly, lung or bladder) disease in which the eggs cause tissue inflammation and destruction.

Diagnosis is by the detection of eggs in the urine or faeces, and treatment is with antiworm medicine. As always, it is best avoided in the first place. Don't swim or walk in lakes, streams or ponds, particularly if the water is stagnant. If you must walk in water that's likely to be infected, wear shoes and dry yourself energetically and thoroughly. You cannot get bilharzia from sea water.

Trypanosomiasis This disease, which is also known as sleeping sickness, is caused by a parasite transmitted by the tsetse fly. The main characteristic of trypanosomiasis is a red, painful nodule appearing on the skin about three to four days after being bitten. The glands in the same area may also become inflamed. After about two weeks the lesion disappears and the sufferer develops a generalised illness of fever, chills, headache and widespread inflammation of the glands. Three to six weeks after the bite, the parasites may invade the nervous system, causing weakness, recurrent fever and a constant headache. A patchy rash may appear and the person may become irritable and develop mood changes. If it is not treated it can be fatal.

You would probably notice if you were bitten by a tsetse fly. It is large (about 12 mm long), with scissor-like wings and a painful bite. The risk of infection is low, but if you think you are developing sleeping sickness seek medical help immediately.

Malaria This disease is widespread in East Africa. The malarial parasite is transmitted by the *Anopheles* mosquito. The infective parasites are stored in the salivary glands of the female mosquito and are injected via the insect bite into the bloodstream. From there they travel to the liver, where they develop and multiply. Then follows the cyclical release of parasites from the liver, which establishes serial infections of the red blood cells. It is this release of parasites and invasion of the red cells that causes periodic sweats and fever, which are characteristic of malaria.

Although mosquitoes may be found at high altitudes, the malarial parasite cannot survive in cold temperatures. However, evidence suggests that the parasites are becoming increasingly resistant to cold conditions. You should continue taking your antimalarial pills at all times, so that you are protected for lowland travel in between mountains.

The incubation period from bite to development of symptoms can vary from about six to 30 days. The onset may be sudden, with violent chills and sweats, and a high temperature. The fever may be constant at first, becoming intermittent. Alternatively, the onset may be more gradual, with symptoms such as diarrhoea, headache, abdominal pain, breathlessness or muscle pain. The fever may not start until later. If malaria is left untreated, serious complications can follow rapidly, including cerebral malaria, which is frequently fatal.

Prevention Don't underestimate malaria. Take your antimalarial tablets, starting a week before you reach East Africa, and finishing four weeks after you leave. Antimalarial recommendations vary, depending on where you live, but generally the current options are proguanil (Paludrine) two tablets every day and chloroquine (several trade names) two tablets once a week, or (where it is licensed for such use) Mefloquin once a week. There are obvious advantages to only having to take a tablet once a week, but on anecdotal evidence at least, Mefloquin seems to have more minor side effects than chloroquine and proguanil. Neither guarantee 100% protection but they may lessen the severity of symptoms if you are unlucky enough to contract malaria while taking the tablets. Avoiding mosquito bites in the first place is the surest protection; cover up in the evenings and use insect repellents and a mosquito net. Make sure that your net is big enough. Don't forget, mosquitoes can bite through the net if part of your body is touching it.

Treatment If you think you have malaria, get a blood test and seek medical advice. A positive blood test result will give you the diagnosis, but a negative result does not necessarily exclude malaria. If you cannot get to a doctor you may have to start treatment yourself. The treatment that used to be recommended was chloroquine 600 mg (four 150-mg tablets) followed by 300 mg six hours later and 300 mg the next day. But because there is now so much chloroquine-resistant malaria in East Africa, it is now recommended to use Mefloquin in a dose of three tablets, followed by two tablets after six hours and, for people over 60 kg, a third dose of one tablet after a further six hours. It is worth carrying a course of Mefloquin in your first-aid kit. This treatment may make you feel worse than you did before, with dizziness, abdominal pain, diarrhoea and vomiting being common side effects. Mefloquin should normally be avoided in pregnancy.

A final word of warning – continue your antimalarial tablets for the recommended period when you get home. If you become ill within about a month of arriving home, tell your doctor where you've been. It could save a lot of people, including yourself, a lot of trouble.

Yellow Fever The vaccine is 100% effective, so get vaccinated to avoid the disease (and being stopped at borders).

Other Diseases & Medical Problems
Tuberculosis This disease is widespread in East Africa. If you have not been immunised, avoid people coughing into your face and don't drink unpasteurized milk. Cheese and yoghurt are safe, as the process used to make them kills the bacilli.

Rabies This virus is transmitted by infected animals. It cannot be transmitted through intact skin – the animal needs to bite you. The incubation period varies from about 10 days to several months, after which symptoms of headache and fever may progress to varying degrees of paralysis, muscle spasm and, eventually, death from respiratory failure. If you think you have been bitten by a rabid animal, clean the bite thoroughly with soap or detergent and seek medical help immediately.

Tetanus Tetanus is caused a bacterium which survives as spores in the soil. The tetanus spores can be introduced into the body through injury – dirty puncture wounds, burns or even relatively minor wounds. The incubation period of the disease is four to 21 days, and the disease produces symptoms of stiff or rigid muscles, 'lockjaw', difficulty swallowing and, later, agonising convulsions of the body. It is difficult to treat, potentially fatal, and can be prevented by immunisation.

Worms Worms can be picked up from contaminated vegetables and undercooked meat, or they can get through your skin if you walk around in bare feet. They don't cause diarrhoea but if left untreated for a long time they may cause complications such as anaemia. Treatment is with a drug called mebendazole, which is safe and widely available.

Sexually Transmitted Diseases If you have had sex with an infected person, symptoms such as genital sores, warts, blisters, rashes and discharge or pain when urinating may indicate that you have caught whatever they had. Celibacy is the best prevention but using a condom certainly helps. Treatment is generally with antibiotics.

AIDS (HIV Virus) AIDS is now highly prevalent in East Africa. The HIV virus is transmitted through blood and semen. If you have any new sexual contacts whilst in Africa you would be well advised to use a condom. Most carriers of the virus are unaware that they are infected.

Avoiding a blood transfusion while away might not be a matter of personal choice. Blood in Nairobi is screened for HIV, but as in the West, that does not fully guarantee its safety. If you need an injection make sure an unopened, disposable or sterile needle is used. It's a good idea to carry a supply of needles and syringes in your first-aid kit.

Hepatitis B This is transmitted in the same way as HIV. The onset of hepatitis is gradual and symptoms are similar to those of Hepatitis A, but it can result in serious long-term complications such as liver cirrhosis and cancer of the liver.

Tropical Ulcers & Skin Infections Tropical ulcers are common, and are often related to an injury or insect bite. They generally occur below the knee, and develop as a small red blister which bursts to form a painful spreading ulcer. The ulcer tends to stop growing after a few weeks, but by this time may be as big as 10 cm in diameter. Treat by cleaning the ulcer with antiseptic and then covering it with a sterile, preferably non-adherent, dressing. Keeping the ulcer clean is of fundamental importance, as is removing dressings very carefully so as to avoid destroying all the healing that has taken place. A course of antibiotics, such as a penicillin, will probably be needed.

Scratches and cuts can become infected, and should be treated in the same way. Infection in the wound is indicated by the skin margins becoming red, painful and swollen. More serious infection can cause swelling of the involved limb and of the neighbouring lymph glands. The sufferer may develop a fever, and will need medical attention.

Snake Bites There are some basic rules about dealing with snake bites. The first is to try to calm and reassure the patient. The second is to clean the wound and cover it with a dressing. (Do *not* cut the wound open and try to suck out the venom – this procedure is not effective and leads to infection.) The third is to get the victim to hospital as quickly as possible – venomous bites are rarely fatal within five hours of the bite occurring. This may not appear to be of much help halfway up a mountain, but the chances of encountering a snake in the mountains are very low anyway.

If someone does get bitten, after cleaning the wound and covering it with a dressing apply a bandage firmly and evenly up the whole limb, or else apply a tourniquet to the limb immediately above the wound. When the bandage or tourniquet is in place, it is vital to make sure you can still feel a pulse below the tourniquet (ie, in the wrist or foot). Do not release the compression until the patient reaches hospital. It is also helpful to immobilise the affected limb.

WOMEN'S HEALTH
Gynaecological Problems
Poor diet, lowered resistance due to the use of antibiotics for stomach upsets, and even contraceptive pills, can lead to vaginal infections when travelling in hot climates. Keeping the genital area clean, and wearing skirts or loose-fitting trousers and cotton underwear will help to prevent infections.

Yeast infections, characterised by a rash, itch and discharge, can be treated with a vinegar or even lemon-juice douche or with yoghurt. Nystatin suppositories are the usual medical prescription. Trichomonas is a more serious infection; symptoms are a discharge and a burning sensation when urinating. Male sexual partners must also be treated and, if a vinegar-water douche is not effective, medical attention should be sought. Flagyl is the prescribed drug.

Pregnancy
The risk of miscarriage is greatest during the first three months of pregnancy, and during the last three months you're unlikely to feel up to trekking across Mt Kenya or Kilimanjaro anyway. If you do travel during pregnancy, discuss it with your doctor first and sort out the most appropriate vaccinations and antimalarial medication you will need.

ACUTE MOUNTAIN SICKNESS
Several of the treks described in this book are on high mountains, where the altitude can lead to an illness called acute mountain sickness (AMS), more usually known as altitude sickness. The symptoms of AMS can be unpleasant enough to spoil your trek, and in some cases cause you to abandon it. It can also be fatal. However, if you understand something about the causes of AMS there are many steps you can take to minimise its effects, or even avoid it completely.

Altitude

Atmospheric pressure and the oxygen content of the air decrease in an approximately exponential manner as altitude increases. This means that as you trek higher, the breaths you take contain less oxygen. Above a certain altitude this can have a detrimental effect on your body's function and performance. For most trekkers, the effects of reduced oxygen become apparent at around 3000 metres.

However, some 15 million people in the world live above 3000 metres, and there are permanent residents in some mountain areas living above 4000 metres. These people are acclimatized to the altitude – their bodies have adapted to cope with the lower oxygen content of the air.

Acclimatization is the resetting of physiological mechanisms which allow the body to return oxygen levels in the tissues to normal or near-normal. In this way, climbers and trekkers can continue to perform reasonably well at altitudes that would otherwise make them incapable of any strenuous exercise, or even render them unconscious.

This process is not instantaneous, and when your rate of ascent is faster than the body's ability to adjust to the gain in altitude then AMS occurs. The symptoms of AMS can be unpleasant, serious or even fatal. It is therefore essential that your own rate of ascent should allow for this adjustment.

There is wide variation between people in their ability to acclimatize. Obviously, it is helpful to be reasonably fit when walking up a mountain, although fitness seems to bear no direct correlation to the speed of acclimatization. Indeed, a very fit person may be tempted to ascend faster than normal, so bringing upon themselves more severe symptoms of AMS. In general, although there is a lot of variation between individuals, each person's response to altitude is fairly constant on different occasions, given similar conditions and speed of ascent.

Symptoms & Treatment

Acute mountain sickness usually develops in the first eight to 24 hours at high altitude. It occurs infrequently at altitudes below 3000 metres. Mild symptoms include headache, poor appetite, nausea, fatigue, and poor sleep quality. At this stage you should stop your ascent. Rest, frequent small meals and mild painkillers may be all that is required to relieve the symptoms. Avoid alcohol. After the symptoms have fully abated, you may be able to continue your ascent.

If the symptoms worsen to severe headache and vomiting, you must not ascend any further, and should descend to an altitude where the symptoms abate. Altitude sickness in its most severe form can progress to either pulmonary oedema (fluid on the lungs) or cerebral oedema (swelling of the brain). Symptoms of fluid on the lungs include shortness of breath and frothy spit, sometimes pink-stained. Symptoms of cerebral oedema include severe headache (which may be worse when lying down), vomiting, dizziness and loss of balance, blurred or double vision, and drowsiness progressing to coma. These conditions can be fatal, and the only treatment is immediate descent.

Prevention

Gradual Ascent The surest way to acclimatize properly and prevent the development of AMS is by gradual ascent. Recommendations from the international mountain rescue organisations vary, and include ascending at a rate of not more than 500 metres per day over an altitude of 3000 metres. Some recommendations follow this method and also advise a rest day every third day. Of course, sometimes it's not possible to do this, because of the position of huts or campsites, in which case you should follow the recommendations as closely as you can.

Staging Another recommended method is that of 'staging', whereby you remain at an intermediate altitude between 3000 and 4000 metres for an extra day before ascending further. This seems to be more appropriate to the high mountains of East Africa. On Mt Kenya, most of the roadhead or low moorland camps (eg Met Station, Judmaier Camp, the Chogoria roadhead, the new Timau roadhead) are between 3000 and 3200 metres; you should try to stay two nights here. On Kilimanjaro the mid-way huts or camps (eg Horombo, Shira Cave, Barranco Hut) are all between 3700 and 4000 metres; two nights here is even more strongly recommended.

In the Rwenzoris, the ascent is more gradual, and on the other mountains above 3000 metres the trekking altitudes are not so high, so AMS is less likely to be a problem. Although a rest day is not essential here, it always helps.

Diamox Proper acclimatization on the high mountains may not always be possible. Many trekkers now use a drug called acetazolamide (generally known as Diamox) to help prevent AMS. Diamox works by imitating the acclimatized state of the body, and has been shown to substantially reduce the frequency of AMS. It also reduces the incidence of pulmonary and cerebral oedema. It may also help in the treatment of AMS, although this is debatable. In any case, it should never be used as substitute for descent to a lower altitude. It must also never be used to allow further ascent by a person with AMS.

Diamox is generally a safe drug when taken in the correct dosage. Side effects are usually mild, and include tingling of the hands, feet and face, and mild gastrointestinal upset. Some trekkers report an increase in urination rate. If you notice this, make sure you increase your liquid intake accordingly. Dizziness, vomiting, confusion and rashes can occur but these are unusual. People who are allergic to sulphonamide antibiotics may also be allergic to Diamox.

Recommended is a trial dose of 250 mg twice daily for two days at your normal altitude, several weeks before your trek starts. If you suffer no distressing side effects, on the ascent take a dose of 250 mg twice a day for three days before reaching an altitude of 3000 metres, and then continue it for two or three days afterwards. Some trekkers find that they get a good response using half the dose, whereas others may need to increase the dose to 250 mg three times a day.

There are plenty of trekkers who reach high altitudes successfully without the use of Diamox, and without suffering from AMS. Taking the drug is a matter of personal choice. Purists may argue that to take Diamox is tantamount to 'cheating'. Diamox may well enhance your enjoyment of the trek and, if you're a peak-bagger, increase your chances of reaching the summits of Mt Kenya or Kilimanjaro.

Getting There & Away

This chapter tells you how to get to East Africa from Europe, the USA, Asia or Australasia. For travelling between Tanzania, Kenya, Uganda and Malawi, see the Getting There & Away sections in the relevant country chapters. General information on travel within each country is given in the Getting Around sections. Specific details about transport to and from the trekking areas are given in the individual mountain sections.

AIR

Most trekkers fly to East Africa, because it's the easiest way of getting there, and many go to Nairobi because there's a greater choice of flights to and from this destination, and they tend to be cheaper. If you're planning to trek in more than one country, or combine trekking with some general travel in this region, Nairobi is a good place to start and finish. There are regular flights to and from Europe and the rest of the world, and other countries in the region.

There's often a bewildering choice of routes and fares. Some flights have restrictions on the maximum or minimum number of days you can be away. Prices depend on the quality and reliability of the airline, the number and length of stopovers, and many other factors. Don't automatically go for the cheapest fare. Sometimes, for a very small extra price, you can get a superior airline, with fewer stopovers and better service. There are some very good deals if you take the time to look, so it's well worth shopping around the specialist flight agencies who normally advertise in travel magazines or in the travel sections of newspapers such as the *Observer* in Britain, the *New York Times* in the USA, or the *Age* or the *Sydney Morning Herald* in Australia.

To/From the UK

London is one of the cheapest places in Europe to buy flights to East Africa. Discount flight centres used to be called 'bucket shops' and had a slightly sleazy image, but these days most have smartened up their act and the flights they sell are all perfectly legal. There are many agencies, but a few stand out as Africa specialists:

Africa Travel Shop
    4 Medway Court, Leigh St, London WC1H 9QX
    (☎ (071) 387 1211)
African Travel Systems
    6 North End Parade, North End Rd, London W14
    0SJ (☎ (071) 602 5091)
STA Travel
    (Africa Desk), 117 Euston Rd, London NW1
    2SX (☎ (071) 465 0486)

On some airlines you can buy an 'open jaw' ticket, which lets you fly into one place and out of another (eg London to Nairobi, return from Kampala to London). Alternatively, the agency might be able to get you a good deal using two one-way tickets. This is useful if you want to trek in two or more areas, and travel overland between. Another option which can be arranged by specialist agencies is a Round-the-World ticket involving one or more stopovers in Africa. The African specialist agencies can also arrange regional flights around East Africa – Nairobi to Kampala, or Nairobi to Lilongwe, for example.

London-Kenya The main airport in Kenya is Nairobi, although a lot of charter planes fly to Mombasa, on the coast. Return London-Nairobi fares start at £400, although they are often more expensive in the high season, starting at about £500. You can sometimes get amazing bargains to Mombasa (around £200 return), although these are usually only available for two or three weeks. There are good transport links between Mombasa and Nairobi, and most of the trekking areas described in the Kenya chapter are within a day's travel of Nairobi.

(For more details, see the Kenya Getting Around section.)

London-Tanzania Tanzania has two main airports: Dar es Salaam and Kilimanjaro International (KIA) which, as the name implies, is nearer the main trekking areas. If you're only trekking in Tanzania it's easier to fly to KIA than to Dar. Return London-KIA fares start at £450, or £500 in the high season.

London-Uganda The main airport is Entebbe, on the outskirts of Kampala. Return flights to Kampala from London start at £420. From Kampala it's a day's journey to Kasese, the main town and trekking base for the Rwenzoris. If you're visiting the Uganda side of Mt Elgon only, it's easier to approach from Nairobi. (Details are given in the Uganda Getting There & Away and Getting Around sections.)

London-Malawi Return flights from London to Malawi start at about £500 in the low season, and from £550 in the high season. International flights arrive at Lilongwe, the administrative capital in the centre of the country. There are internal flights to Blantyre, the commercial capital in the south. Nyika and Mulanje, the main trekking areas, are in the far north and far south of the country, so arriving at Lilongwe is fine if you're doing both. If you're only doing Mulanje, it's easier to fly on to Blantyre, which costs an extra £35 each way. Alternatively, it's an easy day's journey by road between Lilongwe and Blantyre. (For details, see the Malawi Getting Around section.)

To/From Australasia

There are no direct flights from Australia or New Zealand to East Africa. The nearest you can get are flights to Harare in Zimbabwe, or Johannesburg in South Africa, starting at around A$2000 return (although there are sometimes cheaper 'specials' available). From Harare you can get a regional flight to Malawi for around US$300 one way, or to

Nairobi for around US$450. It's usually cheaper to fly from Australia to Nairobi via Asia or Europe. However, things are changing gradually, and some fares between Australia and London via Johannesburg are almost as cheap as going via Asia, so it's well worth shopping around.

African flight specialists include:

African Escape Travel Centre
    Raptis Plaza, Cavill Ave, Surfers Paradise, Queensland 4217 (☎ (075) 755 035)
Africa Travel Centre
    Level 12, 456 Kent St, Sydney NSW 2000 (☎ (02) 267 3048)

To/From the USA

Bargain deals from the USA or Canada straight to East Africa are hard to find. Most flights go to Nairobi via Europe. Some agencies in New York advertise special deals to Nairobi starting at around US$550 one-way, although in reality you'll probably end up paying more like US$1200 one-way and US$1700 return. Many trekkers from North America save money by flying to the UK on a cheap trans-Atlantic deal, then buying the second leg of their flight to Africa in London. This, of course, takes time and a bit more organisation.

To/From Asia

There are cheap flights between India and East Africa, usually Bombay-Nairobi. Flights start at about US$500, either way. If you're coming from another Asian country, most flights will be via Bombay or Karachi. Flights to any other East African city are more expensive and usually via Nairobi anyway.

LAND

If you've got plenty of time, and a fair bit of cash to spare, it's also possible to get to East Africa overland from Europe. Some travellers do it in their own vehicle, while others join an organised trip or 'expedition' in a specially converted truck. You'd normally travel with about 18 other people, a couple of drivers/leaders, and tents and other equipment. Food would be bought along the way and the group would usually cook and eat together.

Most trans-Africa trips start in London and finish in Nairobi, travelling via the Sahara and West Africa, or go all the way down to Harare via Tanzania and Malawi. Some trips go in the opposite direction. Prices vary and depend very much on itinerary and duration. It's also possible to join the trip for just a short section – Lilongwe-Nairobi, for example.

Overland Companies

UK Overland companies based in the UK include:

Exodus Expeditions
    9 Weir Rd, London SW12 0LT (☎ (081) 673 0859)
Geurba
    101 Eden Vale Rd, Westbury BA13 3QX (☎ (0373) 826611)
Tracks Africa
    12 Abingdon Rd, London W8 6AF (☎ (071) 937 3028)
Dragoman
    Camp Green, Kenton Rd, Debenham, IP14 6LA (☎ (0728) 861133)

There are also several smaller outfits offering cheaper deals, but with fewer departures. Check the advertisements in travel magazines and newspapers. Most overland companies are represented by specialist adventure travel agencies in the USA, Canada and Australasia.

Australia In Australia, adventure travel agencies include:

Africa Travel Centre
    Level 12, 456 Kent St, Sydney, NSW 2000 (☎ (02) 267 3048)
African Wildlife Safaris
    259 Coventry St, South Melbourne, Vic 3205 (☎ (03) 696 2899)
Adventure World
    73 Walker St, North Sydney, NSW 2060 (☎ (02) 956 7766)
Exodus
    81a Glebe Point Rd, Glebe, NSW 2037 (☎ (02) 552 6317)

Peregrine Travel
    258 Lonsdale St, Melbourne, Vic 3000 (☎ (03) 663 8611)

New Zealand In New Zealand, try the following:

Adventure World
    101 Great South Rd, Remuera, PO Box 74008, Auckland (☎ (09) 524 5118
Destinations
    4 Durham St East, PO Box 6232, Auckland (☎ (09) 309 0464)

USA Adventure travel agencies operating in the USA include:

Adventure Center
    1311 63rd St, STE 200, Emeryville CA 94608 (☎ (800) 2278747)
Himalayan Travel
    112 Prospect St, Stamford, CT 06901 (☎ (800) 225 2380)

Canada In Canada, agencies worth trying include:

Trek Holidays
    8412, 109 St, Edmonton, Alberta T6G 1E2, Canada (☎ (800) 661 7265)
Market Square Tours
    54 Donald St, Winnipeg, MB, R3C 1L6, Canada (☎ (800) 661 3830)

ORGANISED TREKS

If time is short, or you haven't got the inclination to make all the arrangements yourself, you can arrange a trek in East Africa through a specialist trekking company based in your own country. You can have arrangements made just for you or a group of friends and choose your own schedule, or you can join an existing group on a specific departure date. These companies will arrange either just the trek, leaving you to buy your own flight and make other arrangements, or they can arrange the whole thing, including all your flights, transport, accommodation and so on. If you go for the whole lot, they'll usually provide a trek leader too, to organise porters and guides, and to take care of things along the way. The idea is that you pay one price, then have nothing more to worry about.

Because these companies are set up specifically to run treks, and already have their own contacts on the ground, they can usually arrange to do a lot more in the holiday time (normally two to four weeks) than you could yourself, thus avoiding a lot of the hassle experienced by independent trekkers.

Length, difficulty, standard and quality of organised trekking trips varies enormously between companies. The best thing to do is contact the companies direct, get a brochure and see what you like. Some companies act as overseas sales agents, selling treks organised by local companies, while others operate the whole thing themselves. Agents tend to be cheaper, although operators are in closer contact with trek conditions and usually have more knowledge about the area.

Don't be afraid to phone them if you want to know more. Some of the companies are run by people who are trekkers and walkers themselves, so they'll know how to answer your questions.

The following is not a complete list of companies organising treks in East Africa, but it will give you somewhere to start.

Companies Organising Treks
UK In the UK, try the following:

Exodus Expeditions
    9 Weir Rd, London SW12 0LT (☎ (081) 673 0859)
Explore Worldwide
    1 Frederick St, Aldershot GU11 1LQ (☎ (0252) 319448)
High Places
    Globe Works, Penistone Rd, Sheffield S6 3AE (☎ (0742) 757500)
Natural Action
    16 Swyncombe Ave, London W5 4DS (☎ (081) 758 9157)
Sherpa Expeditions
    131a Heston Rd, Hounslow TW5 0RD (☎ (081) 577 7187)

Australia Companies operating in Australia include:

Adventure World
    73 Walker St, North Sydney, NSW 2060 (☎ (02) 956 7766)

Equatorial Safaris
    Shop 5, Barberry Square, Kalamunda, WA 6076 (☎ (09) 293 4022)
Exodus Expeditions
    81a Glebe Point Rd, Glebe, NSW 2037 (☎ (02) 552 6317)
Outdoor Travel
    55 Hardware St, Melbourne, Vic 3000 (☎ (03) 670 7252)

New Zealand Two companies are:

Adventure World
    101 Great South Rd, Remuera, PO Box 74008, Auckland (☎ (09) 524 5118)
Venture Treks
    PO Box 37610, 164 Parnell Rd, Auckland (☎ (09) 799 855)

USA In the USA, try:

Adventure Center
    1311 63rd St, STE 200, Emeryville CA 94608 (☎ (800) 227 8747)
Himalayan Travel
    112 Prospect St, Stamford, CT 06901 (☎ (800) 225 2380)
International Expeditions, 1 Environs Park, Helena, Alabama 35080 (☎ (800) 633 4734)
Mountain Madness
    7103 California Ave SW, Seattle, WA 98136 (☎ (206) 937 8389)
Mountain Travel
    6420 Fairmount Ave, El Cerrito, CA 94530
Wilderness Travel
    801 Alston Way, Berkeley, CA 94710 (☎ (415) 548 0420)

LEAVING EAST AFRICA
Air
If you came in overland or on a single ticket, Nairobi is one of the best places in Africa to buy a ticket home or onwards after your trek. There are plenty of travel agents who can arrange flights. Most one-way tickets cost about the same whichever direction you go, but some real knock-down bargains are sometimes available. (See the Kenya chapter for more details on travel agents in Nairobi.)

Airport Tax If you fly out of Nairobi, Mombasa, KIA, Dar es Salaam, Kampala, Lilongwe or Blantyre to another country (even the one next door) you have to pay a departure tax of US$20. Only hard currency is acceptable, but even using UK pounds or German marks you tend to lose out. These guys want dollars!

Land

If you flew in on a one-way ticket, you might want to travel back home, or onwards through Africa, on an overland truck (see the Land section earlier in this chapter). If you haven't booked one in advance, Nairobi is also the best place to pick up a seat on a truck, heading either north towards Europe or down towards southern Africa. Agents dealing with overland trucks in Nairobi include:

Africa Travel Centre
    1st Floor, Union Towers, corner of Moi Ave and Mama Ngina Sts, PO Box 63006, Nairobi (☎ (02) 214099)
Geurba Kenya
    1st Floor, International House, Mama Ngina St, PO Box 43935, Nairobi (☎ (02) 216972).

Getting Around

Relatively few people in Africa own private cars, so buses and trains are reasonably priced and frequent on the main routes. Consequently, most trekkers use public road and rail transport, although planes and rental cars are other options to consider.

This section gives you a general idea about travelling around East Africa. For more specific details, see the Getting Around sections in the individual country chapters.

AIR

There are internal and regional flights between all the capital cities and main towns in East Africa. For long distances, regional flights can be quick, but can take a large chunk out of your budget. They also have a habit of being cancelled more often than international flights. Recently, though, the countries of eastern and southern Africa have started sharing planes and cooperating on routes, which means there are now more planes and fewer delays.

If you're planning to trek on Mt Kenya and Kilimanjaro, it's usually not worth flying between Kenya and northern Tanzania, as road travel is just as quick. If you're short of time, and want to combine these two major peaks with the Rwenzoris or Mulanje then you'll certainly find it helpful to use regional flights between Nairobi and Kampala or Lilongwe.

ROAD

Roads in East Africa vary in quality: some main roads have been tarred recently and are in excellent condition. In other places, tarred roads have become badly potholed, and their conditions range from bad to worse. Sometimes, as a bus driver once said to me, they're 'more than worse'.

In most African countries, the main roads are tar-sealed usually as part of an aid project, often paid for by a Western country, but there never seems to be a long-term maintenance plan tied in with the deal, so

after a few years (or even less) of use by heavy trucks and no repairs, the roads often become full of holes again.

Secondary roads are usually untarred. The surface may be graded dirt, making driving a lot better than on a potholed tar-sealed road, or ungraded, making it about the same.

Traffic keeps to the left (or is supposed to) in all the countries covered by this book. If you're driving, watch out for cattle, bikes and people wandering all over the road.

The standard of driving in East Africa is generally bad. Breakdowns are common and accidents frighteningly frequent. Despite this happy thought, most of your travelling will probably be by road.

Bus, Matatu & Taxi

The type of public transport available is determined by the quality of the road, which in turn is based on the size or importance of the towns it connects.

On the main routes there's usually a choice of local buses (which are slow and crowded) and luxury buses (which are fast and comfortable), and often a wide range to choose from in between. Away from the main routes, there's usually no choice – buses are local, slow and uncomfortable, and that's it.

On the main routes, buses usually keep to a vague timetable or at least leave on time. You can often reserve a seat in advance, and sometimes this is essential.

In rural areas, there's often one bus between the main town and each surrounding village. You'll hear the term 'the bus sleeps at...', which means it goes to that village in the afternoon, stays there, and comes back to the main town early next morning.

There are also minibuses (called *matatus* in Kenya and northern Tanzania) which fill in the gaps in the bus schedules around towns and in the country, and shared taxis (usually Peugeot 504 seven-seaters) which ply between the main towns in Kenya, Uganda and northern Tanzania. Although more expensive, these are the fastest and most comfortable way to travel, and the drivers are usually safer than bus or matatu drivers. All matatus and shared taxis leave when they're full.

Taxis are available in the large towns and cities, and can be useful for crossing town at night, or for reaching the airport.

Car

Car hire is available in some countries. This can sometimes save you time and make access to a few of the trekking areas easier, but it's also an expensive way to travel.

Bicycle

More and more people are travelling around by bike these days, and you can easily cycle between the mountain areas covered in this book. A lot of trekkers seem to be mountain bikers too, and some of the routes in this book can even be done by bike.

Traditional touring machines will cope with most tar-sealed and dirt roads without too much trouble, although very narrow tyres and rims are not recommended. But unless you plan to cover long distances on mainly tarred roads, a mountain bike is more suitable.

Cyclists are regarded as second-class citizens in Africa even more than they are in Western countries, and motorists are more cause for alarm than any road surface. Make sure you know what's coming up behind you and be prepared to take evasive action onto the edge of the road, as local cyclists are often forced to do.

If you get tired, or want to cut out the boring bits, bikes can easily be carried on buses and matatus.

For more information about cycling in Africa, contact your national cycling organisation.

Hitching

If you get right off the main routes, there may be no public transport at all, so you'll have to hitch a ride in a truck or pick-up. This could take time (be prepared for an all-day wait) and a payment is usually expected. Ask the price before getting in; it should be cheaper on top than in the cab.

Hitching free lifts is a different matter. On the main routes, you might get picked up by a well-off local or expatriate worker. If the journey is long you should still offer to pay your way by buying lunch or a few drinks for the person who's giving you a lift.

TRAIN

It goes like this: Kenyan trains are good, in both comfort and reliability; Tanzanian trains are not too bad; trains in Malawi are very slow, in bad condition, and not worth using; and in Uganda they're terrible and to be avoided unless you're a train spotter.

In Kenya and Tanzania, 1st class is a twin cabin, sometimes with wood panelling, where you can travel in faded colonial style. Second class is either comfortable seating or sleeping cars divided into men-only and women-only four-berth or six-berth compartments. Third class is usually very crowded, with wooden seats, tons of baggage, and a few goats and chickens stuffed in for good measure.

On the map, you might see railway lines crossing the borders of Kenya, Uganda and Tanzania. They do, but the trains don't. There have been no services across borders since the dissolution of the East African Community in 1977.

Tanzania

For most visitors, Tanzania is famous for the huge wildlife reserves of Serengeti, Lake Manyara and the Ngorongoro Crater, and for the islands of Zanzibar, that lie off the Indian Ocean coast. Tanzania has also been famous for its shortages, restrictions and suffocating bureaucracy. But recently things have changed: public transport runs again, the hotels have electricity, there's food in the shops and it no longer takes all day to change a travellers' cheque. Tanzania is on the up, and there's optimism in the air.

For trekkers, the biggest attraction is, of course, the massif of Kilimanjaro, the highest mountain in Tanzania and on the whole continent of Africa, with several spectacular trekking routes from the forested foothills to the top of the snow-capped summit dome.

Tanzania's other mountains include Mt Meru, the country's second-highest peak, where the trekking is dramatic and exhilarating, and the mysterious, solitary giant, Mt Hanang.

Away from the high peaks, other trekking areas include The Crater Highlands, rising above the floor of the Great Rift Valley, and the Usambara Mountains in the east, a region of fields and villages which contrasts sharply with the uninhabited wilderness zones further north.

Facts about the Country

HISTORY

The early history of Tanzania is closely linked with that of the other East African countries (see the Facts about the Region chapter).

The Colonial Period

After the Berlin Conference of 1884-5, the two largest European powers, Germany and Britain, divided East Africa between them by drawing a line from Lake Victoria to the Indian Ocean coast. North of the border was British territory, to become Kenya and Uganda. South of the border was German East Africa, declared a protectorate in 1891.

For the next 20 years the protectorate was developed by the German colonial government. The sleepy fishing port of Dar es Salaam was declared the new capital, sisal and rubber plantations were established, and a railway was built across the country, from the coast to Lake Tanganyika.

In many parts of the territory, this development was resisted by local African people, who resented the German methods of land control. One of the largest revolts, between 1905 and 1907, became known as the Maji Maji uprising.

During WWI, German and British forces, with conscripted African soldiers, were engaged in a long, senseless campaign in East Africa. After the war, most of the region was mandated by the League of Nations to Britain, who renamed the territory Tanganyika and continued to administer it for the next 40 years. (The extreme western province of Ruanda-Burundi was similarly mandated to Belgium.)

A new series of land laws and a system of local government were established and the railway line was extended to Lake Victoria. But Tanzania was always seen as the least attractive of the East African territories: while it was never settled by Europeans in the same way as Kenya, there was, however, considerable European settlement in the Kilimanjaro and southern highland regions.

Transition & Independence

After WWII, African people were given more opportunities to take part in the politics of the territory and, through the 1950s, several nationalist organisations were founded, including the Tanganyika African National Union (TANU), led by Julius Nyerere. In 1961, Tanganyika gained independence from Britain, and became a republic a year later. Nyerere was the first president, a post he held for over 20 years. In 1964 he combined Tanganyika with the islands of Zanzibar to form the United Republic of Tanzania. Nyerere's most significant move came in 1967, when he introduced his own Ujamaa system of government, combining aspects of Marxist socialism and African tradition, and emphasising the importance of collectivism and self-reliance. Banks and most privately owned businesses were nationalised, and state-managed collective farms established.

During this period Tanzania received aid from China and East Germany, but the schemes were beset by problems and never succeeded.

Tanzania's problems were compounded in 1977, when the East African Economic Community of Tanzania, Kenya and Uganda collapsed, badly affecting Tanzania's economy. The border with Kenya was closed, leading to a reduction in the number of tourists and a further loss of revenue.

The situation worsened further in late 1978 when the army of Idi Amin invaded northern Tanzania. The Tanzanian 'people's

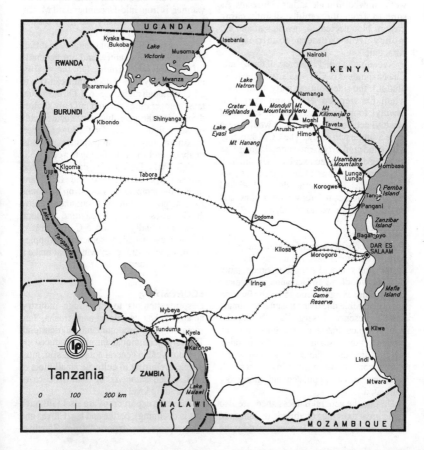

army' finally ousted the Ugandans, but the financial cost of this war (quite apart from the cost in human life and suffering) was something Tanzania could ill afford.

Modern Times

Tanzania continued to be one of the poorest and least-developed countries in Africa until the mid '80s, when Nyerere resigned as president, and Ali Hassan Mwinyi took control. Tanzania struck a deal with the IMF, and the new government made a number of significant changes of policy. Private ownership was once again encouraged and businesses were allowed to trade in hard currency. As support from the rapidly disintegrating Eastern bloc decreased, investment and aid money from Western countries was attracted.

Nyerere remained chairman of the Chama Cha Mapinduzi (CCM, or Party of the Revolution), the sole political party, until 1990, when he stepped down and President Mwinyi took over this post. In mid-1992 Mwinyi declared that Tanzania would cease to be a single party state. The CCM structure within the civil service and armed forces was disbanded and, in the excitement, more than 20 groups announced plans to become opposition parties. Elections are due in 1995, and most people seem happy with a slow and peaceful changeover to pluralism.

GEOGRAPHY

Tanzania consists largely of highland plain, part of the High Plateau that extends across eastern and southern Africa, covered mainly by light woodland and savanna. Settlement on the plains is light. Crop and cattle farming are not possible due to the unsuitable climate and the presence of tsetse flies. The population is concentrated on the hills and low mountains that rise out of the plain, forming a rough arc across the country, from southwest to north-east to north. Most of these hill areas are densely populated and intensively cultivated.

Despite the general flatness, there are also some great extremes of altitude in Tanzania. In the north, the plain is punctuated by the high peaks of Meru and Kilimanjaro, and cut by the western and eastern arms of the Great Rift Valley. The summit of Kilimanjaro is the highest point in Africa, and Lake Tanganyika, in the western Rift, is the deepest lake.

CLIMATE

The climate of Tanzania is technically 'equatorial' but it is actually more tropical, being largely affected by the high altitude of the plateau. Seasons are wet and dry, rather than hot and cold. The long dry season, when conditions are cool, is from June to early October, and the short dry season, when it's warmer, is from mid-December until March. In the south there is only one rainy season, from December to April.

Temperatures vary considerably in different parts of the country, and are generally influenced by altitude. On the plains, maximum daytime temperatures can rise to 28°C, although nights are cool. On the mountains, temperatures rise and fall only slightly throughout the year, but vary considerably between night and day. On the lower slopes, maximum daytime temperatures are normally around 15-20°C, falling to a chilly 5°C at night. At higher altitudes, daytime temperatures range between 10 and 15°C, and night-time temperatures can drop to around freezing point. On the high mountains, above 4000 metres, maximum daytime temperatures are usually around 5°C. It's always below freezing at night, sometimes dropping to -10°C, with strong icy winds that make it seem even colder.

ECONOMY

Despite attempts to encourage industry, notably in Dar es Salaam and Arusha, Tanzania remains predominantly agricultural. The large communal farms introduced by Nyerere were in general not successful, most people preferring to cultivate small plots of land, called *shambas*, at a subsistence or local trading level.

The main export crops are sisal (although this is declining), coffee and tea. Cloves and other spices are exported from Zanzibar.

Tourism is also a major foreign currency earner.

POPULATION & PEOPLE

In 1991, Tanzania's population was estimated at 24 million, and expanding rapidly. There are more than 100 different 'ethnic groups' (see Languages, in the Facts about the Region chapter), mostly of Bantu origin. Other distinct groups are the Maasai (seminomadic people of Nilotic origin), who inhabit the Rift Valley plains and highlands in the north, and the Swahili people, the descendants of intermixing Africans and Arabs over several centuries, on the coast.

RELIGION

Christians, Muslims and people who practice traditional beliefs each make up about a third of the population. There are various Christian groups, including Catholics, Protestants and several local African faiths. Islam is particularly widespread on the coast and in the large towns. (Both Moshi and Arusha have large mosques.)

LANGUAGE

The official languages are English and Swahili (or Kiswahili), although there are many local languages. Swahili is a common language spoken by most people as a second tongue (often simplified and used at a fairly basic level), except on the coast where it is a first language in its own right.

Visitors will find that English is spoken widely in areas used to tourists (eg the towns of Moshi and Arusha) but far less so in rural areas or places off the beaten track. Many of the porters on Kilimanjaro and Mt Meru, for example, speak very little English, although guides and rangers are usually conversant.

Facts for the Trekker

VISAS & CUSTOMS

Visas are required by citizens of most countries, except those from some Commonwealth countries, the USA, Scandinavia and Ireland.

Customs regulations have loosened up since the liberalisation of the currency laws. Declaration forms are no longer used, so there's no need to smuggle cash through in your underwear. However, the regulations are constantly changing. For up-to-date information, contact your nearest Tanzanian embassy, high commission or tourist office.

MONEY

The unit of currency is the Tanzanian shilling (TSh), which is divided into 100 cents, although these are hardly used. With the new currency laws, and the introduction of the 'free' market, the black market demand for money has disappeared and prices have steadied slightly too, so there's a chance the exchange rates quoted here (correct at the end of 1992) might not be too far off the mark by the time you read this.

Free market rates are:

US$1 = TSh 400
UK£1 = TSh 700

To change money at the free market rate you need to go to a private bureau de change. Some banks also operated as bureaus, and change money at free and official rates. Make sure you go to the right desk!

There are several con-artists in Arusha and Dar who offer high rates, then give you a stack of small TSh notes, which are difficult to count and inevitably amount to less than they should. Sometimes they save time by simply pulling a knife and running off with your dollars.

Even with the new regulations, you still won't need too many shillings. Entrance fees for national parks (including Mt Meru and Kilimanjaro), organised treks and safaris, and all but the very cheapest hotels must be paid for in hard currency. Although most hard currencies are officially acceptable, US dollars are the most convenient way to pay, and work out cheaper too. Note that at national parks and some other official places, change is not normally given in dollars, but in shillings, converted at the official (low) rate. Hotels will usually give you change in dollars (if you pay cash, and if they've got any). The best way to carry your money is in a mix of high- and low-denomination US dollar bills and travellers' cheques.

Because most prices in Tanzania are quoted and payable in US dollars, this currency is used throughout this chapter. Where you see the $ symbol it means the US variety. Where shillings are given, this usually indicates that you can pay in shillings. For prices quoted in this book, convert to hard currency at the rate here. Even if it's gone up in shillings, the equivalent price in US dollars or pounds is unlikely to have changed much.

If you are travelling between Tanzania and Kenya, there are no foreign hard currency restrictions, but you are not allowed to import or export more than KSh 200 or TSh 2000, although, if you are coming back and want to keep some money, a search is unlikely. If you have cash you no longer need, there are moneychangers on both sides of the border who will take surplus money off you, but make sure you know the rates. There are also several shops where you can spend your remainder on supplies, or you can haggle with the Maasai women selling souvenirs.

WHEN TO GO

The best time for trekking in Tanzania is during the dry seasons, from mid-December to March, when the weather is generally dry and warm, and June to early October, when it's dry and cool (see the Climate section in this chapter). These dry months are the most popular periods for trekking and are Kilimanjaro's 'high' season.

Over the last few years the weather patterns in East Africa (and all over the world) have become less predictable and the rainy seasons have become less rainy. Trekkers going up Kilimanjaro and Meru in November can often get several days of good weather while still paying cheaper rates. However, paths through the forest are very slippery at this time and the final sections of

routes up to the summit are more likely to be blocked by snow.

Remember that dry seasons are dry only when compared to the wet season! Although rain and snow are less likely during the dry months, you should be prepared for them (they can sometimes be very heavy) at any time of the year.

USEFUL ORGANISATIONS

The Kilimanjaro Mountain Club is made up mainly of expatriates in Tanzania, and does not usually cater for tourists. The club does not have regular meetings, but activities are advertised in the members' newsletter, which is printed a few times per year. The club also produces a journal called *Ice Cap*, but this is rarely seen (there have been eight issues since 1932). The club's address is PO Box 66, Moshi.

The Wildlife Conservation Society of Tanzania is a small but growing organisation campaigning to protect wildlife and areas of wilderness in Tanzania. You can support this cause by joining the society (PO Box 70919, Dar es Salaam). If you join, you'll receive a free magazine which often contains information on the mountain national parks.

HOLIDAYS

Public holidays include:

12 January	Zanzibar Revolution Day
26 April	Union Day
1 May	International Workers' Day
7 July	Saba Saba, Peasants' Day
9 December	Tanzania Independence & Republic Day
25 December	Christmas Day

Other public holidays are the Friday and Monday before Easter Sunday, and the Muslim feasts of Eid-ul-Fitr (the end of Ramadan) and Eid-ul-Haji (the pilgrimage). The dates of Muslim feasts are not fixed, because they are based on the Islamic calendar; in general, they fall eleven or twelve days earlier each year.

GUIDEBOOKS

There are not many general guidebooks on Tanzania, but the country is well covered in Lonely Planet's *East Africa – a travel survival kit*, and in Bradt Publications' *Guide to Tanzania*. Despite its title, *Mountains of Kenya* also covers parts of northern Tanzania (see Guidebooks, in the Kenya chapter).

Guidebooks on individual mountain areas are covered in the relevant sections.

MAPS

For general travel between trekking areas, the BP/Shell 'Map of Tanzania' is very good, although it's available only in Tanzania. Other maps include the roadmap produced by Freytag & Berndt, which is also available from the Tanzanian Tourist Corporation as 'Tanzania, Land of Kilimanjaro', with extra tourist information printed on the back. If you're also trekking in Kenya, most Kenya maps also cover northern Tanzania, including Kilimanjaro and Meru, and sometimes the Usambara Mountains and the Crater Highlands.

Tanzania is covered by DOS/government survey maps at scales of 1:50,000, 1:100,000 and 1:250,000. These are available in Dar es Salaam from the Public Map Office in Ardhi House, next to the Ministry of Foreign Affairs, which is three blocks along from the Kilimanjaro Hotel, Kivukoni Front. Maps cost TSh 1000 and there are no formalities, although the maps of popular areas are often out of stock.

Maps of individual mountain areas are covered in the relevant sections.

TREKKING COMPANIES

Independent trekking is *not* permitted on Kilimanjaro (see the Kilimanjaro section for details). All treks must be arranged through a licensed tour company. Because of this, in Moshi and Arusha (the two towns nearest Kili) there are many companies which arrange treks to suit all budgets and standards. Some companies also organise treks on Mt Meru (although independent trekking is allowed here) and in the Crater Highlands (which is hard to do on your own unless you have a vehicle). Several of the hotels in Marangu Village, at the foot of Kilimanjaro's Marangu Route, also organise treks.

The trekking company you use can make or break your trek, so it's important to choose carefully. Of those who say they do treks, most will just pass you on to a specialist company, charging you a commission in the process. If you go straight to an operating company, instead of an agent, chances are you'll get the trek cheaper.

Obviously, the price you pay depends on what's included (see Organised Treks, in the Facts for the Trekker chapter). On Kilimanjaro or Mt Meru, the minimum you'll be able to get away with is an obligatory guide and a few porters, while you provide your own tent, gear and food, pay your own park fees, and make your own way by public bus to the start of the trek. At the other end of the scale, a trek can include everything: guide, assistant guides, porters, cook, food, utensils, tent, camping equipment, park fees, transport, driver and hotel accommodation before and after the trek. Most trekkers take something in between these two extremes.

Cost

Prices and standards of trekking companies vary. At the bottom end, competition is stiff and, if cheapness is your main criterion, you can find some outfits doing all-inclusive treks on Kilimanjaro for around US$300, and on Mt Meru for around $150, although for trekkers on a tight budget, this still takes a sizeable chunk out of their funds. In the low season, or if you can get a group of eight to 10 people together, the cost can be reduced even further. But, as with anything else, you get what you pay for, and the service offered by some of the cheaper outfits leaves a lot to be desired. If you base your choice on cheapness, it will be harder to justify complaints afterwards if anything goes wrong.

If the price of your trek is not such a problem, there are several companies offering treks between US$500 and US$1000 which are generally of a much higher quality. Usually, the price of the trek falls as the size of the group increases (on Kili, the difference between going alone or in a group of around six to eight can be several hundred dollars). The prices given here are per person, based on a group of four, and include park fees, guides, porters, food and accommodation on the mountain, unless stated otherwise. On Kilimanjaro's Marangu Route, going alone or as a pair will add around 10 to 20% to the price. On other routes (eg the Machame and Umbwe Routes) it can add 25 to 50%. All prices will inevitably increase over the next few years, but these figures are useful for comparisons.

If the cost of a trek on Kilimanjaro or Mt Meru does not include transport, you can usually arrange to hire the company's own vehicle for a drop-off or pickup for an extra US$50 to US$100 (divided between the group), or take public transport (details are given in individual trek descriptions).

Addresses

The trekking companies listed here have been recommended. Most can organise treks almost immediately, or within a couple of days. The treks and safaris mentioned are examples only. Most companies offer a wide range of trips and can also organise things to suit your own requirements.

If writing for more information, use the PO Box number. If phoning from anywhere within Tanzania, Kenya and Uganda, the code for Arusha is 057, and for Moshi is 055. If phoning or faxing from any other country, use the international code for Tanzania (255) and omit the 0.

Arusha In Arusha there are several places you can try:

African Environments
    PO Box 2125, Arusha (☎ 7285, fax 8256). This is one of the most experienced trekking companies in Tanzania. They do a seven-day Kilimanjaro traverse on the little-used western side of the mountain, with one night camping inside the crater, for US$1100 all-inclusive. They also do treks on Mt Meru and wildlife safaris which fit in with the Kilimanjaro trek. You can also contact their US office, Mountain Madness (for their address, see Organised Treks, in the Getting There & Away chapter).

Tropical Trails
    PO Box 6130, Arusha (☎ & fax 8299). This company specialises in treks and walking safaris in all parts of Tanzania, with an emphasis on introducing visitors to the culture and art of local peoples. They do treks on Mt Meru, Kilimanjaro, the Crater Highlands, and Monduli Mountain, where this company has good relations with the local Maasai people. Because trekking is more specialised here, itineraries and costs are flexible. You can visit Tropical Trails (in the Equator Hotel, up the road from the clock tower) and discuss your plans with Mike, the guy who runs the company. He's very friendly and knowledgeable about the area and happy to provide help and advice. Tropical Trails also do self-drive vehicle hire, if you want to combine trekking in the Crater Highlands with a safari.

Equatorial Safaris
    4th floor, Serengeti Wing, Arusha International Conference Centre, PO Box 2156, Arusha (☎ & fax 7006). This company does a good value five-day trek on Kili's Marangu Route for US$475, which covers everything, including transport both ways between Arusha and the park gate. This is ideal if you're based in Arusha and short of time. A seven-day luxury version of the same trip, including two full-board hotel nights, costs US$810. They also do wildlife safaris that fit in with the Kilimanjaro trek.

Jeff's Tours and Safaris
    PO Box 1469, Arusha (☎ & fax 8172). This company does treks on Kilimanjaro and Meru, as well as wildlife safaris and some very interesting walking safaris in the Maasai Steppe and Crater Highlands. A seven-day trek on Kili's Marangu Route, with five days on the mountain plus two nights in the Kibo Hotel, costs US$800. Seven-day treks in the Crater Highlands, walking with Maasai guides and using donkeys to carry the gear, plus a day's wildlife viewing in the Ngorongoro Crater, cost US$580. Walks on the Maasai Steppe are very flexible, so Jeff, the owner, can plan a trek that fits your budget and time. The office is behind the Aresco Building, on the corner of School and Uhuru Rds.

Sengo Safaris
    1st floor, Arusha International Conference Centre, PO Box 207, Arusha (☎ 3181, 6982). This company does good mid-range wildlife safaris, and also organises treks in the Lengai area, north of the Crater Highlands.

Moshi Three trekking companies you can try are:

Shah Tours and Travel
    PO Box 1821, Moshi (☎ 52370, fax 51449). This company specialises in good-quality treks on the

Marangu, Machame and Umbwe routes on Kilimanjaro. Five-day treks up the Marangu Route cost US$400. Six-day treks cost US$555 – for five days trekking, two full-board hotel nights (before and after the trek) and all transport. Six-day treks on the Machame or Umbwe Route cost US$720. Shah Tours also organise treks on Mt Meru, and arrange wildlife safaris to fit in with the trek. The office is on Mawenzi Rd between the clock tower and the bus station.

Trans-Kibo Travels

PO Box 1320, Moshi (☎ /fax 52017). This company is based at the YMCA. Five-day treks on the Marangu Route start at US$400, although prices seem to be negotiable. Prices for six-day treks on the Machame route start at US$680 including park fees, transport, guide and porters, but you provide your own tent and food. Not all Trans-Kibo's guides are familiar with the Machame or Umbwe routes, however. Unless the tour is arranged in advance, you may have to wait for some days until a suitable guide becomes available.

Tropicana Safari Tours

PO Box 1622, Moshi (☎ 54977). This company is worth trying for bargain treks on the Marangu Route. Groups have been known to negotiate prices below US$300 all-inclusive. The office is near the clock tower on Kibo Rd.

Marangu Village The following Kilimanjaro treks are all organised by hotels. For accommodation details, see Places to Stay in the Kilimanjaro section.

Kibo Hotel

PO Box 102, Marangu (☎ Marangu 4). Five-day treks on the Marangu Route cost US$300, plus US$100 per extra day. A six-day trek on the Machame Route costs US$700, plus US$150 per extra day. These charges cover transport to and from the park gate, food, guides and porters, but do *not* include park fees, which you pay direct to the national park (see Park Fees & Regulations, in the Kilimanjaro section).

Marangu Hotel

PO Box 40, Moshi (☎ Marangu 11). The two women who own the hotel have been running trips up the Marangu Route (only) since time began. (Their brochure still wistfully refers to Kaiser Wilhelm Spitze!) Five-day treks cost US$300, plus US$80 per extra day, including transport to and from the park gate, food, guides and porters, but excluding park fees (US$160 for trekkers, plus US$20 for each guide and porter). If you're really strapped for cash, the hotel can also help you do the Marangu Route 'the hard way', by reserving huts and providing the man-

datory guide and his porter, while you provide your own food and equipment, and carry your own rucksack. You must pay all park fees, plus wages for the guide (US$45 for the five-day trip) and porters (US$30), as well as their food. The hotel charges US$35 for this service.

Babylon Hotel

PO Box 227, Marangu. Standard five-day treks on the Marangu Route go for US$330 per person, and six days on the Machame for US$550. Prices are all-inclusive and negotiable.

Ashanti Lodge

PO Box 6004, Arusha. Standard five-day Marangu Route treks for US$300, plus park fees and transport (US$20).

Remember that national park entrance fees may be increased at any time. If this happens, the trekking and safari companies will increase their prices too.

TRAVEL AGENTS

Some of the trekking companies in Arusha also act as travel agents, and can help you with reservations for international and internal flights, safaris and so on. In Moshi, Shah Tours seems to be the best; they can make all the usual arrangements, and also sort out reservations for the train to Dar, which can be useful if the train is 'full'.

EQUIPMENT HIRE & SUPPLY

Trekking equipment, including sleeping bags, boots, rucksacks, jackets and hats, can be hired for around US$5 per item per trek, from the Mountain Inn, the Kibo Hotel or Kilimanjaro Mountain Lodge (for addresses, see the Kilimanjaro Places to Stay section). Quality varies, and some of the stuff is ex-military, and quite heavy, but it does the job. The best place to hire good gear, although at a higher cost, is in Nairobi (see the Kenya chapter).

ACCOMMODATION IN DAR ES SALAAM

You might arrive in Dar es Salaam if you're flying in from Europe or southern Africa, or you might pass through on your way between the trekking areas of northern Tanzania and Malawi. This is not an exhaustive list of places to stay in Dar es Salaam, but it will give you an idea of what's available there. For information on accommodation in Moshi, Arusha and other places nearer the trekking areas, see the individual mountain sections.

Rooms always seem to be hard to find in Dar, whatever your budget, so it's best to arrive in the morning if you can, to give yourself more of a chance of finding something.

At the top end, probably the best hotel in town is the *Motel Agip*, just round the corner from the junction of Samora Ave and Maktaba St. It's run by the Italian oil company, and has singles/doubles at US$74/79; it also has a good restaurant serving (you've guessed it) Italian food. Nearby is the *New Africa Hotel*, run by the state travel service, fading and vastly overpriced at US$68/78 including breakfast. At the end of Maktaba St is the *Mawenzi Hotel*, which has clean, reasonably priced singles/doubles for US$25/30, triples for US$40, and a better restaurant than the New Africa.

Down the scale a bit, and on the other side of town, is the *Starlight Hotel*, on the continuation of UWT St towards the junction of Uhuru and Libya Sts, with doubles at TSh 7500. Apart from the carpets (which are getting threadbare), it's no different to the other mid-range hotels around the corner – the *Safari Hotel* and the *Jambo Inn* – both of which are much better value, with clean doubles for around TSh 3000 including breakfast.

A bit further from the centre (towards Kariakoo Market) but more likely to have a room available, is the *Hotel Eshmail* on Lumumba St, with doubles at TSh 2500, a restaurant, and a mosque on the top floor.

Just off Lumumba St, on the junction of Kariakoo and Ukami Sts, is the new *Harare Hotel*. This is a real gem – clean and safe, with good singles/doubles at TSh 2500/3500 including breakfast. At the top of Lumumba St, near its junction with Morogoro Rd, is the *New Happy Hotel*, another basic place with singles/doubles at TSh 2000/2400 and a cheap restaurant.

Back towards the city centre, other cheapies include the *Kiboyda Hotel*, just along Nkrumah St from the clock tower, with

doubles at TSh 2000, and the popular Holiday Hotel on Jamhuri St, run by the friendly Mr Ali, with rooms at TSh 900/1000/1100.

Getting There & Away

You can travel between Tanzania and the neighbouring East African countries of Kenya, Malawi and Uganda using air, road or rail transport. How you travel depends on how much time you've got, and the amount of travelling (as opposed to trekking) you want to do. In this section it's presumed you want to take fairly direct routes between the trekking areas in the various countries.

TO/FROM KENYA
Air
There are international flights between Dar es Salaam and Nairobi every day for around US$110 one way. You can also fly between Dar and Kilimanjaro International Airport (KIA) which is in northern Tanzania, nearer the main trekking areas. There are also direct flights between Nairobi and KIA for around US$60, but these are likely to be discontinued soon. Generally, it's not worth flying between Kenya and northern Tanzania, as the road connections are very good.

Road
There is a good sealed road all the way between Arusha (the first/last town in Tanzania) and Nairobi. The border is at Namanga, roughly halfway between the two. This is the route most trekkers take for the journey between Kili and Mt Kenya. Formalities at the Namanga border posts are straightforward. You need to complete an arrival/departure form and get your passport stamped.

Bus The journey between Arusha and Nairobi can be done by direct public bus, without changing at the border. The main service is run by the Kilimanjaro Bus

Company, but there are other lines doing this route, some even going all the way between Nairobi and Dar. There's normally a bus about four or five times a week in each direction. In Arusha, the booking office for this bus is in the bus station. In Nairobi, the office is on the junction of Accra and Cross Rds. Arusha to Nairobi costs about KSh 250 (US$8), about the same as a shared taxi. But bus is slower, and takes hours to cross the border, as all passengers have to be individually stamped through and customs officials have to check each item amongst the tons of luggage on the roof.

Shuttle Bus By far the most comfortable way of doing the journey between Arusha and Nairobi is by luxury shuttle bus, operated by DHL, the international parcel service. They have a 20-seater bus leaving every morning from Nairobi at 8 am, arriving Arusha at 1 pm. It then leaves Arusha at 2 pm and gets back to Nairobi by 7 pm. This takes about the same time as a shared taxi, but it's safer and more comfortable, and only takes about half an hour to cross the border. The DHL bus costs KSh 575 or TSh 6000 (about $20). In Nairobi, you can book a seat at the office of Kasana Tours, in Town House on Kaunda St, opposite the cinema (☎ 212804). In Arusha, book at VMT Ltd, on Ngoliondoi St.

More recently, some other outfits in Arusha have also started luxury Nairobi-Arusha shuttle services. Prices are about the same, but departure days and times vary, whereas the DHL bus has guaranteed departures (they've got to get those parcels through!). Agents for these shuttles in Arusha include Coopers & Kearsley and the Naaz Hotel, both on the main street, down from the clock tower, and Tropical Trails, in the Equator Hotel (☎ 8299). In Moshi, Shah Tours and Travel (☎ 52370; address in the Trekking Companies section) are agents. In Nairobi, contact Tayler's Travel on Tubman Rd (☎ 335365).

Shared Taxi Most people do the journey by shared taxi, although these vehicles do not actually cross the border. Shared taxis from Arusha to Namanga leave from a corner of the main bus station, and cost about TSh 1200. In Nairobi, shared taxis for Namanga leave from the junction of Accra and River Rds in downtown Nairobi, and cost about KSh 130. The trip costs the equivalent of about US$8. Drivers will accept Kenyan shillings, Tanzanian shillings or US dollars for either stage of the journey, usually at a fair rate (but make sure you know what it should be).

You have to walk between the two customs posts and pick up another vehicle on the other side. It's only a few hundred metres' walk; if you've got more gear than you can carry, young boys with barrows will help you, for a small fee.

If you arrive by air in Mombasa, you can go direct to Moshi or Arusha, avoiding Nairobi, by crossing the border at Taveta. There is a daily bus between Mombasa and Moshi, costing TSh 1700 or KSh 160. Alternatively, there are matatus and shared taxis between Moshi, the border and Voi (on the Mombasa-Nairobi road), and buses between Voi and Mombasa. There is at least one bus per day between Mombasa and Taveta, or you might need to change at Voi.

Train
Some maps show a railway line from Mombasa to Moshi, but there are no international services.

TO/FROM MALAWI
Air
International direct flights between Dar and Lilongwe go twice a week and cost around US$200 one way. There are daily flights between Dar and KIA, which is nearer Tanzania's main trekking areas (see Getting Around in this section), but it is probably easier to fly between Nairobi and Lilongwe, and travel between Arusha or Moshi and Nairobi by road (as already described in To/From Kenya).

Road

The only land crossing between Tanzania and Malawi is at Kaporo, in the far north of Malawi. This is the one used by most trekkers on the journey between Kili and the Malawi trekking areas.

On the Tanzanian side, from Mbeya (the first/last main town) hitch or take a bus to Kyela, dropping off at the junction where the road goes to the border, about five km before you reach Kyela town. You'll have to walk to the Tanzanian border post, then across the bridge to the Malawi guard post. The Tanzanian border opens between 6 am and 7 am, but the bus on the Malawi side between the border and Karonga (the first/last town) leaves at 6 am, so by the time you've completed formalities and walked across the bridge, it will already have left. So you'll either have to wait all day and night, or hope for a lift.

The Tanzanian border officials here used to have a reputation for being the toughest in East Africa, but as Tanzania's entry and exit regulations have been relaxed, so the guys at Kaporo have mellowed a bit too.

There's supposed to be a direct bus service that runs between Dar and Mzuzu, the first/last main town in Malawi. Days and times are vague, so inquire at the bus station in Mzuzu.

A new road is being built between Mbeya and Karonga, so you might find a lift in either direction with one of the construction workers. When the road is finished it is likely that public transport links between these two towns will improve.

If you're coming into Tanzania from Malawi, see the Malawi Getting There & Away section for more details.

TO/FROM UGANDA

Air

International direct flights between Dar es Salaam and Kampala go about three times a week, and cost about US$200 one way, or you can fly via Nairobi. There are daily flights between Dar and KIA, which is nearer Tanzania's main trekking areas (see Getting Around, in this section). But it's much easier to fly between Nairobi and Kampala, and travel between Arusha or Moshi and Nairobi by road (as already described in To/From Kenya).

Road

The Tanzania-Uganda border, on the west side of Lake Victoria, is closed to foreign visitors, and there are no buses anyway. There are rumours of a boat between Bukoba and Kampala, but no firm information.

The easiest way to get between the trekking areas of Tanzania and Uganda is by road through Kenya, via Nairobi (see Getting There & Away, in the Kenya chapter).

Boat/Lake

Ferry services on Lake Victoria between Tanzania and Ugana have been reintroduced. A Tanzanian boat runs from Mwanza to Port Bell (Kampala) once a week, and a Ugandan boat runs from Port Bell to Mwanza, Musoma and Butoba once a week. Timetables are vague, and the services may not be totally reliable

Getting Around

The normal way of travelling between Tanzania's trekking areas is by road, but if you're travelling to/from Malawi you'll probably use the train or an internal flight.

AIR

The only internal flight you're likely to use is between Dar es Salaam and Kilimanjaor International Airport (KIA). The Air Tanzania Corporation (ATC) holds the dubious honour of being entrusted with this busy route. Even though the service is slowly improving, ATC is notoriously unreliable – planes often break down, and endless delays are par for the course. Try to avoid flying with ATC and never rely on anything they tell you. If you have no other choice, be prepared for cancellations and long waits. The fare is US$123 one way, and usually needs to be booked at least one week in advance, although even then it's not reliable.

To/From the Airport If you arrive by air at KIA (about midway between Arusha and Moshi), the nearest public transport is on the main Arusha-Moshi road, seven km from the airport. You can walk, try hitching, or take a taxi to the junction and catch a bus to Moshi or Arusha from there.

ROAD
The main route in Tanzania likely to be used by trekkers is from Namanga (the border post) on the Kenya-Tanzania border, through Arusha and Moshi, down to Dar es Salaam, then south-west across the country to Mbeya and the borders with Zambia and Malawi. The road from Namanga to Moshi is tarred and of reasonable quality. The section from Moshi to Dar used to be one of the worst main roads in East Africa, but the road has been tarred in several sections now and should be completely repaired, end to end, by now, making the journey much less of a nightmare. From Dar to Mbeya the road is still very bad, although there are plans to repair it after the Moshi-Dar section is finished. Until then, most people use the train.

Bus & Matatu
On the main routes, especially between Namanga, Arusha and Moshi, there are regular buses, minibuses *(matatus)* and shared taxis. To give you an idea of costs, Namanga-Arusha costs about TSh 1200, Arusha-Moshi TSh 1000. From Arusha and Moshi to Dar there are buses only. Basically there are two types of bus: fast or slow. The fast buses are often called 'express' or 'luxury', although the seats may not be any more comfortable than those on a slow bus. But they stop less often and are less crowded, so it makes your journey more enjoyable. Arusha-Dar costs between TSh 8000 and TSh 12,000. Off the main routes there is usually no choice: the buses are slow and basic.

Long-distance Bus Seats on long-distance buses usually need to be reserved in advance.

In the main towns, each bus has its own office at the bus station. For shorter distances, and destinations off the main routes, buses and matatus leave when full. Routes around towns, or between towns and their surrounding villages, are served by local matatus. In Dar es Salaam, and most of southern Tanzania, matatus are called *dala dala*.

Long-distance buses used to travel through the night, but there were so many accidents that this has now been banned, so all buses now have to stop between about 10 pm and 5 am. Usually they stop in a town and you can either sleep on the bus or find yourself a small hotel. The only routes used by trekkers where this is likely to happen are Moshi-Dar or Dar-Mbeya. If you're travelling to Moshi, getting an early bus from Dar means you've got a good chance of getting there in one day. If you're going the other way, an early bus from Moshi means you'll get to Dar in the evening. On the other hand, if you get a later bus, which stops somewhere before Dar, you'll get in next morning and will have more chance of finding somewhere to stay.

Stations Most towns have one bus station where all buses and matatus arrive and leave. Unfortunately, this is not the case in Dar, where there are several bus stations, each for different destinations. The station for buses to Moshi and Arusha is on the corner of Libya St and Morogoro Rd, just outside the city centre.

Car Rental
For most trekkers, the idea is to get away from vehicles, but if you're planning to trek on Hanang or in the Crater Highlands, a vehicle might make access easier. You can even combine trekking with a wildlife safari.

There are a few car rental places in Dar, but for trekkers it's more useful to hire a vehicle in Arusha. At the moment, Tropical Trails, with an office in the Equator Hotel (PO Box 6130, ☎ & fax 8299) is the only outfit renting cars here. Landrovers start at about US$100 per day, or more if you plan to reach areas where the roads are really bad. They're not cheap, but they take five people easily, so costs can be reduced if there's a group of you. You pay for fuel, but there's no kilometre charge, and the deal includes a full set of cooking and camping equipment. If you're not sure about handling Tanzania's rough roads, you can even hire a driver as well, for very little more, but still choose your own itinerary. Tropical Trails can advise on road conditions, wildlife areas, trekking routes, and so on.

Petrol costs about TSh 200 per litre, diesel about TSH 150. Landrovers do between five and 10 km to the litre, or less if the roads are very bad.

Hitching

Hitching free lifts on the main routes is feasible, particularly between Moshi, Arusha and Namanga. Leaving Dar, heading towards Moshi, take a dala dala from Kariakoo Market to the suburb of Ubungo, a major intersection where the new Port Access Ring Road crosses the main Moshi road, or to Kimara suburb, which is even further out, and start hitching there.

On smaller roads, you might have to hitch a lift on a truck, especially if there is no bus, but you'll be expected to pay. This is fair enough, as local people have to.

TRAIN

If you're travelling between the trekking areas of northern Tanzania and Malawi, you can use the Dar-Moshi line and the Dar-Mbeya (Tazara) line. Trains are usually slower than buses on the same route, but they are cheaper, generally more comfortable and safer than road transport. There are three or four classes on each train: 1st class consists of double compartments; 2nd class consists of either sleeping compartments of six, or comfortable seating; 3rd class is crowded and very basic, with wooden seats and no glass in the windows.

Timetables are unreliable but there are usually three trains a week in each direction between Dar and Moshi, and there are supposed to be five each way per week between Dar and Mbeya. Fares are reasonable: Moshi-Dar costs TSh 5500/3400 in 1st/2nd (sleeper) class, or TSh 2500/1000 in 2nd (seat)/3rd class. But you must book seats three days to a week in advance, although you might be lucky and be able to do it nearer the day when you want to go. Sometimes booking clerks will tell you that the train is full, just to get a bribe out of you, so a certain degree of tact and diplomacy, and (if it comes to it) a small fee, may be required.

Stations In Dar, the main train station for the Dar-Moshi line is in the city centre, but the Tazara station (for the Dar-Mbeya line) is in a southern suburb on the main road towards the airport. In Mbeya, the Tazara station is also on the outskirts of town; there are taxis and minibuses from the station to the city centre.

Kilimanjaro

Kilimanjaro's huge snow-capped summit dome, rising high above the surrounding savanna, often with a giraffe conveniently posing in the foreground, is one of Africa's all-time classic images. At 5896 metres (19,344 feet), Kilimanjaro is the highest mountain in Africa, and one of the highest volcanoes in the world. The lure is irresistible, and a trek up 'Kili' is an essential part of a visit to Tanzania. The trek is even more attractive because, with the right preparation, you can walk all the way to the summit without the need of ropes or technical climbing experience.

HISTORY

For the local Chagga people who farm Kilimanjaro's foothills, the mountain has always been revered. When Johannes Rebmann reached this area in 1848, and became the first European to see Kilimanjaro, he reported that his guide had once tried to bring down the 'silver' from the summit, which mysteriously turned to water on the descent. A later explorer, Charles New, who reached the foothills of Kilimanjaro in 1871, heard stories from the local chief, Mandara, about spirits on the mountain jealously guarding piles of silver and precious stones. It was said that anybody trying to reach the summit would be punished by the spirits with illness and severe cold.

New was later followed by other explorers: Gustav Fischer and Joseph Thomson both reached the lower slopes of Kilimanjaro, and in 1887 Count Samuel Teleki managed to get to a point only 400 metres below the top of Kibo. The summit was eventually reached in October 1889 by Hans Mayer, a German professor of geology, accompanied by Ludwig Purtcheller, an experienced Alpinist, and Yohannes Lauwo, a local guide from the village of Marangu. Mayer named the summit Kaiser Wilhelm Spitze, after the German emperor. When mainland Tanzania (then called Tanganyika) gained independence in 1961, the name of the summit was changed to Uhuru (Freedom) Peak.

The derivation of the name Kilimanjaro has never been satisfactorily explained. Rebmann believed that the name meant 'Mountain of Greatness' or 'Mountain of Caravans'. (Slaving caravans travelling between the coast and the interior would have used the mountain as a landmark.) Other writers have since suggested that the name means 'Shining Mountain', 'White Mountain' or 'Mountain of Water'.

There is certainly a reliable supply of water which, together with the rich volcanic soil in the area, makes the foothills of Kilimanjaro ideal for cultivation. Of course, the Chagga knew this and when a group of British settlers, led by Sir Harry Johnston, the writer and naturalist, arrived here in 1884 they also took advantage of these conditions. They cleared and planted an area of land near Taveta, to the east of Kilimanjaro's foothills. Johnston had visions of the region becoming a 'second Ceylon'.

In 1886, when the governments of Germany and Britain agreed on a border to officially define their territories, the line they drew – from Lake Victoria to the coast – was perfectly straight, broken only by an untidy curve around Kilimanjaro. This divided the original British territory claimed by Johnston, now in Kenya, from the rest of the area around Kilimanjaro, now in Tanzania.

You may be told that the border curves around Kilimanjaro because Queen Victoria gave the mountain to Kaiser Wilhelm (her grandson) as a birthday present. While such an action would have been no different to the arbitrary partitioning of East Africa by these two monarchs' own governments, there is no evidence that this story is true. But it remains one of many popular myths that add to the mystique and attraction of Kilimanjaro.

GEOGRAPHY

The massif of Kilimanjaro is roughly oval in shape, 40 to 60 km in diameter, and rising almost 5000 metres above the surrounding plains. Kilimanjaro is even more distinctive because is not part of a chain or extended range. As well as being the highest mountain in Africa, Kili is one of the highest freestanding mountains in the world.

The two main peak areas are Kibo, the flat-topped dome at the centre of the massif, and Mawenzi, a group of jagged points and pinnacles on the eastern side. In fact, the top of Kibo is not flat, but dips inwards to form a crater which cannot be seen from below. Kibo and Mawenzi are separated by a broad plain called The Saddle. A third peak area, Shira, lies at the western end of the massif but is lower and less distinctive than Kibo and Mawenzi.

The highest point on Kibo and the whole Kilimanjaro massif is Uhuru Peak at 5896 metres (19,344 ft), and this is the goal for most trekkers. The highest point on Mawenzi is Hans Mayer Point, at 5149 metres (16,894 ft) but this cannot be reached by trekkers, and is only rarely visited by mountaineers.

GUIDEBOOKS

For detailed background information, and specific details on technical mountaineering routes, the *Guide to Mount Kenya and Kilimanjaro*, published by the Mountain Club of Kenya, has recently been reprinted, and is available in Nairobi. This is mainly a technical climber's guide, with detailed descriptions of the rock and ice routes on Kibo and Mawenzi, but it also contains good background information on history, glaciation, geology, wildlife, and so on. Beware of old copies of this book; many of the huts (and even a few of the glaciers!) have disappeared since it was printed. The *East Africa International Mountain Guide* (with a brief section on Kilimanjaro) is also mainly for technical climbers (see Books, in the Facts for the Trekker chapter).

MAPS

Kilimanjaro and the surrounding area is covered by DOS/government survey maps (1:50,000), sheet numbers 56/1, 56/2, 56/3 and 56/4. The main part of the mountain is on sheet 56/2. A special 1:100,000 map (number 522) of the whole area was also produced. Unfortunately, some of these maps are now out of print, but these numbers will be the same if there's been a reprint.

Some commercially produced maps are also available. These include the Ordnance Survey (UK) Worldmaps Series map, 'Kilimanjaro' (1:100,000) which is an updated reprint of the old sheet 522, and the 'Kilimanjaro Map' (1:50,000) published by Mark Savage (West Col, UK) and sometimes available from shops or trek operators in Moshi or Arusha. Both maps contain a few small errors, so if you're a stickler for detail, it's better to use them both together.

TREKKING INFORMATION
Costs

At the bottom end, an organised trek up Kili starts at US$300 to US$400, which can take a large chunk out of your funds if you're travelling on a tight budget. For longer, better-quality treks you should expect to pay upwards of US$600 to US$700.

Between US$150 and US$400 of this goes on park fees, depending on your trek (see the Park Fees & Regulations section). The rest of the money goes to the trekking company organising your trek. Don't think you can make things cheaper by doing it

yourself: since 1991, independent trekkers have not been allowed on Kilimanjaro. Guides are obligatory and all treks have to be arranged through a licensed travel company (see the Trekking Companies section earlier in this chapter).

Actually, this has not changed things very much. Even before the new regulation, it was still obligatory to take a guide and one porter, and it was virtually impossible to do anything other than the Marangu Route without going through a trekking company anyway. Kili used to have a reputation for hassle, requiring all sorts of wheeling and dealing between guides, porters and park officials, which often spoilt the trek itself. But now procedures are much simpler, without affecting prices much either. There are now a lot of new trekking companies competing for business at the bottom end of the market. Some arrange treks that are only slightly more expensive than the old DIY price.

To put it in perspective, you should also remember that organised treks on Kili are no more expensive than organised treks of the same length and quality on, say, Mt Kenya or some mountains in other parts of the world.

Unfortunately, because trekking on Kili is seen as expensive, many people try to walk up and down in the shortest time possible. You should not feel that it is essential to reach Uhuru Peak, or that you have 'failed' if you don't. If time (or money) is limited, it is far better to walk up to one of the midway huts and appreciate the splendour of the mountain from there before descending, instead of stubbornly pushing for the summit regardless of everything else.

If your budget is really tight, do *not* be tempted to enter the park illegally. Park rangers occasionally go on patrol, and guides will report unaccompanied walkers to the park authorities. Fines are heavy and imprisonment is not unknown. I met three lads from New Zealand who had tried to sneak past the park gate and go up the mountain on their own. They were spotted and chased by rangers with guns and spent two days hiding on the forest on the lower slopes.

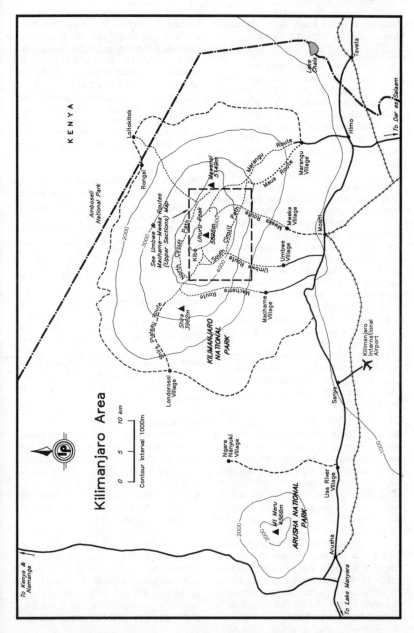

Kilimanjaro Area

0   5   10 km

Contour Interval 1000m

Although it was a funny story afterwards, they were pretty worried at the time...

Route Standard & Days Required

Kilimanjaro is surrounded by a zone of dense forest, so to get to the higher moorlands and main peaks, you have to follow one of the established routes. There are at least ten trekking routes that begin on the lower slopes. Some of these join other routes as they climb, but most routes reach the North and South Circuit Paths that circle the base of the main Kibo dome, roughly following the 4000-metre contour line.

Beyond the Circuit Paths, only three routes continue all the way to the summit of Kili. These are all on the southern side of Kibo, so the trekking routes on the western and southern slopes of the mountain are used more than the north side. The South Circuit Path links all these routes, so several combinations are possible. This makes the treks more interesting, and the extra time also helps acclimatization.

The number of days required for each trek ranges from a minimum of five days (four nights) to eight days or more.

The following section briefly describes two direct routes and one combination route. These routes, as well as other trekking possibilities, are described in detail later in this chapter.

Marangu Route This is the easiest and most popular route up Kilimanjaro, and the one used by most of the trekking companies. The path is straightforward and there are three large, comfortable huts conveniently spaced along the way. A trek on this route usually takes five days (four nights) for the round trip. Most trekkers on this route only go as far as Gillman's Point, on the crater rim at 5685 metres, as from here to the summit at Uhuru Peak and back requires another four hours of walking. You can increase your chances of reaching the summit by spending an extra night on the ascent, ideally at Horombo Hut. Treks on this route usually descend by the same route.

Umbwe Route This is a steep, very direct route, leading straight to Uhuru Peak. It is an interesting and very enjoyable route, if you can resist the temptation to gain height too quickly. Huts on this route are in bad condition or nonexistent, so a tent is essential. A trek on this route usually takes five days (four nights), although an extra night (ideally at Barranco Hut) is recommended to help acclimatization. Treks on this route usually descend by either the Mweka or the Marangu Route.

Machame-Mweka Combination Route This is the most scenic route on the mountain, passing through Kili's complete range of landscape and vegetation types. The ascent is longer and more gradual than the Umbwe Route and, because of the extra time (and expense) required, it is usually quieter than the Marangu Route. Trekkers on this route normally reach Uhuru Peak. The huts along the way are in poor condition, so a tent is strongly recommended. A trek on this route usually takes six days (five nights), although an extra night on the ascent (ideally at Shira Hut) is recommended to help acclimatization. Treks on this route usually descend by either the Mweka or the Marangu Route. (Note that several companies organise treks on this route, but just refer to it as the Machame Route.)

Acclimatization

The number of days quoted for a trek on each of the routes is the usual number most trekkers take. If you can spend an extra night on any of the routes, at about halfway, this will help acclimatization and will also give you time to see some other parts of the mountain. It will also greatly increase your chances of actually getting to the top.

Although many hundreds of trekkers reach Uhuru Peak every year without any real difficulty, many thousands more don't, because they suffer terribly from altitude sickness, having ascended too quickly. Part of the fault lies with some trekking companies who run quick up-and-down trips, although they are only responding to demand. The real fault lies with trekkers who overestimate their own ability, or who simply don't appreciate the serious nature of trekking at altitude and the importance of proper acclimatization. There have been too many sad cases of trekkers who went too high too quickly on Kili; at best, they felt ill and went down; at worst, they became so sick that they had to be carried down; others have even died.

Most people seem to forget that Uhuru Peak, at 5896 metres, is 500 metres *higher* than Everest Base Camp in the Nepal Himalaya, which trekkers often take at least two weeks to reach from Kathmandu. All trekkers should read and observe the advice on altitude and acclimatization in the Health & First Aid chapter.

If you are not already well-acclimatized, trying to cut days just to save time and money is not recommended – in fact, it's just plain stupid.

Guides & Porters

Guides, and at least one porter (for the guide), are obligatory on all routes on Kilimanjaro. You can carry your own gear on the Marangu Route, although porters are generally used, but at least one porter per trekker is essential on all other routes. Most trekking companies allow two to three porters per trekker depending on the length of the trek. Guides and porters on Kilimanjaro are freelancers and will be arranged by the company organising your trek.

All guides must be registered with the national park authorities. If in doubt, check that your guide's permit is up to date. On Kili, the guide's job is to show you the way, and even then they're not always totally reliable (see Warning, later in this section). Only the very best guides, working for good trekking companies, will be able to tell you about wildlife, birds, flowers, or any of the other features on the mountain.

Porters will carry bags weighing up to 15 kg (not including their own food and clothing, which they strap to the outside of your bag). Heavier bags will be carried for a negotiable extra fee.

The guides and porters provided by some of the cheaper trekking outfits leave a lot to be desired. If you're a hardy traveller you might not worry about basic meals and substandard tents, but you might be more concerned about incompetent guides or dishonest porters. I've even heard stories about guides who leave the last hut deliberately late on the summit day, so as to avoid going all the way to the top. But if you use this book – so that you know about all aspects of the route – and are polite but firm with your guide, you should avoid problems like this.

Tipping Most guides and porters are honest and hard-working, so you will probably want to give them a tip after your trek. Over the years, some high-rolling trekkers on Kili have tipped very generously, causing the local guys to expect large tips at the end of every trek. This situation is understandable. The porters know that you have just paid anything from US$300 to US$1000 for the trek. Even if you think of yourself as a budget traveller, they will regard you as a wealthy tourist, with a lot of spare cash to throw around. So don't plead poverty. If the service has been good, pay a fair tip.

As a guideline, a tip could be around 10% of the total bill paid for the trek (or the trekking section of the tour, if it also includes other items like transport or hotels) divided between the guides and porters. Some guides and porters may imply that official 'tipping rates' are set by the park authorities, but this is not true. Tipping in dollars is preferred. If you tip in Tanzanian shillings, convert at the free, rather than the official, exchange rate – otherwise the porters and guides will lose out.

If each member of a group paid US$450 for a short trek, everyone could pay around US$40 in tips, to be divided between the guide and porters. Generally, for a trip up the Marangu route, guides get about US$30 (more with a large group, especially if they've also done the cooking) and porters around US$10. For longer treks, guides usually get US$40 to US$50 and porters around US$15. Of course, you can pay more if you're particularly impressed, and less if you're not. But explain why you're doing this – it will help porters and future trekkers if it's understood that tips are not automatic.

Some disreputable characters have been known to use a variety of methods to extract large tips from visitors. Techniques range from pathetic pleading, through aggressive demands, to virtual strikes. To avoid misunderstandings, it may be necessary to agree on all tips before the start of the trek. Writing down the agreed amount will help memory on both sides. But even after a tip has been agreed, you should make it quite clear that it will only be paid if the service is satisfactory.

Warning Although guides are obligatory, and provided with every organised trek, you should still familiarise yourself with all aspects of the route, such as distances between huts or camping places, availability of water, and condition of the paths. This is particularly important on the unusual routes (everything except the Marangu Route) as guides are not necessarily always as experienced as they claim, or may suggest itineraries and changes to the route which are completely unsuitable, or may even be dangerous.

Park Fees & Regulations

The forest around Kilimanjaro is an official reserve and the area beyond this, mostly above 2700 metres, is Kilimanjaro National Park, and fees must be paid. Although it is obligatory to organise your trek through a company, you may have to pay your park fees directly at the park gates. Other companies quote a price that includes park fees and handle everything for you. It is therefore very important, when arranging your trek, to check whether park fees are included in the price.

If you're paying fees yourself, you must do so in hard currency. US dollars (travellers' cheques or cash) are recommended as all prices are quoted in this currency. For non-Tanzanians, fees are:

Entrance fee	US$15 per day
Hut fee	US$15 per night
(mandatory on the Marangu Route even if you camp)	
Camping fee	US$40 per night
(mandatory on all other routes)	
Rescue fee	US$20 per trip
Park commission	US$5 per trip

Citizens and residents of Tanzania pay lower park entrance and hut fees. Guides and porters also have to pay fees, but this should be handled directly by your trekking company.

For a standard five-day trek on the Marangu Route, park fees come to a total of US$160 per trekker. For six days (five nights) on one of the other routes (coming down the Marangu) the fees total US$290. An extra day puts it up to US$345. Avoiding the Marangu Route on your descent adds yet another US$25. (These prices were correct in late 1992 but increases are likely.) These fees certainly bump up the cost of a trek on Kili, but to complain that they are too high is to miss the point. There is no reason why Tanzania shouldn't earn money from tourists (see National Parks, in the Facts for the Trekker chapter). The problem is that the revenue earnt by Kilimanjaro National Park does not seem to benefit the local people who inhabit the area around the park, and does not seem to benefit the park itself.

For example, some of the revenue could go towards cleaning up the huts and campsites, particularly on the Marangu Route. Horombo Hut is getting more like a shanty town every year. On the other routes some money could go towards building proper rubbish pits or toilets although, ideally, rubbish pits should not be needed, as anything brought up should be taken down again. Guides and porters could be paid a 'trash bonus' for everything they carry down.

Toilets are a different matter: deep, 'long-drop' toilets should be constructed and maintained at every hut and campsite. Some people say that providing facilities of this nature destroys the wilderness aspect of trekking on the mountain. But piles of crap and toilet paper everywhere are unpleasant too.

Top: Kibo crater rim: the jagged spires of Mawenzi seen from Stella Point, Kilimanjaro (DE)

Bottom: On Uhuru Peak, Kilimanjaro's summit, with the Northern Icefields behind (DE)

Top: Sunrise behind Kilimanjaro from Mt Meru (DE)
Bottom: The Ash Cone from Rhino Point, Mt Meru (CE)

Certificates If you reach Uhuru Peak you will be awarded a certificate when you get back down to Marangu Gate, signed by the park warden and your guide. If you make it to the rim you can get one saying you reached Gillman's Point.

Supplies

Most organised treks on Kili include food, but you can sometimes save money by providing your own, or you might just prefer to cook for yourself. There are no shops inside the national park, although you can buy beer and *sodas* at the hut on the Marangu Route. In Marangu Village there are some small shops and stalls selling vegetables, and there's a shop at Marangu Gate selling a limited range or dried and tinned food. In Moshi, the nearest town, you'll find everything you need for a trek, and there's even more choice in Arusha, if you're coming that way.

PLACES TO STAY

Most of the hotels mentioned here can arrange treks on Kili. See the Tanzania Trekking Companies section for details.

Moshi

In the centre of Moshi town, within walking distance of the railway and bus stations, is the *Moshi Hotel*, a large, plain hotel with a terrace bar and restaurant serving African and international food. Singles/doubles cost US$31/47 including breakfast. Nearby is the *Coffee Tree Hotel*, on the top floor of the KNCU Coffee Growers Union office block, with clean rooms for TSh 1500/3000, as well as a bar and restaurant.

Slightly further from the centre is the *Keys Hotel*, recently renovated and quite smart, with doubles for US$50. Camping is free if you eat in the hotel restaurant. In the same part of town is the *YMCA*, which has been popular with trekkers and travellers for many years. Although some Ys in East Africa have hit hard times, the one in Moshi is a great place to stay. The bedrooms and bathrooms are clean (although there's sometimes a shortage of water), the staff friendly and the food excellent value. There's also a small

shop and a travel agency specialising in treks up Kilimanjaro. All they need to do is get some water in the pool and the place would be perfect! Doubles cost US$13 (there are no singles). If the Y is full, just up the road is the *Green Cottage Hostel*, which is a private house with a few rooms; it's small, quiet and cheap, and a bargain at TSh 2000 for doubles.

In the area around the market and the bus station are several cheap lodging houses with very basic accommodation for around TSh 1000.

Around Moshi

The *Mountain Inn* is a fairly new hotel set in nice gardens four km from the YMCA on the road towards Hino and Marangu. The self-contained rooms at US$35/70 including breakfast are clean and there's always plenty of hot water. There's a restaurant serving good-value food if you fancy a splurge.

Further from Moshi, in Marangu Village, near the start of the Marangu Route, is the *Kibo Hotel*, an old colonial-style place with a great atmosphere. People climbing Kili have been staying here for years and the walls are covered with old maps and mementoes. Rooms cost US$70/80 including breakfast, and the hotel has a lounge with a large open fire in the centre of the room. Camping in the grounds costs TSh 2280 or US$12. Just down the road is the *Marangu Hotel*, with rooms and cottages (US$50 per person with dinner and breakfast) set among trees and manicured gardens. Camping costs US$10 per night.

Also in Marangu Village, one km down the dirt road towards Rombo, is the *Babylon Hotel*. This is a new place, owned and run by the affable Mr Stephen. Clean, self-contained doubles cost US$30 including breakfast. Another two km down the same road is *Ashanti Lodge*. Rooms in the main hotel or in the bandas in the garden cost US$20/30 including breakfast. Camping is free if you arrange your trek here.

Next to the Marangu Gate is *Kilimanjaro Mountain Lodge*. This used to be the Youth Hostel, but in the new era of free enterprise it's been sold to a private developer who's smartened the place up and now charges US$45 including breakfast. Camping in the garden costs US$10. There's a restaurant and bar attached.

On the other side of Moshi, near the start of the Machame Route, is the *Aishi Hotel*, a small but fairly stylish hotel, with comfortable, self-contained doubles at US$55.

Arusha

Arusha has a much wider choice of hotels, and this is particularly useful if you're coming from Nairobi or doing a trek on Mt Meru as well as Kilimanjaro. For details, see Places to Stay, in the Mt Meru section of this chapter.

On Kilimanjaro

Accommodation on Kilimanjaro is limited to the Marangu Route, which has three large, well-built huts spaced at convenient intervals, about six to eight hours' (or a day's) walk apart. The huts are administered by the national park and you pay hut fees with your entrance fees. You can also camp on this route but, amazingly, you still have to pay hut fees.

All the other routes have small metal huts called 'uniports', usually dirty and in very bad condition, and only used by local guides and porters. Consequently, on routes other than the Marangu Route, trekkers usually camp. It is usual to camp near the huts so that the guides and porters have somewhere to sleep, as very few trekking companies provide tents for their staff. Also, the only reliable water sources are those near huts.

(It's possible that all the small metal huts on Kili may be removed by the park authorities, as they are unsightly and rarely used by tourists. This means all trekking companies using these routes will have to provide tents and equipment for their staff. If the huts are removed, the campsites will remain in the same places, or nearby, as these are generally flat spots at a suitable position between daily stages. The lower sites also have water supplies nearby.)

Huts and campsites on the mountain are covered more fully in the route descriptions.

GETTING THERE & AWAY

The Kilimanjaro massif lies in north-eastern Tanzania, about 500 km from Dar es Salaam, just below the border with Kenya. It's quicker and easier to reach Moshi, the nearest town, from Nairobi than from Dar. Nairobi is also easier and cheaper to get to from Europe, so most trekkers visiting Kilimanjaro come by this route.

Air

Kilimanjaro International Airport (KIA) is 40 km from Moshi on the main Moshi-Arusha road. There are daily flights between KIA and Dar. (See the Tanzania Getting Around section for more details.)

Bus, Matatu & Taxi

At least five public buses run every day between Moshi and Dar, usually taking a day or 1½ days, with a night stopover. The fare is between TSh 8000 and TSh 12,000 depending on the quality and speed of the bus.

Moshi is also linked to Nairobi, in Kenya, via Arusha and Namanga (the border) on good tar roads. There is no train service but buses, matatus and shared taxis run regularly between these main points. (Details in the Tanzania Getting There & Away section). There are regular buses between Moshi and Arusha for about TSh 1000.

Train

The train between Moshi and Dar es Salaam is more enjoyable than the bus. It can be a longer journey, but it's comfortable (in 1st and 2nd class), safe and reasonably priced. The train goes three times per week in each direction, overnight. From Dar it's usually necessary to reserve seats of the train at least three days in advance, but from Moshi you can sometimes find a seat on the day. The train costs TSh 5500/3400/2500 in 1st class sleeper/2nd class sleeper/2nd class seat. Third class costs only TSh 1000 but is crowded and uncomfortable.

THE MARANGU ROUTE

The Marangu Route is the most popular route on Kilimanjaro. It's the easiest, and the huts provide the best accommodation, so more than 90% of trekkers go up and down this route. During the busy season the huts are very full, often at double capacity, with people sleeping two to a bunk and all over the floor.

The route goes up the south-east side of the mountain and approaches the summit of Kibo via the crater rim at Gillman's Point. Treks on this route usually descend the same way.

Because most people do the whole trek in five days (four nights), very few actually get to the summit at Uhuru Peak. About half get to Gillman's Point, and the rest bail out somewhere between there and Kibo Hut. To increase your chances of reaching Uhuru, or even getting to Gillman's in a reasonable state, an extra day can be spent on the ascent, ideally at Horombo Hut, to help acclimatization.

Access

The route starts at Marangu Gate, near Marangu Village, on the south-eastern side of Kilimanjaro, about 40 km by road from Moshi. Most trekking companies provide transport to the gate, and this will probably be included in your organised trek.

If you're making your own way there by car, from Moshi take the tarred road towards Dar. After about 20 km, in the small town of Himo, turn left (north) and follow this road for a further 13 km to reach Marangu Village. Marangu Gate is a further five km up the hill. The road is tarred all the way. Vehicles can be left at the park gate.

If you're taking public transport, the bus between Moshi and Marangu runs several times each day and costs about TSh 150. The bus goes only as far as the village, as the road up to the gate is too steep. You might be lucky and hitch a ride up to the gate. Otherwise you'll have to walk – look on it as a good warm up!

Stage 1: Marangu Gate to Mandara Hut
(7 km, 4-5 hours, 700 metres ascent)
From Marangu Gate (1980 metres) the path is wide and clear, passing through forest. A short distance from the gate the path divides: the right fork is the 'main' track and the usual way to Mandara Hut; the left fork is a slightly longer alternative route designed to give you more opportunity to observe the wildlife and

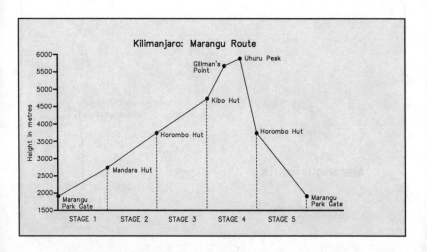

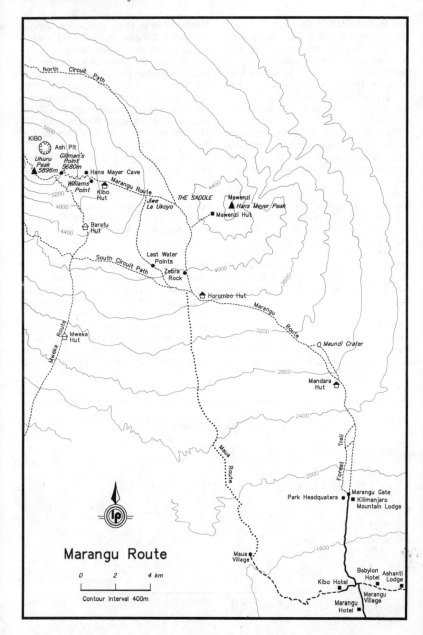

KIBO
Ash Pit
Uhuru
Peak
5896m
Gillman's
Point
5680m
Williams
Point
Hans Mayer Cave
Marangu Route
Kibo Hut
Jiwe
La Ukoyo
THE SADDLE
Mawenzi
Hans Meyer Peak
Mawenzi Hut
Barafu
Hut
North Circuit Path
South Circuit Path
Last Water
Points
Zebra
Rock
Horombo Hut
Marangu Route
Mweka Route
Mweka
Hut
Maundi Crater
Mandara Hut
Forest Trail
Maua Route
Park Headquaters
Marangu Gate
Kilimanjaro
Mountain Lodge
Maua
Village
Kibo Hotel
Babylon
Hotel
Ashanti
Lodge
Marangu
Village
Marangu
Hotel

Marangu Route

0   2   4 km

Contour Interval 400m

enjoy the forest. The forest trail is clearly marked, although not as wide as the main path because fewer people use it. The paths rejoin after 1½ to two hours, and again after two to 2½ hours. From this final junction it's another one to 1½ hours to Mandara Hut.

Mandara Hut (2700 metres) is actually a group of bunkhouses, in good condition, with beds for 80 people, toilets and a clean water supply.

Sidetrack: Maundi Crater
(2 hours)
From Mandara Hut you can visit nearby Maundi Crater, a small mound rising out of the trees to the north. Views from the top, over the forest up to the main peaks of Kibo and Mawenzi, provide plenty of inspiration for the trek to come. The path is clearly signposted.

Stage 2: Mandara Hut to Horombo Hut
(11 km, 5-7 hours, 1000 metres ascent)
From Mandara Hut the path continues through forest, and then a narrow band of heather, before entering the moorland. As you leave the forest you'll get your first clear view of the top of the Kibo dome. To the right are the jagged peaks of Mawenzi, looking higher than Kibo from this angle. The path, although undulating and steep in places, is easy to follow all the way to Horombo Hut.

Horombo Hut (3700 metres) is a large

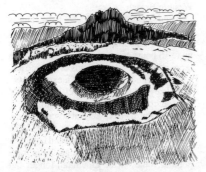

Ice cliffs & crater atop Kibo, with Mawenzi in background

group of bunkhouses, similar to those at Mandara, with space for about 120 people.

Most trekkers spend their second night here and push on to Kibo Hut on the following day. If you've got more time to spare you may prefer to spend two nights at Horombo to help acclimatization. A good rest-day walk is up to The Saddle by the eastern path, where you can explore the area around the lower slopes of Mawenzi for some of the day.

Stage 3: Horombo Hut to Kibo Hut
(10 km, 5-7 hours, 1000 metres ascent)
After Horombo Hut the path divides. Take the left fork (the western path) and continue, gradually gaining height, past the Last Water point (signposted), which is the highest running water on this route. You will fill up containers here. Continue until you join the eastern path on the Kibo side of The Saddle at a point called Jiwe La Ukoyo. From here to Kibo Hut takes one to 1½ hours.

The right fork after Horombo (the eastern path) is steep and rough, and not used much, passing the black-and-white striped Zebra Rock and a Last Water point (marked by a signpost), and reaching The Saddle on the Mawenzi Peak side.

Kibo Hut (4700 metres) is more basic than Horombo and Mandara, with space for about 60 people. There is no reliable water supply. All water must be carried from Horombo or one of the Last Water points. The hut caretake sells bottled drinks at high prices – allowing for porterage costs.

Stage 4: Kibo Hut to Horombo Hut via Uhuru Peak
(4 km, 7-8½ hours, 1200 metres ascent plus 14 km, 4½-7 hours, 2200 metres descent)
Most trekkers spend their third night at Kibo Hut and walk up towards the summit on the fourth day. This stage of the trek can involve up to 16 hours of walking, which is very strenuous, but it's easy to bail out on this route at any point and return the way you've come.

It's usual to start this day's walking very early in the morning, to see the sunrise from the crater rim, and to give you more chance of avoiding the mist. Also, the scree slope up to Gillman's Point, and the snow on the path to Uhuru Peak, will still be frozen, which will make the walking safer and less strenuous. Sunrise is around 6 am, and you should allow five to six hours to get from Kibo Hut to Gillman's Point (5680 metres), plus another two hours to reach Uhuru Peak (5896 metres). This normally means leaving Kibo Hut between midnight and 1 am.

From Kibo Hut, the path is easy to follow as it zig-zags up the scree. You pass Williams Point (5000 metres) and Hans Mayer Cave (5182 metres) which are useful markers, helping you to pace the walk. After the cave the gradient gets steeper and the walk becomes, without doubt, a slog. It seems endless but, some five or six hours later, when you finally get to the rim at Gillman's Point, it's all worth it. From here you can see down into the snow-filled crater, across to the spectacular stepped cliffs of the Eastern Icefields, back down to The Saddle with the dark bulk of Mawenzi behind, and along the edge of the crater rim to Uhuru Peak.

It is important not to arrive at Gillman's Peak too early, as this will mean waiting, sometimes in extremely cold conditions, for sunrise. Experienced guides will have assessed the abilities of their clients and pace the walk up the scree to arrive on the rim at exactly the right time.

Most people are happy with reaching Gillman's Point, especially when they see how much further it is to Uhuru Peak, but if you're feeling good and there's still time, it's well worth carrying on to the summit. The walk around the crater rim, with the steep drop into the crater on one side and the smooth snow-covered outer slopes of the dome on the other, is one of the most spectacular in Africa. From Gillman's to Uhuru takes another two to 2½ hours.

At the summit there's a flag pole, a plaque inscribed with a quote of President Nyerere, and a book where you can sign your name. If the weather's good you might want to hang around up here to revel in your success and take in the views. If the weather is bad, you'll probably be content with a quick photo and high- tailing it down again.

From Uhuru Peak or Gillman's Point it's usual for trekkers on the Marangu Route to descend by the same route. The return from Uhuru Peak to Gillman's Point takes about one to 1½ hours. You should aim to be back at Gillman's about three hours after sunrise, as after this time the top layer of snow becomes wet, slippery and much harder for walking.

From Gillman's back down to Kibo Hut the scree is blissfully easy going compared with the slog up. An easy walk takes 1½ to 2½ hours. If you've got strong knees and nerves of steel you can run down the scree and be back at Kibo Hut in less than an hour.

From Kibo, retrace the path to Horombo Hut – this will take two to three hours.

Stage 5: Horombo Hut to Marangu Gate
(18 km, 4-6 hours, 1900 metres descent)
On the last day, retrace the route, following the clearly marked path down to the park gate at Marangu. Mandara Hut is about half-way down, a good place for a break.

THE UMBWE ROUTE
This is a very direct route to Uhuru Peak, suitable for more experienced trekkers. If followed sensibly (not rushed), it offers a pleasant walk through forest and moorland on the lower slopes and an exhilarating final approach to the summit of Kibo via the Western Breach.

Although the paths are steep, the distances walked on most days are short, except on Stage 4, the summit section, which involves up to 15 hours of walking, and is made even more strenuous by the effects of altitude and extreme cold. If you're unfit, inexperienced, or unlikely to acclimatize well, you should not attempt this top section of the route.

From Uhuru Peak, you can descend on the Mweka Route or the Marangu Route. The Mweka has fewer trekkers on it and is shorter but much steeper; the Marangu is the most popular route on the mountain, longer but with an easier gradient. Both options are described in this section.

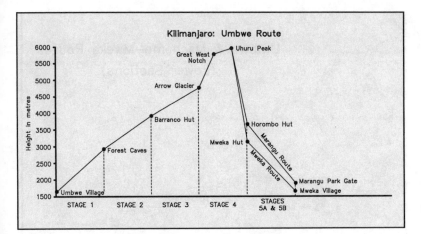

Kilimanjaro: Umbwe Route

The whole trek can be completed in five days (four nights), although an extra day spent on the ascent, ideally at Barranco Hut, is strongly recommended to help acclimatization.

Access
The route starts at Umbwe Gate, near Umbwe Mission on the southern side of the mountain, about 15 km from Moshi. There are several dirt roads and tracks from Moshi to Umbwe Village and the start of the route, but all organised treks on this route include transport to the village or gate.

Stage 1: Umbwe Gate to Forest Caves
(13 km, 4-5 hours, 1450 metres ascent)
From the gate (1400 metres) follow the track up through the forest. The track turns into a path and continues through the forest on a ridge between two valleys. In some places you may have to scramble up steep sections of the path using tree roots for support. Continue following the path, and the occasional red paint marks on the trees, to reach Forest Caves (2850 metres).

The 'caves' are little more than overhanging rocks and, although dry, provide only limited shelter; a tent is recommended. Next to the caves is a small flat area suitable for camping. Guides and porters usually sleep in the caves. Water is available from a small pool 20 metres back down the path.

Stage 2: Forest Caves to Barranco Hut
(5 km, 3-4 hours, 1100 metres ascent)
From the caves, continue following the path up the ridge. The path leaves the forest and passes through heather, and then open moorland, where the main peaks first come into clear view. After about an hour you'll reach the Upper Caves – these are slightly overhanging cliffs which don't provide much shelter.

The path keeps to high ground (as the Great Barranco Valley drops steeply down to the right), following cairns to reach a solitary signpost at an indistinct junction (The left path leads to Arrow Glacier and Lava Tower Hut.) Keep right to reach Barranco Hut (3950 metres).

Barranco Hut is a single uniport with an earth floor. Around the hut are some flat spaces where about eight tents can be pitched. Water is available from a stream (five minutes further along the path). There's more space for camping about ten minutes further along the path, next to another stream, and ten minutes beyond that, right at the foot of the Barranco Wall, is a large boulder with a cave underneath which makes

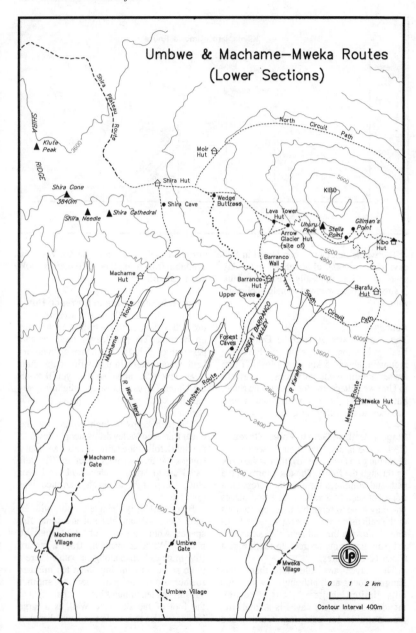

Umbwe & Machame–Mweka Routes
(Lower Sections)

a good shelter (often used by guides and porters), and more space for camping nearby.

From Barranco Hut the Umbwe Route continues up to Arrow Glacier and approaches Uhuru Peak via the Western Breach. This route is described here. Alternatively, from Barranco Hut you can follow the South Circuit Path to Barafu Hut and approach Uhuru Peak from there. (For details of this second option see the Machame-Mweka Combination Route description.)

Sidetrack: The Barranco Wall
(5-6 hours)
From the campsites near Barranco Hut, the Barranco Wall can be clearly seen as a huge dark cliff on the opposite side of the Great Barranco Valley. If you plan to spend two nights at Barranco Hut, the route up the Barranco Wall, and then up to the base of the Heim Glacier is a good sidetrack. The route up the wall is steep and exposed, requiring scrambling in places, but marked by cairns. At the top of the wall, the views of the glaciers and lava fields make even the most indifferent trekkers shut up and simply stare. The South Circuit Path continues in an easterly direction towards Barafu Hut; another path, also cairned, leads directly to the foot of the Heim Glacier, an ice mountaineering route aiming directly up to the Kibo rim. (From Barranco Hut to the top of the Barranco Wall takes one to 1½ hours, then another two to 2½ to get to below the glacier snout. Allow about an hour back from there to the top of the wall, and the same again down into the valley.)

Stage 3: Barranco Hut to Arrow Glacier
(5 km, 4-5 hours, 850 metres ascent)
From the hut, take the path which climbs steeply up onto the main ridge on the west side of the Great Barranco Valley. The path then leads north-west along the ridge top, aiming directly towards the Western Breach, a section of the main wall of Kibo where a giant chunk has been eroded away, so that the gradient is slightly less steep than the sheer cliffs on either side. (The most distinc-

tive feature of the Western Breach is the series of high cliffs that form the Breach Wall on the right (east) side of the Breach itself. This is one of the hardest areas for technical mountaineering on Kilimanjaro, and has been compared in seriousness to the north face of the Eiger.)

On the ridge, the vegetation thins out completely and the path crosses bare rock and scree, but is well cairned. Two hours from Barranco Hut is a junction marked by several signs and some painted animal bones. (Shira Hut and the South Circuit Path are signposted left.) Keep right (east) and continue up steeply over scree, with the high orange cliffs of the Lava Tower to the left (west), to reach a flat platform, the site of Arrow Glacier Hut (4800 metres) and the base of the Western Breach.

Arrow Glacier Hut was damaged by a rock fall in the mid-1980s, and is now nonexistent, so a tent is essential if you are going to spend the night here before taking the route up the Western Breach the next morning. There is a good flat area for camping – you'll have to pitch your tent on snow or fine scree, depending on the time of year. Water has to be melted from ice, or carried from Barranco Hut.

Alternatively, from Arrow Glacier it is possible to descend to Lava Tower Hut, another uniport also damaged by a rockfall, about an hour's walk down to the west. This hut is just about unusable and staying here adds at least 1½ hours on to the next day's walking time, which is already very long, so coming down here to camp is not recommended.

Stage 4: Arrow Glacier to Mweka Hut or Horombo Hut via Uhuru Peak
(3 km, 6-7½ hours, 1100 metres ascent
plus 12 km, 4½-7 hours, 2800 metres descent (Mweka Route)
or plus 14 km, 4½-7 hours, 2200 metres descent (Marangu Route))
This stage of the trek involves between 10½ and 14½ hours of walking, which is made even more strenuous by the effects of altitude and extreme cold. You can descend

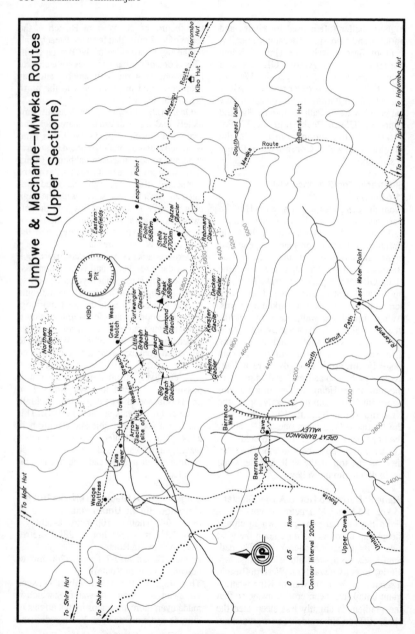

Umbwe & Machame–Mweka Routes
(Upper Sections)

by either the Mweka Route or the Marangu Route. (Although it's also possible to descend by returning down the Western Breach, it is usual to descend by another route.) Unlike the Marangu Route, where you can go as far as the rim at Gillman's or bail out before that, you don't have such a choice on the trek described here. There are no real shortcuts, so you must go all the way, unless you're planning to come back down the Western Breach after reaching the summit. If you don't feel up to this section, you can walk from Arrow Glacier back to either Mweka or Horombo Hut (depending on your descent route).

You need only your guide on this section of the route. Your porters will go straight to the next hut (depending on the descent route) and wait there. Porters should not depart immediately, in case anyone in your group returns from the Western Breach. They can then walk with the porters to the next hut and rejoin the rest of the group.

After heavy snow (which occurs occasionally in the dry season), this section of the route may be impassable for trekkers. Do not attempt it unless you've got rope and ice-axes for protection, and know how to use them (although this is verging on mountaineering techniques). It's better to go straight to Mweka or Horombo Hut.

It is usual to start this day's walking very early in the morning, to see the sunrise at the crater rim and to avoid the mist. Also, the scree and snow on the ascent will still be frozen, which will make the journey safer and less strenuous. Sunrise is at about 6 am, and it takes four to five hours to get from Arrow Glacier to the rim at the Great West Notch, plus another two to 2½ to reach Uhuru Peak. This normally means leaving Arrow Glacier between 1 and 2 am.

Although no technical climbing is involved, this section is the steepest nontechnical route on the mountain and should not be taken lightly. Great care should be exercised, as the rock is very loose in places and a fall could result in serious injury. A torch is essential (preferably a head-mounted torch, as this leaves your hands free) and

ski-poles (or even a long-shaft ice-axe) are highly recommended for balance. (The section of scree can be avoided if you have crampons – and know how to use them – by taking a parallel route up the glacier itself.)

Also note that there is no water supply on this route until Mweka or Horombo Hut (although the caretaker at Kibo Hut sells bottled drinks at high prices!). Take all you need for this stage.

From the site of Arrow Glacier Hut, the path climbs steeply, over loose scree, marked by cairns (some with fluorescent strips attached), keeping to the left (west) of the Little Breach Glacier. Beyond the top of the glacier, the path continues, with a few short stretches of easy scrambling, to reach the crater rim at a low point, sometimes called the Great West Notch, after about four to five hours.

From this point on the crater rim Uhuru Peak can be seen to the right (south-east). The path, which may be obscured by snow, does not aim directly for the peak but contours round the north side of the Furtwangler Glacier. Keeping the cliffs of the glacier to your right, head east, then south-east, back towards the edge of the rim to the north-west of Uhuru Peak Go up an easy gully (shallow snowfield after snow) to reach Uhuru Peak (about two to 2½ hours from the Great West Notch).

For details of Uhuru Peak (5896 metres) and the views of the crater, see the Marangu Route description.

Mweka Route Descent From the summit, follow the path eastwards around the rim to reach Stella Point, a gap in the crater rim, after one hour. The path then leads steeply down, crossing some snow on the upper section, then scree with occasional cairns. You should reach Barafu Hut after another 1½ to 2½ hours. Aim to be at Stella Point two hours after sunrise, as after this time the top layer of snow becomes wet and slippery, which can be harder for walking and more dangerous on the descent.

From Barafu Hut, continue down the clear path to the junction with the South Circuit

Path, and go straight on, steeply downhill through patchy giant heather to reach Mweka Hut (3100 metres), on the edge of the forest, after another two to three hours.

Mweka Hut is two uniports, not in bad condition, as this route is rarely used. Nearby are some places for camping, and water is available from a nearby stream.

Marangu Route Descent From the summit, follow the path through the snow eastwards around the rim to reach Stella Point after one hour, then continue round the rim to reach Gillman's Point after another 30 minutes. You should aim to be at Gillman's about three hours after sunrise, as after this time the top layer of snow becomes wet, slippery and much harder for walking.

From Gillman's Point, descend to Kibo Hut and then to Horombo Hut. For full details of this section see the Marangu Route description.

Stage 5A (Mweka Route): Mweka Hut to Mweka Village

(10 km, 3-4 hours, 1600 metres descent)
From Mweka Hut, descend steeply through the forest on a narrow path, along the crest of a broad ridge between two river valleys. After a few hours, the path widens into a track which leads out of the forest into the shambas around Mweka Village. There is no park gate on this route yet, but there are plans to build one in 1993.

Stage 5B (Marangu Route): Horombo Hut to Marangu Gate

(18 km, 4-6 hours, 1900 metres descent)
This is a very pleasant walk through moorland, heather and forest. Mandara Hut is reached in two to three hours, and Marangu Gate after a further two to three hours.

THE MACHAME-MWEKA COMBINATION ROUTE

This route offers a varied and gradual ascent of Kilimanjaro, linking the Machame and Mweka Routes with a section of the South Circuit path, and approaching the summit of Kibo via Stella Point. (The top section of this route, from Barafu Hut up to Stella Point, is sometimes referred to as the Barafu Route.)

Proper acclimatization is important on any Kili trek (see Acclimatisation, earlier in this chapter), and this route gives you the best chance of acclimatising properly, although the distances walked each day are longer than on any other route, and this can be strenuous. The summit stage is particularly long, involving up to 15 hours of walking, which is made even more strenuous by the effects of altitude and extreme cold.

From Uhuru Peak, you can descend via Barafu Hut and then down the Mweka Route, or you can go down the Marangu Route. Both options are described in this section.

The whole trek usually takes six days (five nights), although an extra day can be spent on the ascent, to help acclimatization. An ideal place for a rest day is the Shira Plateau, spending two nights at Shira Hut.

Access

The route starts at Machame Gate, near Machame Village, on the south-western side of the mountain, about 30 km by road from Moshi. Most organised treks on this route include transport to Machame Village, but you can get here by matatu from Moshi.

From the village green, continue up the dirt road for three km (about a one-hour walk) to reach Machame Gate.

Stage 1: Machame Gate to Machame Hut

(10 km, 5-7 hours, 1200 metres ascent)
From the gate, continue up the track, which becomes a path after about an hour. It is easy to follow (passing occasional red paint marks) as it continues up through the dense montane forest.

The path continues to follow a ridge, rising steadily with some steep sections, the gradient easing slightly as the forest merges into giant heather, to reach Machame Hut (3000 metres). Cloud permitting, the summit of Kibo will be visible beyond the foothills.

Machame Hut is two uniports, both in bad condition. There is space to pitch about four tents next to the huts and space for about 10 more, 20 metres up from the hut. There are also extra spaces about 100 metres back along the ridge. Water is available from a stream 30 metres down a steep slope to the north-west of the huts. In the dry season this stops flowing, so you must go a further 10 minutes down the stream-bed to collect water from pools.

Warning There have been a few isolated incidents of local people coming up from Machame Village during the night and stealing from the campsite. Keep all your stuff inside while asleep and make sure someone from your group keeps an eye on the tents during the evening.

Stage 2: Machame Hut to Shira Hut
(6 km, 5-7 hours, 840 metres ascent)
From Machame Hut, cross the stream onto its west bank and follow the path, which is clear and marked by red paint on rocks and trees, up the steep rocky ridge, crossing and re-crossing the crest a few times. Two hours from the hut you'll reach a steep semi-circular wall of rock. Scramble up this wall to reach easier ground and a good rest spot. From here there are excellent views of the Shira Plateau and the towers and pinnacles on its southern edge.

The path continues up and then left, across several small stream beds (all empty in the dry season), to reach the flatter ground of the Shira Plateau after another hour. From here the path is almost level, winding through thin bush, clumps of grass and across patches of bare sand and ash. After half an hour you'll reach a flat area with plenty of room for camping, with the large Shira Cave nearby.

The path climbs over a small ridge, then drops to cross a stream, before another small rise up to Shira Hut (3840 metres), on a rocky platform overlooking the flat expanse of Shira Plateau. From the cave to the hut takes less than half an hour.

Shira Hut is a uniport in bad condition, with space to camp nearby and water available from the stream 50 metres north of the hut. In the dry season, this source is not reliable, so you have to get water from the stream bed below Shira Cave.

Sidetrack: The Shira Plateau Edge
Shira Cave or Shira Hut are good places to spend two nights to give yourself a rest day. If you're feeling fit, the edge of the Shira Plateau is a fascinating area to explore on this day. There are no paths, and very few people (or guides) come this way. You need to be competent with a map and compass here and

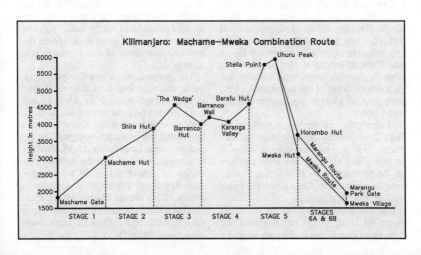

Kilimanjaro: Machame–Mweka Combination Route

should not rely on your guide. If the weather is bad, and visibility low, forget it.

From Shira Hut take the Shira Plateau Route, downhill in a westerly direction, towards the flat floor of the plateau. After half an hour drop down a steep section to meet an old track at its roadhead. (There's a turning circle here and some flat places for camping, but no water.) Follow the track for about two km and then, as it swings right, aim left (south-west) and uphill slightly towards the top of the ridge. From here follow the crest of the ridge as it leads to a cairn on a small summit. From this small summit, it's possible to follow the ridge-crest to the summit of Shira Cathedral, a huge buttress of rock surrounded by steep spires and pinnacles. This is an excellent walk but the crest of the ridge is very steep in places, with sheer drops down several hundred metres on the southern side. Take great care if you decide to follow the crest of the ridge. Some sections require serious scrambling, while others are completely impassable. If in doubt, tend right (north) and down to easier ground and walk through the grassland, keeping parallel to the ridge. Eland are sometimes seen in this area.

Beyond the Shira Cathedral, descent is essential, as the ridge ends at a sheer cliff. But beyond this it's possible to scramble back up again to the summit of the Shira Needle. This ascent requires a few moves of rock climbing and you'll need a head for heights on the top, which is not much bigger than a few tables end to end, but the views from the summit, across the Cathedral and the southern slopes of the mountain, with the main peak of Kibo in the background, are well worth it.

Further away, but far less exposed, is the Shira Cone (marked on some maps as Cone Place). This is a rounded conical hill with smooth grassy sides. To reach the top, aim for the shoulder on its left (southern) side, and go up from there. Once again, the views from the top are superb.

Allow at least seven hours for the return trip to the Shira Needle or the Shira Cone from Shira Hut. If this is not your idea of a rest day, you could just take a short walk in the area. Alternatively, you could stay at your campsite and snooze in the sun all day...

Eland

Stage 3: Shira Hut to Barranco Hut
(10 km, 5-7 hours, 110 metres ascent)
From Shira Hut the path is clear and well marked by red paint as it climbs gradually, in an easterly direction, towards the main peak of Kibo, passing between increasingly large boulders, to reach a very large (six metres high) lone boulder with a cairn on top, after one to $1\frac{1}{2}$ hours. After another 30 minutes, a line of cairns leads off to the left (north). An arrow and the words 'Moyr Hut' (sic) are painted on a nearby rock. This is the start of the North Circuit Path. Ignore this path and continue uphill directly towards the main peak.

The gradient eases and the path tends right, dropping into a broad valley, then climbing steeply up the other side to a ridge-crest. Fifteen minutes further on, the route divides, with paths going either side of a large black wedge-shaped buttress. (The left path goes up to Lava Tower Hut.) Keep right, to contour below and to the right of 'the wedge'. Continue following the contour, then drop down a scree slope and cross a stream. (This stream always seems to be running and is a rest place for porters.) Up to the left, the orange cliffs of the Lava Tower can be seen. Behind the Tower is the Western

Breach, a section of the main wall of Kibo where a giant chunk has been eroded away, so that the gradient is slightly less steep than sheer cliffs on either side.

From the stream the path undulates and crosses a boggy section before climbing back up onto a ridge. One hour from 'the wedge' a path down from the Lava Tower and Arrow Glacier comes in from the left at a junction marked by several signposts and painted animal bones. The path continues down the ridge, with the deep sides of the Great Barranco Valley falling away to the left, for another hour until Barranco Hut becomes visible directly below and to the left (east). The path drops steeply down the side of the ridge, into the Great Barranco Valley, to reach Barranco Hut (3950 metres).

Barranco Hut is a single uniport with an earth floor. Around the hut are some flat spaces where about eight tents can be pitched. Water is available from a stream (five minutes further along the path). There's more space for camping, about ten minutes further along the path, next to another stream, and ten minutes beyond that, right at the foot of the Barranco Wall (the large, dark cliff on the opposite side of the valley) is a large boulder with a cave underneath, which makes a good shelter (often used by guides and porters), and more space for camping nearby.

Stage 4: Barranco Hut to Barafu Hut
(8 km, 8-9 hours, 650 metres ascent)
From Barranco Hut, follow the path across the floor of the Great Barranco Valley, crossing several streams, up to the huge boulder at the base of the Barranco Wall. The path passes to the right of the boulder, and then very steeply up the Barranco Wall, following cairns and red paint marks to the top. It takes about one to 1½ hours to reach the top of the Wall. The path is steep and exposed in sections; great care should be taken.

From the top of the Wall you'll get some truly excellent views of the main bulk of Kibo up to your left. Now you'll really feel you're on a big mountain!

The path aims generally south-east, undulating slightly, crossing several small valleys and streams, but generally keeping level, until dropping steeply down into the Karanga Valley, after a further two hours. If you intend to camp at Barafu Hut, the Karanga River is the last water point; make sure your porters fill up here for all your needs until you get down to Horombo (on the following day). Large containers are essential. Trekking companies who organise treks regularly on this route will have a supply of containers for you to use. Allow around seven litres per person for the time at the hut and the following day's walk, and arrange for the porters to carry the extra weight.

Continue on the path as it crosses two shallow valleys and then a flat desolate area of dry heather and moorland, and up towards the crest of a broad ridge, following cairns. After 2½ hours you'll reach a junction. Turn left (north) at this junction and follow the path up the broad ridge, and a final steep section over rocky slabs, to reach Barafu Hut (4600 metres) after another 2½ hours.

Barafu Hut is two small uniports with space to pitch about 15 tents on the rocky ground nearby. There is no water at the hut, or anywhere nearby. It must be carried from the Karanga River. To compensate for the difficulties with water, the views from Barafu Hut are among the most impressive on the whole mountain: up to the main peak of Kibo, across The Saddle to Mawenzi and down to the plains below.

Stage 5: Barafu Hut to Mweka Hut or Horombo Hut via Uhuru Peak
(5 km, 6-7½ hours, 1300 m ascent
plus 12 km, 4½-7 hours, 2800 metres descent (Mweka Route)
or plus 14 km, 4½-7 hours, 2200 metres descent (Marangu Route))
This stage of the trek involves between 10½ and 14½ hours of walking, which is made even more strenuous by the effects of altitude and extreme cold. You can descend on either the Mweka Route or the Marangu Route on this trek, so if you decide not to do the summit stage you can go straight to

Mweka Hut or Horombo Hut (depending on your descent route).

You need only your guide on this section of the route. Your porters will go straight to your next hut. Porters should not depart immediately in case anyone on your group turns back on this section. They can then walk with the porters to the next hut and rejoin the rest of the group.

This section of the route may occasionally be impassable after heavy snow, and should not be attempted if this is the case. Instead, you should go straight to Mweka Hut or Horombo Hut.

It is usual to start this day's walking very early in the morning, to see the sunrise at the crater rim and to try to avoid the mist. Also, the scree and snow on the ascent will still be frozen, which will make it safer and less strenuous. Sunrise is about 6 am, and it takes five to six hours to get from Barafu Hut to the rim at Stella Point, plus another one to 1½ hours to reach Uhuru Peak. This normally means leaving Barafu Hut between midnight and 1 am.

Although no technical climbing is involved, this section is one of the steepest non-technical routes on the mountain, and should not be taken lightly. A torch is essential (preferably a head-mounted torch, as this leaves the hands free), and ski-poles are highly recommended for balance.

From Barafu Hut the path leads up the western ridge of the South-east Valley. The ridge blends into the main wall of Kibo and the path becomes very steep, zigzagging up across scree and snow. The path is fairly clear and well cairned until you cross a section of steep snow, to the right of the Rebmann Glacier, to reach the crater rim at Stella Point (5700 metres). At this point on the rim, the Barafu Route joins the route from Gillman's Point, which continues westward (clockwise) round the Kibo rim, gaining height gradually, to reach Uhuru Peak (5896 metres) after another one to 1½ hours. For information about this section of the route, and the summit itself, see the Marangu Route description.

Mweka Route Descent From the summit, retrace the path eastwards around the rim to get back to Stella Point after one hour, then retrace the top section of the Mweka Route to Barafu Hut, reached after another 1½ to 2½ hours. Aim to be back at Stella Point two hours after sunrise, because after this time the top layer of snow becomes wet and slippery, which can be more difficult for walking and more dangerous on the descent.

From Barafu Hut, continue down the clear path to the junction with the South Circuit Path, and go straight on, steeply downhill through patchy giant heather to reach Mweka Hut (3100 metres), on the edge of the forest, after another two to three hours.

Mweka Hut is two uniports, not in bad condition, as this route is rarely used. Nearby are some places for camping, and water is available from a nearby stream.

Marangu Route Descent From the summit, follow the path through the snow eastwards around the rim to reach Stella Point after one hour, then continue round the rim to reach Gillman's Point after another 30 minutes. You should aim to be at Gillman's about three hours after sunrise, as after this time the top layer of snow becomes wet, slippery and much harder for walking.

From Gillman's Point, descend to Kibo Hut and then to Horombo Hut. For details of this section see the Marangu Route description.

Stage 6A (Mweka Route): Mweka Hut to Mweka Village
(10 km, 3-4 hours, 1600 metres descent)
From Mweka Hut, descend steeply through the forest on a narrow path, along the crest of a broad ridge between two river valleys. After a few hours, the path widens into a track which leads out of the forest into the shambas around Mweka Village. There is no park gate on this route yet, but there are plans to build one during 1993.

Stage 6B (Marangu Route): Horombo Hut to Marangu Gate
(18 km, 4-6 hours, 1900 metres descent)
A very pleasant walk through moorland,

heather and forest. Mandara Hut is reached in two to three hours, and Marangu Gate after a further two to three hours. (For details of this route, and the huts on it, see the Marangu Route description.)

OTHER ROUTES

Routes other than those described here are possible, but usually fairly complex to arrange. They normally involve longer and more difficult approach drives, and trekking groups usually need to be completely self-contained, with tents and equipment for local guides and porters. As all treks on the mountain have to be organised through a trekking company, these logistical problems tend to make treks on these routes very expensive, which in turn means they are seldom used.

Northern Routes

There are some trekking routes on the northern side of the mountain, and a North Circuit Path, but none of them lead to the summit of Kibo. The approach from the foot of the mountain on this side can also involve crossing the border from Kenya, which is strictly forbidden by both Kenyan and Tanzanian authorities, so these routes are rarely used.

Maua Route

This is on the south-eastern side of the mountain, linking Maua Village to Horombo Hut, and is parallel to the Marangu Route. It used to be preferred by some mountain aficionados as an alternative route between Marangu and Horombo because it avoided the main 'tourist route'. Today, it is very rarely used and is reported to be overgrown in the forest section, although the park authorities could consider opening it again, to relieve some of the pressure on the Marangu Route.

Mweka Route (Ascent)

Also on the southern side of the mountain, the top section of this route is used in the Machame-Mweka Combination Route described earlier. The whole route is one of the most direct ways up to the summit of Kibo, but it is very steep and strenuous and not normally recommended as an *ascent* route, although it makes a good *descent* route if you want to avoid the Marangu Route.

If you decide to use the Mweka Route for an ascent, it starts near Mweka Village, about 12 km from Moshi. Mweka Hut is at about 3100 metres, and is usable. Barafu Hut (4600 metres) is in bad condition so a tent is recommended. There is no water after Mweka Hut, which means carrying supplies for two days. Very fit and well-acclimatized trekkers ascending this route can do the whole trek in four days (three nights).

Shira Plateau Route

On the far western side of the mountain, this route is rarely used because the approach track is long and in bad condition. However, once on the route, the scenery is fascinating; the flat grasslands of the plateau, ringed by sharp ridges that are the remains of the ancient Shira Crater, are unlike any other part of the Kilimanjaro massif. The route starts at Londorossi Gate, on the western side of the mountain, about 80 km by road from Moshi, and leads to Lava Tower Hut, via Shira Hut. From Lava Tower Hut the summit can be approached via the Western Breach or the Southern Circuit Route and the top of the Mweka Route, as described earlier. From Londorossi Gate to Shira Hut is usually a two- to three-day walk. A track leads to within a one-hour walk of Shira Hut, but this is in very poor condition (the top section is rarely used and may be closed off completely by the park authorities in the future). Even if you had a powerful 4WD vehicle and got up this high, it would be worth spending at least one extra day at Shira Hut to acclimatize before your trek.

Mt Meru

At 4566 metres (14,979 feet), Mt Meru is the second-highest mountain in Tanzania, although it is overshadowed by Kilimanjaro, its famous neighbour, and frequently overlooked by trekkers in East Africa. But Meru is a spectacular mountain, a classic volcanic cone, with its crater wall broken to create a gigantic horseshoe. It's well worth a visit: a trek to the summit involves some beautiful hiking through the grassland and lush forest on the mountain's lower slopes, followed by a dramatic and exhilarating walk along the knife-edge rim of the crater horseshoe.

Like most of the mountains in this region, Meru was formed by volcanic action associated with the creation of the Great Rift Valley. The circular wall of the crater was broken by subsequent explosions, and more recent volcanic activity has created the ash cone that stands inside the crater. Small eruptions have been reported in the last 100 years, indicating that Meru is still not quite extinct.

The local Warusha people who live in the area regard the mountain as sacred. Every year a bull or sheep is sacrificed and offered to the mountain to ensure rain in the coming season. While it is likely that local people have been visiting the forest, and even the area on the crater floor, for generations it is not known whether anybody ever reached the summit. The exposed nature of the walk, the unpredictable weather and the effects of altitude would probably have deterred casual curiosity.

HISTORY

The first European to record a sighting of Meru was the German explorer, Karl von der Decken, who reached this area in 1862. The mountain was later seen and described by other explorers, including Gustav Fischer in 1882 and Joseph Thomson the following year. In 1887, the Austro-Hungarian Count Samuel Teleki and members of his team penetrated the dense forest on the lower slopes and reached a point where the trees thinned out enough for them to see Kilimanjaro, which they planned to climb later in their expedition. The first ascent to the summit of Meru is credited to either Carl Uhlig in 1901 or Fritz Jaeger in 1904.

By the end of the 1880s, the area around Meru had become part of German East Africa. In 1907, the land east of the mountain was cleared and farmed by a settler family.

Although used mainly for ranching, part of their land was set aside as a reserve for indigenous wildlife and this area remained the property of the family until 1960, when the Ngurdoto Crater National Park, which included the farm, was established.

In 1967 the boundaries were extended to include Mt Meru, and the park was renamed Arusha National Park. During the early days of Tanzania's independence, the summit of Meru was named Socialist Peak, although this title was never commonly used. In more recent years, the Tanzanian government has abandoned many of its socialist principles, so it's likely that this name will soon be forgotten.

GEOGRAPHY

Mount Meru has a circular base, some 20 km across at 2000 metres, where it rises steeply above the foothills and plains. The mountain is an almost perfect cone, with an internal crater, or caldera, surrounded by a steep wall of cliffs. At about 2500 metres, the wall has been broken away, so the top half of the mountain is shaped like a giant crescent, or horseshoe, with the opening of the crescent on the east side of the cone, and the highest point directly opposite. The cliffs of the inner wall below the summit are over 1500 metres high, which makes them among the tallest in Africa. Inside the crater, more recent volcanic eruptions have created a subsidiary peak, called the Ash Cone.

GUIDEBOOKS & MAPS

The *Guide to Arusha National Park* is a very good booklet produced by Tanzania National Parks and the African Wildlife Foundation. It has a section on Mt Meru, with information on animals and birds, vegetation, geology, and so on. It is available from bookshops in Arusha.

Mount Meru is covered by the DOS/government survey maps (1:50,000) sheet numbers 55/1 (Oldoinyo Sambu), 55/2 (Ngare Nanyuki), 55/3 (Arusha), and 55/4 (Usa River). These four sheets join right in the centre of Mt Meru crater, but 55/2 is available in an expanded version which

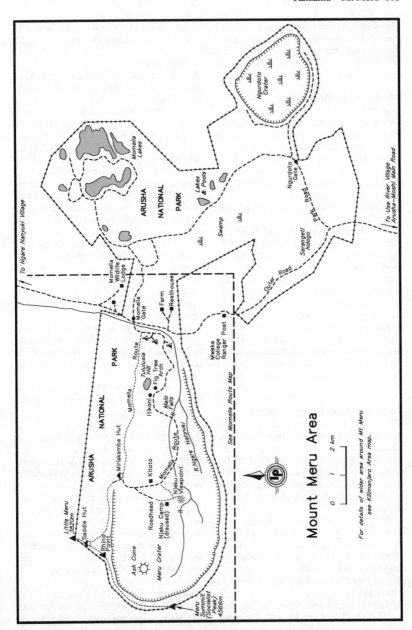

Mount Meru Area

0   1   2 km

For details of wider area around Mt Meru
see Kilimanjaro Area map.

shows the whole of Mt Meru on the one sheet. It is not possible to buy these maps in Arusha or at the park gate, but they are sometimes available from the map office in Dar es Salaam.

TREKKING INFORMATION

Despite its attractions, Meru remains a relatively obscure mountain, completely overshadowed by its more famous neighbour, Kilimanjaro, whose lower slopes are only 40 km away to the north-east. For trekkers, this obscurity is an advantage. You will probably meet only one or two other trekking groups on the mountain, and for the rest of the time have the whole place completely to yourself.

Although Meru appears small compared with Kilimanjaro, don't be fooled into thinking that conditions won't be as serious as those on the larger mountain. The effects of altitude can be a problem too so, if you are not properly acclimatized, you shouldn't try to rush up Meru.

If you've got the time and money, a visit to Meru is a great way to prepare for Kilimanjaro. It helps you build up acclimatization, and the view from Meru, across the plains to Kili's great dome rising above the clouds, provides plenty of inspiration for the major trek to come.

Route Standard & Days Required

The Momella Route is currently the only straightforward route up Meru. It starts at Momella Gate on the eastern side of the mountain and goes to the summit along the northern arm of the crater horseshoe. This route is described in detail, and some other trekking possibilities are outlined, later in this section.

The trek up Mt Meru on the Momella Route is steep but not very strenuous. It can be done comfortably in four days (three nights), although trekkers often do it in three days by combining Stages 3 and 4; some fit and very well-acclimatized trekkers even do it in two days.

Walking to and from the start of the trek, between Usa River and Momella Gate (see Access, in the Momella Route section), will add another two days to the trek.

Guides & Porters

A guide is mandatory. Unlike those on Kilimanjaro, guides here are national park rangers provided to protect you in case you meet some of the park's buffalo or elephant, rather than to show you the way (although they do know the route). The rangers are well-trained and professional and will be as informative or unobtrusive as you like. They all speak English, and most trekkers find them friendly and knowledgeable companions. They carry guns and, even though it is unlikely that an animal will have to be shot, you should not underestimate the danger and walk too far away from your guide.

Guides are arranged at Momella Gate. The fee of US$10 is paid to the national park (not to the guide himself). An extra TSh 1000 per day is paid to the guide for his food. He receives no additional payment from the park for guiding, so a tip for good service is appropriate.

Most trekkers go up Mt Meru with only a guide, but if you want porters, they are also available at Momella Gate. They come from one of the nearby villages, and are not park employees.

The charge is TSh 1000 per porter per day. This is paid at the gate and given to the porters after the trip.

You also have to pay park entrance and hut fees of TSh 300 per night for porters. Porters will carry rucksacks weighing up to 15kg (not including their own food and clothing). Heavier bags will be carried for a negotiable extra fee.

Generally, the guides and porters on Mt Meru are hard-working and reliable. They do not expect the huge tips sometimes demanded by their counterparts on Kilimanjaro. For a standard-length trip, reasonable tips might be US$15 to US$20 for the guide and US$5 to US$10 for each porter.

Park Fees

Mount Meru is in Arusha National Park and all visitors have to pay national park entrance fees in hard currency. US dollars (travellers' cheques or cash) are recommended as all prices are quoted in this currency. For non-Tanzanians, national park fees are:

Entrance fee	US$15 per day
Hut fee	US$10 per night
Rescue fee	US$20 per trek
Services of guide	US$10 per trek
Park commission	US$5 per trek

All fees are payable at Momella Gate. If you enter the park at Ngurdoto Gate you must pay your entrance fees there, but your mountain fees at Momella. A 'day' is a 24-hour period. Entry permits are marked with the time of entry. If you enter at noon on Monday morning and leave before noon on Wednesday you should only need to pay two days' fees, although this might be difficult to agree with the rangers at the gate. Fees may rise in June 1993.

Supplies
There are no shops inside the park or at the gate. In Arusha, you can buy all the food required for a trek. There's a very good market, several large shops, and even a few supermarkets.

PLACES TO STAY
The town nearest Mt Meru is Arusha. This is the centre of Tanzania's safari industry, and has a wide range of hotels. Most trekkers stay at least a few nights in Arusha as it's the best place to arrange a safari in the famous wildlife areas of Serengeti and Ngorongoro, as well as treks on Meru, Kilimanjaro and the Crater Highlands. (See the Trekking Companies section earlier in this chapter.)

Arusha
Top End The up-market places are on the eastern outskirts: the *Mount Meru Novotel*, generally regarded as the best hotel in town, with singles/doubles at US$80/65 including breakfast; the *Hotel 77*, with double rooms in individual chalets at US$50 including breakfast; and the *Motel Impala*, which is probably the best value for money in town,

with a good restaurant, efficient staff and clean, self-contained rooms for US$30/40 including breakfast.

In the town centre, next to the clock tower, the *New Arusha Hotel* has rooms at US$65/70 including breakfast, but it's pretty sleazy and service is slow, although the garden bar is good for a lunchtime refresher. Nearby, the similarly tatty *New Safari Hotel* has doubles at US$50. The adjoining New Safari Grill has reasonable food.

Just down from the clock tower is the *Arusha Resort Centre*. This is a good hotel with clean, self-contained rooms, most with a balcony (from where Meru can be seen, clouds permitting), a restaurant and a garden bar. Doubles cost US$35 including breakfast. If you're in a group, the hotel's self-contained apartments are a good deal at US$70; each apartment has two double rooms, a bathroom and a fully equipped kitchen where you can prepare your own food.

Middle & Bottom End Down the scale a bit is the interestingly titled *Hotel Arusha By Night*, near the central market, with doubles at US$25 including breakfast, a roof garden bar and 'the best disco in town'. The very popular *Naaz Hotel*, on Sokoine Rd (the main street down from the clock tower), has clean doubles for US$15. There's usually hot water, night security staff and a good serve-yourself snack-bar. There's a *YMCA* on India Street (behind the New Safari Hotel), but US$10 a double is a bit on the steep side for basic rooms, dirty toilets and a meagre breakfast. *Friends Corner House*, on the main street, about 1½ km from the clock tower, is basic but better value at TSh 1500 for doubles, and *St Teresa's Catholic Mission Guest House*, in the green area near the river off Sokoine Rd, is still the cheapest place in town, costing TSh 500 for a bed in the dormitory.

Camping If you've got a tent, there's a campsite on the outskirts of town, along the Old Moshi Road, about three km past the crossroads near the Motel Impala. Camping costs US$3 per person. There are toilets, hot showers, a bar and restaurant. The site guards are a gang of Maasai warriors, armed with spears, so there's no problem with security! The campsite is run by Tropical Trails; if you need directions, their office is in the Equator Hotel, or phone Arusha 8299.

Around Arusha

The *Momella Wildlife Lodge* is on the edge of Arusha National Park, near Momella Gate and the start of the route up Mt Meru. There's a large main building, with restaurant, bar and conference rooms, surrounded by separate bungalows and chalets. Singles/doubles cost US$50/63 including breakfast. The main building was once the home of John Wayne and Hardy Kruger, who used the house while making the adventure film *Hatari*, and later developed it as a hunting lodge. From the terrace there are excellent views of Meru and Kilimanjaro. Camping is also possible here (US$6 per night). The Lodge is run by Lion's Safari International, PO Box 999, Arusha, (☎ 6423).

The *National Park Resthouse* is an old colonial farm cottage near Momella Gate. It has five beds (although there's space for more people on the floor), a kitchen and a bathroom, for US$10 per person. There are three campsites near Momella Gate, and at Ngurdoto Gate (US$10 per night). As the campsites and resthouse are inside the park you also have to pay the US$15 entrance fee, which makes it expensive unless you're paying park fees for that day anyway. The resthouse can be reserved in advance by writing to the Mount Meru National Park, Tanzania National Parks Office, PO Box 3134, AICC, Arusha.

The Mweka Wildlife College has a small ranger post on the road to Momella Gate, about five km before the gate. There's a small resthouse here which has fallen into disrepair and is officially closed, but the rangers on duty might let you sleep here for a small fee. There is also an area for camping nearby. Park fees are not payable, as this area is outside the park boundary.

On Mt Meru

There are two large, well-maintained bunk-houses on the main route up the mountain, conveniently spaced for a three-day or four-day trek, so a tent is not usually necessary. You can also camp near the huts, although this won't save you any money. If a large group of trekkers is on the mountain at the same time as you, the huts may be full and you might have to camp, but this is unlikely. Check at the gate before starting your trek. At each bunkhouse there is a separate sleeping area for guides and porters.

GETTING THERE & AWAY

Mount Meru is in north-eastern Tanzania, about 80 km south of the border with Kenya, and about 500 km north-west of Dar es Salaam. The nearest large town is Arusha, which is linked to Moshi and Nairobi (Kenya) by good tar roads. You can travel between Arusha and Dar by air or road. For more details see the Kilimanjaro Getting There & Away section.

It is much easier to reach Arusha from Nairobi than from Dar. (For details see the Tanzania Getting There & Away section and the Tanzania Getting Around section).

THE MOMELLA ROUTE
Access

Arusha National Park consists of two main areas, the Ngurdoto Crater and Momella Lakes on the east side, and Mt Meru in the west, joined by a narrow strip of land. Momella Gate, the start of the trek, is at the centre of this narrow part.

If you're driving, you reach Momella Gate by turning north off the main Moshi-Arusha road one km east of Usa River Village. After about 10 km the track divides: the left fork (the Outer Road) crosses the park, but fees are not required for transit traffic; the right fork (the Park Road) goes through the park proper. The tracks rejoin at Momella Gate.

For trekkers without a car, there is no public transport to Momella Gate. Buses between Arusha and Moshi stop at Usa River, and from there you'll have to hitch or walk. If you get a lift in a vehicle going

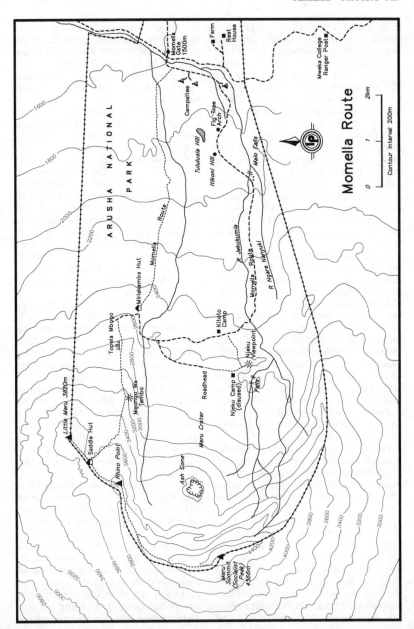

Momella Route

through the park you'll have to pay park fees. This is no problem if you intend to start your trek up Meru on the same day, as fees have to be paid at Momella Gate anyway. If you don't find a lift, the 24-km walk from Usa River to Momella Gate along the Outer Road takes between six and eight hours. Many local people walk this way. The track rises very gently for the first 10 km, passing through farmland and coffee plantations, to reach the fork where the Outer and Park roads divide. Keep left here. After the fork the track passes through an area of grassland called Serengeti Ndogo (Little Serengeti), then becomes rougher and steeper as it climbs towards the gate. Carry some water, as sources are unreliable until the Mweka College Ranger Post, about five km before the gate.

If you have a vehicle you can leave it at Momella Gate, although park fees will have to be paid on it. Vehicles can also be left at Momella Wildlife Lodge, for a more reasonable fee. If you stay at Momella Lodge, you can arrange transport from Arusha to the start of the trek at the offices of Lion's Safari International, the owners of the lodge (see Places to Stay – Around Arusha, for details). Other Arusha tour companies can provide transport to Momella Gate (for around US$100 per vehicle, divided between up to five passengers), or you can arrange a one-day safari to Arusha National Park (for only slightly more) which drops you at Momella Gate at the end of the tour.

Paying park fees and arranging guides and porters at Momella Gate can take a couple of hours. You can save time by making arrangements the night before. The park office officially opens at 6 am, but delays may occur.

Stage 1: Momella Gate to Miriakamba Hut

(10 km, 4-5 hours, 1000 metres ascent)
Two routes are available from Momella Gate. The first is a track that goes through the forest towards the crater floor, and then steeply up to Miriakamba Hut, with a possible diversion onto the crater floor. The second is a path that climbs gradually through the grassland, along the lower section of the northern spur of the crater, direct to the hut. The first option is more interesting, and described here. The second option is shorter, and makes a suitable descent route.

Although Miriakamba Hut could be reached by a powerful 4WD, this track is rarely used by vehicles, so you are unlikely to be disturbed.

From Momella Gate, cross the Ngare Nanyuki River and follow the track past the campsites into the forest. The track winds uphill, and there are a couple of narrow paths which cut across the bends (the guide will show you). One hour from the gate is Fig Tree Arch. This is a parasitic wild fig which originally formed around two other trees, eventually strangling them. Now only the fig tree remains, with its distinctive arch, big enough to drive a car (or a medium-sized elephant) through.

The track continues to climb, reaching Itikoni Clearing on the left side of the track, after another 15 minutes. From a small hill on the right, you can often see buffalo grazing in the clearing. Half an hour further on, the track crosses a large stream just above the Maio Falls, which are signposted down to the left. Continue for another hour, crossing the Jekukumia River (the last reliable water source until Miriakamba Hut), to reach Kitoto Camp, a wide open space overlooking the forest below, with excellent views over the Momella Lakes and plains beyond to Kilimanjaro in the distance. There is a ruined hut nearby.

(From here, a path leads steeply up to Meru Crater floor, but this path is overgrown and difficult to follow. An easier alternative, described in the next section, is available.) Continue following the track, passing a few faint grassy paths branching off, to reach a junction after half an hour. There's an old wooden signpost leaning on a rock. (The left track leads to the crater floor.) Take the right track, over flat ground, to cross a rocky stream bed (usually dry) and descend slightly through trees, ignoring the path that comes in from the left, to reach Miriakamba Hut (2514 metres), one hour from Kitoto Camp.

Miriakamba consists of two bunkhouses, large and well built, each with room for about 40 people. They contain bunk beds (most with mattresses) and a separate room to be used as a kitchen, although no cooking equipment is provided. The caretaker will provide a lamp if he has fuel. There are toilets, and a good supply of water.

Sidetrack: Meru Crater Floor
(2-3 hours)
If you leave Momella Gate in the morning, there is time to take a sidetrack to the crater floor on your way to Miriakamba Hut. You can divert this way from the junction marked by the old wooden sign, 30 minutes back from the hut, or go straight to the hut, dump your gear, and then return to the junction. (Alternatively, you can do this sidetrack before beginning Stage 2.)

At the junction, take the track by the old wooden sign heading south-west to reach a roadhead marked by a signpost reading 'Meru Crater, Njeku Camp'. A path continues, crossing two open grassy areas, to reach the remains of Njeku Camp (an old forest station) and Njeku Viewpoint. Other parts of the crater floor are steep, rocky and covered with dense vegetation, and so virtually impossible to walk through. The viewpoint is a platform on a high cliff overlooking a

waterfall, with excellent views of the ash cone and the whole extent of the crater.

Stage 2: Miriakamba Hut to Saddle Hut
(4 km, 2-3 hours, 1050 metres ascent)
From the bunkhouses, retrace the end of Stage 1 for about 50 metres to reach a fork. Take the right track and follow it uphill slightly until it peters out into a path which climbs steeply up through pleasant glades between the trees, to reach Topela Mbogo (Buffalo Swamp) after 45 minutes and Mgongo Wa Tembo (Elephant Ridge) after another half an hour. From the top of Elephant Ridge there are great views down into the crater and up to the main cliffs below the summit.

Continue up the path, through some open grassy clearings and over several stream beds (usually dry) to Saddle Hut (3570 metres) on a wide col between the slopes of Meru and the smaller peak of Little Meru.

Saddle Hut consists of an old metal hut, used by the caretaker, and a newer bunkhouse similar to the ones at Miriakamba. There is a toilet (with no door, but a fine view!), and water available from a small stream 10 minutes away.

Sidetracks: Little Meru & Rhino Point
(2 hours return for both)
From Saddle Hut you can walk up to the summit of Little Meru (3820 metres) in about an hour on a clear path. From the top you'll get impressive views of Meru Summit, the crater horseshoe, the top of the ash cone, and the sheer cliffs of the crater's inner wall. In the other direction, across the top of the clouds, you can see the great dome of Kilimanjaro. As the sun sets behind Meru, casting huge jagged shadows across the clouds, the snows on Kili turn orange, then pink, as the light fades. Allow 45 minutes to get back to Saddle Hut.

Alternatively, you can go to Rhino Point (also about one hour up from Saddle Hut), which is on the main route towards Meru summit. From here the views of Kili are similarly stunning and you can also see down into Meru Crater, to the base of the ash cone, and across the crater floor. You'll pass this way again on your way up and back from the summit, but the views are so impressive it's worth going at least twice.

Stage 3: Saddle Hut to Meru Summit and Return

(5 km, 4-5 hours, 1000 metres ascent
plus 5 km, 2-3 hours, 1000 metres descent)
Many trekkers combine Stages 3 and 4, which is possible, but turns the trek into a bit of a rush. Whatever you decide to do, it's usual to leave Saddle Hut very early in the morning (about 2 to 3 am) to reach the summit in time to see the sun rising from behind Kilimanjaro, and to stand a chance of avoiding the late morning mist.

The walk up to the summit, along a very narrow ridge between the sloping outer wall of the crater and the sheer cliffs of the inner wall, is one of the most dramatic and exhilarating sections of trekking anywhere in East Africa. However, some trekkers find this section too exposed for comfort, especially when done in the dark, or they find that the altitude makes the going beyond Saddle Hut a bit on the tough side. If the sunrise is your main point of interest, there's no need to go to the top. It's just as impressive from Rhino Point (about an hour from Saddle Hut), or even more so because you also see the main cliffs of the inner wall of the crater slowly being illuminated by the rising sun.

If you decide to go for the summit, take plenty of water. Even though it can be below freezing just before dawn, as soon as the sun comes up the going becomes hot and hard. During the rainy season, ice and snow can occur on this section of the route, so take great care.

The ideal combination is sunrise at Rhino Point, then up to the summit for the views (depending on the mist). If you spend two nights at Saddle Hut you can still see the sunrise at Rhino Point, then trek up to the summit and back in daylight. If you're combining Stages 3 and 4, it's just about possible to see the sunrise from Rhino Point, do the summit, and get back to Momella Gate before dark, although this doesn't leave much of a margin for delays.

To reach Rhino Point, take the path from behind Saddle Hut, across a flat area, tending left then steeply up through bushes. After an hour the vegetation gives way to bare rock and ash. Rhino Point is marked by a cairn and a pile of bones (presumably rhino, but what was it doing up here?!).

From Rhino Point the path drops slightly then rises again to climb steeply round the edge of the rim over ash scree and bare rock patches. Continue for three to four hours to reach the summit (4566 metres). The views are, of course, spectacular. To the west, if it's clear, you can see towards the Rift Valley, and the volcanoes of Kitumbeini and Lengai, while down below you can see the town of Arusha, and the plains of the Maasai Steppe beyond.

To descend from the summit, simply retrace the route round the rim, back to Saddle Hut (two to three hours).

Stage 4: Saddle Hut to Momella Gate

(9 km, 3-5½ hours, 2000 metres descent)
From Saddle Hut, retrace the route of Stage 2 to reach Miriakamba Hut after 1½ to 2½ hours.

From Miriakamba Hut, you can either return through the forest (2½ to three hours), or take a more direct route down the ridge which leads almost directly to Momella Gate (1½ to 2½ hours). This direct route goes through forest for some of the way, then through open grassland, where giraffe and zebra are often seen.

OTHER ROUTES

There used to be two other routes up to the summit of Meru, on the north and west sides of the mountain, but these fell into disuse after the national park was extended to include the mountain. The current route from Momella Gate is easier than these two old routes, as it makes a more gradual ascent. The paths that do exist on the north and west sides of the mountain have been cut through the forest by local woodcutters and poachers, and are not permanent.

Even if you could find any of the old routes or poachers' paths, special permission to use them has to be granted by the national park chief warden (as it involves entering the park at a point other than Momella Gate), and this process can take several months. The only company organising treks up Mt Meru on these other routes (with permission from the National Park) is Tropical Trails (address in the Tanzania Trekking Companies section).

If you want to wander around on the lower slopes of Mt Meru for a few days, outside the park (which avoids the need to pay fees), there's an old Maasai man named Sanches who does some guiding on the western foothills. Sanches normally stays in his village, but the various 'agents' who lurk around the budget hotels in Arusha can put you in touch with him. You can join Sanches and walk in the area for one to three days. Prices for his services start at about US$40 per person per day but, according to the agents, are 'very negotiable'. You provide your own tent, gear, food and so on.

An Aussie guy I met in Arusha had spent a few days with Sanches and said it was relaxed and interesting, although not very energetic. They spent most of their time walking slowly between the villages and sitting in the sun. Most of Sanches' walks stay on the lower slopes.

It is possible to go up into the forest, although this is technically illegal. It's also possible to get to the summit, which is definitely illegal, by leaving the edge of the forest at 3 am to get to the top by sunrise. This probably follows the disused route from the site of an old forestry hut at about 3600 metres, going straight up the steep scree on the western side of the mountain, to come out on the crater rim only a short distance down from the summit. An illegal attempt on the summit cannot be recommended – this route is very strenuous and if you get into trouble you'll be on your own. Nobody will come and rescue you. In fact, it's likely that your 'guides' will abandon you for fear of being reported to the police. There have also been reports of a lot of Maasai ganja being grown in secret parts of the forest. Going for the top of Meru 'the back way' would be even more worrying if your guide was stoned out of his brain!

The Crater Highlands

The Crater Highlands is a range of extinct volcanoes that rise steeply from the side of the Great Rift Valley in northern Tanzania. Peter Matthiessen, who wrote about this area in his classic book *The Tree Where Man Was Born* (HarperCollins, UK), called it 'the strangest and most beautiful of all regions that I have come across in Africa'.

West of the range are the great savanna plains of the Serengeti National Park, while to the south and east the land drops to the Rift Valley floor and Lake Manyara, another national park. At the centre of the range is Ngorongoro Crater, probably one of the best-known wildlife areas in Africa, attracting many thousands of visitors every year.

For most people, a visit to the Crater Highlands means a day driving and wild-life-viewing in the spectacular Ngorongoro Crater itself. Its fame is undeniably justified, for nowhere else in Africa can you see so many different animals in such a small area. But the Crater Highlands consist of much more than just Ngorongoro.

To the north and south of Ngorongoro are several impressive peaks, with steep escarpments, crater lakes, dense forests and grassy ridges, streams and waterfalls. There's even an active volcano. It's also home to many Maasai people who have grazed cattle on the grassy hillsides here for hundreds of years. This part of the highlands is an excellent walking area, but is very seldom visited, and is completely upstaged by the Ngorongoro Crater just a few km to the south.

GEOGRAPHY
The Crater Highlands range is roughly oval in shape, measuring about 80 km by 40 km,

and is pinched at one end. The range rises steeply from the surrounding plains at about 1500 metres to heights of between 2500 and 3500 metres.

Like many of East Africa's mountains, the Highlands are volcanic in origin, although the different peaks were created over many millions of years by a series of eruptions connected with the formation of the Great Rift Valley. The older volcanoes have been eroded and most have collapsed to form the craters (more correctly known as calderas) from where the range takes its name.

At the southern end of the Crater Highlands are the oldest volcanoes, Oldeani and Lemagrut, with both summits at around 3100 metres. North-east of these lies the Ngorongoro Crater, measuring some 20 km across, making it one of the largest calderas in the world. The rim of the crater is at about 2200 metres. Inside the crater is an example of just about every type of vegetation and wildlife habitat, including forest, grassland, swamp, salt pans and a freshwater lake, with a wide range of animals to match.

To the north of Ngorongoro Crater is the main part of the highlands, where the trekking described in this section takes place. Only a few km away, the mountain of Olmoti rises to 3100 metres on its western side, with a flat-topped peak which can easily be seen from Ngorongoro. This mountain also has a small crater. To the east of Olmoti is Loolmalasin, the highest peak on the range, at 3648 metres, with its eastern side dropping steeply down to the plains near Engaruka. North of these two peaks is Empakaai (also spelt Embagai), with a steep-sided circular crater, half-filled by a lake. In between the peaks of Olmoti, Loolmalasin and Empakaai the ground dips to form the large Embulbul Depression.

At the northern end of the range is Kerimasi, one of the more recent volcanoes, rising to 2300 metres. Beyond this lies the Crater Highlands' northernmost mountain, Oldoinyo Lengai (2878 metres), a classic volcanic cone with steep sides rising to a small flat-topped peak. Lengai was the last volcano of the Crater Highlands to be formed, and is still active. The last big eruption was in the mid-1960s, and at the top of the mountain today you can see hot steam vents and growing ash-cones.

GUIDEBOOKS & MAPS

The *Ngorongoro Conservation Area* booklet, produced by David Bygott and the Wildlife Conservation Society of Tanzania, has a lot of good information about the wildlife and vegetation in the different zones within the NCA, plus sections on ecology, geography, history, and many other subjects. This book is usually available in Arusha.

For details on walking and driving routes beyond those given in this book, and further ideas about other mountains in the Crater Highlands area, the *Mountains of Kenya* guidebook (see the Kenya chapter for more detail) has a section on Northern Tanzania which provides good information. This book is available in Nairobi.

The trekking area described in this section is covered in detail by the DOS/government survey maps (1:50,000), sheets 53/1 (Ngorongoro), 53/2 (Kitete), 39/4 (Oldoinyo Lengai) and 39/2 (Mosonik). Gelai Mountain is on sheet 40/1 (Gelai). These are available from the map office in Dar, but not in Arusha.

The whole Crater Highlands area is also covered by the Survey of Kenya 1:250,000 map sheets SA-36-16 (Oldeani) and SA-36-12 (Loliondo), which might also be available in the map office in Dar.

TREKKING INFORMATION

Most of the Crater Highlands range is within the boundaries of the Ngorongoro Conservation Area (NCA), which is not a national park like Serengeti or Kilimanjaro, as it contains settlements and a permanent human population living alongside the wildlife. Unfortunately, the coexistence is not always completely peaceful: the Maasai resent being excluded from some of their traditional grazing grounds (for example, they are not normally allowed into the Ngorongoro Crater) and feel that they are regarded as less important than the conservation of wildlife or the needs of tourists. The Maasai also complain about being excluded from the revenue that is earned by the NCA – the treks across the Crater Highlands are one way in which they can benefit from tourism in the area.

Because of the rugged nature of the terrain, and the presence of some fairly rugged animals, unaccompanied walking is not allowed, but it would be virtually impossible anyway for independent walkers to trek here without guides and logistical support. However, some of the local Maasai people have recently started organising treks right across the highlands, from Ngorongoro Crater in the south to Oldoinyo Lengai in the north, allowing several days of excellent walking through this fascinating landscape, which provides an interesting contrast to the mountain wilderness areas of Mt Meru and Kilimanjaro. Maasai *morans* (warriors) act as guides, and donkeys are used to carry food and gear. Water is also carried for some stages, as parts of the highlands are very dry.

Organised treks across the Crater Highlands with the Maasai can be arranged in Arusha. They usually include a visit by vehicle to the Ngorongoro Crater, or the trek can be included in a longer safari, taking in Serengeti and Lake Manyara as well. If you were thinking of doing a safari here anyway, this is an ideal way to combine some good-quality trekking and wildlife-viewing, and provides a chance to meet the local people in their own environment.

Route Standard & Days Required

Trekking in the Crater Highlands is a fairly new activity, and there are no established routes yet, although the local Maasai cooperative use some campsites and paths. Most treks start just north of Ngorongoro Crater, and head north, via the Olmoti and Empakaai Craters, down to Oldoinyo Lengai, the active volcano at the end of the range.

There are various ways of doing this trek, and the routes and stages outlined here are suggestions only, to give you an idea of what's available.

Trekking in the Crater Highlands is not as strenuous as on the mountains of Kiliman-

jaro and Meru. You generally follow tracks and paths, although some sections require cutting across open bush and grassland. Some paths can be very dusty, but conditions underfoot are generally good.

Daytime temperatures on the high ground can be hot (up to 28°C), although nights can be chilly, with mist and rain not uncommon, especially in June, July and August. On the lower areas, around Lengai, it gets very hot, with maximum daytime temperatures often above 35°C during the warm season (see the Tanzania Climate section).

Most of the walking is at around 3000 metres, so you might feel some slight effects of altitude, such as shortness of breath for the first day or two, but this is unlikely to be a problem.

There are many options available, but the minimum number of days required for the trek from Ngorongoro to Lengai is four, although five or six is more usual and more comfortable, with the option of an extra day or two, to go up Lengai (an all-day walk) or to reach Lake Natron. You should also allow another day at either end of the trek for travelling to and from Arusha. This usually includes time for wildlife viewing in the Ngorongoro Crater.

Fees

All visitors inside the NCA have to pay fees. For non-residents these are:

Entrance fee	US$15 per day (ie, per 24-hour period)
Camping fee	US$10 per night for public sites US$40 per night for special sites

(Camping fees are not payable if you're staying in a lodge.)

Foreign-registered vehicle	US$30 to US$100
Local vehicle	TSh 300
Tanzanian citizen	TSh 100
Tanzanian resident	TSh 2000

You also have to pay an extra fee to enter the Ngorongoro Crater. This is US$10 and includes the services of a park ranger, who acts as guide.

You may pay these fees yourself at the gate. Non-residents have to pay in hard currency; it's easiest to deal in US dollars (cash or travellers' cheques). If you are on an organised trek, the fees are likely to be included in the total price that you pay the trekking company, so you shouldn't need to worry about this.

You'll also have to hire a NCA ranger for the treks, for US$20 per day, for every day he is away from the headquarters (ie including travelling days).

Note that part of the trek covered in this section is outside the NCA, so you only pay for days you are inside the area. The northern boundary of the NCA passes about midway between Empakaai and Lengai. The area may be extended in the future to include Lengai and the southern shore of Lake Natron. This will probably have no effect on the trekking itself, but it will mean having to pay a few days' extra fees.

The NCA fees comprise a considerable chunk of the cost of the trek. The prices are on a par with a good trek on Kili, and the cost can be prohibitive for some people. To help put the payment of fees into perspective, see National Parks, in the Facts for the Trekker chapter.

Supplies

There are small shops at Ngorongoro Village, plus a post office and petrol station, but only basics are available here. There's a lot more choice in Arusha. On most organised treks food will usually be arranged, and included in the price.

PLACES TO STAY

Arusha is Tanzania's safari capital, with plenty of accommodation to choose from (for details, see the Mt Meru Places to Stay section).

Inside the NCA, where you stay depends on the type of safari or trek you arrange. On the southern side of Ngorongoro Crater are (in ascending price order): *The Drivers' Hostel*, *Rhino Lodge*, *Wildlife Lodge* and *Crater Lodge*. There's also *Simba Campsite* on the crater rim. Camping is no longer permitted on the crater floor. On the north side of the crater is the very up-market *Sopa Lodge*.

In the trekking area, there is nothing in the way of solid accommodation, so you must camp. There are some NCA 'special' campsites with no facilities, or you can camp near the Maasai villages. To the north of the range, around Lengai and Lake Natron, which is outside the NCA, there are a few permanent tented camps, where you can stay in large walk-in tents, or camp nearby.

GETTING THERE & AWAY

The Crater Highlands are in the Ngorongoro Conservation Area (NCA), about 200 km west of Arusha by road. The main entrance gate into the NCA is at Lodoare, just south of the Ngorongoro Crater. There's no public transport going all the way, but a public bus may be introduced in 1993. Visitors are not allowed to enter the NCA without a vehicle.

If you have a vehicle, you can drive to the NCA headquarters at Ngorongoro Village, and make arrangements there, as the NCA staff are in touch with the Maasai trekking cooperative. This means you'll need to arrange all your own gear and food for the duration of the trek. You'll also have to arrange for someone to drive the car to the end of the trek to collect you, and to bring the ranger back to Ngorongoro later.

If you don't have a vehicle, it's generally not worth hiring one to do this trek, as it will be parked for several days while you're trekking, which is a complete waste of money.

The usual way of doing things is to arrange a complete deal in Arusha with the Maasai cooperative's agent. This is straightforward, cuts all the hassles about vehicles, guides, accommodation, food and so on, and is probably the cheapest way of doing things. The agent is Jeff's Tours, a trekking and safari company (PO Box 1469, Arusha (☎ (057) 8172)). The office is behind the Aresco Building, on the corner of School and Uhuru Rds, just down from the clock tower.

There's a standard seven-day trip which involves five days of trekking, and a visit to Ngorongoro Crater, for US$580 if you're in

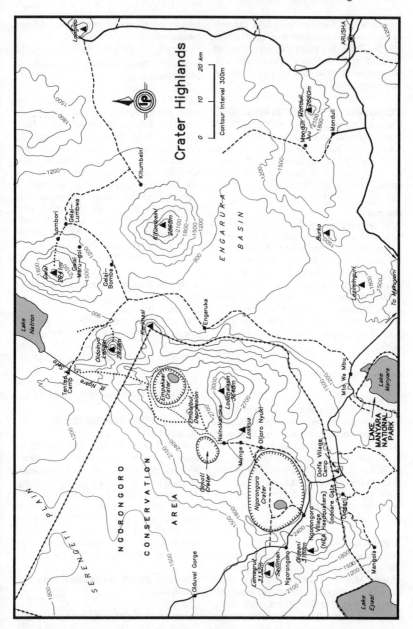

a group of four. Extra trekking days, to reach Lake Natron, or the summit of Lengai, cost US$50. Things are pretty flexible – you can also choose the number of trekking days and the number of safari days in other areas that you're interested in.

NGORONGORO TO LENGAI ROUTES
There are no set routes in the Crater Highlands, but the ones outlined here, from Ngorongoro Crater north across the range to Oldoinyo Lengai, pass through some beautiful and very varied landscape, taking in several of the area's 'highlights'.

Access
After driving from Arusha, it is usual to camp or stay in one of the lodges at Ngorongoro Village on your first night and go down into the crater for a few hours' wildlife viewing. Late afternoon or early morning is best, as this is when the animals are more likely to be active. On the second day, you can drive across Ngorongoro Crater and leave by the northern track. In the area north of the crater you'll meet your Maasai guides and donkeys.

Stage 1: Ngorongoro Crater to Nainokanoka
(12 km, 4-5 hours)
From the northern side of the crater, you walk through the forest on a good track to reach the ranger post near the village of Nainokanoka, your first night's camp on the trek proper. (Some treks start at Nainokanoka, in which case you can drive to this point.) Your vehicle returns to Ngorongoro Village, and then drives round to Ol Doinyo Lengai to collect you in a few days' time.

Sidetrack: Olmoti
From Nainokanoka, you can sidetrack up through open forest to reach the summit of Olmoti Mountain, where there's a small crater and the spectacular Munge Waterfall. Water collected in the Olmoti crater flows down this waterfall and eventually into the lake in Ngorongoro Crater. This sidetrack takes about two to three hours.

Stage 2A: Olmoti to Empakaai Crater (West Rim)
(20 km, 6-8 hours)
From the base of Olmoti, continue on the track, aiming north around the edge of the Embulbul Depression, towards Empakaai Crater. As you gradually gain height, the forest thins out and you pass through open grassland on the dry side of the mountain, to reach the highest point on the western rim. The view from here down into the crater is stunning. The steep inner walls are densely forested and drop to the flat crater floor, partly covered in grass, and partly submerged under a lake. The Maasai are not allowed to graze cattle here, and there's a good chance of seeing wildlife.

Stage 2B: Olmoti to Empakaai Crater (East Rim)
(25 km, 7-10 hours)
Alternatively, if your guides know the way, you can take this route from Olmoti northeast, to reach the eastern side of the Empakaai Crater. This is a harder route and some Masai guides will not want to take it. You can camp on the rim here, or descend into the crater itself and camp by the lake.

Sidetrack: Empakaai Rim Circuit
(32 km, 1 day)
You could base yourself at Empakaai for an extra day and do a complete circuit of the spectacular rim. This is about 32 km, mainly on good paths and tracks, and takes all day. The northern side of the mountain is particularly impressive, with great views down into the crater to the south and north to the conical peak of Lengai some 13 km away, with Lake Natron and the flat plains of the Rift Valley sometimes visible beyond.

Stage 2C: Olmoti to Empakaai Crater (Long Route)
(2 days)
From Olmoti, the Maasai have another route

Kilimanjaro from Little Meru summit (DE)

Top: Trekking through the Loroghi Hills with Samburu warrior as guide (DE)
Left: Suguta Valley: Looking down to Lake Logipi and Cathedral Rock (DE)
Right: Mbere Route: View of the crater from Lookout Block, Mt Elgon (DE)

Euphorbia bussei

which takes you off the Empakaai track, further west than routes 2A and 2B. This one goes gradually uphill out of the Embulbul Depression, following cattle trails through the forest and grassland, to a waterhole, called Kamnana, south-west of Empakaai. (This takes five to six hours of walking.) You camp here in the bush.

Next day, you go up to the crater rim of Empakaai on the western side, then circle round the crater rim to the north before dropping down the north-western side to reach a scattered Maasai settlement about four km from the crater, called Naiyobi (five to seven hours of walking). The local people are very friendly, and seem genuinely pleased to see visitors. This is a good opportunity to meet and talk with the locals, rather than just snap away with your camera.

Stage 3: Empakaai to Ngare Sero
(30 km, 1-2 days)
From Empakaai Crater (or Naiyobi), follow winding dusty paths downhill all day, off the edge of the Highlands and out of the NCA. It gets hotter as you descend, and your guides may want to break this stage and camp another night, in an area called Mouwongoni (carry water from Naiyobi). From here it's another three to four hours across bares rock and lava. Conditions are usually very hot, so

when you meet the Ngare Sero River, which flows north from the Crater Highlands into Lake Natron, the running water will be very refreshing. Another two km further on is a permanent tented camp situated on the bank of the river. You can camp near the river and go to the tented camp for meals and cold beer! (Another tented camp might be established in the Ngare Sero area during 1993.)

Your vehicle will probably meet you here, and the Maasai guides and donkeys will go back to Ngorongoro or Nainokanoka. From the camp, a rough dirt road leads south, along the eastern edge of the Crater Highlands, back towards Mto Wa Mbu and the main dirt road to Arusha. You can end the trek at Ngare Sero and return to Arusha the next day, or spend two nights camped in this area and go to the summit of Oldoinyo Lengai on the day in between.

Stage 4: Ngare Sero to Oldoinyo Lengai summit & return
(9-11 hours)
From the Ngare Sero camp, Lengai is best approached on its northern side. This is a long walk, and it's common to use the vehicle to drive up a large gully on the north side to cut some of the walking time. A very early start is important in order to gain as much altitude as possible in the cool of the morning. It is usual to drive to the mountain in the afternoon, then camp in the gully overnight, so you'll be on the spot next morning and able to start walking immediately. You can hire a Maasai guide from Ngae Sero camp. Prices seem negotiable (around $20 per day).

Although this walk is normally done in a day, it is possible to camp on the summit, but this means taking up all your gear and food, plus water, as there's none anywhere on the mountain.

The walk is through volcanic dust and ash for much of the way (from the 1966 eruption); it's very steep. You work you way along narrow exposed ridges between steep furrows and gullies for much of the way, which can be difficult. It is also very hot: a

Maasai warrior

sun hat is strongly recommended and a large water intake is essential.

At the summit of the mountain there are two craters, one of which is still active. It's possible to walk inside this live crater, and see steam outlets and the growing cones of volcanic ash. Obviously, this is a potentially dangerous area, and you should take great care where you step.

From the summit, the view back to the rest of the Crater Highlands is usually obscured by cloud, but to the north you can look over Lake Natron to the dome of Shompole at its northern end, just over the Kenyan border.

OTHER ROUTES

Your trekking in the Crater Highlands area can be extended for several more days, and will be restricted only by your own time and money.

Ngorongoro to Oldeani Summit

From the village of Ngorongoro, on the south side of Ngorongoro Crater, you can walk up to the summit of Oldeani, the large dome-shaped peak that overlooks the village from the south. This requires about 1000 metres of ascent, mainly across open grassland, although there are a few patches of bamboo. ('Oldeani' is the Maasai word for 'bamboo'. It grows nowhere else on the Crater Highlands.)

From the summit you can look north-east across Ngorongoro and the whole Crater Highlands range, with excellent views all the way to Lengai, if the weather is clear. To the north-west, the plains of the Serengeti stretch to the horizon, broken only by a few rocky kopjes and 'inselbergs'. Also to the north-west are Oldeani's neighbouring peaks of Lemagrut and Sadiman. Together these three ancient mountains form the oldest part of the highlands.

Oldeani is shaped like a semicircle at the top, where a giant chunk has been blasted away by a volcanic eruption. The existing rim dips in the middle, forming north and south summits. To the south-west, the land drops steeply to the hot low area around Lake Eyasi. Along the northern shore of the lake runs the Eyasi Escarpment, also called Ol Doinyo Ailipi, an ancient fault-line that is part of the Rift Valley system. Eyasi is a *soda* (saline) lake and the surrounding land is hot and dry, except for a few spots where clear springs of water, running underground from Oldeani, emerge by the lake shore.

This area is inhabited by the Hadza (or Watindiga), a very ancient people who are believed to have lived here for over 10,000 years. Their language is vaguely similar to that of the bush dwellers in southern Africa. Also in this area are the Mbulu, another old people (of Cushitic origin), although they are comparative newcomers compared with the Hadza, having arrived in the area only about 2000 years ago. This area is virtually unique as, with the Nilotic Maasai and various Bantu groups, it contains peoples from the four main language groups of East Africa.

Oldeani Mountain to Lake Eyasi

It's possible to do a two- or three-day trek from Oldeani Mountain, through the bush on local paths, down to Lake Eyasi. This trek is currently being developed by the owner of Lake View Lodge, a small house and campsite in a beautiful position overlooking the eastern end of the lake. The trek could also be done from the lake up to Oldeani Mountain. Again, Jeff's Tours are the agents in Arusha, so they will have the details.

Gelai

At the other end of the Crater Highlands, standing apart from the main range, to the north-east of Lengai, is the mountain of Gelai. This is a huge dome-shaped mountain, about the same height as Lengai, but appearing much larger, as the surrounding plains are lower. Using your vehicle, you could extend your Crater Highlands trek by another day or two and bag this summit as well.

Note that tracks are very faint here and you may find yourself driving across bare open country. This is a harsh and remote area, and driving here can be a serious enterprise, although this is all part of the attraction. If you add Gelai to your trek, you should ensure your vehicle is well-equipped with water, fuel and spares. Very few drivers know this area, and only the specialised trekking and safari companies come here. This is no place for self-drive unless you are very experienced.

Access To reach Gelai from Lengai, follow the rough dirt road back towards Mto Wa Mbu, then branch off left on another track (if you can find it) heading east, then north-east round the base of Gelai, passing through the settlement of Gelai Bomba on the southern side, to finally reach another settlement called Gelai Lumbwa, on the eastern side of the mountain. A local guide can usually be arranged here (although you'll probably need some basic Swahili). Leave your vehicle here.

Route From Gelai Lumbwa, a path leads west, up a small ridge towards a small collection of huts. This area is called Lombori. Continue in the same direction, through a grassy area which becomes more densely vegetated. There are many paths and cattle trails, but keep heading in the same direction. The final section, near the summit, is densely vegetated, so a *panga* (local machete) will come in useful. Allow eight to 11 hours to get to the summit and back to Gelai Lumbwa.

From Gelai, the usual way back to Arusha is on the track past Kitumbeini, to meet the main tarred Namanga-Arusha road opposite the rocky peak of Longido.

Other Trekking Areas

The mountains and routes covered in detail in the Tanzania chapter have been chosen because they provide interesting and exciting treks, and because most of them can be reached fairly easily by visitors. The following mountains will also be of interest to competent and adventurous trekkers looking for more areas to explore.

MONDULI MOUNTAINS

The Monduli Mountains lie to the north-west of Arusha. This small range appears low and unimpressive when viewed from the southern side, but on the northern side it has high peaks, steep escarpments and some fine open ridges which are ideal for walking. This is a good area to consider if you want do something other than Kili or Meru, but can't afford the time and money required for a trek in the Crater Highlands.

The northern side of the range has some very contrasting landscapes within a fairly small area. On the lower slopes, at about 1000 metres, the landscape is dry scrub-land. On the middle slopes are Maasai settlements and a few small areas of cultivation, and the higher sections consist of open grassland or are covered in forest. The highest point of the range is the summit of Monduli Mountain itself (2660 metres). There are several smaller peaks forming a long ridge running west-east through the middle of the range. From the high ground, you can get great views down into the Rift Valley, and see the giant dome of Kitumbeini rising above the plains to the north, and sometimes the distant cone of Lengai, faint on the horizon.

Trekking Routes

The base for trekking in this area is a campsite at Monduli Juu, a small village on the north-west side of the range. This can be reached by road if you have a car, or by public transport as far as Monduli town, a larger settlement on the south side of the range. From Monduli town to Monduli Juu you can walk up the dirt road which climbs gently through forest and curves round the western end of the range, or follow steep paths straight over the top of the main ridge. Guides are recommended for this second option and for any other walks in the area, unless you are a fairly used to African bush conditions. They are often essential to help you locate water, which can be hard to find on the lower slopes of the range. Guides can be arranged at the campsite.

There are no set routes here, and from Monduli Juu you can walk for as many days as you like in the surrounding area.

Plains & Escarpment One good trek follows steep gullies from the high land down onto the plains to the north of the range, to camp near springs at the bottom of the escarpment. Then make a broad eastward arc across the plains to cross the dirt road leading to Kitumbeini Village and eventually meet a cattle trail heading back up towards the eastern end of the range. A second camp is made here. The route then goes up to the main ridge, which you follow back westwards to drop down into Monduli Juu near the large open grassy area in front of the primary school.

Monduli Ridge Another good trekking route is a complete traverse of the main ridge, starting at Monduli Juu and heading eastward to finally meet the main Namanga-Arusha road near Oldoinyo Sambu. This trek takes three days, and can also be done in the opposite direction.

You have to get permission to use the Monduli Juu campsite from Tropical Trails, a trekking and safari company based in Arusha (details in in the Tanzania Trekking Companies section). They can advise on other trekking routes in the area, and arrange local Maasai guides. They also operate walking safaris in this area, including treks on Monduli, Gelai and Lengai.

MT HANANG

Some 180 km south-west of Arusha is Mt Hanang. At 3417 metres (11,212 feet) it is the fourth-highest mountain in Tanzania. It is a grand volcanic cone, rising steeply above the surrounding plains, with an excellent trek to the summit but very few visitors know of its existence.

Getting There & Away

To reach Hanang, first get to Katesh, on the mountain's southern side. The road goes via Makuyuni and Babati, and buses to Singida pass through Katesh. From here, drive or walk to Ngendabi, on the mountain's west side, and ask around for a local guide. There is no accommodation here, so be completely self-contained. Ask permission to camp outside the village.

Starting early, you can reach the summit and return in a day. An overnight trip would make the trek less arduous. Water supplies up high are unreliable, and local porters are available.

The Route

From Ngendabi, the route follows old cattle tracks and paths through dense bush, then the crest of a large ridge, leading south-easterly up the mountain. After a few hours the bush thins out and you pass through trees and grassland, as the gradient gets steeper. The trees give way to protea bushes as you gain height and the ridge narrows. Five to six hours from Ngendabi you reach the southern summit, after some loose scrambling.

The southern summit is linked to the main summit by a very narrow rocky ridge-crest, which requires some scrambling. Follow this crest with care for about one to 1½ hours, aiming north-east, to the main summit of Hanang (3417 metres). From the main summit, return to the southern summit and then retrace the route down to Ngendabi (five to six hours total for the descent).

It may also be possible to reach the southern summit directly from Katesh via the ridge up the left (western) side of the large valley. Or you could take this ridge down from the southern summit.

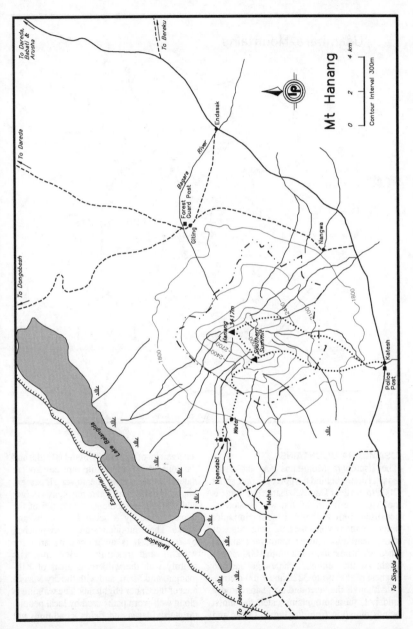

Mt Hanang

Contour Interval 300m

0   2   4 km

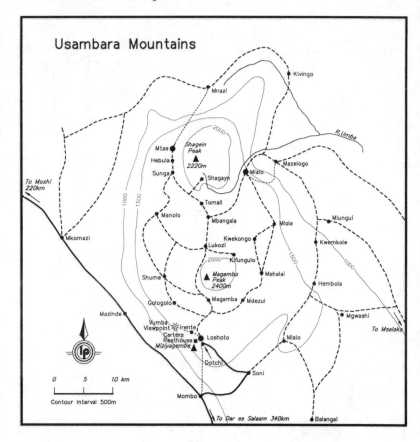

USAMBARA MOUNTAINS

The Usambara Mountains rise above the coastal plains behind the port of Tanga, about 200 km north of Dar es Salaam. The range is not volcanic in origin, but was created by localised uplift. Rather than the sloping sides found on many volcanoes, the outer edges of the Usambaras consist mainly of almost sheer escarpments, some up to 1000 metres high. At the centre of the range the two highest peaks rise to 2220 and 2400 metres.

Although the surrounding plains are dry and hot, these mountains catch the moist winds blown in from the Indian Ocean and receive a lot of rainfall. The land is fertile and the tops of the mountains are covered in natural forest, while the lower slopes are intensely cultivated. There are many villages and scattered settlements on the top of the range, linked by a network of paths and tracks. These mountains are rarely reached by tourists. It is an interesting area for walking and trekking, which contrasts sharply with the wilderness areas of Kilimanjaro and Meru, and with the dry Maasai area of the Crater Highlands. The walking is along well-worn paths used by local people, through villages and fields, conditions not dissimilar to those encountered by trekkers in the foothills of the Himalaya or the lower Atlas Mountains.

The mountains' title is a corruption of the name of the local people – the Shambali or Washambala, which means 'scattered'. The mountains were seen in the 1840s by the missionary explorers Krapf and Rebmann, who were the first Europeans to see Kilimanjaro and Mt Kenya. They were impressed by the fertile conditions and friendly people, and planned to build a mission station here.

When this area was part of German East Africa, the main town in the Usambaras, Loshoto, was an administrative centre and was even proposed as the colony's capital – a far healthier alternative to Dar es Salaam. There were plans to bring a wide road, and even a railway, up the steep escarpments on the west side of the range. But after WWI, Tanganyika became a British protectorate and these plans were never realised, although Loshoto is the centre of various church and missionary organisations in Tanzania.

Places to Stay

Loshoto is the main town in the Usambaras. On its south side, up a dirt track on the left if you're walking in, is the *Lawns Hotel*, a faded colonial-style place with singles/doubles at TSh 3500/4600 including breakfast. Nearby is the *Kilimani Resthouse*, a local place with 'cubes' built round a courtyard, and basic bathrooms out back; doubles cost TSh 600. The women who run the resthouse are friendly, and the place has a good atmosphere. The courtyard becomes a bar at night. Down the hill, nearer the town centre is the quieter *Kimunyu Hotel* with similar prices and facilities. There are vague plans for a church guesthouse on the north side of town, near the bishop's offices.

Loshoto has a market, post office, shops, and a surprising number of snack-bars selling tea and cakes.

Outside Loshoto, at Miziyagembe, a peak jutting out from the western escarpment you can stay in a small resthouse built by Carter, a near-legendary American hang-glider, who lives nearby. Carter and his friend George regularly fly off the escarpment here, and are also training a pair of augur buzzards to fly with them to indicate the best air currents and thermals. Strange but true. It costs TSh 2000 to stay in the resthouse, and the money goes to a local tree-planting scheme. You can stay and help with the planting if you want.

Getting There & Away

Loshoto can be reached by bus from Mombo, on the main road between Moshi and Dar es Salaam. The road up is steep and twisting, with some sheer drops off the edge of the road down into the valley below, and the ancient old bus goes very slowly. The road was tarred in 1987. It must have been a nightmare before this.

You can also walk from Mombo to Loshoto up the old dirt road. This is now badly eroded and no longer used by vehicles, but it makes a good path, and is used regularly by local people. To reach the start of the path, get to the north side of Mombo, just beyond the junction by the petrol station where the tar road to Loshoto branches off. A dirt track runs alongside the river. Follow this, over a bridge, past a wood yard and the secondary school. After this the path crosses some flat fields then starts climbing up the escarpment. It's clear and wide most of the way, and some narrow paths cut off some of the larger loops. There are many people around to ask the way if you're not sure. Allow five to six hours for the ascent. You meet the main tarred road just south of Loshoto at a village called Dotchi. (There are quite a few places with this name in the area; it's a corruption of the word 'Deutsch', from the German colonial period.)

Trekking Routes

There are no set trekking routes in the Usambaras. Basically, you can go where you like for as many days as you like, along the network of paths and tracks covering the area. A few destinations are suggested here. To reach some places, you can combine trekking with rides on the local bus. Any kind of schedule is hard to pin down. Ask at the bus station for information. Some of the larger tracks link Loshoto with the large villages of Mtae on the north-western corner of the range, and to Mlalo, on the north-eastern side (not to be confused with Mlola, to the east, or with another small village called Mlalo, in the south), and buses go this way once each day.

A local guide is useful, although not essential. Without a guide, some words of Swahili are helpful when asking for directions. A well-known guide is Ibrahim Sabali (always called Bula). In Loshoto you can ask for him at the Kilimani or the Kimunyu Hotel or go to Dotchi, just south of Loshoto, and ask for him there. He will walk with you for as many days as you like, for a negotiable fee starting at around TSh 2000 per day. Bula is very knowledgeable about local birds and plants. He also understands the local bus 'timetables'.

Gologolo Forest Places you can reach from Loshoto include Carter's resthouse, about two to three hours' walk away. From there you can work your way northwards along the escarpment (although you have to come away from it in several places to get round deep gullies and ravines) to reach Vumba Viewpoint, near the village of Irente. From here you can continue north into the Gologolo Forest, which has many indigenous trees and other plants, some unique to these mountains.

Magambo Peak North of Loshoto lies Magambo Peak (2400 metres) the highest point in the Usambaras. It's best to take a bus to Magamba Village and follow paths from there. A guide is almost essential.

Mtae & Shagein Peak Further north is Mtae, a large village to the west of Shagein Peak. There's a small resthouse here and you can walk from the village along a narrow ridge that extends northwards from the main range. It is noticeably drier on this side of the range; the views from the end of the ridge are spectacular over the South Pare Hills and north across the plains of Tsavo in neighbouring Kenya. On a clear day, even Kilimanjaro can be seen on the horizon to the north-west. To reach the summit of Shagein (2220 metres) take the logging track on the south side, starting near the village of Tomali. There are also several smaller paths up to the summit, but again, a guide is recommended.

EASTERN USAMBARA MOUNTAINS

Separate from the main range, this smaller group of mountains enjoys similar weather conditions to the main Usambara range, and is also well-populated. Near the small town of Amani is a fascinating Forest Reserve and Botanical Garden, with several long and short walks possible in the area. The place was founded in 1902 by the 'Deutsch Ost-Afrika Geselschaft', which fell on hard times when the research centre was moved to Nairobi in the mid-1980s. The reserve and gardens have recently been revived by IUCN, the international conservation organisation. It has an extensive collection of tropical spice and fruit trees, and is used to promote the conservation of several endemic and endangered species of tree and shrub, many of which have medical properties.

Amani can be reached by public transport from Muheza, which is on the Tanga-Segara road. There's a resthouse at the reserve headquarters, and camping is sometimes permitted. For the short walks, you can follow well-marked paths, but guides are necessary (and provided) for longer all-day walks in the forest.

Kenya

Kenya is one of the most popular tourist destinations in sub-Saharan Africa. Some visitors come for the world-famous wildlife reserves of Tsavo and the Maasai Mara, while others come for the Indian Ocean coast: package tourists from Europe head to the Mombasa resorts, while travellers head for Lamu, the 'Kathmandu of East Africa'.

For trekkers, the main attraction is, of course, Mt Kenya, the highest mountain in the country and the second-highest in Africa, with an excellent selection of long and short treks. But Kenya has more than just this one high mountain: other places for high-altitude trekking are the mountain wilderness areas of the Aberdare (Nyandarua) Range, in the Aberdare National Park, and Mt Elgon, straddling the Kenya-Uganda border in the far west of the country. Away from these high mountains, trekking is also possible on the Rift Valley escarpment and through the forests of the Loroghi Hills. Further north, you can trek through the blistering desert of the Suguta Valley, as far removed from the glaciers, mist and hail of the highlands as it's possible to get.

Facts about the Country

HISTORY

The early history of Kenya up to the end of the 19th century is closely linked with that of other East African countries, and this is covered in the Facts about the Region chapter.

The Colonial Period

By 1886, after the Berlin Conference, the European powers had neatly divided Africa into spheres of influence, and the territories claimed by Germany and Britain were divided by a line drawn between the coast and Lake Victoria. To the south of this line was German East Africa, to become Tangan-

yika and then Tanzania, while to the north was the protectorate of British East Africa, to become Kenya and Uganda.

But the British government was reluctant to get more involved in the development of the Kenya Protectorate. The fertile lands of Uganda, at the head of the Nile, were seen as more valuable.

To link Uganda to the coast, the British administration built a railway through Kenya, from Mombasa to the shores of Lake Victoria. This massive project, which became known as the Lunatic Line, was completed in 1903. Thousands of labourers from the British colony of India were brought in for the construction work, and many remained in East Africa after the line was finished.

To fund the railway, Britain tried to exploit the surrounding land and actively encouraged European settlement, although, to make conditions attractive to the settlers, the requirements of the African population were generally ignored. This policy continued after WWI, when demobbed British soldiers were offered cheap land in various parts of Kenya.

By this time, Nairobi, originally built as a temporary railway depot, had become the capital. In 1920, the protectorate became the Kenya Colony, but although this changed things for the European settlers (and, to a lesser extent, the Indians), it had little effect on the African population. So during the '20s and '30s several African organisations – including the Kenya Central Association, led by Jomo Kenyatta – campaigned for land rights and improved working conditions.

Transition & Independence

After WWII, opposition finally crystallised into the Mau Mau rebellion, or The Emergency, which lasted from 1950 until 1960. During this time, guerrilla fighters from the forests around Mt Kenya and the Aberdares attacked government targets. The British retaliated by confining local people to restricted villages, which some writers have compared to concentration camps.

At the end of The Emergency, the need to include more Africans in the running of the colony was recognised. By 1960, there were more African than European members in the colony's legislative council, and two African political parties had been formed: the Kenya African Democratic Union and the Kenya African National Union (or KANU), led by Kenyatta. In 1963, Kenya gained full independence and a year later the country became a republic, with Kenyatta as president.

Kenyatta (unlike President Nyerere of neighbouring Tanzania) advocated a mixed economy of agriculture and industry with private and state investment. He encouraged personal effort and group cooperation in a doctrine called Harambee, meaning 'all pull together'.

Kenyatta died in 1978 and was succeeded by his vice-president, Daniel Arap Moi, who continued to encourage the development of Kenya as a nation, while at the same time (and usually with more priority) strengthening his position and consolidating the power of KANU.

Modern Times

In 1982, Kenya became a one-party state, and by the end of the '80s Moi's power-base was virtually unassailable, as all opposition had been outlawed or crushed. But in 1990 things began to change. In the new era of post Cold War global politics, some Western countries encouraged Moi to release political detainees and legalise opposition parties, and there were several large demonstrations in Nairobi, calling for political reform.

At the end of 1991, Moi gave way to the pressure and multi-party politics were once again introduced. The pressure group Forum for the Restoration of Democracy (FORD) became a legal party, and the main opposition to KANU. During late 1991 and most of 1992, there were sporadic outbursts of rioting in various parts of the country between over-enthusiastic supporters of the

different groups, but the expected government crackdown never came.

Kenya's first multi-party elections for 20 years were held in December 1992. The opposition parties were split by in-fighting and KANU retained power by a narrow majority.

GEOGRAPHY

Kenya measures about 900 km north to south and 750 km east to west, at its widest points, covering around 600,000 sq km, or just over half the size of Tanzania. Within this relatively small area, Kenya has a wide variety of landscapes, ranging from sparsely inhabited desert in the north, through farmland, forest and snow-capped mountains in the central region, and grassy plains and savanna in the south, to a humid coastal plain bordering the Indian Ocean in the east.

The Great Rift Valley runs the length of the country. Its lowest points are Lake Magadi in the far south, and around Lake Turkana in the north, where the floor of the Rift drops to only 250 metres above sea level. At its highest point, the valley floor rises to about 1800 metres, with the top of the Rift escarpment a further 700 metres above that, as it passes through the Central Highlands, to the west of the Aberdare Range. To the east of the Aberdares, at the centre of the highland region, is Mt Kenya. The country's other major mountain area, Mt Elgon, is in the west of the country, on the border with Uganda.

The population is predominantly rural, dense in the well-watered highland regions and in the lower areas around Lake Victoria, where farming is the main activity.

CLIMATE

Kenya's climate is determined by the band of rain that moves north and south over the East African region, giving the country two wet seasons and two dry seasons each year. For most of the country, the dry seasons are from the end of May to early October, when it's dry and cool, and from late November to early March, when it's generally warmer. Within these broad seasons, the climate is

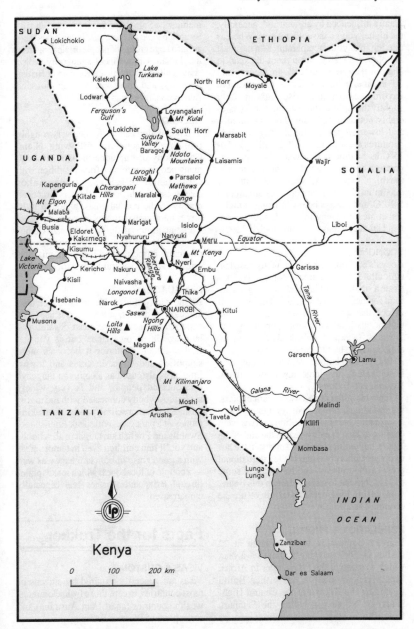

Kenya

0   100   200 km

greatly influenced by altitude and, generally, the higher you go the colder it gets. Whereas maximum daytime temperatures on the coast are often over 28°C throughout the year, in Nairobi they're about 24°C in January and 20° in June. In highland areas, the maximum daytime temperatures rise and fall only slightly throughout the year, but vary considerably between night and day. On the hills and lower slopes, maximum daytime temperatures are around 15-20°C, falling to 10-15°C in the moorland zones, where the temperature hovers around freezing at night. On the high mountains, above 4000 metres, maximum daytime temperatures are around 5-10°C, and always below freezing at night, sometimes dropping to -10°C, with violent winds that can make it seem much colder.

ECONOMY

Kenya's economy is predominantly based on agriculture. In rural areas people either cultivate a small plot of land (shamba), growing food for their own needs plus a surplus to sell in local markets, or work on larger farms and plantations producing crops for sale in the towns or for export. Industrial development, although high by the standards of the region, is limited to Nairobi, Mombasa and, to a lesser extent, the large towns of Nakuru, Kisumu and Eldoret.

Tea and coffee are Kenya's main exports, but the largest provider of foreign currency is tourism. Over half a million tourists were coming to Kenya every year at the end of the 1980s, but political and civil unrest in the last two years, plus coverage in the international press of the murders and robberies of some tourists, has led to a sharp drop in this figure, with an obvious detrimental effect on the economy as a whole.

POPULATION & PEOPLE

Kenya's population was estimated at 22 million in 1991, growing at about 4% a year, which was one of the fastest rates in Africa. Most African people are either Bantu (including the Kikuyu of the Central Highlands) or Nilotic (including the Samburu from the north). Other distinct groups include the Somalis in the north-east, and the Swahili people on the coast. In the cities there are also large groups of people originating from the Indian sub-continent (generally called Asians although many are Kenyan or British citizens), and there are several thousand Europeans, mainly in Nairobi.

RELIGION

The population can be divided very roughly into thirds, each third following Islam, Christianity or traditional beliefs, although many people combine African tradition with established religions, which makes categorisation difficult. Islam is practised mainly in the coastal areas, although most large up-country towns have a mosque. Christian groups include mainstream Catholics, Protestants and Nonconformists, originally introduced by European missionaries, as well as several local African faiths.

LANGUAGE

All the main groups in Kenya have their own language or dialect, and Swahili is used as a common tongue. On the coast, Swahili is a language in its own right, but as you get further into the interior it becomes more simplified and basic. In cities and towns, English is also used as a common language by educated people, and is very widely spoken. Anybody connected with the tourist business, whether selling you a trek or taking money at a park gate, will speak English too. Swahili and English are taught in all schools, and you'll find children even in remote areas with a good grasp of both languages, as well as a couple of local ones, which make monolingual Brits and Aussies feel especially embarrassed.

Facts for the Trekker

VISAS & CUSTOMS

Visas are generally required by citizens of most countries, except those from Commonwealth countries (apart from Australia) and some parts of Western Europe.

There are no restrictions on the amounts of hard currency you can carry, but you are not allowed to import or export more than KSh 200. Currency declaration forms are not used, although there's always a possibility of them being reintroduced.

Entry regulations are always liable to change, so it's worth checking the latest situation at your nearest Kenyan embassy, high commission or tourist office.

MONEY

The unit of currency in Kenya is the Kenyan shilling (KSh), divided into 100 cents. Inflation in Kenya is high so the official exchange rates given here may be out of date by the time you read this, but it should give you an idea. When converting prices quoted in KSh, use the rates here; the actual cost in hard currency is unlikely to change much.

US$1 = KSh 35
UK£1 = KSh 60

Also, look out for banks offering so-called 'free' and 'premium' rates, where you can sometimes (legally) get KSh 10 or KSh 15 more for a US dollar, although this may not continue indefinitely.

The black market demand for hard currency was all over the place during 1992 with the abolition of declaration forms, and banks offering free and premium rates. Sometimes you could get up to 50% more for your cash on the black, but at other times nobody was interested. If you do use the black market, check the situation carefully before doing any deals.

International air tickets generally have to be paid for in hard currency. Because exchange rates are uncertain, some large hotels and safari companies quote in US dollars, although you can pay in KSh at the current rate (sometimes without having to show a bank receipt). Where this is the case, the prices are quoted in US dollars in this book.

WHEN TO GO

The best time for trekking in Kenya is during the dry seasons, from the end of May to early October, when the weather is cool, and from late November to early March, when it's generally warmer (see the Climate section).

Because weather patterns in East Africa are becoming less predictable, you could take a chance on going up Mt Kenya in mid-November and might get several days of good weather. Alternatively, it could still be raining heavily in December, which might mean snow blocking the route up to Lenana.

Don't forget that even in the dry seasons it can still rain. I've seen thick snow on the summit of Mt Kenya in August, and hail on Mt Elgon at the same time of year. You should be prepared for bad weather at *any* time.

USEFUL ORGANISATIONS

The Mountain Club of Kenya (PO Box 45741, Nairobi) is primarily a members' club for local climbers. Meetings are held every Tuesday at 8 pm in the clubhouse at Wilson Airport. Members of the club have considerable knowledge of conditions and routes on mountains within the region, and the club produces guidebooks for climbing Mt Kenya, Kilimanjaro and other mountains and crags in Kenya.

The club can provide information to genuinely interested climbing parties and to members of other mountain and hiking organisations. However, it is not a travel agency, and cannot help you with general queries on the more straightforward aspects of trekking or travel in Kenya.

The East African Wildlife Society is a non-profit organisation whose main aim is to safeguard the habitat in all its forms. The membership fee helps them continue this campaign. You can join the society in Nairobi at their office and shop in the Hilton Hotel shopping mall, or write direct to EAWLS, PO Box 20110, Nairobi. Members get a free bimonthly magazine.

HOLIDAYS

As well as Christmas Day, Boxing Day, New Year's Day and Easter Friday and Monday, public holidays include:

1 May	Labour Day
1 June	Madaraka, or Self-government Day
10 October	Moi Day
20 October	Kenyatta Day
12 December	Independence Day

GUIDEBOOKS
General

Amongst the many general guidebooks that have been written about Kenya, Lonely Planet's *Kenya – a travel survival kit* is highly recommended and an excellent companion to this book, with detailed information on the whole country for independent and budget travellers. Other books, which have more emphasis on photography and mainstream background information than practical advice, include the *Insight Guide to Kenya* (Apa, Hong Kong, 1990), the *Insider's Guide to Kenya* (Moorland Press, UK, 1989), *Kenya* (Nelles Verlag, Germany, 1991) and the *Spectrum Guide to Kenya* (Camerapix, Kenya, 1990). Most of these guidebooks contain detailed bibliographies, listing books with more specific information on the history, geography and people of Kenya, plus travelogues, biographies, African novels, field guides, and coffee-table picture books.

Specialist

The Mountain Club of Kenya has published *The Mountains of Kenya*, which is a 'blatant peak-baggers' guide' to almost 100 mountain summits in Kenya, ranging from Furole on the Kenya-Ethiopia border to Kasigau in the south near Tanzania, and is aimed mainly at residents or visitors with their own vehicles. *Mountain Walking in Kenya* (McCarta, UK, 1990) is written more specifically for visitors, and covers a selection of long and short walks in various parts of the country, with an emphasis on the more accessible and interesting areas.

The *Guide to Mount Kenya and Kilimanjaro* (also published by the Mountain Club of Kenya) is mainly for rock climbers and mountaineers, although it does have some brief sections on trekking routes, and a lot of

good background information on the history, geology and wildlife of these two mountains. The book was reprinted in 1992, and altered slightly, mainly to take account of the receding glaciers and disappearing ice routes.

Another useful book is the *Camping Guide to Kenya* (Bradt, UK/Hunter, USA, 1990) which covers every campsite in Kenya, including towns and the coast, as well as mountains and national parks.

Several very good bookshops in Nairobi carry huge stocks of maps and books (local and foreign) on Kenya, including most of the ones mentioned in this list. The Nation Bookshop (next to the New Stanley Hotel in the city centre) and the Text Book Centre (several outlets around the city – they sell all kinds of books) are recommended.

Guidebooks on individual mountains and trekking areas are covered in the relevant sections.

MAPS

For general travel around the country, or in between trekking areas, the 'Kenya' map published by Nelles/McCarta is one of the best. Other maps of the whole country are published by Macmillan, Freytag & Berndt and the Survey of Kenya (SK). Most of these are good, but of limited use if you leave the main routes, and are not suitable for trekking. For the mountains and trekking areas covered in this chapter, some more detailed maps are available (for details, see the individual trekking sections).

Common bulbul

The country is covered by SK maps to scales of 1:50,000, 1:100,000 and 1:250,000, but they cannot be sold to the public, for security reasons. This regulation may change, however, so details on SK maps are given in the individual trekking sections. The SK Public Map Office is on Harambee Ave, near the Kenyatta International Conference Centre.

TREKKING COMPANIES

You can trek independently in all the areas covered by this chapter but it's also possible to join an organised trek or a safari that includes some trekking. If your time is limited, this can save a lot of messing about and sometimes it's not a lot more expensive than arranging a trek of the same length and standard yourself (see Organised Trekking, in the Facts for the Trekker chapter).

Most organised treks can be arranged in Nairobi, where there's an infinite number of safari companies, but only a few that actually operate genuine treks. Most of the outfits who offer Mt Kenya trips act as agents only, and are unlikely to be able to help with specific advice. Unless they've got a good deal going, you might as well go straight to the real operators.

Costs

The price of the trek you take will depend on the number of days, the quality of transport, equipment and food provided (if any), the knowledge and experience of the guides, and many other factors. When comparing prices, check whether they include park fees, as most of the highland trekking areas are in national parks, and this can make a big difference to the overall cost. The prices quoted here include transport to the start of the trek and back to Nairobi, all park fees, food, accommodation in bunkhouses or tents, guides and porters, unless otherwise stated.

Addresses

The companies listed here have been recommended. Most can organise a trek almost immediately, or within a couple of days. Some have treks and safaris with scheduled departures, which you can join if the dates suit you.

You can contact them for more information by writing in advance or calling when in Nairobi. If writing, include the PO Box number. If phoning from anywhere inside Kenya, Tanzania or Uganda, the code for Nairobi is 02. If phoning from any other country, use the international code for Kenya (254) and omit the 0.

Nairobi There are several companies in Nairobi that you can try:

Natural Action
    1st floor, Museum Hill Shopping Centre (opposite the National Museum), PO Box 12516, Nairobi (☎ 740214). A specialist mountain company doing high-quality treks and technical mountaineering on Mt Kenya, Kilimanjaro and the Rwenzoris, plus treks on Mt Elgon, the Aberdare Range and several other parts of Kenya. Their six-day Mt Kenya trek traverses the mountain, ascending via an unusual route on the east side, for US$580. Natural Action's mountain guides are properly trained and equipped, very knowledgeable, and even offer a short 'Swahili for Mountaineers' language course! The Natural Action office is also a shop selling/hiring mountain equipment, guidebooks and maps. They even sell compasses specially calibrated for equatorial conditions (see Equipment, in the Facts for the Trekker chapter), and the staff (who are off-duty mountain guides) don't mind giving advice to independent trekkers. There's a message board in the shop, for people selling/wanting gear or looking for trekking/climbing companions.

Kenya Hiking & Cycling
    2nd floor, Arrow House, Koinange St (opposite the City Market), PO Box 39439, Nairobi (☎ 218336/8, fax 224212). The name says it all. This company organises good-quality budget safaris of five to eleven days, with sections of walking or mountain biking. Areas include Mt Elgon, Mt Longonot, Maasai Mara, Hell's Gate and the Suguta Valley. Hiking & Cycling also organises a very reasonable five-day Mt Kenya trek, using bunkhouses, for around $400 per person. Lake Turkana is their specialist area – they have boats on the lake to take trekkers from the Suguta to Loyangalani, South Island or the archaeological dig at Koobi Fora. The company says 'our safaris are active; we ask you to make an effort, but they are NOT survival courses!'. Even if you can't join an organised trek, the

people in their office are happy to provide advice and assistance for independent trekkers.

Tropical Ice
PO Box 57341, Nairobi (☎ 740811, fax 740826). This is an up-market company which pioneered Nepal-style trekking in Kenya almost 20 years ago. They offer very high-quality treks across Mt Kenya and the Loita Hills in Maasailand, and some unique lowland bush walks through wildlife areas along the Tsavo and Galana Rivers in eastern Kenya. All treks and hikes are five days long, with scheduled departures, so you need to book in advance. Prices are between US$600 and US$750.

Bushbuck Adventures
Gilfillan House, Kenyatta Ave (near African Heritage), PO Box 67449, Nairobi (☎ 212975/7, fax 218735). This mid-market company specialises in trekking and walking safaris in mountain and wildlife areas all over Kenya, including Mt Kenya, Mt Elgon and the Maasai Mara. Five-day treks based at Bushbuck's own private camps in the Aberdares and several other lowland parks cost US$595. They also have camping equipment for hire.

Executive Wilderness Programmes
PO Box 15014, Nairobi (☎ 891049). This company offers trekking and technical mountaineering on Mt Kenya, Mt Elgon, Kilimanjaro and the Rwenzoris. Treks can be designed to suit your budget, experience and time-limit.

Gametrackers
1st floor, Kenya Cinema Plaza, Moi Ave, PO Box 62042, Nairobi (☎ 338927, 212830/2, fax 330903). Frequently recommended for their safaris to Lake Turkana, Maasai Mara and the other national parks, Gametrackers also do canoe and mountain bike safaris, and four-day treks in the Aberdares.

Bike Treks
PO Box 14237, Nairobi. Nairobi agent: Let's Go Travel, Standard Street, PO Box 60342, Nairobi (☎ 340331, fax 336890). Again, the name says it all: mountain bike trips in various parts of Kenya, plus treks of two to six days through the Maasai Mara and Loita Hills area, combined with game viewing in the reserve. A six-day trek costs US$480.

Kentracks
Nairobi agent: Special Camping Safaris, Gilfillan House, Kenyatta Ave, PO Box 51512, Nairobi (☎ 338325, fax 211828). This is a bushwalking specialist outfit doing five-day treks in the Great Rift Valley for US$495.

Mt Kenya On the east side of Mt Kenya are two hotels (see the Mt Kenya Places to Stay section for accommodation details) offering a range of fully supported treks on the mountain. Contact the hotels, or their Nairobi agents, to make reservations, or just turn up: treks can usually be arranged with one day's notice, and you might meet some other people and get together to reduce costs.

Naro Moru River Lodge
PO Box 18, Naro Moru (☎ (0176) 62622). The lodge is a old country-house hotel with rooms, cottages, a bunkhouse and campsite, near the start of the Naro Moru Route up Mt Kenya. The lodge also has two bunkhouses on the Naro Moru Route and most of their treks stay overnight there. A four-day trek, going up and down the Naro Moru Route, costs US$535 per person, or US$385 each for a group of four. An extra day, to do a circuit of the peaks, will add US$125/90. A five-day trek up the Sirimon Route and down the Naro Moru Route costs US$680/495.

Mountain Rock Hotel
PO Box 333, Nanyuki (☎ (0176) 62051). Nairobi agent: Yare Safaris, 1st floor Union Towers, corner Moi Ave/Mama Ngina St, PO Box 63006, Nairobi (☎ 214099, fax 722338). This hotel, originally called Bantu Lodge, is eight km north of Naro Moru, with rooms and a campsite. The hotel has two bunkhouses on the Sirimon Route and most of their treks go this way. A four-day trek going up and down the Sirimon Route costs US$485 per person, or US$315 each for a group of four. If you want to come down the Naro Moru Route, add an extra $10 per person. An extra day to do a circuit of the peaks adds US$100/70 to the price.

If you want something between an organised trek and a completely independent trek, the hotels near Mt Kenya can arrange guides and porters only, or make reservations in the bunkhouses, while you plan your own route, provide your own gear and food, and make all the other arrangements yourself (see the Mt Kenya section for details).

TRAVEL AGENTS

Like safari companies, there are hundreds of travel agents in Nairobi, handling international and internal flights, safaris, car hire and so on. Some are a lot cheaper than others, and offer different deals, so you'll need to shop around. For trekkers, there are a couple of particularly useful places:

Let's Go Travel
    Caxton House, Standard Street, PO Box 60342, Nairobi (☎ 340331, fax 336890). This company is useful because it is the agent for several of the specialist trekking companies already mentioned. They do car hire, make reservations for trains and flights, and also handle bookings for huts and bunkhouses on Mt Kenya and the Aberdares.

Africa Travel Centre (Yare Safaris)
    1st floor, Union Towers, corner Moi Ave/Mama Ngina St, PO Box 63006, Nairobi (☎ 214099, fax 722338). Part of the Africa Travel Centre chain, which has branches in London and Sydney, this company can make all the usual travel arrangements. They are also the agents for Mountain Rock Hotel on Mt Kenya, and the Nairobi office for the Maralal Hostel in the Loroghi Hills trekking area.

EQUIPMENT HIRE & SUPPLY

There's not much choice in Nairobi. For specialist, lightweight trekking equipment, Natural Action (see Trekking Companies) has a good range. Bushbuck (also listed earlier) has a smaller range of specialist stuff, but just about anything you need for camping and walking safaris. In town, Atul's shop on Biashara St has locally made tents and sleeping bags, and a lot of second-hand walking and camping gear, all for sale or hire. Naro Moru River Lodge and Mountain Rock Hotel, near Mt Kenya, also have gear for hire (see the Mt Kenya Places to Stay section).

ACCOMMODATION IN NAIROBI

Most trekkers start and end their journey through East Africa in Nairobi and spend a few days here arranging an organised trek or safari, sorting out paperwork, or passing through to stock up on supplies in between treks.

Nairobi is one of the largest cities in Africa (although the centre is still not big enough to get lost in), and there's a wide range of hotels. This brief selection will give you an idea.

To stay at most of the hotels in the top and mid-range, it's sometimes worth booking through a travel agent or trekking company, as they can often get good discounts.

More details on places to stay in or near the trekking areas are given in the relevant sections.

Places to Stay – top end

At the top end are the *Hilton*, the *Inter-Continental* and the historic *Norfolk Hotel,* with singles from US$100 to US$150 and doubles from US$150 to US$200.

Places to Stay – middle

Down the scale a bit, in the centre of town, is the large and impersonal but reasonably priced *Six-Eighty Hotel*, with singles/doubles at KSh 1000/1500. Also central, and better value, is the small and friendly *Oakwood Hotel*, which has self-contained doubles for KSh 1300 including breakfast.

Outside the city centre, also in the middle-range, is the recently modernised *Fairview Hotel*, set in pleasant gardens, with self-contained rooms for US$34/56 including breakfast. In the same part of town is the mid-range *Milimani Hotel*, with rooms for KSh 1200/1500 including breakfast and the *Sagret Hotel* with rooms for KSh 950/750 including breakfast. Nearby is the *Youth Hostel*, on Ralph Bunche Rd, where a bed in the dorm costs KSh 100, but the communal style means security is not good.

Places to Stay – bottom end

Back in town, nearer the bottom end of the range, one of the best value for money places is the *Dolat Hotel* on Mfangano St, where basic but clean self-contained doubles go for about KSh 300. Most of the really cheap and basic places are in the same area, around River and Latema Rds: these include the *New Kenya Lodge*, a legendary hippy hangout where you sometimes have to watch your gear, the *Iqbal Hotel*, which has a good restaurant, and the *Sunrise Lodge*, where the security is good and there's usually hot water, all with singles/doubles for about KSh 150/250.

Places to Stay – camping

The only place for camping, where there are also cheap rooms and a place to safely park a vehicle, is *Mrs Roche's House*, on 3rd Parklands Ave, about three km from the city centre. This is another legendary travellers' stopover, with beds at KSh 75 and KSh 50 for camping, but its popularity means it gets very crowded these days, although nobody is ever turned away.

Getting There & Away

You can travel between Kenya and the neighbouring East African countries using air, road or rail transport. How you travel depends on how much time you've got, and the amount of travelling (as opposed to trekking) you want to do. This section presumes you want to take a fairly direct route between the trekking areas in the various countries.

TO/FROM UGANDA
Air

There are regular services between Nairobi and Kampala – usually about five or six flights per week in each direction. The one-way fare is about US$100.

Road

The main border crossing between Kenya and Uganda is at Malaba, which is linked to Nairobi and Kampala by good tarred roads. The Akamba Bus Company operates a direct overnight bus between Nairobi and Kampala, which you can book in advance at their office on Lagos Rd, just off Latema Rd; the one-way fare is KSh 500. Alternatively, you can do the journey in stages. On the Kenya side, there are buses, *matatus* and shared taxis between Nairobi and Bungoma, the first/last big town in Kenya. In Nairobi, these leave from the River and Accra Rds area, and from the Country Bus Station. The bus costs about KSh 200. In Bungoma, get off at the junction on the outskirts of town, where the new road to the border goes straight on. (If you get stuck here, the nearby Kanduyi Inn has self-contained doubles for KSh 170.) Matatus run regularly between Bungoma and the border. You can easily walk across the border.

Formalities at the Malaba border point are straightforward for both countries, although the Ugandan side is a bit of a maze. Arrival/departure forms need to be completed, but there are no currency forms to worry about on either side. You are not allowed to import or export more than KSh 200 or USh 5000, but if you're going to be crossing back across the border after a few weeks and want to keep some money, a search is unlikely. There is a bank and foreign exchange bureau on the Ugandan side and plenty of moneychangers on both sides. Know the rates and you'll get a good deal.

On the Uganda side, there are matatus between the border and Tororo, and buses and matatus between Tororo and Mbale or Kampala (see the Uganda chapter for details).

Train

The train between Nairobi and Malaba goes three times a week in each direction, overnight: Nairobi to Malaba on Tuesdays, Fridays and Saturdays, the other way on Wednesdays, Saturdays and Sundays. The service is fairly reliable, costing KSh 350/700 for 2nd/1st-class sleeping compartment, plus a charge for bedding if you want it. Meals are available in the restaurant car.

Although a rusty track crosses the border there are no international services. On the Uganda side, there is a line from Tororo to Kampala, but the trains are very slow and unreliable, and you're better off going by road.

TO/FROM TANZANIA
Air

There are international flights between Nairobi and Dar es Salaam every day, starting at about US$110 one way. From Dar you can fly to Kilimanjaro International Airport (KIA), in northern Tanzania, near the trekking areas. But this is expensive and a very long way round, and delays are inevitable. There are also direct flights between Nairobi and KIA, although these are likely to be discontinued soon. By far the easiest way of travelling between the trekking areas of Kenya and Tanzania is by road.

Road

There's a good tarmac road all the way between Nairobi and Arusha, the first/last main town in Tanzania. This road goes to Moshi, the base for Kilimanjaro, and eventually to Dar. The main Kenya-Tanzania border is at Namanga, roughly halfway between Nairobi and Arusha.

Most people do the journey by matatu or shared taxi, although these vehicles do not actually cross the border. You have to walk between the two customs posts and pick up another vehicle on the other side. There are regular matatus and shared taxis between Arusha or Nairobi and the border.

The journey between Arusha or Moshi and Nairobi can also be done by direct public bus or by luxury shuttle-bus, without the need to change at the border.

If you arrive by air at Mombasa, and want to go straight to Moshi or Arusha for Kilimanjaro, you can avoid Nairobi by crossing the border at Taveta, to the east of Moshi.

For more details on transport between Kenya and Tanzania, see Getting There & Away, in the Tanzania chapter.

TO/FROM MALAWI
Air

Flights between Nairobi and Lilongwe go about four times a week in each direction. One-way fares cost between US$200 and US$300, depending on the airline.

Road

Kenya and Malawi do not have a common border, so all overland journeys between these two countries have to go through Tanzania by road or rail. For details see the Getting Around and Getting There & Away sections of the Kenya and Tanzania chapters.

Getting Around

You can reach the trekking areas in Kenya by air or, more usually, by road and rail. Generally things are fairly efficient, but bad roads and long waits become more common as you get further away from the main routes and centres.

AIR

If you arrived in Kenya at Mombasa, Kenya Airways have several flights a day between Nairobi and Mombasa, for around KSh 2000.

ROAD

Main roads in Kenya are generally good, and usually tarred, although some of the busier routes have become increasingly pot-holed in recent years, because of overloaded trucks and general lack of maintenance. The main routes likely to be used by trekkers are: south from Nairobi to the Tanzanian border at Namanga; north-west to the Ugandan border at Malaba; and north to Mt Kenya and the Central Highlands. All these main routes are tarred, and many secondary roads are also tarred or well graded. Minor dirt roads tend to be in bad condition or impassable after rains.

Bus, Matatu & Shared Taxi

On all the main routes, there are regular buses, matatus and shared taxis. Express buses, which tend to be faster and less crowded, run between the main towns, with definite departure (if not arrival) times. On long-distance buses, seats can be reserved in advance at the bus company's office, which is usually a wooden shed at the bus station. In Nairobi, several bus companies also have offices on the streets in the area around Accra and River Rds. Fares are cheap. For example, Nairobi-Kitale (KSh 180), Nairobi-Nyeri (KSh 110), Nairobi-Mombasa (KSh 200 to KSh 250).

Shared taxis (sometimes called taxi-matatus) are a good way of getting around between the main towns in Kenya, although some drivers tend to be on the crazy side. Towns linked to Nairobi by shared taxis include Nanyuki and Meru (near Mt Kenya), Nyeri (near the Aberdare National Park), and Kitale (near Mt Elgon). They also run to the border at Namanga. Fares are generally between 1½ and two times the cost of a bus. In Nairobi, shared taxis to different towns leave from various streets or junctions, all in the area around Accra and River Rds. In the other towns they generally leave from a corner of the bus station. Most take seven people, and leave when full. On the main routes there's usually at least one going every couple of hours throughout the day.

Away from the main routes, in rural areas, local buses and matatus are often slow and uncomfortable, running to no fixed schedule, and leaving when full.

Taxi

In Nairobi there are several taxi ranks. Rates are slightly negotiable, but always ask before getting in. Across town costs KSh 100, and between the city and the airport about KSh 350.

Car Rental

For most trekkers, the plan is to get away from cars, but a vehicle might be useful for visiting some of the mountain areas, or if you want to combine trekking with a safari.

Nairobi has many car hire companies, and costs vary considerably. Rates for a small saloon car (sedan) hired from a budget outfit start at about KSh 500 per day and can go up to almost double that if you get a new car from a smart multi-national. Add to this the daily insurance charge of KSh 300 to KSh 400, and a distance charge of between KSh 6 and KSh 10 per km.

A small 4WD is likely to be more useful for reaching the trekking areas. Budget rates start at KSh 700 and can double with the smarter companies. Insurance for this vehicle usually costs KSh 400 to KSh 500, and the distance charge somewhere between KSh 7 and KSh 12.

For a week's trip in a small 4WD, covering about 1000 km, you're looking at between US$260 and US$370, depending on your rate of exchange. Most companies also do weekly rates which include insurance and up to 1200 'free' km, and these deals can often work out cheaper. In the low season you can get some incredible bargains. I met four British lads who hired a small 4WD for a week, just at the end of the rains, for only US$100, and did some good trekking with it on Elgon and the Aberdares. They finished at the foot of Mt Kenya, where they were going to do another trek, while one of them took the car to Nairobi and then hitched back next day to join the others.

To compare prices you need a good idea of your intended route and distance, so you can weigh up the various options and shop around the companies. Don't forget to add petrol costs. A small 4WD does about 10 km to the litre, on a mix of tar and dirt roads, and petrol costs about KSh 18 a litre.

International rental companies, such as Hertz, Avis and Europcar have offices all over the world and you can often make inquiries and even reservations at an office in your own country. Recommended car hire companies in Nairobi include:

Kesana Car Hire, 8th floor, Town House, Kaunda St, PO Box 7154, Nairobi (☎ 749062)
Let's Go Travel, Caxton House, Standard St, PO Box 60342, Nairobi (☎ 340331)
Payless Car Hire, Olympic House, Koinange St (near the City Market), PO Box 49713, Nairobi (☎ 338400), and other offices in the Hilton shopping block and at the airport
Crossways Car Hire, Banda St (behind African Heritage), PO Box 10228, Nairobi (☎ 223949)
Market Car Hire, Market Filling Station, corner Koinange and Banda Sts, PO Box 49713, Nairobi (☎ 335735)

Hitching

Hitching free lifts on the main routes is feasible, but on the quieter roads you may have to wait a long time – you'll probably have to rely on lifts in trucks or government vehicles, where a payment is usually expected.

TRAIN

From Nairobi, the main railway lines go south to Mombasa and north-west to the Ugandan border at Malaba. These services are generally reliable. Trains compare favourably with buses and matatus on the same route in terms of speed, and probably come out on top for comfort and safety.

Each train usually has double-berth 1st-class cabins, four- or six-bed 2nd-class compartments, and seats-only in the 3rd-class carriages, which can be very crowded. Cabins and compartments are either men or women only unless you reserve both/all beds.

Between Nairobi and Mombasa, there are two overnight trains in each direction every weekday, and one at weekends. There are three trains a week in each direction between Nairobi and Malaba. Trains have restaurant cars, and fares are reasonable: Nairobi-Mombasa costs KSh400/750 in 2nd/1st class

one way. Reservations at least three days in advance are recommended, although you can be lucky and get one at shorter notice. If you want to avoid queues at the station, tickets can be arranged by Let's Go Travel in Nairobi.

Mt Kenya

Roughly in the centre of Kenya is an area of high ground called, not surprisingly, the Central Highlands. Mount Kenya, from where the country takes its name, stands at the centre of the Highlands, and is often visible from Nairobi, some 130 km to the south. Of all East Africa's mountains, this is where you get nearest to equatorial ice-caps. Mount Kenya's glaciers are only 16 km north of the equator, just pipping the Rwenzoris, which lie 40 km above the equator, and beating Kilimanjaro by more than 300 km.

Like Kilimanjaro, Mt Kenya was formed by volcanic action associated with the creation of the Rift Valley. But Mt Kenya is much older than Kili and geologists believe it once stretched at least 1500 metres above its current height of 5199 metres (17,057 feet). Mount Kenya has been trimmed to its present size by glacial erosion. Today the jagged central peaks of Batian and Nelion contrast sharply with the smooth dome of Kibo. But despite being a mere shadow of its former self, Mt Kenya is still the highest mountain in the country, and the second-highest in Africa after Kili.

Mount Kenya is also East Africa's second-favourite mountain, with a wide range of top-quality walking and climbing routes attracting trekkers and mountaineers from all over the world.

To reach the highest summits of Mt Kenya – the twin peaks of Batian and Nelion – you need to be a technical mountaineer, armed with ropes and a full harness of climbing gear. The trekkers' summit is Lenana, the third-highest point on the mountain, and most visitors try to bag this peak during their trek.

HISTORY

The Kikuyu people, who settled in the Central Highlands some 200 to 300 years ago, cultivated the foothills and hunted in the forests surrounding the mountain, but it's unlikely that any went above the high moorland. Cold, and respect for Ngai (God) who they believed lived on the top of Mt Kenya, would have prevented any high-altitude hunting forays. The mountain was revered and Kikuyu houses were always built with the door towards the mountain as a sign of respect. Its Kikuyu name is Kirinyaga, meaning 'White (or Bright) Mountain', although its modern title is more likely to come from the language of the neighbouring Kamba people, who called it Kee Nyaa (also spelt in several other ways), meaning 'Place of the Ostrich'. The black and white stripes of bare rock and ice on the high peaks looked like an ostrich's feathers.

The first sighting of the mountain by a European was in 1849, when Ludwig Krapf, a Swiss missionary and colleague of Johannes Rebmann, who had earlier spotted Kilimanjaro, saw the twin peaks and glaciers from the area near the present-day town of Kitui. Forty years later, Count Samuel Teleki, passing through on his way to Lake Turkana, managed to cut through the forest and reach a point above the moorland on the south-west side of the mountain. The explorer/geologist J W Gregory went further in 1893, and got as far as the top of the Lewis Glacier, just below Point Lenana, before turning back. The high peaks were first climbed in 1899 by the British mountaineer Halford Mackinder and his two Alpine guides Cesar Ollier and Joseph Brocherel. Several features on the mountain, including the Mackinder Valley and the Cesar and Joseph glaciers, bear the names of these three men.

GEOGRAPHY

The Mt Kenya massif is roughly circular, about 60km across at the 2000-metre contour, where the steep foothills rise out of the more gradual slopes of the Central Highlands. At the centre of the massif, the main peaks rise sharply from around 4500 metres to the summits at just under 5200 metres.

For the record, Batian is 5199 metres (17,054 feet), Nelion is 5188 metres (17,025

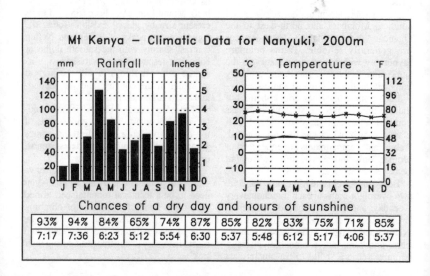

Mt Kenya – Climatic Data for Nanyuki, 2000m

Chances of a dry day and hours of sunshine

| 93% | 94% | 84% | 65% | 74% | 87% | 85% | 82% | 83% | 75% | 71% | 85% |
| 7:17 | 7:36 | 6:23 | 5:12 | 5:54 | 6:30 | 5:37 | 5:48 | 6:12 | 5:17 | 4:06 | 5:37 |

feet) and Lenana is 4985 metres (16,355 feet). Other major summits on the mountain include Point Pigott (4957 metres), Point Dutton (4885 metres) and Point John (4883 metres).

From the main peaks, which are the remains of the volcanic plug, a series of large U-shaped valleys descend in a radial pattern towards the lower foothills. The largest of these valleys are the Teleki, the Hohnel, the Hobley, the Gorges, the Mackinder and the Hausberg. In between the valleys are broad ridges that become increasingly steep and narrow where they join the main peaks.

GUIDEBOOKS & MAPS

The Mountain Club of Kenya's *Guide to Mount Kenya and Kilimanjaro* is available in Nairobi and due for reprint in 1993. The *East Africa International Mountain Guide* also has a section on Mt Kenya. Both these books are mainly for mountaineers and technical rock climbers (see Books, in the Facts for the Trekker chapter).

The Survey of Kenya (SK) 1:50,000 map of Mt Kenya is not usually available, but you may be able to find copies of the SK 1:125,000 'Tourist Map of Mount Kenya' in some bookshops. This map has recently been reissued by Ordnance Survey UK in their Worldmaps series, with some updated information, but the scale of the peaks section is too limiting to be useful. The best map available is 'Mount Kenya Map & Guide', produced by Andrew Wielochowski (published by West Col), and available in Nairobi. It's clearly drawn, with good detail, although there are a few errors on it, but these get corrected with each new edition.

TREKKING INFORMATION

Mount Kenya is completely surrounded by dense forest, so to get to the moorlands and main peaks you have to follow one of the cut routes. There are at least seven trekking routes from the lower slopes of Mt Kenya up to the main peaks area, although those not in regular use have become overgrown and difficult to follow. These ascent routes are all connected by the Summit Circuit Path which

Giant groundsel

circles the main peaks between the 4300-metre and 4800-metre contour lines. Beyond the Summit Circuit Path, two routes lead up to the summit of Point Lenana, the highest peak on the mountain that can be reached by trekkers.

All the routes up the mountain follow a major valley or ridge to reach the main peak area, and the Summit Circuit Path around the peaks goes over several high cols (passes) as it crosses from the head of one valley to the next. High cols which can be reached by trekkers include Simba Col (4620 metres), Hausberg Col (4591 metres) and Tooth Col (4720 metres).

Mount Kenya is the only mountain in the country with a permanent covering of ice. The largest glacier is the Lewis Glacier, which you pass on the trek from the Teleki Valley to Point Lenana, via Austrian Hut, and there are several others on the main peaks. Since records were first kept, it appears that the glaciers on Mt Kenya have been shrinking. In the last 20 years, this rate has increased noticeably, and some glaciers have completely disappeared. On maps produced

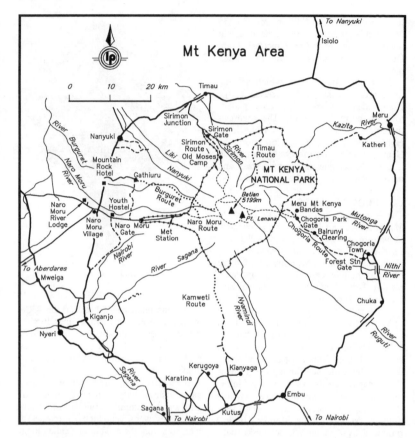

in the early 1960s the Lewis Glacier is shown descending from the ridge between Lenana and the main peaks all the way to the Lewis Tarn at 4700 metres. Today, the snout of the glacier is almost 100 metres above the tarn.

Route Standard & Days Required

On your Mt Kenya trek you can go up and down the same route, or use the Summit Circuit Path to link different routes and do a complete traverse of the mountain.

The number of days required varies from a two-day sprint for the fit and well-acclimatized to a leisurely seven-day traverse which takes in many of Mt Kenya's highlights.

Extra days are always recommended (see Warning, later in this section, and Acute Mountain Sickness in the Health & First Aid chapter).

The number of days given for each route is the 'usual' amount, but it's much better to spend an extra day ascending on any of the routes, or stop for two nights at about halfway, as this helps you acclimatize (see the Health & First Aid chapter).

If you are fit and well-acclimatized you can do these routes in a day less, although this normally means combining two stages into one, rather than doing an extra bit every day. But if you're not acclimatized, don't even think about cutting a day just to save time or money (see Warning, later in this section). Remember that Point Lenana is just under 5000 metres; this is higher than a lot of Himalayan passes that trekkers there take several days to reach. If you rush up Mt Kenya, the chances are you'll get sick, and wish you'd never come up at all, thereby wasting the cash you have paid out.

This section describes one short straight-up-and-down route, a traverse which is longer and more satisfying, and some other routes which can also be linked into a traverse of the mountain. These routes are described in detail, and other trekking possibilities are outlined, later in this chapter. The main routes are first described briefly here.

Naro Moru Route This is the most popular route on the mountain, with easy access, good bunkhouses, and the quickest way to Point Lenana. You don't even need a tent. The path is generally easy to follow and not difficult underfoot, although steep and boggy in places. Most stages are mildly strenuous, although the summit day is long and hard. A trek on this route can take two days and two nights for the round trip, but three or four days allows you more time to acclimatise. If you use another route to approach Lenana, you can descend on this route.

Burguret Route This is a very rarely used route, which joins the Naro Moru Route or the Summit Circuit Path (from where the Sirimon Route can be reached) to the west of the main peaks. It can be linked with any other route to make a good traverse of the mountain. The route passes through a wide band of dense bamboo on its lower sections, and paths are indistinct, so a local guide is essential, although porters are not generally used, as there are no huts or facilities of any kind. (If you want porters you have to provide tents – which can be hired – for them.)

This route is hard, with the going underfoot very muddy in the forest sections, and rough on the open moorland, and with buffalo and elephant in the forest, so this will appeal to real wilderness aficionados.

It normally takes three days to meet the Naro Moru or Sirimon Route, and Point Lenana can be reached on the morning of the fourth day.

This route can also be used as a descent, which takes two or three days, but a guide is absolutely essential to find the path down through the bamboo.

Sirimon-Chogoria Traverse This trek combines two routes which are used less frequently than the Naro Moru ascent and provide much better quality trekking. It is especially good for independent trekkers without a car, who are planning to camp all the way, as access is easy and there are several good campsites. The main routes are generally clear to follow, and most days are mildly strenuous, although some alternative stages are longer and more demanding, with indistinct or non-existent paths. The summit days are long but most other long stages can be split into two. There are several extra stages which can be added to the 'basic' trek. This traverse takes a minimum of five days (four nights) but it is much more satisfying spread over seven to eight days. This trek can be done in either direction.

Timau Route This is a very rarely used route, which joins the Chogoria Route east of the main peaks and can be linked with any other route to make a very good traverse of the mountain. For the higher part of the route, there is no path at all and you walk through open country, relying totally on your map and compass for navigation. Some stages are long and strenuous, and there are no facilities of any kind, although there are several good places to camp, making this is an excellent route for experienced, self-contained trekkers. Guides and porters are generally not used on this route.

From the start of the route to its junction with the Chogoria Route usually takes three days. From here, you can reach Point Lenana by various ways in anything from a few hours to a few days, depending on your route (see the Chogoria-Sirimon Traverse for details). After Lenana, you can descend on the Sirimon, the Chogoria or the Naro Moru Route, with one or two more nights, to reach the foot of the mountain. The Timau Route cannot be done easily in reverse, for logistical reasons.

Other Options Different sections of the routes outlined here can be combined to create several other good treks on Mt Kenya. For example, if you have no tent, it's still possible to do a traverse by going up the Sirimon and coming down the Naro Moru, as there are bunkhouses on both routes. (You'll still need a sleeping bag and cooking gear though.)

Alternatively, you can link the Chogoria and Naro Moru routes, and go in either direction. If you are fully self-contained and looking for something more adventurous, you can tie in either the Timau or the Burguret Route. It is better to use these routes as ascents, and then descend on one of the other more regularly used routes. However, a Burguret-Timau traverse in either direction would be the ultimate Mt Kenya wilderness trek.

Guides & Porters

Guides and porters are not obligatory, and many people do treks on Mt Kenya completely independently, and for experienced trekkers this is fine (see Guides & Porters, in the Facts for the Trekker chapter). If you decide to take a guide and/or porters, they can be arranged at Naro Moru River Lodge, Mt Kenya Youth Hostel and Mountain Rock Hotel on the west side of the mountain, and at any of the hotels in Chogoria town on the east side of the mountain. It is not normally possible to arrange guides and porters at the park gates.

Guides and porters are either tied to one of the hotels, or work as freelancers. Many have formed clubs or associations, in an attempt to standardise rates and improve conditions. Rates for a guide are about KSh 150 to KSh 200, and about KSh 120 to KSh 180 for porters, per stage (ie the distance

between two huts/bunkhouses, or a usual day's walking). If you combine two stages in one day, you'll still have to pay for both stages. If you have a rest day, and stay two nights at one hut/bunkhouse, that counts as a stage. The access and exit days of your trek, where you might be using a vehicle, also count as stages, even if your porters get a lift as well. This is fair enough: it may be an easy day's work for the porters but it's still a day when they could be working on their farm or carrying bags for somebody else – and time, as they say, is money.

The price covers food, which guides and porters provide and cook themselves. Make sure your guides and porters know how long your trek is going to be, and that they bring enough to eat. It's not unknown for porters to run out of food after a few days and then expect trekkers to provide for them. You also have to pay national park entrance fees for guides and porters.

Porters' loads are limited to 16 kg (or 18 kg if the trek is less than four days), to which they add their own kit. They do not have their own rucksacks. If you hire a guide first, he can arrange porters for you.

Guides are normally experienced and knowledgeable but, particularly among the freelancers, there are a few cowboys on the loose, so beware. The national park issues the more reliable organisations with entry vouchers for porters and guides. This makes it cheaper for them to enter the park and is also a way of controlling the unreliable ones. The park recommends to all visitors that they hire guides and porters who hold entry vouchers. Even so, if you want to do something different (such as the Burguret Route) or even slightly unusual (such as a circuit of the peaks), make absolutely sure your guide knows the way. A few questions to check won't do any harm.

On Mt Kenya, the distinction between porters and guides is normally clear: porters carry loads and that's all; guides show you the way and may require a porter to carry their own gear, even if you're carrying yours. Sometimes, though, the difference is blurred – you can find porters who will also act as guides for an extra fee (but, again, make sure they know their stuff before hiring them).

Tipping After your trek you will probably want to give a tip to the guide and porters who have worked for you. Some get a bit pushy towards the end of a trek when it comes to tipping time, although you can't always blame them (see Guides & Porters, in the Facts for the Trekker chapter). As a guideline, for a five-day trek on Mt Kenya, a tip should be an extra day's wages for each porter and guide, or slightly less for short treks and more for a longer one.

Park Fees & Regulations

All of the area above 3200 metres is Mt Kenya National Park. Below this, down to 2000 metres on the south of the mountain and 3000 metres on the north, is forest reserve. Two tongues of park land (called 'salients') descend through the forest to the Naro Moru and Sirimon gates at about 2500 metres.

To enter the park all visitors have to pay park fees. For non-residents, these are: KSh 540 per day and KSh 180 per night. In 1992 this was about US$18 and US$6. Even if the park rates go up, which they inevitably will, the actual cost to visitors is likely to remain about the same. There are proposals to reduce the daily entrance fee to KSh 300 for people staying in the park for more than two days. This is to encourage visitors to allow extra time for acclimatization, and is a very positive move. For Kenya residents, park fees are KSh 55 per day and KSh 30 per night, although these are likely to rise also.

These fees are paid at the gate where you enter the park, and receipts are checked when you leave. You're supposed to pay in advance for all the days you spend in the park, but if you stay longer than planned, you can pay for the extra days on your way out.

If you come up the Chogoria Route you have to pay an extra track maintenance fee of KSh 12 per person. If you're descending on the Chogoria Route, the last stage (from the Park Gate down to Chogoria town) is outside the park and park fees are not payable for that day.

The most important regulation to remember is that trekkers are not allowed to enter the park alone. This is a sensible rule, with your safety in mind, so all you lone wolves out there will have to find companions or a local guide.

Supplies

There are no shops inside the park, and only a small store at Naro Moru Gate. Basics can be bought in Naro Moru village or Chogoria town, and most things in the large towns of Embu and Nyeri. In Nairobi, you can buy almost anything (see Where to Buy Food, in the Facts for the Trekker chapter).

Warning

An important feature of Mt Kenya, and where it differs from the other major mountains of East Africa, is the speed at which you can get up to high altitudes. It's possible to drive from Nairobi up to one of the roadheads, walk to a high hut, and be on the summit of Lenana the next morning. This may be fine for fit and very well-acclimatized mountain athletes (although even for them it seems to be a bit of an endurance test), but for most visitors this is just asking for trouble. Many of the organised treks on offer only spend two nights on the mountain, which is just about OK for some people, but a lot of trekkers still get altitude sickness, which means they miss the summit and generally have a miserable time. It is not by chance that a great proportion of reported cases of pulmonary oedema (a severe, often fatal, form of altitude sickness) occur on Mt Kenya.

The situation is made worse by some tour companies (and some guidebooks) billing the trek to Lenana as an easy hike, something to tick off along with Lamu and the Maasai Mara. This has led to many people going up completely unprepared for the conditions, and suffering terribly from the cold or the altitude, or both. It's not difficult for ill-prepared independent trekkers to go off-route and have an accident, or even get hopelessly lost, sometimes fatally. Most years there are reports of trekkers simply disappearing on the mountain.

It is important to remember that Mt Kenya is a big mountain, where conditions can be very serious. There's no doubt that if you can spend at least three nights on the ascent, before going to the summit of Lenana, you stand a much better chance of enjoying yourself. And if you're prepared, with proper clothes and equipment, you stand a much better chance of surviving too! If you're not a regular mountain walker, and don't know how to use a map and compass, going up and down anything other than the Naro Moru Route, or trekking without a competent companion or a local guide, is not recommended.

PLACES TO STAY
Around Mt Kenya

On the western side of the mountain is the *Naro Moru River Lodge*, just outside Naro Moru village, off the main road. The lodge is an old-style country hotel catering for all types of trekker, with singles/doubles for US$72/94 (including bed, breakfast and evening meal), self-catering cottages from US$15 per person, a bunkhouse for US$6 a bed, and a good campsite for US$4 per person. (Room and cottage prices are cheaper in the low seasons – mid-April to June, and mid-September to mid-December. All prices are quoted in dollars, but payable in shillings.) There's a restaurant and bar, and even a swimming pool and tennis court, if trekking isn't already enough exercise. The lodge arranges all-inclusive treks, mainly on the Naro Moru Route (see the Kenya Trekking Companies section), and can also supply guides and porters if you want to make your own arrangements. The staff can also help with information and advice. The lodge has been arranging treks on the mountain for years, so they know their stuff. They also hire out equipment like rucksacks, boots, jackets and sleeping bags, although prices are on the steep side (KSh 200 per night for a sleeping bag, KSh 150 for a rucksack), and the quality is varied: there's some modern gear, while other items are

pretty basic. The lodge administers the two bunkhouses on the Naro Moru Route, at Met Station and Mackinder's Camp, and bookings for these have to be made here. Reservations for rooms, treks or beds in the mountain bunkhouses can be made direct to the lodge, PO Box 18, Naro Moru, or to their agents Let's Go Travel, Caxton House, Standard St, PO Box 60342, Nairobi.

In Naro Moru village there are a couple of basic lodging houses behind the 'main street', although they're seldom used by trekkers.

On the other side of the main road, about seven km up the dirt road towards the Naro Moru park gate, is the *Mount Kenya Youth Hostel*. The original hostel burnt down a few years ago, but there are now some simple *bandas* (cabins) and a campsite. Porters and guides can also be arranged here at reasonable rates for a straightforward service.

Towards Nanyuki, eight km north of Naro Moru village, is *Mountain Rock Hotel* (formerly *Bantu Lodge*), with singles/ doubles/triples at US$26/32/48 including breakfast, and camping at US$4 per night (all prices quoted in dollars, but payable in shillings). The campsite is a good deal: there's a kitchen, plenty of firewood, hot showers and even a bath! The hotel has a bar and restaurant and can also arrange trout fishing and horse-riding, for those idle moments. Mountain Rock also arrange treks on the mountain, mainly on the Sirimon Route (see the Trekking Companies section), where they have two bunkhouses at Old Moses Camp and Shipton's Camp. They also hire out mountain gear, although again the quality varies and prices are on the steep side, with tents going at US$12 per day, rucksacks for US$5 and gloves for US$3! Reservations for rooms, treks or beds in the bunkhouses can be made direct to the lodge, PO Box 333, Nanyuki, or to their agents, Yare Safaris, 1st floor, Union Towers, corner of Moi Ave and Mama Ngina St, PO Box 63006, Nairobi.

On the other side of the mountain, in Chogoria town, at the start of the Chogoria Route, there's a choice of places to stay. Opposite the hospital, on the main street, are the *Chogoria Guest House* and the *Chogoria Cool Inn*, both with rooms for KSh 100 per person. The Guest House is in slightly better condition. The Cool Inn also has a restaurant and bar, and can be noisy at night. About two km away from the main street, is the slightly more up-market *Chogoria Transit Motel*, with doubles for KSh 300 and a restaurant with good food (although it has to be ordered several hours in advance). All the Chogoria hotels can arrange porters and guides, and transport up to the Chogoria Park Gate (see Access).

At the top of the dirt track up to the park gate, just outside the park boundary, are the *Meru Mount Kenya Bandas*, administered by Meru County Council. The bandas are good quality wooden cabins, set in a pleasant forest clearing, and cost KSh 500 per person. As they're outside the park, entrance fees are not payable. Each banda has a bedroom sleeping three or four (the beds have clean sheets and blankets), a bathroom (with hot showers), a sitting room (with log fire) and fully equipped kitchen. There's even a shop selling beer. After a long, tough trek on Mt Kenya the luxury here is almost too much to take! You can just turn up and take a place, if there's room, or make an advance booking at Let's Go Travel in Nairobi. There is also camping here.

On Mt Kenya

Inside the national park, there are four bunkhouses with simple facilities, and about five huts, which are very basic. Bunkhouses have bunk-beds, an eating area with tables and benches, toilets outside and a tap or stream nearby. There's a separate hut for porters, and the whole place is looked after by a caretaker. It's perfectly possible to do a trek on Mt Kenya without a tent if you stay in the bunkhouses, and you can even do it using the huts, but some of these are in unpleasantly bad condition and only provide rudimentary shelter. It's also possible to camp, either near the bunkhouses or huts, or at any of several other good sites elsewhere on the mountain. If you're camping, and have hired a guide or

porters, you'll need to camp near a hut or bunkhouse every night, so they have somewhere to sleep, unless you provide tents for them. (There are also some huts exclusively for the use of Mountain Club of Kenya members and some basic bivvy shelters for mountaineers on the main peaks, but these are of no use for trekkers.)

On the Naro Moru Route the bunkhouses are at the Meteorological Station (always shortened to Met Station) and Teleki Lodge at Mackinder's Camp, both administered by Naro Moru Lodge. It costs US$8 per night at Met Station, and US$9 at Mackinder's. Payments for the bunkhouses have to be made in advance at Naro Moru Lodge, or their agents in Nairobi, Let's Go Travel, but if you just turn up the caretaker might be able to help you if there's space. You can camp near the bunkhouses and use their facilities for KSh 15. On the Sirimon Route the bunkhouses are at Old Moses Camp and Shipton's Camp, both administered by Mountain Rock Hotel. It costs US$8 per night at Old Moses, and US$9 at Shipton's or US$2 to camp. Payments have to be made in advance at Mountain Rock, or their Nairobi agents, Yare Safaris (all addresses given earlier). There are no bunkhouses on any of the other trekking routes.

The huts on Mt Kenya belong to the Mountain Club of Kenya (MCK) and you're supposed to pay a fee to the club to use them. This is payable at Naro Moru River Lodge or Let's Go Travel (not to some of the sharper porters who take the money and 'promise to pass it on'). Many trekkers don't pay at all, but the fee is only KSh 40 and it's only fair to contribute to the maintenance of the huts, even though they don't actually seem to get any. In fact, the MCK seem to have abandoned most of their huts on Mt Kenya's trekking routes. They are often in bad condition, and are used mainly by porters, while most trekkers camp. The only hut which is still in reasonable condition is Austrian Hut, just below Point Lenana, but every year it becomes slightly more dilapidated and unless something is done, it will soon be in a similar state of disrepair to the others.

It is possible that some of the old small huts may be removed in the future. This will have little effect on self-contained trekkers, but if you're planning to rely on these old huts for yourself or porters, check the latest situation at the gate before starting your trek.

Full details of bunkhouses, huts and campsites are given in the route descriptions.

GETTING THERE & AWAY

The main towns near the Mt Kenya massif are Nyeri and Nanyuki on the west side, and Embu and Meru on the east. The road north from Nairobi divides near Sagana and completely circles the mountain. It's tarred all the way, and there are frequent buses, matatus and shared taxis, making access very easy. If you're in a group, you can arrange to hire a shared taxi. This will cost seven times the one-person fare (however many people in your group), but it's an easy way to get to the start of your trek.

There is no single 'base' town for Mt Kenya (like Moshi for Kilimanjaro), so before taking transport to the mountain, first decide what route you're going to do. For routes on the western and northern side of

the mountain, from Nairobi take a direct bus or shared taxi towards Nanyuki. It may be easier to find transport to Nyeri, which is a larger town, and then take a local matatu or bus from there. This total journey costs about KSh 130 on the bus, or KSh 250 in a shared taxi. Naro Moru River Lodge (see the Places to Stay section) run a shuttle-bus between Nairobi and the lodge, costing US$50 per person, with discounts for groups of five or more. Contact the Lodge or Let's Go Travel in Nairobi for more details.

To reach the route on the eastern side of the mountain, take a bus or shared taxi to Meru, via Embu, and get off at the road junction near the small town of Chogoria. It may be easier to find transport to Embu, then take a local matatu to Chogoria town from there. From Nairobi this will cost about the same as getting to Nanyuki.

THE NARO MORU ROUTE

This is the most popular trekking route on the mountain, with easy access to the start of the route and good facilities on the way up. There are two good bunkhouses, one hut, and several places to camp.

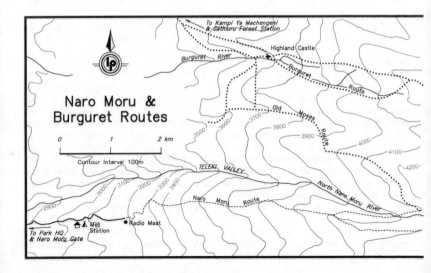

This route also allows a very quick ascent to Point Lenana, which is fine if you're well-acclimatized. But most people who do this route aren't, and they get altitude sickness because they do it too quickly (see Acute Mountain Sickness in the Health & First Aid chapter). The usual way of doing a trek on this route is to be dropped off by vehicle at Met Station (the first bunkhouse), then on the following day walk up to Mackinder's Camp (the second bunkhouse), and attempt to reach the summit of Point Lenana the next morning (only the second day of walking), before returning all the way to Met Station. Thus, a trek on this route can take as little as two days, not enough to give you a good chance of getting to Lenana, and very little chance at all of actually enjoying the trek. You are strongly recommended to walk to Met Station from the park gate, and to spend one extra night at either Met Station or Mackinder's Camp on the way up. This makes four days (three nights) for the round trip. Some alternative ways of making a slower ascent (involving an extra day) are outlined in Stage 3.

Access

The route starts at the village of Naro Moru, on the west side of Mt Kenya, between the larger towns of Nyeri and Nanyuki, about 200 km by road from Nairobi.

From Naro Moru village to the park gate is about 18 km along a good dirt road. There are a few junctions, but the park is signposted at each one; in any case, there'll be enough people around to ask for directions. It's not a bad walk, through fields and small villages, but if you're itching to get on the mountain you might want to get a lift to the gate. This can be arranged at Naro Moru River Lodge and Mountain Rock Hotel. Prices at Mountain Rock start at US$120 for the vehicle to Naro Moru Gate (although this may be negotiable), while the Lodge charges about US$50 to the Met Station, or less to the gate. These prices can be shared between up to six people, but you can usually get it cheaper than this by asking around locally at the Youth Hostel, or in the village.

Camping is permitted at the gate, but you have to pay park fees. Alternatively you can stay or camp at the Youth Hostel (about

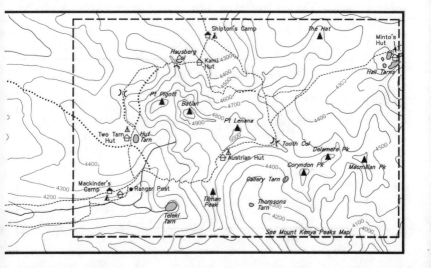

seven km from Naro Moru village) and, with an early start, walk from there to Met Station in a day (a total of 19 km).

Stage 1: Naro Moru Park Gate to Met Station

(10 km, 3-4 hours, 1000 metres ascent)
From the gate, keep to the park track, which follows the crest of a broad ridge between the Northern and Southern Naro Moru valleys. Although lifts are easy to find (for a fee), it's better to walk this section as it helps acclimatization. The going is easy, and it's pleasant walking through the forest.

About two thirds of the way up, after the bridge, there are several good views to your left (north), down into the Northern Naro Moru Valley. The track ends at the Met Station (3050 metres), a group of large bunkhouses surrounding a flat patch of grass for camping.

Stage 2: Met Station to Mackinder's Camp

(10 km, 5-6 hours, 1150 metres ascent)
From the Met Station, head uphill on the track to pass the radio mast on your right after about half an hour. After another 30 minutes you'll reach the end of the forest belt and enter moorland. This area is called the Vertical Bog. Wade or hop across tussocks until the going gets easier and you reach a fork, overlooking the Teleki Valley, about 3½ hours from the Met Station: the left path drops down into the valley, then runs alongside the North Naro Moru River up towards Mackinder's Camp; the right path stays on the ridge and reaches the river higher up. The right path is easier, so more people go this way. The paths meet about an hour later, from where it's another 45 minutes to the Mackinder's Camp area (4200 metres). Camping is possible here, or you can sleep in the bunkhouse, which is officially named Teleki Lodge, although it's more generally called Mackinder's Camp.

Stage 3: Mackinder's Camp to Met Station via Point Lenana

(4 km, 3½-5½ hours, 785 metres ascent plus 14 km, 5-6 hours, 1935 metres descent)
The usual way of doing this stage involves a start around 3 am to get to the summit of Point Lenana by sunrise, or just after, then a walk all the way back down to Met Station on the same day. This is long and hard, and the speed of ascent is one of the major reasons why so many people get sick and don't enjoy their trek on this route. Nevertheless, if you're only interested in bagging the summit in the shortest possible time, this is the way to go.

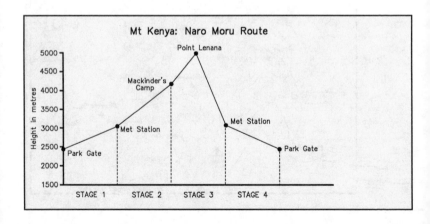

If you can afford an extra day, it's far better to go up in the daylight as far as Austrian Hut and spend the night of Stage 3 there before going up Lenana next morning, and descending to Met Station the same day. Alternatively, you can spend a second night at Mackinder's after Lenana, and go down to Met the next day. Even better, spend two nights at Mackinder's before going up to Lenana, to give yourself more time to acclimatise and a much better chance of enjoying the walk to the top.

Whatever you decide to do, to reach Austrian Hut from Mackinder's head north-east up the valley, past the ranger post, then tend right, across the head of the valley, so that the main peaks are up to your left. After half an hour you'll reach the bottom of a large scree slope. The path zig-zags up this to reach the crest of a ridge then tends left across easier ground to reach Austrian Hut (4790 metres). This section takes between two and four hours depending on how you feel.

Austrian Hut is in a reasonable state, with wooden sleeping platforms, windows and doors, but it has no caretaker, so its condition gets worse every year. There's a toilet, and water is available from the small tarn nearby called the Curling Pond (although this is fast becoming polluted). Next to Austrian Hut is the old Top Hut, in a very bad state of repair, and not suitable for sleeping in.

From Austrian Hut you get excellent views: north-east up to the summit of Point Lenana, with the area on the left (west) of the main South-west Ridge usually a snowfield covering the Lewis Glacier; west, across the Lewis Glacier itself, to the steep south-east face of Nelion; and south-east, down into the Hobley Valley, with Gallery Tarn over to the left (north) side of the valley.

To reach Lenana from Austrian Hut, aim north-east, following the clear path up the rocky South-west Ridge, aiming directly towards the summit. You can usually follow footprints, as most days there's a group of trekkers going up this way. If there has been snow, the path up to the summit may be hidden and extra care must be taken. If bad

weather obscures the route or the view up to the summit, this section should not be attempted by inexperienced trekkers without a guide.

About 20 to 30 minutes from Austrian Hut, tend left onto the edge of the snowfield, keeping the crest of the ridge to your right. Do not go too far left, onto the main glacier itself, as there are crevasses. Do not go too far right as you'll get onto steep rock. If the going becomes difficult or unsafe, you're on the wrong route. About 45 minutes to one hour from Austrian Hut, you'll pass below and to the left of the summit, then up to reach a metre-high rock step. Scramble up this and keep right to reach the summit, marked by a white painted rock. There's also a large metal cross with a Latin inscription (a gift from the Pope in the 1930s), and a star and crescent on a pole, erected more recently.

From the summit of Point Lenana, especially at dawn, the views are spectacular. To the west, across the top of the Lewis Glacier, the main south-east face of Nelion glows orange in the rising sunlight. Just below the top of the peak you can make out the tiny silver square of Howell Hut, a climbers' bivvy built in the 1970s by Iain Howell, one of Mt Kenya's pioneering technical mountaineers. From Nelion, looking round to the right (north), you can see the head of the Mackinder Valley, with the two subsidiary peaks of Terere and Sendeo on the ridge beyond. Further to the right, you can look down the Gorges Valley and see the sheer cliffs of The Temple, with Hall Tarns on top of the cliffs, appearing to slope sideways. Beyond them, you can see the huge mound of Ithanguni, with the flat-topped hill called the Giants' Billiards Table down to its right (south). Further round again, to the south of The Temple, you can see the three large peaks of Macmillan, Coryndon and Delamere on top of the ridge between the Gorges and Hobley valleys. To your south you can look back down to Austrian Hut and the steep U-shaped Teleki Valley, with the Mackinder's Camp bunkhouse visible at its head. And to the right of that, at the base of Nelion and the Lewis Glacier, is the leaning tower of Point John. If it's really clear, far to the south you can sometimes see the faint purple dome of Kilimanjaro rising above the clouds, some 300 km away.

If you can tear yourself away from Lenana, descent is by the same route. Retrace to Austrian Hut, then down to Mackinder's (about two hours) or the Met Station (another four to five hours).

THE BURGURET ROUTE

This is a very rarely used route on the western side of the mountain, following narrow paths through a wide zone of dense bamboo on its lower sections, and open moorland on the higher slopes. It gives you a taste of what the Naro Moru and Chogoria routes were like before the tracks were cut through the forest.

Because the vegetation is so dense you can get hopelessly lost on this route, even with a good map and compass, so a local guide is essential. Guides who are familiar with this route are available from Mountain Rock Hotel, which is also within walking distance of the start of the route.

There are no huts or facilities of any kind on this route, so porters are not normally used as there is nowhere for them to stay

(unless you hire tents for them). You will have to provide tent-space for your guide, or hire a tent for him from the hotel.

The route follows a ridge to the north of the Burguret River, and leads to Mackinder's Camp on the Naro Moru Route, or to Hut Tarn, south-west of the main peaks, from where Shipton's Camp on the Sirimon Route can be reached.

It normally takes three days to get to Mackinder's or Shipton's, and Point Lenana can be reached on the morning of the fourth day. Some of the first stage can be driven, which reduces the ascent by a day, but this is not so good for acclimatization. This route can also be used as a descent, which takes two or three days, but a guide is absolutely essential, to find the path down through the bamboo.

There is no park gate on this route, so you have to go to Naro Moru Gate or Sirimon Gate to pay your park fees. Mountain Rock Lodge can help you with this. If you descend this route you have to return to either of these routes to sign out. If you come down another way you can sign out at the gate on your descent route. It may be tempting to avoid park fees, but guides will play it by the book. And you shouldn't do it without a guide.

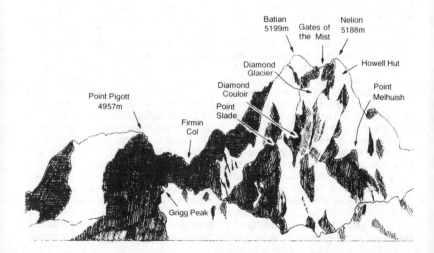

Access

The route proper starts at Gathiuru Forest Station. If you're driving, this is reached by turning off the main road between Nanyuki and Nyeri 12 km north of Naro Moru Village. The Forest Station is another 11 km along dirt tracks. Mountain Rock Lodge can also arrange transport to the Forest Station for US$60 for up to 10 people.

It is also possible to walk through the forest direct from Mountain Rock Hotel to the Forest Station, via the caves where Mau Mau fighters were based during The Emergency (see the Kenya History section). There are many tracks in the forest, so a guide is essential here. The 13-km walk takes four to five hours.

In the Forest Station compound a barrier crosses the track, and the route starts here.

Stage 1: Gathiuru Forest Station to Kampi Ya Machengeni

(10 km, 4-5 hours, 600 metres ascent)
In the forest station there's a barrier which is closed in wet conditions. Beyond the forest station there are many logging tracks which cause confusion, but keep heading roughly eastwards for about one hour, to leave the plantation area and enter natural forest. Soon after this, the path widens slightly: this grassy area is called Elephant Camp. If you walked from Mountain Rock Hotel, you could camp here. Water is available from the nearby stream.

After Elephant Camp you enter the bamboo forest and continue following a faint path along a vague ridge. There are buffalo and elephant in this section of the forest so make a noise as you walk. (You probably will be anyway.) After three to four hours you reach a clearing in the forest. This is Kampi Ya Machengeni (3000 metres). Water is available from the nearby stream.

Stage 2: Kampi Ya Machengeni to Highland Castle

(5 km, 4-5 hours, 700 metres)
From Kampi Ya Machengeni, the gradient gets steeper. Continue through the bamboo for about one hour, then enter the heathland zone, and after another 30 to 45 minutes you leave the trees behind and reach the moorland. There are a few old marker posts around, but no path. Head right and up, across a broad expanse of moorland, until you reach a point overlooking the Burguret River, after another one to two hours. Do not go down to this river but traverse below the crags of Highland Castle which are above you on the left. At the base of one of the crags is a large cave (3700 metres). This is a good site, with room to pitch your tent inside the cave if you wanted. Water is available from the Burguret River, about 10 minutes away.

Stage 3A: Highland Castle to Mackinder's Camp

(8 km, 6-8 hours, 500 metres)
(This stage follows the top section of the Old Moses Route. The lower section of this route

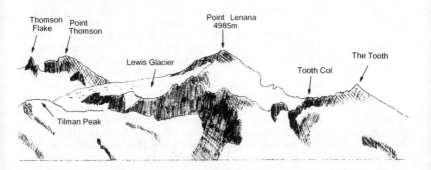

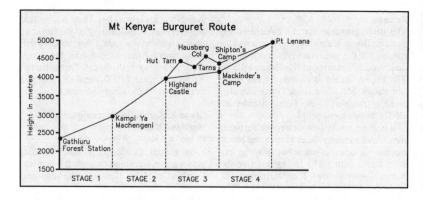

Mt Kenya: Burguret Route

is completely overgrown and no longer used.) From Highland Castle, drop to cross the Burguret River then aim south-west, over the next ridge, or contour round it, descending slightly to reach a small col. The going can be hard over tussock grass and takes one to two hours. Drop down into the next valley, to reach the stream that flows into the North Naro Moru River, and follow this uphill, keeping to its north bank for another hour until you see another larger col on the ridge to your south with a large rocky outcrop at its western side. Work your way up though mud and tussock grass to reach this col, then aim east along the crest of a broad ridge, passing several small outcrops. There is no clear path. After 1½ to two hours from the larger col, start to tend right then contour off the ridge-crest to reach the main North Naro Moru River and the path which runs along its north bank leading to Mackinder's Camp (4200 metres), reached after another 1½ to two hours.

From Mackinder's you can reach the summit of Point Lenana the following morning, as detailed in Stage 3 of the Naro Moru Route description.

Stage 3B: Highland Castle to Shipton's Camp

(9 km, 6½ to 8½ hours, 530 metres)
From the cave below Highland Castle, pass beneath the other crags and then go up to regain the crest of the ridge.

Continue heading east, as the ridge becomes broad and featureless. There is a faint path in places and occasional cairns. Two to three hours from Highland Castle the ridge levels out for a short section, and you cross some flat areas of gravel.

Continue gaining height, keeping right (south-east), aiming to the right of the main peaks which are now clearly visible. The path becomes clearer as you swing back eastwards and descend slightly to reach Hut Tarn (4490 metres) four to five hours from Highland Castle. Camping is possible here, if you want to break this stage. There is also a small hut (Two Tarn Hut), but this may be removed in the future.

You are now on the Summit Circuit Path. Looking north from Hut Tarn, you can see a large ridge called Arthur's Seat extending westwards out from the main peaks, and ending abruptly at a large cliff-face called the Eastern Terminal. North of this is another cliff-face called the Western Terminal.

Keeping Hut Tarn to your right, follow the path, keeping left, down to reach Nanyuki Tarn and then round the west side of the Eastern Terminal. With the cliffs on your right, follow the path over a small col between Arthur's Seat and the Western Terminal (the path to the right (east) of Arthur's Seat is harder and very steep down on the other side), then descend to Hausberg Tarn and Oblong Tarn, about one to two hours from Hut Tarn.

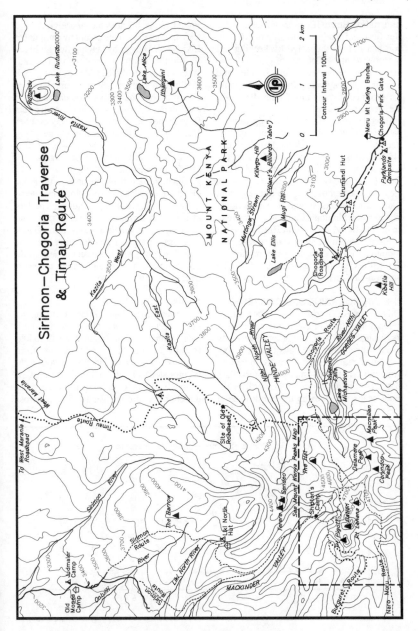

Sirimon–Chogoria Traverse & Timau Route

Alternative Route If you are not camping at Hut Tarn, and heading on to Shipton's Camp, you can reduce this stage by keeping left (north-east) at the flat area of gravel two to three hours from Highland Castle, and making your way below (north of) Nanyuki Tarn to meet the Summit Circuit Path near the Western Terminal.

From Hausberg Tarn and Oblong Tarn the path goes between the two tarns and zig-zags steeply up scree to reach the Hausberg Col (4591 metres). From here, you drop steeply down a slope of yellow scree to reach Kami Tarn. (There are two old huts here, although they may be removed in the future.) From Kami Tarn continue straight down the valley side to reach Shipton's Camp (4230 metres), about 2½ to 3½ hours from Hut Tarn.

From Shipton's Camp, you can reach the summit of Point Lenana on the morning of the following day, as described in the Sirimon-Chogoria Traverse.

THE SIRIMON-CHOGORIA TRAVERSE

This is an ideal trek for self-contained, independent trekkers, with several alternative stages available. The shortest way you can do it requires five days (four nights), and goes via the campsites at Judmaier, Shipton's, Hall Tarns and the Chogoria Park Gate. This route passes to the north of the main peaks and goes up the North Face of Point Lenana. It's possible (and advisable) to take another day on the ascent by camping at Liki North Hut, or by staying two nights at Shipton's before ascending to Lenana. Another day can also be added by going back to Shipton's after Lenana, completing a circuit of the main peaks. You can also add another day by going south of the main peaks from Shipton's, camping on the way at either Hut Tarn or American Camp, before going up to Lenana via the South-west Ridge. These additions turn the traverse into a very satisfying trek of seven or eight days.

The traverse can also be done in the other direction. An advantage of doing it in reverse is that it's easier to arrange guides and porters in Chogoria town, at the start of the route (they are not available at the Sirimon Gate). The disadvantage of this direction is a very long first stage, which is easier done coming down, although you can arrange transport over most of it in Chogoria.

Access

This route starts at the Sirimon Gate, on the north-west side of the mountain. The park gate is linked to the main Nanyuki-Isiolo road by a dirt track. If you're driving from Nanyuki, look for the junction on your right (signposted) about 15 km north-east of Nanyuki. If you're coming from the other direction, go through Timau Village, across

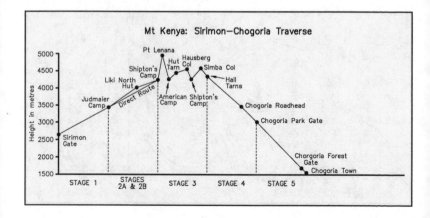

Mt Kenya: Sirimon–Chogoria Traverse

a large bridge over the Sirimon River, and the dirt track is on your left, about one km from the bridge. If you're on public transport, ask to be dropped at the Sirimon junction.

From the junction to the gate is nine km along the dirt track, which climbs gently through the forest. If you have no transport, the walk is useful for limbering up. There are three forks along the way – keep left at each one to reach the gate.

Camping is permitted here and it's outside the park so no entrance fee is payable, although you might need to pay an overnight fee.

Stage 1: Sirimon Gate to Judmaier Camp

(9 km, 3-4 hours, 690 metres ascent)
From the gate follow the park track as it winds uphill through the forest, which becomes heathland after about three hours. After another hour, the track veers right and crosses a small stream next to some concrete blocks and an old barrier. Just before the stream, on the left, is Judmaier Camp (3340 metres), a flat area in between large clumps of heather. If you're not camping, ten minutes further up the hill is the Old Moses Camp bunkhouse.

From Judmaier Camp, the summits of Batian and Nelion are visible to the south, just to the right of two other peaks called Terere and Sendeo, which look larger than the main peaks when viewed from this angle. When the main peaks are obscured by cloud, Terere and Sendeo do a good imitation, and this confuses a lot of people!

Stage 2A: Judmaier Camp to Shipton's Camp (direct)

(13 km, 6-7 hours, 890 metres ascent)
From Judmaier Camp, follow the track uphill, forking left at the junction after ten minutes (right goes to the Old Moses Camp bunkhouse). Continue, passing three more forks: keep right at each. One hour from Judmaier the track crosses a stream and reaches a fork (straight on goes to Liki North Hut). Go right, contouring through moorland

on a disused track for half an hour, until a path forks off the track on the left, aiming uphill towards a ridge. You should reach the crest of this ridge 2½ to three hours from Judmaier Camp.

Drop to cross the Liki North River and go up to the top of another large ridge overlooking the Mackinder Valley, reached after another hour. From here you get good views up the valley towards the main peaks.

The path goes up the left (east) side of the Mackinder Valley, gradually gaining height and getting nearer the main Liki River, which is down to your right. After one to 1½ hours the path from Liki North Hut comes in from the left. Continue up the valley for another hour to cross the river and reach a flat grassy area below a cliff of small overhangs called Shipton's Caves. The path goes steeply up the valley side to the right of the caves to reach easier ground and the Shipton's Camp campsite after another 30 minutes (4230 metres). The campsite has a toilet block, and water is available from the stream. If you're not camping, the Shipton's Camp bunkhouse is another five minutes up the path. The campsite has an excellent setting, below the looming north faces of Nelion and Batian.

Stage 2B: Judmaier Camp to Shipton's Camp (via Liki North Hut)

(13 km, 8-9½ hours, 890 metres, total 1 or 2 days)
This stage is harder than Stage 2A, as it crosses more ridges, and it is less frequently used, but the scenery is better. The path is not clear, so care and good map-reading are required. This stage can be broken into two by overnighting at Liki North Hut. Porters do not like going this way, and usually refuse to sleep at Liki North Hut, but this is no problem if you're trekking independently. (If you have porters, you could send them on to Shipton's Camp and meet them the following day.)

From Judmaier Camp, follow the directions in Stage 2A, until you reach the fork

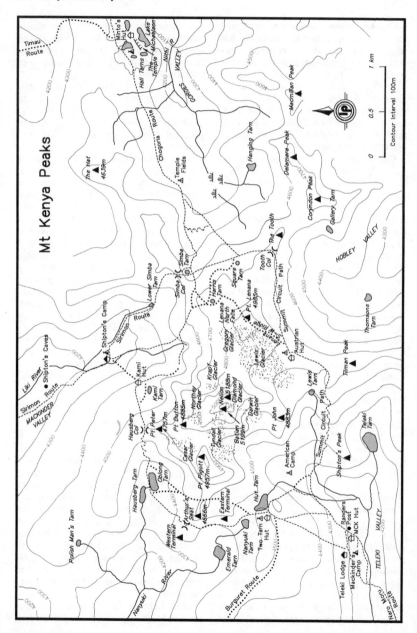

Mt Kenya Peaks

after one hour. (The path off to the right is the direct route to Shipton's.) Go straight on, aiming towards a rounded hill on the near skyline called The Barrow, then tend right (south) round the head of a large valley, crossing several small streams to reach a ridge crest between the Ontulili and Liki North valleys, three to four hours from Judmaier Camp. Drop to cross the stream and reach Liki North Hut (3990 metres), after another hour. The hut is small and basic (and may be removed in future) but there's plenty of room for camping nearby.

From Liki North Hut the path leads up the west side of the valley, over a ridge, then down into the Mackinder Valley to meet the direct route after 1½ to two hours. From here follow the directions in Stage 2A, to reach Shipton's Camp.

Options from Shipton's Camp

For the next stage of this trek, from Shipton's Camp to Hall Tarns, you have four main options:

Stage 3A You can go from Shipton's Camp direct to Hall Tarns via Point Lenana;

Stage 3B You can stay two nights at Shipton's, and on the day in between go to Point Lenana and come back down the same route;

Stage 3C You can stay two nights at Shipton's, and on the day in between go to Point Lenana, then come back a longer way, south of the main peaks.

Stage 3D You can go south of the main peaks first, via Hut Tarn and American Camp, to reach Lenana then continue to Hall Tarns.

Stage 3A is the shortest (only one day), but this means carrying your gear to the summit (unless you've got porters). All the other stages require two days. On stages 3B and 3C, after returning to Shipton's, you go to Hall Tarns next day direct via Simba Col. Either of these options is better if you don't want to carry your gear all the way up to the

summit. Stage 3C is one of the most spectacular sections of trekking on the whole mountain, and well worth spending the extra day on. Stage 3D does part of 3C in reverse, and ideally takes two days, but also means taking your gear to the summit.

Stage 3A: Shipton's Camp to Hall Tarns Hut (via Harris Tarn & Point Lenana)

(3½-5 hours, 755 metres ascent,
plus 2-3 hours, 685 metres descent)
Some parties with guides do the first section of this stage in the dark, to reach Harris Tarn by first light, and Point Lenana by sunrise, but the path is not always clear and this is not recommended for independent trekkers, especially if weather conditions obscure the route. If you'd like to do this section in the dark, and there's a group with a guide in the bunkhouse, you could ask to join them, offering to make a small payment to the guide or leader. Alternatively, ask one of the workers at the bunkhouse to show you the way (again, for a small fee).

From the campsite and bunkhouse, go up a steep stony gully that cuts through a cliff, clearly visible a few hundred metres directly in front of the bunkhouse. (Do not go left (east) on the path towards Lower Simba Tarn.) At the top of the gully, head right across open ground then go steeply up the crest of a broad ridge of scree, aiming roughly due south, keeping the main peaks on your right side on the other side of a large valley. This section is a long, hard slog, and the path is indistinct in places, although marked by occasional cairns. After two to three hours of walking from Shipton's you'll reach Harris Tarn. Near the ridge crest, keep aiming up and avoid heading left too far. From Harris Tarn, the entire north face of Lenana, rising to the pointed summit, is visible. Note two *gendarmes* (pinnacles) at the end of a short ridge to the right (northwest) of the summit. From the tarn, the path first tends right of the tarn, then up and leftwards across the top of the slope behind (west of) the tarn, aiming for the left (east) side of the face, then swings back right (west) at the foot of a series of cliffs below the summit, aiming for a point on the ridge in between the summit and the gendarmes. From here the route goes up the ridge, tending right after 50 metres, to meet the route up from Austrian Hut just below a short rock step. Scramble up this to reach the summit, marked by white rocks, a cross and several marker-poles. This is one of the most exhilarating sections of walking on the whole mountain, but it can be serious in bad weather and impassable after snow. Allow another 1½ to two hours to get from Harris Tarn to the summit.

(If this section of the route is impassable, you can still reach Lenana from Harris Tarn. Drop to Simba Tarn then follow a faint path southwards to Square Tarn and go round to the south side of Lenana via Tooth Col to reach Austrian Hut. From here, approach Lenana by the South-west Ridge, as outlined in the Naro Moru Route description.)

Views from the summit of Lenana are spectacular (see the Naro Moru Route description).

Options from Lenana to Hall Tarns

From the summit of Lenana, there are two ways down to Hall Tarns. If the ascent route up the North Face from Harris Tarn was not passable, do not attempt to descend it. If it was clear, you can retrace this back to Harris Tarn and from there go down to Simba Tarn and the top of the Gorges Valley. Go down the valley, keeping right to avoid large cliffs just after the tarn, to meet a clear path leading to Hall Tarns (about two hours from Lenana).

Alternatively, you can drop down the South-west Ridge to Austrian Hut, and from there come round the south side of Lenana.

If it is misty, the section between Austrian Hut and Tooth Col can be difficult to follow. Several trekkers have become seriously lost here. If you lose the path, it is very important not to drop steeply down into the Hobley Valley. The path contours round the head of the valley, dropping only gradually, before a short steep section up to Tooth Col. Some green marker posts have recently been put along this route. From Tooth Col, drop to Square Tarn and then steeply down into the

top of the Gorges Valley on the scree-slope overlooking a flat grassy area called Temple Fields. Here you'll meet the clear path coming down from Simba Tarn leading to Hall Tarns (about three hours from Lenana).

Hall Tarns Area

There are several good places for camping around the picturesque Hall Tarns (4300 metres). Nearby is Minto's Hut, a tin shack in bad condition, used mainly by porters, although some trekkers without tents do sleep there. (This hut may be removed in the future.)

Water used to be available here, but the tarns have been polluted by the washing of countless greasy billy-cans by thoughtless trekkers and their porters, so now you have to get it from a stream back up the path, about 20 minutes before you reach the tarns. Do not wash anything in the tarns and they might recover.

As a short sidetrack, you can go to the top of the nearby huge cliff, called The Temple, which overlooks Lake Michaelson and the Gorges Valley. To get to the edge of the cliff from the tarns, aim south, across the bare rock slabs for about five minutes. It's a sheer drop of over 300 metres to the valley bottom, so don't wander around on the top of The Temple in misty conditions!

Stage 3B: Shipton's Camp to Point Lenana & return (direct)

(3½-5 hours, 755 metres ascent,
plus 2-4 hours, 755 metres descent)
From Shipton's Camp, follow the directions to the summit of Lenana as in Stage 3A. From the summit, return to Shipton's either direct via the North Face or the longer way via the South-west Ridge, Tooth Col (as described in Options from Lenana) and either Harris Tarn or Simba Col.

Stage 3C: Shipton's Camp to Point Lenana & return (via American Camp and Hut Tarn)

(3½-5 hours, 755 metres ascent,
plus 5½-7½ hours, 755 metres descent)
This stage goes to Point Lenana then returns

to Shipton's by going south of the main peaks along the Summit Circuit Path. It is one of the most spectacular stages on the mountain and should not be missed. With an early start, fit trekkers can do this stage in a day, which means you can leave your tent and gear at Shipton's and travel light. Alternatively, you can do this stage in two days in the other direction, as described in Stage 3D.

From Shipton's Camp, follow the directions to the summit of Lenana as in Stage 3A. From Lenana, descend the South-west Ridge to Austrian Hut, then follow the clear path south and then south-west, steeply down scree into the head of the Teleki Valley towards Mackinder's Camp. At the bottom of the steep scree slope, head-right, away from the path across an area of groundsels and boulders, then up the other side of the valley to reach American Camp, a small patch of grass on the northern side of the head of the valley (1½ to two hours from Lenana). Up to your left is the classic view of Mt Kenya's south-west face, with the long, thin Diamond Glacier leading up to the Gates of the Mists between the summits of Batian and Nelion.

From here go steeply up the scree to the north-west of American Camp to reach Hut Tarn (4490 metres) after less than an hour. (Next to the tarn is Two Tarn Hut, although this may be removed in the future.)

From Hut Tarn, you can see a large ridge extending westwards out from the main peaks. This is called Arthur's Seat, after a rocky hill in Edinburgh which it resembles, and it ends abruptly at a large cliff-face called the Eastern Terminal. North of this is another cliff-face called the Western Terminal.

Keeping Hut Tarn to your right, follow the path, tending left, down to reach Nanyuki Tarn and then round the west side of the Eastern Terminal, scrambling over large boulders. With the cliffs on your right, the path climbs over a small col between Arthur's Seat and the Western Terminal, then descends to Hausberg Tarn and Oblong Tarn, about one to two hours from Hut Tarn.

The path goes between the two tarns and zig-zags steeply up a scree slope to reach the

Hausberg Col (4591 metres). From here, you drop steeply down a slope of yellow scree to reach Kami Tarn. There are two huts here: one belongs to the MCK and is supposedly for members only, although in recent years the lock has been forced several times and the hut may soon become disused; the other is a public hut, with tin walls and a dirt floor, providing very basic shelter. (Both huts may be removed in the future.)

From Kami Tarn continue straight down the valley side to reach Shipton's Camp, about one to 1½ hours from Hausberg Col.

Stage 3D: Shipton's Camp to Hall Tarns (via American Camp & Point Lenana)

(6-9½ hours, 755 metres ascent,
plus 2-3 hours, 685 metres descent,
total 1 or 2 days)

This route follows most of Stage 3C in reverse, going to the south of the main peaks along a spectacular section of the Summit Circuit Path on the way to Point Lenana, so only brief directions are given here. Although this stage can be done in a day by fit and well-acclimatized trekkers, it means getting to the summit of Lenana in the afternoon, when there might be more chance of mist. It's far better to camp an extra night on the way, at either Hut Tarn or American Camp, and spread this stage over two days.

From Shipton's Camp a faint path leads steeply up the valley side to the south-west, aiming for a ridge-crest to the right (north) of the main peaks. Go up this path to reach Kami Tarn.

From the tarn the path climbs up a yellow scree slope to a low point on the next ridge, Hausberg Col (4591 metres), about 1½ to two hours from Shipton's. Drop down the scree on the other side of the col, heading towards Oblong Tarn and Hausberg Tarn, reached after another 30 minutes. Beyond the tarns, a large ridge called Arthur's Seat extends westwards out from the main peaks and ends abruptly at a large cliff-face called the Western Terminal. The main path leads between the two tarns then climbs up scree to a col in between the Western Terminal and the highest point of Arthur's Seat. (Avoid tending too far left immediately after the tarns, as this leads to another faint path which climbs much more steeply over serious scree to reach a col on the east side of Arthur's Seat summit.)

The path drops down the other side of the col and crosses large boulders at the base of steep cliffs to reach Nanyuki Tarn. Keep this tarn on your right, then go up over rock terraces to reach Hut Tarn (4490 metres), one to 1½ hours from Oblong Tarn. You can camp here or stay in the small Two Tarn Hut (which may be removed in future), or drop down the scree slope to the south of the tarn to reach American Camp (4300 metres) after another 30 minutes. This is a flat grassy area with plenty of room for tents, and fine views of the south-west side of the main peaks. There are no facilities here. Water is available from the nearby stream, so far unpolluted. Keep it that way.

From American Camp a path aims south to the head of the Teleki Valley and meets the main path from Mackinder's Camp leading up to Austrian Hut and Point Lenana, at the foot of the large scree slope, half an hour from Mackinder's. For details of this section see the Naro Moru Route description. From American Camp to Austrian Hut takes two to four hours. From Austrian Hut to the summit of Lenana, via the South-west Ridge, takes another 45 minutes to one hour.

From the summit of Lenana you have two choices for descending to Hall Tarns: via Austrian Hut and Tooth Col (three hours), or via Harris Tarn and Simba Tarn (two hours), as described in Options from Lenana. The second option should not be taken in bad visibility, or if snow obscures the route, as the path zig-zags between steep cliffs and a route-finding error could be fatal.

Stage 4A: Hall Tarns to Chogoria Gate (direct)

(14 km, 4½-6½ hours, 1280 metres descent)
This is the usual way of descending from Hall Tarns to the Chogoria Park Gate, although an alternative route, via the Gorges Valley, is possible (see Stage 4B). On the direct route there's no water between the hut

and the stream near the roadhead (three to four hours).

From Hall Tarns Hut the path aims easterly, through some bowl-like depressions then past an area of rocks eroded like mushrooms, to follow a broad ridge crest with the main Gorges Valley down to the right (south). On clear days you get spectacular views down into the valley, past huge rock towers and pinnacles, with Lake Michaelson and the Vivienne Falls below. Looking the other way, to the left (north-east), you can see across the moorland to the subsidiary peaks of Ithanguni and Rutundu, and to their right (south) to the flat-topped hill called Kilingo, or the Giant's Billiards Table. After three to four hours the path crosses a stream. Go up the far bank to reach the Chogoria Roadhead. You could camp here (there's a toilet block and water available from the stream), but it's normally used only by trekkers coming up this route.

From the roadhead, follow the track down through the giant heather and forest for another 1½ to two hours, ignoring a track that comes in from the left about one km from the roadhead, to reach the park gate (3017 metres).

Alternatively, from the roadhead you can follow the path that leads through heather and bush to the south of the track. This path is overgrown in places and crossed by animal trails, so a compass is essential. This is also a favourite area for buffalo, so make a lot of noise as you walk. After an hour you'll reach the edge of the forest and Urumandi Hut. The hut is in bad condition, but there's plenty of room for camping in the pleasant glade (more useful if you're coming up this route). Just before the hut the path crosses a stream, which is on a high natural bridge; water is available from the stream, which is reached by a steep path that goes down the gorge side on the east side of the bridge. (Urumandi means 'the place where water flows underground'.) From Urumandi Hut a track leads in an easterly direction through the forest (keep making anti-buffalo noises) to reach the gate after 1½ hours.

Just before the park gate, on the right side of the track, is the Parklands campsite. You can also camp at the gate itself (with permission from the rangers), but if you've already paid park fees for this day, it won't save you any money. Accommodation is also available in the Meru Mt Kenya Bandas, a group of simple log cabins about 500 metres from the gate. Beds with sheets and blankets, log fires, hot showers, and a small shop selling beer and chocolate tempt many a hardened camper after a long Mt Kenya trek (see the Places to Stay section)!

Note that the Chogoria Park Gate may be moved to a position lower down the mountain in the future. Make inquiries locally before starting your trek.

Stage 4B: Hall Tarns to Chogoria Gate (via Gorges Valley)

(15 km, 6½-9 hours, 1280 metres descent)
This alternative stage is for experienced trekkers only, and not advisable if you're feeling tired from the previous day's summit push. It is extremely rarely used and very few guides know the way. A compass (that you know how to use) is essential. There is no path to follow, and you must wade through bog, tussock grass and dense bush for much of the distance. However, it is a spectacular route, along the floor of the valley, round the shore of Lake Michaelson, down beside the Vivienne Falls, and below the giant caves and pinnacles that cannot be seen from the main route.

From Hall Tarns aim west for a short distance, back towards the main peaks, then swing right (south) and descend steeply in to the valley, with the main cliffs of The Temple to your left. Cross the stream and follow it in an easterly direction through the gorge. Recross it just above a waterfall overlooking Lake Michaelson. Keep right, away from the stream and drop to the lake, re-crossing the stream again just before the lake. From this viewpoint the sheer size of The Temple is apparent. The cliffs are made up of lava columns, and at one point they have been eroded from below to overhang, resembling organ pipes.

Hack through the tussock grass round the right (south) side of the lake to cross the stream where it leaves the lake, just above a small waterfall and a point where the stream flows underground.

Descend steeply to cross a wide, very boggy section, where a stream crosses from the left. You can see the 'mushroom rocks' on the skyline up on the left. At the end of the boggy section the valley drops very steeply down and the stream plunges over the Vivienne Falls. You need to keep right to avoid the large cliffs, but it's still very steep and hard going through dense bush. Where the valley floor levels out again you get a great view back up to the falls. Up to your left (north) are several huge pyramidal rock buttresses, dominating this section of the valley. Continue down the valley, through high tussock grass, crossing and re-crossing the stream several times. About an hour from the foot of the falls, keep to the left side of the stream and go up the valley side to avoid several boggy sections, and cross some sections of exposed boulders. The large, rounded Kibatia Hill should be on your right. Cross to the right side of the river and contour round the base of the hill until you can see a path leading down the opposite bank to the river. Cross the stream to gain this path, which leads uphill to meet the main path coming down from Hall Tarns about 20 minutes above the Chogoria Roadhead. From Hall Tarns to the roadhead by this route takes five to seven hours. It's then another 1½ to two hours to the park gate (see Stage 4A).

Stage 5: Chogoria Park Gate to Chogoria Town

(29 km, 6-8 hours, 1500 metres descent)
From the park gate a dirt track winds down through the forest for 23 km to the forest gate. The track is sometimes impassable for cars after rain, but you'll have no problem getting through on foot. The walk is not hard, but it can seem very long after several days trekking on the mountain. There are no junctions to worry about, but unfortunately no views either, as the route passes through thick bamboo and forest; after a while you'll switch into automatic pilot and just keep plodding down.

From the Forest Station gate at the end of

the track, it's still about six km through fields and villages to Chogoria town. If the first 23 km is enough for one day, you can ask to camp at the Forest Station here. Supplies are available from nearby *dukas*.

If you don't want to walk, you might be lucky and find a lift going down some of the way. Vehicles from Chogoria town often bring trekkers up to this point and go down empty. You'll still need to negotiate a fair fee, though. The drivers will look to see how tired you seem and raise the price accordingly! You can sometimes also arrange a lift in the landrover from the bandas. The starting price is around 2000 KSh (US$40) for the vehicle (but don't expect to have it all to yourself).

THE CHOGORIA-SIRIMON TRAVERSE

The Sirimon-Chogoria Traverse already described can also be done in reverse. Much of the information required is in that description, but a few things are important to know if you're going in this direction, so the route is described briefly here.

Stage 1: Chogoria Town to Chogoria Park Gate

(29 km, 7-10 hours, 1500 metres ascent)
This is a long stage, along a dirt road through the forest, although conditions underfoot are not too strenuous and route-finding is no problem. To reduce this walk you can camp at the bottom forest gate, near the Forest Station six km from the town, and only have 23 km to walk the next day. This stage can also be broken in two by camping at Bairunyi Clearing, about two-thirds of the way up, but water supplies here are not reliable, so you'll have to carry all you need for a night's stop, which makes the walk even harder. It's better to make an early start and go for it in one day. Alternatively, arrange a lift up to the park gate at one of the hotels in Chogoria town mentioned in the Places to Stay section. This will cost between KSh 1500 and KSh 2000 for the vehicle. Note that the track is sometimes impassable after rain, especially the last seven km, which are very steep. To cut costs you might be able to arrange a lift as

far as Bairunyi Clearing or the bottom of the steep section, and walk the rest of the way.

Note that the Chogoria Park Gate may be moved to a position lower down the mountain in the future. Make enquiries locally before starting your trek.

Sidetrack: Lake Ellis, Mugi Hill & Kilingo
If you do get a lift up to Chogoria Gate, it's worth spending two days here or at the Chogoria Roadhead, to help acclimatization. On the day in between you can sidetrack to Mugi Hill, Lake Ellis and Kilingo Hill (also called the Giant's Billiards Table). To reach these, take the branch that heads right off the track about one km below the roadhead. A small track descends to a stream. Just before the stream a faint path leads uphill with the stream on the left. Continue this way for 1½ to two hours to reach the lake. About halfway up this path you can cross the stream and walk through light bush to reach the summit of Mugi Hill. There is no path.

From the summit of Mugi Hill, you can make out the easiest way to the top of the flat-topped Kilingo Hill. Again there is no path. The best way is to aim east from Mugi Hill, down across the Mutonga stream and then up Kilingo on its north-eastern side.

Vervet monkey

Stage 2: Chogoria Park Gate to Hall Tarns

(14 km, 6-9 hours, 1280 metres ascent)

From the park gate follow the track up to the Chogoria Roadhead (two to three hours). Camping is possible here. There are toilets, and water is available from the stream, but there are no other facilities.

From the roadhead, the path drops to cross a stream then follows the broad ridge to the east of the Gorges Valley to reach Hall Tarns (4297 metres), about four to six hours from the roadhead. The longer alternative stage, via the Gorges Valley, is not recommended as an ascent route.

Stage 3A: Hall Tarns to Shipton's Camp (via Harris Tarn & Point Lenana)

(4½-7 hours, 685 metres ascent, plus 2-4 hours, 755 metres descent)

From Hall Tarns the path aims westwards towards the main peaks and divides after about an hour, above a flat green area at the head of the valley known as Temple Fields. (The left path aims south-west steeply up to Square Tarn and Tooth Col.) Go straight on, then keep left to avoid steep cliffs, to reach Simba Tarn, and from there follow a faint path up steep scree to Harris Tarn (reached after another two to three hours). For details of the route from Harris Tarn to Point Lenana by the North Face see Stage 3A of the Sirimon-Chogoria Traverse description.

The North Face is a serious route and can be blocked by snow. If it is blocked, Lenana can still be reached if you go to Square Tarn and through Tooth Col to reach Austrian Hut. If it is misty, the section between Tooth Col and Austrian Hut can be tricky, and several trekkers have become seriously lost here. The important thing is not to drop down into the Hobley Valley. The path contours round the head of the valley and rises slightly to reach Austrian Hut. Some green marker posts have recently been put along this route. From Austrian Hut, approach the summit of Lenana by the South-west Ridge (for details see Stage 3 of the Naro Moru Route description).

From the summit of Lenana you have two choices. If the section up the North Face from Harris Tarn is passable, you can retrace this way, back to Harris Tarn, and from there down the scree to Shipton's Camp (two to three hours). If the North Face is blocked by snow, do not attempt to descend this way. The other way is down the South-west Ridge to Austrian Hut, then east, round the head of the Hobley Valley, through Tooth Col, past Square Tarn and Simba Col, and down to Shipton's (three to four hours).

Stage 3B: Hall Tarns to Shipton's Camp via Point Lenana & American Camp

(4½-7 hours, 685 metres ascent, plus 4-5½ hours, 755 metres descent)

This is a long route which can be done in a day if you're fit and well-acclimatized, but it is much better split into two with a night at either American Camp or Hut Tarn.

Follow the same directions from Hall Tarns to Lenana as described in Stage 3A, ascending either via Harris Tarn or via Tooth Col and Austrian Hut. From Lenana, descend to Austrian Hut, then head west, keeping south of the main peaks, to American Camp (1½ to two hours from Lenana) and round the Summit Circuit Path, via Oblong Tarn and Kami Hut, as described in Stage 3D of the Sirimon-Chogoria Traverse, to Shipton's (four to 5½ hours from American Camp).

Stage 4A: Shipton's Camp to Judmaier Camp (direct)

(13 km, 3-4 hours, 890 metres descent)

From Shipton's, the path aims north-west down the Mackinder Valley. About an hour from Shipton's Camp, the path divides: fork left, closer to the river, for the direct route. (Right is the longer route – see Stage 4B.) Continue down the valley, over the ridge at the end, across the Liki North River, to descend and meet the old track down to Judmaier Camp.

Stage 4B: Shipton's Camp to Judmaier Camp (via Liki North Hut)

(13 km, 4-5 hours, 890 metres descent)

From Shipton's follow the Stage 4A directions to the fork. (Left is the direct route.) Go right, slightly up then more steeply, to cross a ridge and descend to Liki North Hut. The path climbs over the next ridge, then descends and swings round the head of a broad valley with the Barrow up to the right (north-east), to drop and meet the track that leads down to Judmaier Camp.

Stage 5: Judmaier Camp to Sirimon Park Gate

(9 km, 2-3 hours, 690 metres descent)
The track down to the park gate is easy to follow.

THE TIMAU ROUTE

This is a very rarely used route on the northern side of Mt Kenya, which joins the Chogoria Route at Hall Tarns to the east of the main peaks. It follows a good track on the lower slopes, but this deteriorates gradually into nothing about halfway up the mountain. For the final section of the route, there is no path at all and you walk through open country, relying totally on your map and compass for navigation. There are no facilities of any kind, although there are several good places to camp, making this is an excellent route for experienced, self-contained trekkers.

From the start of the route to Hall Tarns usually takes three days (two nights, with the third night at Hall Tarns). The long first stage

can be driven, which cuts the walking by one day, although if you do this you should camp two nights on the ascent to help acclimatization. If you're walking, this stage can be split into two sections, and the second section can be joined to Stage 2. From Hall Tarns you can reach Point Lenana by various ways in anything from a few hours to a few days, depending on your route (see the Chogoria-Sirimon Traverse for details). After Lenana, you can descend on the Sirimon, the Chogoria or the Naro Moru route, with one or two more nights, to reach the foot of the mountain.

There is no park gate on this route, so before starting out you have to pay park fees at either the Sirimon Gate (which is nearer) or the Naro Moru Gate. For safety reasons, all trekkers on the mountain have to sign out at a park gate after their trek. If you come down the Timau, you'll have to go to the Naro Moru or Sirimon Gate again afterwards.

It may be tempting to go up this route without paying park fees. Don't try it. The national park warden patrols the whole mountain by plane, and there are armed park rangers protecting the forest and moorland from poachers. If you're caught without tickets you could be arrested and fined.

Access

This route starts near Timau Village, which is 20 km north-east of Nanyuki, on the main

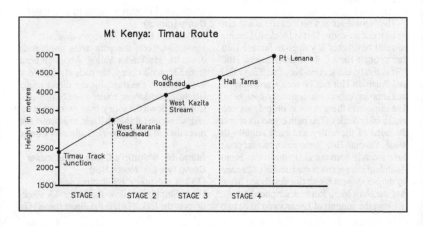

sealed road that circles the mountain. The first stage of this route follows vehicle tracks for 29 km to the West Marania roadhead at about 3300 metres, so if you have a car you can cut the first day's walking. It is also possible to arrange a lift to the roadhead at either Mountain Rock Hotel or Naro Moru River Lodge. (Naro Moru vehicles do not use the tracks described here but pass through the lodge's own farm to the west of this route.) But transport is by no means essential: the walk is not unpleasant or difficult, and also helps acclimatization. The first stage can also be split into two sections.

Stage 1: Timau Track Junction to West Marania Roadhead
(29 km, 8-10 hours, 860 metres ascent)
About six km east of Timau Village, the Timau track turns off the sealed road on the right, signposted to 'District Officer Timau', and 'CCM Nkiria Primary School'. If you're on public transport, get off at this junction. If you're driving from Nanyuki, turn right here.

From the junction, the dirt road passes through a small settlement then enters farmland, climbing gradually. There are many tracks in this area, so it's important to follow these directions closely. If you get lost, ask for the primary school. About three km from the main road junction, cross a bridge over a stream and immediately fork left, and 100 metres later go left again. After another one km, turn left. After another one km go straight on at a crossroads. After another one km turn right at a T-junction. About seven km from the main road junction you enter a forested area and reach another T-junction, where you go left and ignore the right fork immediately afterwards. The track fords a stream and after another one km leaves the forest and re-enters farmland. About 14 km from the main road junction you reach the CCM Primary School. After this there are fewer forks and the track is easier to follow, although driving conditions get a lot worse.

Continue uphill from the school. Leave the farmland and enter low heath. About two

km from the school, a firetower is visible on the top of a conical hill straight ahead. About five km from the school you pass a concrete water tank and some buildings. The track appears to stop at a gate, but actually turns right about 100 metres before this gate. This area, 19 km from the main road, is a good place to camp if you want to split this section. The next 10-km section could be done on its own, or joined to Stage 2.

As you continue up the track, you can see a radio mast on top of a hill to your right. About two km from the gate, the track swings sharply right and heads directly for the mast. After two km the track turns sharp left up the hillside opposite the mast. After one km more you emerge suddenly onto the edge of Mbaru Crater, the remains of a small volcano. To your left (south-east) you can see across the open moorland to the huge dome of Ithanguni, a subsidiary peak of Mt Kenya, with the smaller dome of Rutundu to its left (north). Follow the spectacular crest of the crater ridge for two km to meet a larger track (coming from Embari Farm), and pass two upright posts (which once had a sign attached). About one km beyond the posts (or four km from the first view of Mbaru Crater) the track reaches a steep rock-step. This is the West Marania roadhead (3300 metres). Vehicles should be left here as the track beyond is badly eroded in places. (Even if you drive to this point, it is recommended that you walk from here to help acclimatization.) To the left is the West Marania stream. Camping is possible here amongst the heather.

Stage 2: West Marania Roadhead to West Kazita Stream
(14 km, 4-5 hours, 550 metres ascent)
From the West Marania Roadhead follow the old track away from the stream and gradually uphill. Ten minutes from the roadhead, the path swings round to the left and you head towards a prominent peak to the south-west with an obvious rock-band. Behind you, to the north, the views open out. On a clear day, you can see across the dusty plains around

Isiolo, beyond the Ewaso Nyiro River, to the red block of Ololokwe Peak.

Continue gaining altitude gradually. About 1½ hours from the roadhead, a large bowl-shaped valley lies down to the left. The path meets an old dry stream bed and undulates slightly. Old wheel-tracks lead all over the place, but you should keep the stream on your left and continue, to reach a fairly flat section of the West Marania Valley in between two hills. About three to four hours from the roadhead you can see through a broad col on your left (east) towards the dome of Ithanguni.

Soon after this, the Sirimon Valley is clearly visible below and to the right (north-west). The path goes left and up to a col at the end of a ridge between the Sirimon and Kazita valleys, reached after another hour. (Several sections of the path are faint or non-existent in this area, so great care should be taken. Check frequently with your compass against the map.)

Go through the col, and drop down, keeping right (south-east), to cross two streams. By the second stream (20 minutes from the col) is an excellent camping spot (3850 metres).

Stage 3: West Kazita Stream to Hall Tarns

(9 km, 5½-7 hours, 450 metres ascent)
From the camping spot by the second stream, the path climbs to a spur on the east side of the valley, then turns sharply right (north) to follow the crest of the ridge between the West and East Kazita Valleys. Continue up the ridge for two to 2½ hours to reach a patch of boulders where the path seems to disappear. Keep right for a short distance, then up, rejoining the crest after a few minutes, to find the path again. After another 20 minutes the path stops abruptly. This is the old roadhead. You can still see the remains of a turning circle (4150 metres).

From the old roadhead you can see a flat spot in the ridge on the opposite (south) side of the East Kazita Valley. There is no path, so either drop down to cross the stream and go up to this flat spot, or contour round the valley sides. Next to the stream is another good area for camping if you want to break the trek here.

You'll reach the flat spot, which is marked by some small cairns, about one to 1½ hours from the old roadhead. There is no path but very little vegetation, so the going underfoot is not too hard. Pass through the flat spot and drop steeply down to cross the Nithi North stream, then steeply up the other side of the valley on scree and tussock grass to reach another col about two to three hours from the old roadhead.

Through the col is a steep, bouldery scree-slope. Go up this for about 30 minutes, tending slightly right, to reach the crest of the ridge running eastwards from the peak called The Hat, in between the Nithi and Gorges valleys. Hall Tarns are directly below, reached after another half hour.

For full details on the campsite at Hall Tarns, and nearby Minto's Hut, see the Sirimon-Chogoria Traverse description, noting especially the advice about water. The hut may be removed in the future, but this will not worry trekkers on the Timau route, who have to be completely self-contained anyway.

OTHER ROUTES

On old maps of Mt Kenya, you may notice several other routes from the foothills up to the main peak area of the mountain. No paths of any sort exist on these routes and the going is generally very hard. They are rarely, if ever, used and should not be attempted unless you are a very experienced trekker and have skilled local guides to accompany you. These include:

The Kamweti Route

On the south side of the massif, this route involves several days of hacking through the forest zone where it is at its most dense and impenetrable, followed by a long stretch across empty moorland on the upper slopes. The route runs from the old Castle Forest Resthouse, north of Kianyaga Village, and leads up the Hobley Valley. Trekkers attempting to follow this route as a descent, from the section of the Summit Circuit Path between Austrian Hut and Tooth Col, have become hopelessly lost.

The Old Moses Route

On the west side of the mountain, in between the Naro Moru Route and the Burguret Route, the lower section of this route also passes through a large section of dense forest. It is very rarely used and there is no path. Conditions in the forest are more serious than on the Burguret Route (see that route description for more details). The upper section of the route can be followed, and is described in the Burguret Route section.

The Kazita Route

On the north-east side of the mountain, the lower section of this route is also called the Meru Route. It starts near the village of Katheri, near Meru town, and leads past Rutundu Hill, before crossing a very wide area of open, pathless moorland to finally link with the Timau Route north of Hall Tarns.

The Aberdare Range

Many trekkers are surprised to find a Kenyan mountain range named after a town in Wales. These mountains, which stand between Mt Kenya and the Great Rift Valley, were named after Lord Aberdare, president of the Royal Geographical Society, by the explorer Joseph Thomson when he walked round the range in 1883.

The local Kikuyu people, who farmed the mountains' well-watered eastern slopes, called them Nyandarua, which means 'drying hide'. The shape of the range resembled an animal skin, pegged out to dry in the traditional way, with sticks under the spinal ridge to keep it clear of the ground. Although this African name is used, the range is still more generally known as The Aberdares.

To the west of the range, the Maasai herders on the Rift Valley plains used another name. They called the highest peak Oldoinyo Lesatima, 'the mountain of the bull-calf', and this name is used today, although it's usually shortened to the more manageable Satima. The summit is just over 4000 metres (13,120 feet), which makes the Aberdares the third-highest range in Kenya.

Like many of the mountains in East Africa, the Aberdares are volcanic in origin, but the magma which formed the range erupted from an elongated fissure and created an extended range of several peaks rather than the more usual single cone or dome. Most of the range falls within the boundaries of the Aberdare National Park, which also encloses a large area of forest, covering the lower hills on the east side of the main range, called The Salient. This is where most of the park's big game, including elephant, rhino, buffalo, lion and leopard are found, and most visitors who come to the park remain in this section, normally holed up at one of the famous 'tree-hotels'.

Above the forest, the peaks are surrounded by areas of bush and open grassy moorland, which make the Aberdares an ideal place for wilderness trekking. But The Salient gets most of the limelight and the high moorlands remain very little-visited and almost unknown as a trekking area.

One reason why trekkers don't come here very often is that the lions in the Aberdares are notoriously aggressive. During the 1980s some walkers were attacked and other visitors staying at remote campsites suffered from inquisitive lions pummelling tents during the night. In recent years there have been no reports of any more attacks, but all trekkers and wilderness campers in the park still have to be accompanied by an armed park ranger. Elephant and buffalo also come up from The Salient onto the high forest and moorland and, although you're fairly unlikely to see any wildlife while walking, the ranger is definitely not there for decoration.

The park regulations have led in turn to another problem, especially for independent trekkers – to do a trek in the Aberdares you need a car. There is no public transport into the park and you are not allowed to walk in. A car is also required to collect the ranger from the park headquarters, which is a long distance from the trekking area. Also, some campsites are several kilometres from the nearest water and, as porters are not available, again the vehicle comes in useful.

GEOGRAPHY

The Aberdare Range is a long, narrow massif, stretching north-south for about 70 km on the western side of the Central Highlands, in between Mt Kenya and the Great Rift Valley, with its southern end about 80 km north of Nairobi. Along the centre of the range, roughly following the north-south line, are the main peaks: Chebuswa (3364 metres), Satima (4001 metres) and Table Mountain (3791 metres) are in the Northern Moorland section of the park; Rurimueria (3860 metres) and Maratini (3698 metres) are in the Central Moorland; Kinangop (3906 metres) and The Elephant (3590 metres) are in the Southern Moorland. The Central Moorland is undulating, with rolling hills and deep valleys, but has no major peaks.

MAPS

The Survey of Kenya (SK) produces a tourist map of the Aberdare National Park which should be available from bookshops, but is usually hard to find (although it may have recently been re-printed). If you need more detail, the Aberdare Range is covered on the SK 1:50,000 sheets 120/1 (Ndaragwa), 120/3 (Kipipiri) and 134/1 (Kinangop) (but see notes on availability in the Kenya Maps section).

TREKKING INFORMATION

The usual way of doing a trek in the Aberdares is to use the vehicle to carry tents and gear from one campsite to the next, with one person driving while the others walk along tracks or through the bush with the ranger. Rental costs can be reduced if you get a group together. If you hire a car for about a week you can tie in an Aberdares trek with some game-viewing in The Salient, or with a visit to the nearby lakes Nakuru and Naivasha in the Rift Valley. Alternatively, you can join an organised trek.

Once you're up on the high moorland, you can walk for days here and see no other people or cars. This is the only trek in this book where a vehicle is required and, if you've got the money and inclination, it's highly recommended.

The trek described starts at an altitude of around 2900 metres and the highest point reached is the summit of Satima (4001 metres). If you're unacclimatized, you'll certainly feel the effects of altitude, especially on the Satima section, but you're unlikely to have any serious symptoms. If you do start to suffer, the advice is the same as on any other mountain – go down.

The nearest large town to the Aberdare Range is Nyeri, on the east side of the range, about 150 km by road from Nairobi. The national park headquarters is at Mweiga, seven km north of Nyeri on the main tarred road to Nyahururu. This is where you collect the park ranger.

Route Standard & Days Required

There are no set trekking routes in the Aberdares like those on Mt Kenya or the other major mountains. The lower slopes of the range are covered in thick forest, cut through in only a few places where dirt tracks lead to the park gates. On the upper slopes of the range, although the forest cover is not quite so dense, no footpaths exist and the going is still hard. So trekkers in this area usually follow the park tracks, although this part of the park sees very few vehicles and you're unlikely to be disturbed.

The trek described has no official name. It goes through several different types of vegetation zone, including woodland, giant heather, open moor and bamboo forest and also takes in the highest point of the Aberdares, and passes many of the range's most spectacular waterfalls, so I've called it the Aberdare Contrasts Trek. It is a suggestion only: experienced trekkers can put together many other routes.

Most of the trek keeps to park tracks and

although some of the daily distances are long, the going is easy underfoot and there are no major gradients. With your ranger, it is also possible to leave the tracks, and make your own way across open grassland or follow animal trails through forest and dense bush. In the forest areas, the going is hard and a few hours' bush-bashing each day is usually enough for most people. It also gets the adrenalin going when there are fresh buffalo or elephant droppings on the ground and you can never see more than a few metres in front of you. You never know what you might run into and it can be quite a relief to get back on the track!

Stage 3 of the trek goes above the forest and passes through open moorland. This is the most spectacular section of the route, with some excellent views. For the first half of this stage there is a faint path to follow and the going is not too hard, with only a gradual ascent. The second half involves making your own way through bog and tussock grass, which can be tiring (although there is an easier alternative return route).

The route described in this section takes four days, involving at least four nights in the park, although it can be reduced by omitting the first or last stage. The trek can also be extended by keen trekkers looking for more of a challenge (see the end of the trek description for details).

The trek can also be done in reverse, although the direction described here is better for acclimatization.

Guides & Porters

All trekkers in the park must be accompanied by an armed park ranger. He is provided to protect you in case of encounters with some of the lion or buffalo that inhabit the upper forest and moorlands. The ranger will also act as a guide during your trek, and will be particularly useful if you want to leave the park track for a while and go through the bush. All the rangers are well trained and speak English. Even though you are unlikely to see any large animals on your trek, do not underestimate the danger of wild animals in

the Aberdares: you should never walk too far away from your ranger.

Rangers have to be collected from the park headquarters at Mweiga, and cannot be picked up from any of the entrance gates. Although it may be possible to arrive at the headquarters in the afternoon and organise a ranger for the next day, it's better if you phone or write beforehand to make a reservation. Write to Assistant Warden, Aberdare National Park, PO Box 22, Nyeri (☎ (0171) 55024), saying that you need a ranger for trekking. State the number of days involved, and the dates when you will pick up and drop off the ranger. The fee for a ranger is KSh 200 per day. This goes to the national park; an extra tip for the ranger himself is appropriate after the trek if the service has been good.

The ranger will provide his own sleeping bag and waterproof jacket. You must provide him with food and a place to sleep. If tent space is limited, there are some huts near the route where the ranger will sleep (see the trek description for details).

Porters cannot be arranged. Because trekking in the Aberdares is unusual, there is no tradition in nearby villages of local men working as porters. This is not normally a problem, though, because a car is necessary anyway and can be used to transport gear and water supplies between camps.

Park Fees & Regulations

All visitors to the Aberdares National Park have to pay entrance fees. For non-residents these are: KSh 540 per day, KSh 180 per night for camping, KSh 85 per day for car. Residents pay KSh 55 per day and 30 per night. To stay in the Fishing Bandas costs KSh 340 per night (Ksh 60 for residents). These charges are likely to increase (see the note on Park Fees in the Mt Kenya section).

For the 'special' campsites in The Salient you pay all the usual entrance and camping fees, plus an extra KSh 1000 fee. This gives you exclusive use of the campsite.

There is only one track linking the Salient area to the upper forest and moorlands. To use this track you have to pass through a barrier near Ruhuruini Gate. The barrier is kept locked but you can get a key from the park headquarters. A refundable deposit of Ksh 600 is required.

Supplies

There is nowhere to buy food inside the park or at any of the entrance gates. The best place for shopping is Nyeri, where you can find most food items required for a trek. Alternatively, buy all the stuff you need in Nairobi (see Where to Buy Food, in the Facts for the Trekker chapter).

PLACES TO STAY
Nyeri

At the top end, *The Outspan Hotel* has most facilities and doubles at around US$62 including breakfast. Even smarter is the *Aberdare Country Club* near Mweiga, with doubles at US$129. (Both these places advertise car hire, but the vehicles are not self-drive, and are intended for game viewing in The Salient, rather than supporting moorland treks.)

In the main part of town, and down the scale in price and standard, is the *White Rhino Hotel*, an old colonial-style inn, with a bar and restaurant and doubles for KSh 700.

For something cheaper, try the *Central Hotel*, near the start of the road to Kiandongoro Gate at the top end of town, with doubles for about KSh 450. Even cheaper is the *Bahati Boarding & Lodging*, in the centre of town, with basic doubles for KSh 150.

In the National Park

The Salient This is the lower forested part of the national park, with the two 'tree-hotels', *Treetops* and *The Ark*. Both are famous and expensive, and a major highlight for many visitors to Kenya. Built on stilts overlooking waterholes, they are recommended for game viewing, especially at night, although with salt-licks and floodlights they seem slightly artificial. Prices vary according to season, but start at around US$150 for Treetops, or US$200 for The

Ark (although you can sometimes get good deals at travel agents in Nairobi). The experience is said to be worth it and it might be a good way to round off your trek. It's probably the only way you'll get a proper look at any of the Aberdares' wildlife.

In the same part of the park are eight 'special campsites' which can be hired exclusively by groups. There are five sites at Muringato, two at Kigui, all in the far eastern part of The Salient, and one – the Prince Charles site – a few km to the west. Facilities are limited to a water supply and toilet.

The High Moorland On the high moorland part of the national park the only public campsite is *Reedbuck Campsite*, a few km from Kiandongoro Gate. This is a small, grassy site, with tap, toilets and a useful cooking shelter. To stay here, you can just turn up. You do not need to be accompanied by a ranger. All the other public campsites on the high moorland have been closed due to the lion danger. Next to Reedbuck Campsite are the *Fishing Bandas*, a set of wooden cabins, basic but in very good condition, each with a fireplace, beds and benches, but no other facilities or equipment. A caretaker lives nearby. To stay here costs KSh 340 per person. To reserve space in the bandas, contact the national park (see Guides & Porters for the address).

There are several other excellent places to camp in the high moorland, but you can only stay here if you're accompanied by a ranger (more details are given in the trek description).

GETTING THERE & AWAY

Because it is virtually impossible to do a trek in this range without the help of a vehicle, it's presumed you'll have driven from Nairobi to Mweiga. (For details about car hire in Nairobi see the Kenya Getting Around section.)

The national park has six public entrance gates. To reach the start of the trek described in this section from Mweiga you need to drive about 40 km, mostly on dirt road, to enter the park through Kiandongoro Gate.

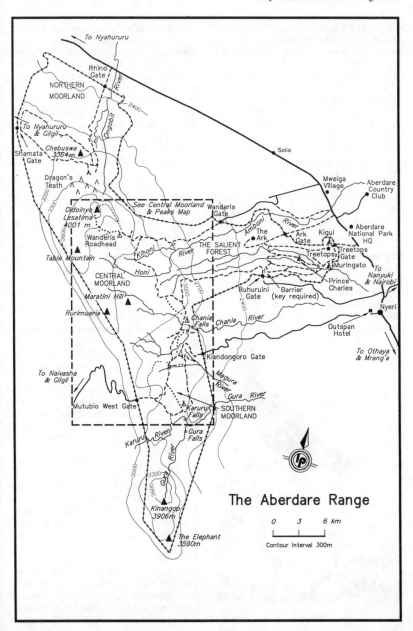

To Nyahururu

NORTHERN
MOORLAND

Rhino
Gate

2400

Ongobit River

To Nyahururu
& Gilgil

Chebuswa
3364m

Shamata
Gate

Solio

Dragon's
Teeth

3000

3600

Oldoinyo
Lesatima
4001 m

See Central Moorland
& Peaks Map

Wanderis
Gate

Mweiga
Village

Aberdare
Country
Club

Wanderis
Roadhead

Kihoni

River

Amboni

The
Ark

River

Ark
Gate

Kigui

Aberdare
National Park
HQ

Table Mountain

Honi

THE SALIENT
FOREST

Treetops

Treetops
Gate

CENTRAL
MOORLAND

Muringato

To
Nanyuki
& Nairobi

Maratini Hill

3000

2700

Prince
Charles

Rurimueria

Ruhuruini
Gate

Barrier
(key required)

2400

Nyeri

Chania
Falls

Chania

Chania

River

To Naivasha
& Gilgil

Kiandongoro Gate

Outspan
Hotel

To Othaya
& Mrang'a

Magura
River

Gura   River

Mutubio West Gate

Karuru
Falls

SOUTHERN
MOORLAND

Karuru

River

Gura Falls

3000

Gura

River

3300

3600

Kinangop
3906m

The Elephant
3590m

The Aberdare Range

0   3   6 km

Contour Interval 300m

The roads are usually impassable in the wet season, and 4WD and high clearance are required even when it's dry. There's an AA (Automobile Association of Kenya) office in Nyeri, at the top end of town, near the start of the road towards Kiandongoro Gate, where the staff may be able to give you more information about road conditions in the park. The staff at the park headquarters will also be able to advise.

If you don't want to hire a car to reach the Aberdares, you can take an organised trek, which includes transport and cuts all these hassles. Companies doing treks here include Bushbuck, Gametrackers and Natural Action (see the Kenya Trekking Companies section for details).

THE ABERDARE CONTRASTS TREK
Access
This trek starts at Karuru Falls, in the centre of the Southern Moorland area. From Mweiga Park Headquarters, where you pick up your ranger, follow the main tarred road back towards Nyeri town. As you enter the

Vultures

town, keep right and take the road towards the Outspan Hotel and Kiandongoro Gate (signposted). Follow this dirt road for about 30 km to reach the gate. There are a few junctions, but most are signposted. At the gate, pay your park fees, then continue on the park track, keeping left at the first junction, past the track down to the Fishing Bandas, and continue for about eight km. The road turns sharp right and there's a flat area above the level of the road on the right, with room for about five tents. To the left another track, which soon turns into a path, leads down to the Karuru Falls. There are no facilities at the camping place. For water, follow the path towards the falls: it crosses the river after 100 metres. You cannot stay here without your ranger, so if there's no tent space for him, you'll need to camp at Reedbuck Campsite (where he can sleep in the caretaker's hut), then come to the start of the trek next day by car.

Stage 1: Karuru Falls to Chania Falls
(15-20 km, 4-8 hours depending on route)
Before starting this stage of the trek, it's well worth going to have a look at the Karuru Falls, where the Karuru River plunges over 300 metres down into the valley below. Views are best in the morning, when there's less chance of mist. There are two viewing platforms overlooking the falls and the forest below. South of the Karuru Falls, on the other side of the valley, you can see the equally impressive Gura Falls.

On this stage of the trek, there are a couple of options. You can follow the park track westward for about five km, to meet the road coming in from Mutubio West Gate at a T-junction. Here, you turn right and walk through the rolling moorland to reach a track on the right leading to Queen's Cave after another five km, or you can turn left at the T-junction, then right onto a disused track, which goes to the west of the main track, and take this slightly longer way to Queen's Cave. Alternatively, from Karuru you can cut straight across the bush, roughly north-west, to meet the Mutubio to Queen's Cave track.

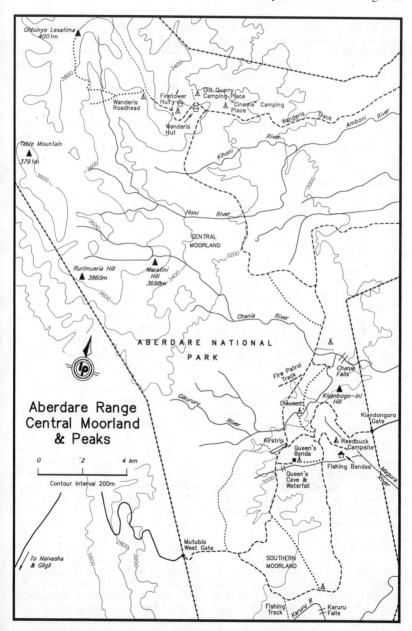

Oldoinyo Lesatima
4001m

Wanderis
Roadhead

Firetower
Hut

Old Quarry
Camping Place

Cinema
Camping
Place

Wanderis Track

Amboni River

Wanderis
Hut

Kihoni River

Table Mountain
3791m

Honi River

CENTRAL
MOORLAND

Rurimueria Hill
3860m

Macatini
Hill
3698m

Chania River

A B E R D A R E   N A T I O N A L

P A R K

Fire Patrol
Track

Chania
Falls

Gikururu

Disused

Kiambogo-ini
Hill

Kiandongoro
Gate

River

Aberdare Range
Central Moorland
& Peaks

Airstrip

Reedbuck
Campsite

Queen's
Banda

0   2   4 km

Fishing Bandas

Contour Interval 200m

Queen's
Cave &
Waterfall

Mutubio
West Gate

To Naivasha
& Gilgil

SOUTHERN
MOORLAND

Fishing
Track

Karuru R

Karuru
Falls

From Karuru to Queen's, allow three to four hours on the tracks, or longer if you go through the bush.

Queen's Cave is a large cave with a picturesque waterfall flowing over its entrance. There's a pool below the falls where you can swim. Large groundsels grow on the steep banks and the hexagonal columns of volcanic rock have been exposed by the water. If the sun's shining, it's a good place for a long lunch break. On your way down to the falls you pass Queen's Banda, a shelter (roof but no walls) built in 1952 for the visit of Princess Elizabeth (who became Queen during her visit to the Aberdares, as her father George VI died while she was staying at Treetops). If you're tempted to stay by the falls for a bit longer than lunch, there's an area for camping next to the banda.

From Queen's Cave you have several options. You can follow the track for about five km, to reach a bridge across the Chania River, where a path leads down through the forest to the Chania Falls, another fine waterfall, flowing off a semicircular cliff into a large natural bowl. You can also reach Chania Falls by following the track north for about one km across the Gikururu River, then branching off right, through the bush, to reach a disused campsite, continuing to the west of the river to reach Chania Falls. From Queen's Cave you can also go eastward, along the north side of the river down towards the Fishing Bandas, meeting a park track and following it north for about two km, before branching off left as the track bends round to the right, to go over Kiambogo-ini Hill and come out on the Chania River, opposite the old campsite. Allow 1½ hours to go from Queen's Cave to Chania Falls if you keep to the tracks, and anything up to four hours if you're bush-bashing.

The camping place at Chania Falls is just off the track where it crosses the river above the falls. Water is available from the river. Take heed of the 'Beware Lions' notice painted on a rock nearby. (If you have no tent space for your ranger you'll need to return to Reedbuck Campsite at the end of this stage.)

Stage 2: Chania Falls to Wanderis Track
(16 km, 4-5 hours, 500 metres ascent)

The distance and time given here are if you keep to the track, but there are also some routes through the bush which will add a bit of distance and a lot of time. The most pleasant section is through the area to the north of the falls, bounded to the east and north by the track. This is good going for part of the way, through grass and open forest glade, although there are also some dense patches of bush, and a few bogs, which slow progress.

After meeting the park track again, continue following it north, over the Honi and Kihoni rivers (the last water point before the Wanderis camping places) to meet the Wanderis Track, which links the Wanderis Gate and the Wanderis Roadhead.

There are several places for camping in this area. If you turn right and go downhill for about 500 metres, there's a grassy area on the left, called 'Cinema' by the rangers because the film crew making *Gorillas in the Mist* camped here. Or you can turn left and go uphill for about one km until a faint fork branches off right to the Old Quarry, another suitable place for camping. Near the fork, on the left side of the main track, is Wanderis Hut, in bad condition but OK for shelter in an emergency. None of these camping places have water nearby.

Alternative Campsites

Continue left up the track, round a sharp hairpin bend, to reach a junction after two km. The right fork goes to Firetower Hut (small but usable), with a place for camping nearby. (This is the best place to stay if you've no tent space for your ranger, as he will sleep in Firetower Hut.) The left fork goes to Wanderis Roadhead (3610 metres), another one km past the junction, a low point on the main ridge extending south-east from Satima, which has a flat area for camping, with excellent views to the east, from where you can often see the peaks of Mt Kenya sticking up above the cloud. This is probably the most dramatic of the camping places in this area, but it's also the most exposed: be prepared for cold winds and driving rain. None of these camping places have a water supply. Bring all you need from the Kihoni River.

Stage 3: Wanderis Roadhead to Satima Summit & return

(7 km, 4-5 hours, 400 metres ascent, plus 4-5 hours, descent)

This stage starts at the Wanderis Roadhead. If you camped at one of the lower places, follow the directions in the Alternative Campsites section to reach the roadhead. It's possible to walk from any of the camping places mentioned here, do the complete Satima circuit and return to the camp in a day. If you get an early start you stand more chance of missing the afternoon cloud and doing the full circuit in good conditions. Overlooking the roadhead, to the south, is a prominent dome buttress. Before you start, note this for reference on the return route.

From the roadhead, aim north, keeping to the left (west) of the crest of the ridge. Down to the left is a large valley (the headwaters of the Honi). There is a faint path, indistinct or non-existent in places. If in doubt, keep high, just below the crest of the ridge. In some places you can go up to the crest of the ridge, which is harder going but gives better views.

Continue for about three hours, as the ridge gradually tends westwards, then swing directly west over a broad col, passing to the right of a rocky buttress in the centre of the col. The head of the Honi Valley is down to your left (south) and the head of the Ongobit River to your right (north). Also to your right, to the west of the Ongobit, are several jagged outcrops, called the Dragon's Teeth. They don't seem to have a local name.

The main peak of Satima is directly ahead (west), like a broad table dipped slightly in the middle. The peak on the right (north) of the dip appears higher, but the actual summit is to the left. Aim directly towards the north peak and scramble up some rocky ledges to its top, which is marked by a small cairn. From there, cross the dip to the south peak, the summit of Satima (4001 metres), marked by a larger cairn. (Alternatively, you can

miss the scramble up to north peak by keeping left below it, aiming straight for the lowest point of the dip between the two peaks, and going straight for Satima summit from there.)

From the summit of Satima, to the south, you can look down the Honi Valley, with two large ridges on each side. To the east, Mt Kenya can sometimes be seen, while to the west the valleys drop away towards the Great Rift Valley.

To get back to the Wanderis Roadhead you can retrace the approach route down the east ridge (about three hours), but it's more satisfying to do a circuit, by going down the west ridge then crossing the valley lower down before going up to the roadhead. This section of the route is hard, because you lose a lot of height when crossing the Honi, and the valley bottom is covered in tussock grass and bog, with no clear path to follow. If weather conditions are bad, it's better to retrace the ascent.

From the summit, aim south, following the crest of the west ridge, or tending left around some of the peaks and buttresses on the ridge. After about an hour, you'll reach a large col. Drop into this then keep left of the main ridge, keeping below and to the left of some large rocky outcrops. After another 45 minutes tend left, following a broad ridge south-east down towards the valley bottom. You'll reach the Honi River at a point below, and almost directly due west of, the large dome buttress that overlooks the roadhead. Go steeply up the valley side to reach the roadhead. Allow at least 2½ hours to cross the valley.

Stage 4: Wanderis Roadhead to Wanderis Gate

(15 km, 3-4 hours, 1000 metres descent)

From the roadhead, retrace to the junction and keep right at the first junction (left goes to the Firetower). Keep going downhill, past Wanderis Hut, to the next junction (about three km from the roadhead), where you go straight on. (A path through the forest bypasses a big loop in the track – your ranger will show you the way.) Continue winding down on the easy track, through forest then bamboo, to reach Wanderis Gate after another 12 km.

Exit

Meet your vehicle at Wanderis Gate, then continue down the track, which turns into a wide dirt road passing through farmland, back to the main tarred Nyeri-Nyahururu road, where you turn right to reach the Mweiga Park headquarters and drop off your ranger. From the gate to the headquarters is about 20 km and takes around 45 minutes to drive.

Alternative finish

From the summit of Satima, instead of returning to the roadhead, it is possible to extend your trek down the north side of Satima, past the Dragon's Teeth to be collected by your car from one of the park tracks near Chebuswa Peak. Before choosing this option, discuss it with your ranger at the park headquarters to make sure he is familiar with the route. The assistant warden has a good map of the whole park on the wall of his office. Note that some of the tracks shown on this map around Chebuswa are in very bad condition and may not be passable. The assistant warden and ranger will advise you. It is also very important to note that the park tracks in the Central Moorland do not connect with those in the Northern Moorland. Maps produced since the 1960s have faithfully recorded a 'road under construction' to the east of Satima, and there are still vague rumours that a track may yet be built, but at the end of 1992 there was absolutely no way you could get a vehicle through. To get there, you need to leave the park at Wanderis Gate, as already described, then take the tarred road towards Nyahururu and re-enter at Rhino Gate. Remember also that you'll have to come back to Mweiga to drop off the ranger.

The Loroghi Hills

The Loroghi Hills rise from the plains around Maralal, to the north of Kenya's Central Highlands. These plains, and the hills scattered across them, are the homeland of the Samburu people, a group of cattle-herding pastoralists, closely related to the Maasai, with whom they share many cultural traditions as well as a taste for beads, ochre and bright red blankets.

The Hills are composed of grassy ridges and lightly forested valleys, and generally enjoy a pleasant climate similar to those of the highlands further south, which makes them ideal for trekking. The area is very seldom visited by tourists, and the only way most travellers see these hills is from the back of a fast-moving safari truck, as the main dirt road from Maralal to Lake Turkana passes this way.

The Samburu people number about 75,000, and their territory is the shape of a triangle with its base between the towns of Rumuruti and Archer's Post, and the apex near the southern tip of Lake Turkana. Their name is thought to mean 'butterfly' in the

Samburu woman

Maa language (which they also share with the Maasai), presumably a reference to their bright and colourful clothing. Brightest of them all are the *morans* (warriors), young men aged between about 15 and 30, who traditionally protect the people and their cattle from wild animals and human enemies. They keep their hair long and platted, coloured orange with thick ochre, with beads at the back and sometimes a peak-like 'comb' at the front. Headbands of beads and buttons, and earrings made from bone, are *de rigueur*, and a thin chain around the ears and across the chin seems to be an essential part of the get-up. Armbands, wristbands and waistbands, all made from beads and strips of leather, are also important. Clothes are minimal: a loin cloth and a blanket worn as a robe (or two if it's cold) and a pair of sandals complete the outfit. Vital accessories are a long thin spear, a broad-bladed knife tied round the waist, and a *runga*, or fighting stick, often with a lump of sharp metal attached to ensure maximum damage to enemies in times of emergency.

The Samburu migrated to these hills and the surrounding plains about 300 years ago from the west of Lake Turkana. The hills provided good water and grazing for their cattle, when the plains were hot and dry. Much later, in the early 1900s, the colonial government of Kenya also recognised the area's potential for farming, but the hills were never settled and stayed safely in the hands of the Samburu.

Today, a trek in the Loroghi Hills is a good way to see the Samburu people, and an ideal way to explore a little-visited part of Kenya, without the expense of the national parks, and avoiding the logistical worries normally connected with some of the more remote areas.

GEOGRAPHY
The Loroghi Hills (also spelt Lerogi or Lorochi) is a relatively small highland area, about 30 km across and 20 km long above 2000 metres, some 160 km north of the Central Highlands around Mt Kenya, and bounded on the west by the Great Rift Valley.

Their highest section is a broad ridge, dotted with several rounded peaks, running east-west across the northern part of the hills, with its highest point, a peak called Poror (2580 metres), roughly in the centre.

To the north of this ridge the ground falls sharply to the dry and dusty Marti Plains. To the west the drop is even steeper and more spectacular where the hills end abruptly at the sheer Lesiolo escarpment, which overlooks the floor of the Rift Valley, almost 600 metres below. To the south and east of the main ridge the incline is more gradual, and the hills are dissected by a series of parallel forested river valleys running between broad grassy ridges.

GUIDEBOOKS & MAPS
For day-walks, the guidebooks *Mountain Walking in Kenya* and *Mountains of Kenya* both have sections on the area around Maralal (see Guidebooks, in the Kenya section).

The Loroghi Hills and the area around Maralal are covered by the Survey of Kenya 1:50,000 map sheet number 78/3 (Maralal).

TREKKING INFORMATION
The trek described here passes through the area south and west of Poror, crossing many of the smaller ridges and valleys, and taking in the Lesiolo escarpment.

On your trek, you'll pass clusters of Samburu huts (usually called *manyattas*, although technically these are for morans only), and meet local people walking between the settlements, or morans herding cattle on the grassy ridges. If you've got the time you can combine a camel safari with some trekking in the Loroghi Hills, using the Maralal Hostel as a base (see Places to Stay, Maralal). The cool, forested highlands contrast sharply with the semi-desert scrubland further south. It's an ideal way to get a taste of the fascinating Samburu lifestyle and landscape.

The nearest town to the Loroghi Hills is Maralal, about 250 km directly north of Nairobi, or about 300 km by road.

Route Standard & Days Required

There are no set routes in the Loroghi Hills, as in the higher mountains more geared to trekking, but across the ridges and through the forest there's a network of tracks and paths used by local people for driving goats and cattle to water, or simply for getting from one manyatta to the next. The trek described here, which I've called the Loroghi Hills Circuit, is only one of many that are possible in this area.

The circuit goes from Maralal up to Poror, crossing several ridges and valleys, then to the edge of the Rift Valley escarpment at Lesiolo, returning to Maralal along a large broad ridge that runs through the centre of the hills. The route follows paths and tracks all the way, through several different sorts of landscape, and the going is generally easy. There's one major sidetrack – a long loop where you can go right down the Lesiolo escarpment wall onto the floor of the Rift, which is highly recommended, although conditions are more demanding.

The trek can be done in three days, or five if you do the Lesiolo Loop sidetrack. The five-day trek involves three long days interspersed with two short days, making the trek less strenuous overall – although, if you're feeling fit, some stages can be combined.

Guides & Porters

It is not absolutely essential to have a guide in this area; with a map, a compass and a sense of direction it's virtually impossible to get dangerously lost. But taking a local guide with you does have several advantages.

With a guide you'll feel less of a stranger when you meet people along the way, either in the villages or out on the ridges, and the guide can help you communicate with the locals, so you'll be able to get to know them as real people rather than as just part of the landscape. This is a small community and the chances are your guide will do a bit of family visiting along the way, and you might be invited into a manyatta. Courtesy and manners are important features of Samburu culture, and it's customary to ask permission before walking though peoples' land. If your

Swahili isn't up to much your guide can help you with the formalities. And, of course, being with a local guide, you can ask questions and learn from him much more about all aspects of Samburu life and the landscape you're passing through.

A guide is also useful when your route passes through the forested valleys where there are buffalo and even lions. This is not a major problem and, if you make enough noise when you pass through these forested areas, you'll scare most animals off long before you even know they were there, but having a guide with a spear, and a general 'feel' for the bush, is a lot more comforting.

The best place to get guides is the Yare Safaris Hostel in Maralal. You can book ahead at Yare's Nairobi office (see the Kenya Trekking Companies section), or just turn up and tell the manager what you want, and he'll arrange an English-speaking moran to accompany you for as long as you want, whether on a short or a long trek. The charge for a guide is KSh 200 per day, payable to the hostel, which then pays the guide. If you are happy with the guide's service, a tip of about KSh 30 to KSh 50 per day is appropriate. Yare Safaris also do an all-inclusive deal for walkers for US$25 per day with full-board accommodation at the hostel, a packed lunch, and the services of a moran-guide for day-walks in a different direction each day.

When arranging a long trek, spending some nights out in the bush, you need a tent, sleeping bag, stove, food, and so on. The moran will provide for himself. It's important to make sure he understands the number of days involved and the route you want to take, and that he carries enough food, or knows where to get some along the way. It's a matter of pride for a moran to be able to walk for days on end with no food or water, but it can be difficult when you stop for lunch and the guide just sits and watches you eating.

If a guide is not available, it is possible to shorten this trek by cutting the first and last stages, and travelling between Maralal and Poror by matatu or hitching. A guide is unnecessary for the walk between Poror and Lesiolo, and a guide for the sidetrack can be

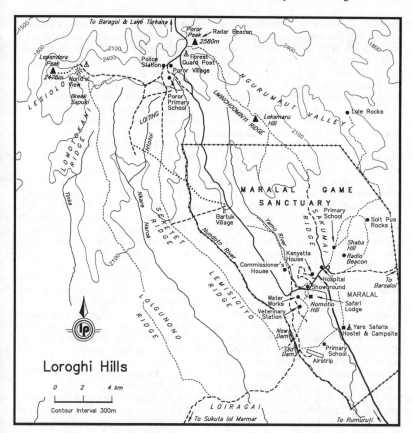

Loroghi Hills

0   2   4 km

Contour Interval 300m

arranged for the day at Lesiolo (see the trek description).

Park Fees & Regulations
Maralal is at the centre of a National Sanctuary wildlife reserve, where hunting is forbidden and grazing restricted, but there are no regulations concerning trekkers. The route passes through the reserve but fees are not required.

Supplies
Maralal has a few shops where you can buy most basic items, such as bread, tins of mar-

garine and jam, tinned meat and fish, biscuits, chocolate, tea, coffee and dried milk. There's a market for fruit and vegetables, but anything else should be brought from Nairobi or one of the bigger towns.

PLACES TO STAY
Maralal
Maralal is a regional administrative centre, and the unofficial Samburu 'capital'. With its four dusty streets and crooked lines of clapperboard shops and bars, complete with verandas and swinging signs, the place has a frontier feel about it, and more than one

writer has drawn obvious Wild West analogies. On the main street is *Buffalo Lodge*, the biggest bar in town, usually with a group of local cowboys lurking on the front step, and reasonable rooms out the back for KSh 150 per person. Other B&Ls, on the street between the town-centre roundabout and the hospital, are more basic and cheaper.

On the west side of town, about three km from the centre is *Maralal Safari Lodge*, an up-market place, with rooms in tastefully decorated wooden cabins for about US$100 a double, including breakfast and dinner. The food is excellent and there's also a bar open to non-residents. Even if you're not staying here, the lodge is a good place to come for a celebratory meal or a beer in luxurious surroundings after your trek.

The most popular place for travellers is the *Yare Safaris Hostel and Campsite*, about three km south of Maralal town. They have self-contained double bandas for KSh 600 including breakfast, beds in the dormitory for KSh 90 (less with a IYHF card), and camping for KSh 80. There's a bar and restaurant for meals or snacks. Yare operate camel-trekking safaris in the area south-east of Maralal, along the Ewaso Nyiro River, and the hostel is the base for these. A shuttle bus from Nairobi ties in with these safaris. If you're on the safari, transport is free, otherwise you pay KSh 200 each way. More details from Yare Safaris. Their office is on the first floor of Union Towers, on the corner of Moi Ave and Mama Ngina St.

On the Hills

This area is not used to tourists (even, or especially, on foot), so there are no huts or lodgings. You need a tent and a full set of camping gear. For details on camping at World's View, see the end of the Stage 2 description.

GETTING THERE & AWAY

There is one daily bus between Maralal and Nairobi (KSh 170), or you can go from Maralal to Nyahururu by matatu or shared taxi, and from there to Maralal by matatu. The last matatu for Maralal leaves Nyahururu about midday. If you're staying at the hostel and campsite (see Places to Stay), get the bus/matatu to drop you before you reach the town. You can also get between Maralal and Nairobi on the Yare Safaris shuttle-bus (see Places to Stay).

If you're doing a Turkana truck trip that passes through Maralal after seeing the lake, you could get dropped off here and make your own way back to Nairobi after your trek.

LOROGHI HILLS CIRCUIT
Access

From Yare Safaris Hostel and Campsite, you can follow the main dirt road into Maralal town, but it's much more pleasant to go by the footpath which runs behind the hostel and continues for three km, roughly parallel to the road, straight into the main street on the southern side of town. From there, go up this street to the roundabout in the town centre, turn left, past the market, then go 500 metres to the next roundabout and the road out of town. If you have no need to go to Maralal, you can cross the main road directly opposite the hostel and go round the base of Nomotio Hill and the back of the Safari Lodge to reach the main road just west of the bridge over the Yamo River.

Stage 1: Maralal to Poror

(25 km, 6-8 hours)

From the roundabout near the government offices on the west side of town, head southwest along the main dirt road that eventually leads to Baragoi and Lake Turkana. It also leads to Poror Village so, if you're not sure, ask for directions to the village. Follow the road out of town, straight on at another roundabout (right leads up to Kenyatta House, where Jomo Kenyatta was imprisoned before Kenya's independence; the building is now a national monument), and just after another road on the right (which you ignore), take a path that leads round the edge of the showground and down to the Yamo River. Cross this river onto the west bank and follow the path northwards, keeping the river on your right, to meet a larger track coming in from the left. Keep on this for about half an hour, passing a large

Top: Loroghi Hills: Samburu morans (warriors) (DE)
Left: Rock hyrax, with Mt Kenya behind (JW)
Right: Loroghi Hills: Samburu woman (DE)

Top: Sasa Route: Jackson's Summit, with groundsels in foreground, Mt Elgon (DE)
Left: Sasa Route: ladders up the Mudangi Cliffs, Mt Elgon (CE)
Right: Approaching hot springs via 'Smugglers' Path', Mt Elgon (JB)

house (the Provincial Commissioner's official residence) up to your left, until a path branches off on the left just before the track goes down to cross the river. Follow the path, as it starts to climb up the valley side through the edge of the forest, keeping the river down to your right. At a fork, take the left path and keep on going up, more steeply through dense bush. The path then levels out, following the crest of a broad ridge until it meets the main dirt road (about 1½ hours from the Commissioner's house).

Turn right and follow the dirt road for about three km, or 45 minutes, to the village of Il Bartuk, where a small track branches off left towards Seketet (about two to three hours from Maralal). Leave the main dirt road here, but keep aiming north-west through the huts of Il Bartuk, passing between the church (up to your right) and the duka (with a red roof, down to your left). Drop gradually down into the forested valley of the Nkare Narok, the upper reaches of the Nundoto River.

There are many paths through the forest and over the ridges in between the river and its tributary valleys. Depending on the way your guide takes you, you'll either cross the Nundoto and a major tributary on its west side to come up onto the eastern ridge of an area called Loiting, or cross another river, the Ntotoi, and come up onto the western ridge of Loiting. Both these ridges have a track running along their crest, climbing gradually, passing occasional huts and manyattas. These ridges blend into the main east-west ridge that runs across the centre of the Loroghi Hills, and the tracks pass through wheat fields. (The farm is managed by a European farmer on land he leases from the local Samburu people. You may see tractors or combine harvesters, looking slightly incongruous in this pocket of cultivation surrounded by manyattas and natural forest.) Some of the tracks around the wheat farm may be changed each year but at least one will lead towards Poror Village. Depending on which route you take, you'll pass either the police station or the primary school on the way in (four to five hours from Il Bartuk).

There are no lodgings in Poror, but one of the shopkeepers may let you pitch a tent on the grass behind the shops. You can also ask for permission to camp at the primary school or the police station. Your guide may be able to sleep with friends or family near the village (although you'll need to check whether this will be possible before you leave Maralal, otherwise you'll need a tent for him). Camping is also possible at the Forest Guard Post, about two km from Poror just on the other side of the main Baragoi-Maralal road. The rangers here are friendly and seem happy to have company, although if their head ranger is due to visit then camping may not be allowed. A small tip for their help is appropriate.

Stage 2: Poror to Lesiolo (via Lependera)

(17 km, 4-5 hours)

If you're going for the five-day trek, this is an easy stage. If you're not taking the Lesiolo Loop, and want to do a three-day trek, you can combine this stage with Stage Four and get back to Poror on the same day.

From Poror follow the track through the wheat fields, aiming south-west then west, keeping to the crest of the broad ridge. Keep right at all forks, to reach the end of the track, at a grassy patch on the very edge of the Rift Valley escarpment (two to three hours from Poror).

The Samburu name for this area is Lesiolo, and the viewpoint itself is often called World's View. From here you can see down onto the valley floor and across to the Tiati Hills and the faint outline of the Cherangani Hills, some 120 km away on the other side of the Rift.

To the left (south-west) a spur juts out westwards, perpendicular to the main escarpment. On the end of this spur you can see the peak of Lependera (although it's marked on some maps as Lesiolo). To reach this peak, follow the path that runs south from World's View, parallel to the main escarpment. It drops down into a forested valley and climbs up the other side over a grassy hill, then drops into another valley before climbing again through bushes to reach the summit (2476 metres) about one hour from World's View.

The spur sticks out just far enough so that from the summit of Lependera you can see south down the valley all the way to Lake Baringo, straight across (west) to the Cheranganis, and north up the Rift, towards the blistering heat of the Suguta Valley. When it's cold and misty on the edge of the escarpment, it's hard to imagine that you're only just over 150 km away from one of the hottest places on earth (see the Suguta Valley section).

Retrace your steps to World's View (one hour).

Camping at World's View

In the manyatta near World's View lives a Samburu man called Lele. He's friendly, but doesn't speak much English. His job is to see that nobody camps on the actual viewpoint, but it's OK if you put your tent up near his hut or on the grass just inside the wire fence that separates World's View from the farm land, only 100 metres from the viewpoint.

Lele can guide you to Lependera, or will watch your gear while you're away. He will also show you where to find water, from a spring in a clump of trees on the edge of the escarpment. Local boys will offer to bring you firewood. (Although maybe you shouldn't encourage this as the boys are

likely to tear down live branches in their enthusiasm.) A small fee is appropriate: KSh 30 to Lele for guiding, KSh 70 for a night's watch; and KSh 10 or so to the odd-job boys.

Stage 3: The Lesiolo Loop

(12 km, 8-10 hours)
From Lesiolo you can drop down the spectacular escarpment onto the floor of the Rift Valley, and then come back up on another path to the north which brings you to Lesiolo again. You are strongly recommended to take Lele as a guide for this section, even if you also hired a guide from Maralal. This is serious territory, and no place to start getting lost. A suitable fee for Lele is KSh 75 to KSh 100 for the day, although this may need to be discussed before you leave.

From World's View, you follow the path described at the end of Stage 2, to Lependera, then keep going down the small path which follows the sharp ridge down towards the valley floor. You then tend right (northwards) across the flat section of the floor visible from the summit, along the foot of the escarpment until you cut across another path about five km further north, which climbs up a valley between two of the large spurs, to reach the top of the escarpment to the north of Lele's hut. Another way up and down follows the forested valley that you cross in between World's View and Lependera, but this is harder, especially after rain. (After heavy rain, all the paths up and down the escarpment become wet and slippery, and this section of the route becomes very difficult, and dangerous in places.)

If you leave World's View at sunrise, you'll be on Lependera by 8 am, and down on the valley floor after another two to three hours. It takes two to three hours to work round the base of the escarpment, then at least another two to follow the winding escarpment path back up to the top. Allow eight hours, minimum. Carry plenty of water, as it can get very hot on the valley floor and supplies there are not reliable. This section of the trek requires commitment, but is well worth the effort.

Stage 4: Lesiolo to Poror

(10 km, 2-3 hours)

For this section of the trek you simply retrace the route of Stage 2. This is a short stage so, if you're fit, it could be done after the Lesiolo Loop (if you started early), or combined with Stage 5.

Sidetrack: Poror Peak

If you're a peak bagger, you might want to reach the summit of Poror, the highest point of the Loroghi Hills. This is no North Face of the Eiger; a small dirt road leads all the way to the top, servicing the radar station. Walk up the track, but make sure it's OK with the guards for you to be there. Photos are not a good idea.

Stage 5: Poror to Maralal

(21 km, 6-7 hours)

This route follows an old track that runs down the Lminchoominyi and Sakumai Ridges, some five km east of the main dirt road. Since the new road was built this track has fallen into disuse. It's now impassable for vehicles, but makes a very good path.

From the Forest Guard Post to the east of Poror Village, follow a path down into the valley on the left (north) side of the rangers' hut, then up the other side, contouring around the base of Poror peak, with the radar beacon on the summit visible up to the left, to meet the old track. Turn right onto this and follow it as it swings south-east and keeps going in this direction, along the crest of a broad ridge, through light bush and areas of grass.

After an hour you reach a fork. Keep right, on the main track (the left goes down into the valley of Ngurumaut), following the ridge. The Samburu word for the bushes that grow in this area is Lminchoominyi, which give the ridge its name.

After another hour the track descends more steeply through dense bush, although it's still easy to pass, then goes in a big curve round the side of a hill called Lekamaru. To the left you can see across the Ngurumaut Valley to the exposed outcrop of Lole Rocks, directly to the east. About 45 minutes from

Lekamaru you reach an indistinct fork, which is easy to miss. Take the left path up through trees, keeping Lole Rocks in view (the right goes downhill towards Il Bartuk).

The track becomes more distinct as you continue descending towards Maralal. About four to five hours from Poror are the first outlying huts. Down on the left is the Loikas Valley, with huts and shambas spreading up the hillside. Another hour and you'll reach Maralal town, passing the hospital on your right, to reach the roundabout in the town centre.

From here it's another hour back to the Yare Safaris Hostel & Campsite.

The Suguta Valley

The Suguta Valley is a large section of the Great Rift Valley, between Lake Baringo and Lake Turkana, in the far north of Kenya. At its northern end, the valley floor is only a few hundred metres above sea level, making it one of the lowest parts of inland Kenya and the entire Rift Valley system. It's also one of the hottest parts of Kenya; a harsh and inhospitable region of desert, salt lakes, volcanic cones and jagged lava-fields. It's not the most obvious place to go for a long walk.

But despite the unrelenting heat and the rugged landscape (or perhaps because of it), the Suguta area, between the southern tip of Lake Turkana, Mt Nyiro and the Loriyu Plateau, offers some exciting wilderness treks. It's a fascinating contrast to the alpine moorlands and snowy peaks of the high mountains further south. The treks described in this section start at the small town of Baragoi and end at Loyangalani, on the south-east shore of Lake Turkana, either following the edge of the Suguta Valley, or crossing at its lowest (and hottest!) point, and including a few days of walking alongside the lake.

The Suguta is also where the homelands of the Samburu and Turkana people meet. The Samburu herd cattle, travelling vast distances across the plains in search of grazing, returning to the high ground around Mt Nyiro, their sacred mountain, which has grass and good water even in the dry season. The Turkana live in remote settlements, herding goats through the harsh wilderness from one patch of scrub grass to the next, or catching fish from the lake.

The Samburu and the Turkana had already been here for a couple of centuries when the Austro-Hungarian Count Samuel Teleki and Ludwig Von Hohnel became the first Europeans to reach the area in 1888. Their journey, sometimes called the last of the great East African expeditions, had also taken them past Kilimanjaro and Mt Kenya, as well as the Suguta Valley, before they reached the southern shore of Lake Turkana. They named this vast inland sea Lake Rudolph, after the prince of Austria, and the name stuck until the 1970s, when it was named after the people who inhabit its shores.

Today, very few visitors come to this area. Due to the harsh nature of the terrain and climate, the logistics of a trek can be complicated and time-consuming to arrange. Getting to and from the area is also hard, although organised treks are available. But, if you've got the time and energy, the trekking is undeniably worth it.

GEOGRAPHY

The whole section of the Rift, from just north of Lake Baringo to the southern tip of Lake Turkana, is the Suguta Valley, but the area crossed by the routes described here is its far northern section, between Mt Nyiro in the east and the Loriyu Plateau in the west.

Mt Nyiro (also spelt Ngiro or Ngiru) stands to the east of the Suguta. Even though it is surrounded by desert, its higher slopes are covered in forest, and small springs emerge lower down to feed the villages of Tum and South Horr, and several other small settlements in the foothills.

From the top of Nyiro to the bottom of the Suguta, the land drops over 2500 metres in less than 20 km. This area is sliced through by deep ravines, called *luggas*, which are usually dry but become awash with sudden flash floods after rain.

North of the Suguta, several volcanoes have erupted from the Rift Valley floor to create a gigantic natural dam, called The Barrier, which holds back the waters of Lake Turkana. These volcanoes are still active: even since Teleki's time there have been small eruptions. On the trek described here you can walk and scramble across huge lava-fields, now solidified, like spilt treacle set in mid-flow.

The tops of the volcanoes that formed The Barrier have collapsed to form craters, or calderas, which cannot be seen from below, so there are no definite peaks which can easily be made out. The highest point is called Kakorinya, and nearby are the remains of Teleki's Volcano, named after the great explorer himself, although it's unlikely that he actually went to this exact spot.

On the south side of The Barrier, the seasonal Suguta River flows into Lake Logipi Namakat, over 100 metres lower than the surface of Lake Turkana. The water cannot flow out, and evaporation is high, so the lake is saline and the shores encrusted with vast deposits of 'soda'. The name of the lake means, not surprisingly, 'salt water' in the local Turkana language.

An obvious feature of Logipi is a large outcrop of yellow rock, rising like an island in the middle of the lake, called Naperito, or Cathedral Rock. The other main feature is the large flock of flamingos which feed on algae in the shallows at the lake's edge. Although not as pink as their cousins in the lakes further south, these birds are still a fascinating sight.

Across The Barrier, on the southern shore of Lake Turkana, are more volcanic outcrops. The most distinctive peaks are the jagged ridge of Abili Agituk, and the perfect cone of Nabuyatom ('the elephant's stomach') right on the edge of the lake, with the waters of Turkana lapping its northern side.

Lake Turkana is the largest of Kenya's Rift Valley lakes, and one of the largest desert lakes in the world. The lake is often, rather romantically, called the Jade Sea, and in certain light conditions it does have a muddy green tinge. More noticeable are the white-capped waves which often skip across its surface, kicked up by the strong winds that blow in from the desert to the east. Sometimes these winds get up to hurricane force, transforming the lake into a stormy sea.

MAPS
The Suguta area and the southern part of Lake Turkana are covered on Survey of Kenya 1:250,000 maps sheets NA-37-5 (South Horr) and NA-37-9 (Maralal), although the Maralal map only covers Stage 1. More detail on the stages between Parkati and Nabuyatom is shown on the 1:100,000 sheet number 53 (Ng'iro) (see the Kenya Maps section).

TREKKING INFORMATION
The routes described in this section cross the northern section of the Suguta Valley and then follow the southern shores of Lake Turkana. There's also an optional sidetrack up Mt Nyiro, to the east of the valley.

Route Standard & Days Required
This section describes two routes between Baragoi, a small town on the main dirt road between Maralal and Lake Turkana, about 450 km north of Nairobi, and Loyangalani (also spelt Loiengalani and Loiyangelani), a village on the south-east shore of Lake Turkana. They are not established routes with names as on the bigger mountains, so I've given them imaginative titles for ease of reference: The Suguta Valley Long Route and The Suguta Valley Shorter Route. By their nature, routes in this environment do not always follow a set path, and cannot be described in step-by-step detail. It cannot be emphasised enough that conditions in the Suguta Valley area are very tough. The central and final sections are probably the most demanding trekking described in this book. A trek in this area is a unique and fascinating experience but the right preparations and the right frame of mind are essential.

The first three sections of both routes are the same. From Baragoi to Tum, the route is not difficult underfoot, although distances are on the long side. You follow the dirt tracks, or use your guide's local knowledge to take shortcut paths through scrubby bush. From Tum you can follow a rough, little-used track down to Parkati, or take an interesting but more demanding path steeply down the escarpment into a lugga which joins the track just south of Parkati. From Baragoi to Parkati takes three days.

After Parkati the routes divide. The Shorter Route goes along the eastern edge of the Suguta Valley, crossing The Barrier to the east of Kakorinya, to reach Lake Turkana's south shore after one more day. The Long Route goes across the floor of the Suguta Valley, then crosses The Barrier to the west of Kakorinya, to reach Lake Turkana's south shore, and then Nabuyatom, after three more days. On both routes the going is tough underfoot, mainly across boulders and rough lava.

The routes rejoin at Nabuyatom. From here to Loyangalani is rough going for the first section, over broken lava and boulders. After the Salima Lugga (also spelt Sirima), you can follow a rough track and a dirt road where conditions underfoot are easier, although it's still very hot and water is only available from the lake. This section takes two to three more days.

To do either of these treks independently you're looking at eight or nine days for the Long Route and six or seven for the Shorter Route, plus another one or two if you do the sidetrack up Mt Nyiro.

Whichever route you decide to take, the most important aspect to consider is your water supply. Baragoi, Kowop and Tum have clean water, but after Tum there are no reliable sources of good water until you reach Loyangalani. There is a spring in Parkati, with water which is salty but drinkable. The water in Lake Logipi is completely undrinkable even if you could reach it through the soda flats and quicksands that surround its edge, although there is one small spring on its north-east corner, called Maji Moto, with warm, very salty water which local people and their goats can survive on, but you'd really be pushing yourself to the limit to rely on this. Lake Turkana is also quite saline at its southern end. You can live by drinking it, but it never actually quenches your thirst. Unless you've had some experience of desert survival techniques, it's strongly recommended that you carry most of your water requirements for the trek.

The second important aspect is the route itself. Paths are not always clear to follow, and some stages involve following rough trails made by wild animals or people herding goats. A local guide is strongly recommended.

Guides & Porters

The trickle of adventurous travellers passing through this area has created a demand for local guides and donkeys (instead of human porters). This has led, inevitably, to a fledgeling guide and donkey-hire business in Baragoi.

You can ask for a guide at any of the hotels or restaurants in Baragoi, but it's more likely that one will find you, soon after you step off the matatu. It is very important to choose your guide carefully. Most are reliable, although even the good ones generally know only the Shorter Route, from Parkati straight to the lake. Very few guides know the more interesting Long Route past Lake Logipi and over The Barrier to the west of Kakorinya. Once you've arranged your guide, he can help you sort out the donkeys to carry your water supplies and kit. If you're doing the Shorter Route, and happy to rough it, you can get by with one or two donkeys per trekker. On the Long Route you may need two or three each. After Tum, you should allow for at least seven litres of water per person per day, although this can be reduced to about five on some days, if you cook with the saline water from the springs or from Lake Turkana. Check whether the guides and handlers will be drinking spring water or relying on the supply being carried. A litre of water

weighs a kilogram, and donkeys can carry about 40 kg each in these conditions. You can carry your own food and kit, but it makes the walking much easier if you get a donkey for this as well.

Daily rates for a guide are between KSh 75 and KSh 100 per day. A donkey costs KSh 50 to KSh 100 depending on how many you need, and the fee normally includes the handler. (The guide may offer to be the handler as well, but it's better to have somebody extra to look after the donkeys. Make sure they are experienced; donkey driving is quite a skill.) It usually takes at least one day to sort out guides and donkeys in Baragoi.

If the logistics of a trek in the Suguta put you off, Kenya Hiking & Cycling (Arrow House, Koinange Street, PO Box 39439, Nairobi; ☎ 218336) are the only company to run organised treks here. Their Suguta trek starts in Tum and goes to the south shore of Lake Turkana via Parkati, Lake Logipi and the west side of The Barrier. After Nabuyatom, the long slog up the side of the lake to Loyangalani is avoided by using a boat, which stops off at South Island and El Molo Village on the way. This trek is only available as part of Hiking & Cycling's own Turkana safari, which is similar to the other Turkana truck trips in this area (although slightly more expensive), so if you were thinking of going to Turkana anyway, this might be an option to consider. Even if you want to do this trek independently, the staff at Hiking & Cycling will be happy to advise you about routes, guides, donkeys and so on.

Supplies

You can buy enough food in Baragoi to get by on. The shops are surprisingly well stocked, although there's not much in the way of fresh fruit and veg. There's more choice, and a better market, in Maralal, or you can bring stuff from Nairobi.

You'll need plastic jerrycans to carry water. These are not usually available in Baragoi. You can sometimes hire some with your donkeys, but not always. Even old ones left behind by other trekkers tend to be split, or badly patched, and are not reliable. It's better to buy your own, either from Maralal, or from Nairobi, where they're cheaper (see the Kenya Equipment Hire & Supply section).

Warnings

There have been occasional outbreaks of cattle rustling and inter-tribal fighting in the area around Lake Turkana. Be aware of this and check the latest situation before you leave for Baragoi. Hiking & Cycling (in Nairobi) will be able to advise you, as they have good contacts with the people in the area.

A dangerous feature of Lake Turkana is its population of Nile crocodiles. At one time the lake was much larger, filling much of the Suguta Valley and emptying into the River Nile. When the lake shrank, the crocs got cut off; there's now more of them in Lake Turkana than in the Nile. The crocs of Lake Turkana are supposed to be fairly timid, but you should still be very careful about going for a swim!

Nile crocodile

By far the most dangerous feature of a trek in this area is the heat. The Suguta Valley around Lake Logipi is certainly the hottest place in Kenya (and probably one of the hottest places on earth), with daytime temperatures often above 50°C. There's very little shade anywhere on the whole route, and the heat is intensified even more by the black lava.

One trek described in this chapter goes across the valley floor, which means you might be subject to this inferno for at least a day. The second trek keeps to the higher edges of the valley, but even there, and on several other stages, temperatures are still very high, and you should be properly prepared for these conditions.

PLACES TO STAY

Baragoi

The *Morning Star Hotel* is fairly clean (although the adjoining butchery gives off a bit of a stink) with rooms for KSh 150. Along the main street are a couple more lodging houses, where a bed costs about KSh 100. About three km north of the town is a campsite, used mainly by the Turkana trucks, where you can pitch a tent for KSh 50 per night. Ask for directions in the town.

Loyangalani

Loyangalani is the Turkana truck terminus. *The Oasis Lodge* caters mainly for exclusive fly-in visitors, but if you've got KSh 2000 you can rent a self-contained bungalow. There's a bar, restaurant and swimming pool which is open to non-residents for a daily fee of KSh 250.

Just north of the town are two campsites – *Sunset Strip* and *El Molo Lodge*, where you can pitch a tent for KSh 100; both are about the same standard. El Molo Lodge also has some concrete bungalows, which get incredibly hot, for about KSh 1000.

A new campsite is due to open about 10 km south of the town sometime in 1993. For more details, contact Gametrackers in Nairobi (see the Kenya Trekking Companies section).

On the Treks

There is no accommodation along the routes described here. You need to be completely self-contained. A tent is not essential, as rain is very unlikely, but a mosquito net is useful to keep out the sand-flies. A sleeping bag is worth taking for the few hours each night, usually just before sunrise, when the temperature gets cool.

GETTING THERE & AWAY

The treks described start at Baragoi. The only public transport is a matatu from Maralal, usually once a day in each direction. (To reach Maralal from Nairobi, see the Loroghi Hills section.)

The treks end at Loyangalani. There is no public transport and your only way in or out

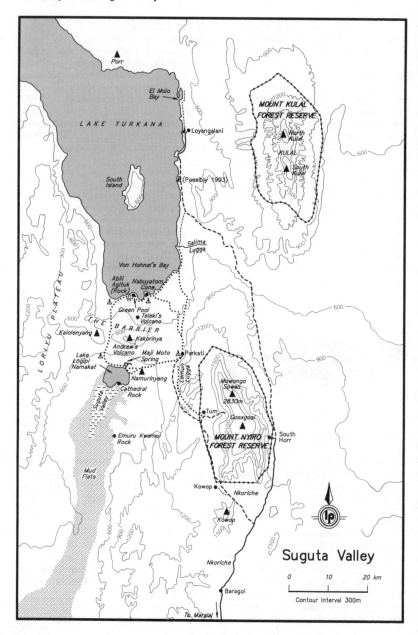

is by hitching. Most of the vehicles you'll see are the safari trucks which run between Nairobi and Lake Turkana, but these are usually full of people who have paid for the whole trip and they don't stop to pick up hitchers! You might see a few cars, but you'll be competing for that valuable space with several local people, who have probably been waiting longer than you.

THE SUGUTA VALLEY LONG ROUTE
Stage 1: Baragoi to Kowop
(32 km, 7-10 hours)

This is a long walk, but straightforward and not too bad if you get an early start. From Baragoi follow the dirt road north towards Lake Turkana, with Mt Kowop, a southerly outlyer of Mt Nyiro to your north, then to your north-west (left). About 18 km from Baragoi you reach a smaller track on the left, heading north-west between Kowop and Nyiro. Follow this to reach the small settlement of Kowop. Ask permission to camp nearby. Alternatively, from Baragoi, your guide should be able to show you shortcut paths that lead more directly from the dirt road to Kowop, but can be harder underfoot. Follow the dirt road for at least 10 km, until you pass a high area called Nkoriche, before branching off onto the paths.

Stage 2: Kowop to Tum
(22 km, 5-6 hours)

Continue northwards on the small track. Up to your right, the densely forested slopes of Mt Nyiro contrast sharply with the dry, dusty landscape you're walking through. There are a few faint junctions, where paths and tracks branch off, but keep to the clear track to reach Tum, a one-street village of tin-roofed dukas surrounded by Turkana and Samburu huts. There are some patches of tough grass around the lower end of Tum, although you might find somewhere better for camping further up the slope towards the Forest Station. If you're planning to do the sidetrack up to the summit of Mt Nyiro, you can camp at the Forest Station, about one to 1½ hours above the village. (A small fee is expected.)

Sidetrack: Tum Forest Station to Mt Nyiro Summit & return
(5-6½ hours, 1300 metres ascent, plus 4-5 hours descent)

If you stay at Tum for two nights this is a good diversion for a day; up to the cool, forested high ground which makes a pleasant (and surprising) change to the heat of the semi-desert below. With an early start you can do this sidetrack in a day. If your guide is not sure of the way, you can arrange for somebody else in Tum or at the Forest Station to show you.

From the Forest Station, a clear path climbs steeply up to a low point on the main Nyiro ridge, reached after two to three hours. Turn left (north) and follow faint paths through the forest, keeping to the ridge and rising gradually. You'll reach the summit, called Mowongo Sowan (or Mowo Ngosowan – 'Buffalo Horns', 2830 metres) after another three to 3½ hours. Just beyond the summit is another outcrop where the views are spectacular. From here you can see down to Cathedral Rock and the Suguta and across The Barrier to Lake Turkana, with Nabuyatom and South Island clearly visible.

(From the low point, two to three hours from the Forest Station, it is also possible to turn right (south) and follow the ridge to Gosagosi (also written Kusi Kusi), Nyiro's southern summit. This route is used by local people crossing from Tum to South Horr.)

From Mowongo Sowan, return to Tum by the same route.

Stage 3A: Tum to Parkati (track)
(22 km, 6-7 hours)

This section of the trek is the only way loaded donkeys can go. An alternative route is available (see Stage 3B).

From Tum, retrace the last part of the Stage 2 route, ignoring the first very faint track that branches right (north), and taking the next track on the right (west), about one km from the edge of Tum. Follow this track, as it swings north, along the crest of a broad ridge, winding gradually downhill, continuing to aim generally northwards. At the end of a long descent, you reach a junction where you take the right track, keeping Mt Nyiro on your right shoulder, to reach the small settlement of Parkati.

Stage 3B: Tum to Parkati (path, via Lemun Lugga)

(20 km, 7-9 hours)

If you've got a good guide and reliable donkey handlers you can walk this route, while the donkeys go the easier way round, as described in Stage 3A.

From Tum, aim north-east, following faint paths or crossing bare rocks and boulders, to reach the edge of the escarpment from where you can see down into the Suguta and north-west to The Barrier, with Lake Turkana behind. A steep path zig-zags down into the Laraguti Lugga then follows it northwards until it meets the larger Lemun Lugga coming in from the right. Keep going down the lugga as it gets broader and the cliffs on either side get higher. At the end of the lugga, tend right to cut across rocky mounds to reach the small track which comes down the ridge to the east. Keeping Nyiro on your right shoulder, follow this track up the left side of another lugga to reach Parkati.

Stage 4: Parkati to Lake Logipi

(20 km, 6-8 hours)

This section, by far the most serious part of the trek, takes six to eight hours of walking time, but you should allow for a long stop in the middle of the day to avoid the worst of the heat.

From Parkati aim west, over a stony plain, crossing an old airstrip and a couple of faint tracks, aiming for a very distinctive yellow mountain visible over the near skyline. This is Namurinyang, which means (surprisingly) 'yellow mountain'. Cross the right (northern) shoulder of Namurinyang, where the yellow rock meets the brown lava. The ground drops steeply down towards Lake Logipi and Cathedral Rock. Aim for some trees visible on the edge of a ridge in between Namurinyang and the lake. This is a good place to wait out the intense midday heat.

From the trees, continue dropping over ridges of black lava to finally reach the edge

of Lake Logipi. Even in the afternoon, the heat here is unbelievably intense on cloudless days. Pass Maji Moto, the saline spring, and continue heading west, with Lake Logipi to your left (south) and The Barrier up to the right (north). At the far end of the lake, several sandy luggas flow down from a dark mountain called Kalolenyang to meet the lake. Follow the largest of these luggas up away from the lake to reach a clump of stunted palm trees and a good place to camp. There is absolutely no water here.

Stage 5: Lake Logipi to Lake Turkana (South Shore)

(18 km, 5-7 hours)

Walk northwards out of the lugga, away from Lake Logipi, up towards the skyline on the top of The Barrier. As you gain height, there are some excellent views back down to Lake Logipi and, if you're lucky, the hint of a breeze. When you reach the crest of The Barrier, the vista of Lake Turkana opens out before you, with South Island clearly visible in the centre of Von Hohnel's Bay. Behind South Island, appearing like another island further up the lake, is the conical shape of Mt Porr, some 70 km away on the east shore.

From the crest, descend over gravely hills towards the lake. There's a clump of large trees growing by the side of a wide lugga, about 500 metres back from the shore, where a tent can be pitched. Nearby are a few huts used as a temporary camp by local anglers.

Stage 6: Across Lake Turkana South Shore (to Nabuyatom)

(17 km, 5-7 hours)

Although today's distance is relatively short, the second half of the stage is over a recent lava-field, where the setting magma has broken up into huge angular slabs, which makes for slow going. Start as early as possible.

From the camp under the trees, walk down to the shore. Then, keeping the lake on your left, aim towards the large yellow outcrop of Abili Agituk. Watch out for crocodiles as you walk along this section.

Leave the grey stones of 'the beach' and cross black lava to go round the south end of

Abili Agituk, and back down to the lake shore, where there's a perfectly circular pool of vivid green water formed in the remains of a small volcanic crater. In the breeding season, this pool is used as a hatchery and nursery by the local crocs, so step extra carefully!

From the pool keep the lake to your left as you work round the bay between Abili Agituk and Nabuyatom Cone, over huge slabs of lava. Pass to the right (south) of Nabuyatom, leaving the black lava, over a few small rises with a large pool to the right, to reach a small beach to the east side of the cone, with a couple of stunted thorn trees growing at one end. These provide shade, but it's better to camp higher up the beach where it's flatter.

Nearby are the remains of a crashed aircraft, used several years ago to bring in exclusive tourists looking for an exciting place to do a spot of fishing. There's also a pattern of stones on the beach placed by a group of young British explorers to mark the centenary of Teleki's arrival at the lake.

Sidetrack: Up Nabuyatom Cone

From the beach it's possible to walk up to the top of Nabuyatom Cone. The sides of the cone are smooth and very steep, but solid, and provide good traction for shoes. Keep your body vertical, and keep your head (don't panic) to keep your grip. Before you go too far up, try coming down again, which is even harder – it's no good finding you can't do it when you're at the top! Just as you'd expect from an old volcano, the top dips steeply inwards to form a crater. Views from the rim, across the eastern end of The Barrier, with Mt Nyiro in the background, and along the eastern shore of the lake and out to South Island, are worth the scramble.

Stages 7 & 8: Nabuyatom to Loyangalani (via Salima Lugga)

(50 km approx, 2-3 days)

From the beach below Nabuyatom, keep the lake to your left, and aim northwards, across the lava and boulders. For the first hour or two you need to keep away from the lake

shore to get round the end of some long inlets divided by narrow spits of land. It's hard going, although the views of Nabuyatom, back across the lake, are impressive. There is a faint path in places, as the local anglers walk this way, but it's not really any easier than when there is no path. Don't follow the edge of the lake too closely, so that you can cut across peninsulas between the many bays, and avoid the crocodiles. You may meet groups of anglers in temporary camps along the way. The only water supply is the lake. Salima Lugga is large and deep where it enters the lake. Keep near the lake edge here to avoid the steep walls.

Keep heading north on the other side of the gorge to meet the end of a rough track used by the truck which takes the fish to the factory in Loyangalani. You may be amazingly lucky and meet the truck, and get a lift. Otherwise camp the night here, or continue down the track to meet the main dirt road from Baragoi as it comes down the lake escarpment from the right. From here to Loyangalani is another 20 km along the dirt road.

It might take you three days to do these last two stages, if you camp at Salima and somewhere else between there and Loyangalani. There's a new campsite planned 10 km south of Loyangalani, due to open in 1993, which would be an obvious place to break the journey.

THE SUGUTA VALLEY SHORTER ROUTE

Stages 1 to 3

As described in the Long Route.

Stage 4: Parkati to Nabuyatom (direct)

(25 km, 10-12 hours)

This is a long day, but there's no ideal place to break the stage. It's best to start at first light, which also means you can do some of the steep section while it's still cool.

From Parkati, a path leads up a lugga aiming generally north, through scrubby bush. The local people walk this way to the lake and to the settlements north of Mt Nyiro. There are several paths and faint trails, which can be confusing, but generally you keep going north, towards the lowest point on the skyline, to reach the crest of The Barrier. The land flattens out slightly as you pass between small hills and outcrops then starts dropping towards the lake. After you cross the crest of The Barrier another path, which seems to be used more regularly by local people, keeps heading north towards Salima. Ignore this, and tend left (north-west). Nabuyatom Cone is an obvious landmark to aim for. The going is hard, across jagged rocks and lava for much of the way. You'll eventually reach the beach just to the east of Nabuyatom, as described in Stage 6 of the Long Route.

Stages 5 & 6: Nabuyatom to Loyangalani (via Salima Lugga)

Follow the directions in Stages 7 and 8 of the Long Route.

Other Trekking Areas

The mountains and routes covered in detail in this Kenya chapter provide interesting and exciting treks, and are fairly easily reached by independent trekkers.

Kenya has several excellent smaller mountains which can be covered in short walks of a day or two, but they are beyond the scope of this book. These include the Ngong Hills, near Nairobi, and the volcanoes of Suswa and Longonot in the Great Rift Valley, still within easy reach of the capital. Not as high, but just as dramatic is the walk through the gorge in Hell's Gate National Park, also in the Rift Valley near Lake Naivasha. The Mau Escarpment, to the west of the Rift, is mainly farmland with no dramatic peaks, and is not very interesting for walking. Short walks in some of the mountains mentioned in this section are covered in *Mountain Walking in Kenya* or *Mountains of Kenya* (see the Kenya Guidebooks section for more details).

This section outlines mountain areas where experienced trekkers can look for longer, more challenging routes.

MT ELGON

Mt Elgon is a large, extinct volcano which lies in the far west of Kenya, straddling the border with Uganda, about 400 km to the north-west of Nairobi. The mountain is shaped like a broad dome, with a large crater surrounded by several peaks at its highest point. The lower parts of the mountain are covered in dense forest, but on the upper slopes there is a large area of open moorland, which is excellent trekking country. Unfortunately, access to the moorland from the Kenyan side is very difficult for independent trekkers. Part of the mountain is a national park where visitors cannot enter without a vehicle, and the other areas involve long and complex approach routes where a car is also useful. Added to this, the park authorities do not allow walkers in the forest and do not encourage treks (or even walks for more than a day) on the high moorland.

However, the recently established forest park on the Uganda side of Mt Elgon is encouraging walking and trekking. Here you can walk through forest and open moorland to reach the crater and main peaks, and enjoy top-quality mountain wilderness trekking for anything between four and eight days. Also, there are no park fees to worry about, guides and porters are available, and access is straightforward (see the Uganda chapter for more details).

On the Kenyan side, for visitors with a car, some short walks on the moorland are possible. For real adventurers, a long traverse is theoretically feasible, although this is complicated by the national park situation. These options are outlined briefly here.

Any walk or trek on the high moorland of Mt Elgon can be serious. Routes are often indistinct, and the weather can be a lot worse than Mt Kenya's. The mountain is often covered in mist, and hail or driving rain is not uncommon, even in the dry season. Temperatures drop below freezing most nights. You should be properly equipped, and competent with a map and compass.

Altitude sickness can also be a problem on the higher parts of Mt Elgon. It is advisable not to drive straight up to one of the

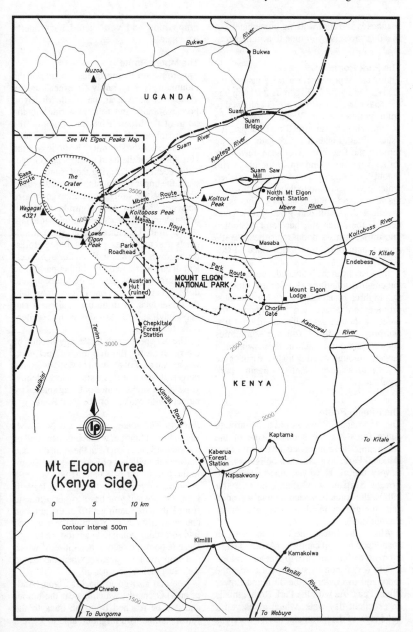

Mt Elgon Area (Kenya Side)

0   5   10 km

Contour Interval 500m

roadheads and start walking immediately, as this does not give you time to acclimatize.

The Park Route

The usual approach for a brief visit to the Kenya side of Mt Elgon is through the national park, where you are not allowed to enter without a car. Walkers have to be accompanied by an armed park ranger. It's usual to camp near the park gate, drive up through the forest to a roadhead, then walk through the moorland up to the crater rim (about three hours). The descent is quicker, which gives you time to drive back down to the campsite in the same day. This is an excellent day-walk and gives you a good taste of the mountain, but don't be fooled into thinking it's a doddle, just because it's shorter than other routes described in this book.

If you camp at the roadhead, you can reach the crater rim and the Hot Springs (another two to three hours each way), but you must provide tent space and blankets for the ranger, although generally they do not like camping overnight. You are sometimes allowed to camp at the roadhead without a ranger, although walking up to the rim or the Hot Springs independently is against park regulations.

The Kimilili Route

This approach follows an old track through dense forest on the southern side of the mountain. The route is outside the Mt Elgon National Park, so a car is not obligatory, but is very useful. However, since Chepkitale Forest Station was abandoned in the 1980s, the track has become badly eroded and overgrown in places (but see Future Possibilities).

Above the forest, the track leads to an abandoned hut and campsite (Austrian Hut). From here it's about three to four hours along a faint (often non-existent) path across the moorland to Lower Elgon Tarn and Lower Elgon Peak. As with the Park Route, this is an excellent day-walk, which gives you a good taste of the mountain, but it's a serious

proposition and you should be properly equipped.

The Mbere Route

This route, on the north-eastern side of the mountain, is very rarely (if ever) used by visitors. It starts near the North Mt Elgon Forest Station, and follows a ridge to the north of the Mbere River to a point on the crater rim near Koitoboss Peak. From here you can reach the summit of Koitoboss or the Hot Springs at the head of the Suam Gorge.

In recent times, during the Ugandan civil wars, the upper section of this route was used by local people smuggling coffee and maize between Kenya and Uganda (see the Smugglers' Path described in the Mt Elgon section of the Uganda chapter). The path still exists in some places, passing through forest on the lower sections and then through excellent open moorland on the higher parts. You need three or four days to do a trek up and down this route, plus one or two to explore the crater area. With proper equipment and good navigational skill this is an excellent route to do.

The only problem is that a large section of the route passes through the national park, where you are not allowed to walk without a ranger. If you did this route independently, you stand a slight chance of being spotted by rangers with walkers on the Park Route.

Access The route starts at the North Mt Elgon Forest Station, which lies at the end of a good track, nine km from the main dirt road between the villages of Endebess and Suam, to the north-west of Kitale. If you've got a vehicle, you can drive this far and leave it here. Otherwise, you have to get a matatu from Kitale to Suam, get off at the junction and walk from there. You might be lucky and find something going to Suam (on the Kenya-Uganda border, closed to non-citizens) which can drop you at the junction where the road to the forest station branches off.

You can also go to the Mt Elgon (Andersen's) Orchards, which is near the border and can be reached from the track to the forest station. You might be able to leave a

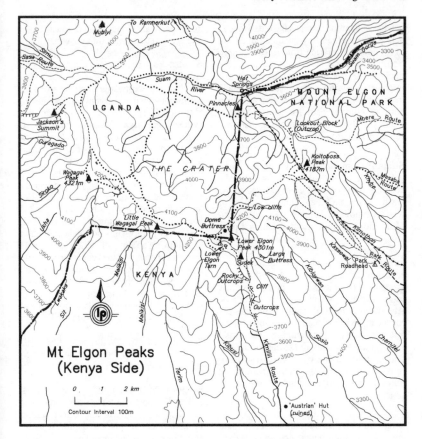

Mt Elgon Peaks
(Kenya Side)

0   1   2 km

Contour Interval 100m

vehicle here and ask about hiring a local guide or camping in the area. Because this route is near the border there have been reports of a few 'bandit' attacks. The people at the forest station or the orchards would be able to update you on the latest security situation.

Stage 1 From the forest station, follow the logging tracks for 12 km through the forest. There's a maze of tracks in this area, so a local guide for this section is strongly recommended. Landmarks to look out for are an old concrete chimney stack by a crossroads,

five km from the forest station, and an old black and white signpost by a fork (where you go left) about one km further up the track.

The track becomes impassable for vehicles where a stream flows across, turning it into a bog. There are some old concrete pipes nearby (the remains of an abandoned project to divert the stream). If you're driving, you'll probably be lucky to even get this far, as the track is blocked lower down by fallen trees. You could camp in this area.

Continue walking up the track, round two sharp hairpin bends and through some patches of bamboo, to reach the old roadhead near a clump of tall fir trees on a ridge (five to six hours of walking from forest station). You can also camp here. Up to this point, the track is very overgrown and hard to follow in places. Look for signs of the old vehicle track which occasionally deteriorates to a narrow winding path for short sections. There are also signs of buffalo in this area, so make a lot of noise as you walk.

Stage 2 From the old roadhead, the going gets easier as the path aims westwards, keeping to the crest of a broad ridge to the north of the main Mbere Valley. The peak of Koitcut is now behind you (east), at the end of the ridge. You are now in national park land.

The path continues to follow the ridge, falling and rising in places, crisscrossing the crest and at one point winding through a group of rocky pinnacles. The path is clear in some places but non-existent in others. About three to four hours from the old roadhead, there's a small stream down on the left and a place for camping. The small stream may be empty at the end of the dry season, in which case you'll have to go down into the main Mbere Valley (about 20 minutes down, 30 minutes back up) to get water.

Stage 3 From this camping place, the path continues gaining height gradually, swinging south round the head of a large valley (a tributary of the Suam), then back east, through fairly level ground. The main peak of Koitoboss is clearly visible to the southwest. The path leads to the north of Koitoboss (keep the peak to your left), then drops steeply, passing beneath high cliffs, to tend left and up round the base of a square-shaped rocky buttress to reach the crater rim, two to three hours from the camping place.

Apparently, smugglers (and probably poachers) on this route used this outcrop as a vantage point to check for border guards and park rangers, and it's known as the Lookout Block. The views are very good:

north-eastwards back down towards the Suam Gorge; and west into the crater itself.

Sidetracks in the Crater From the Lookout Block, you have two options. You can follow the clear path westwards along the broad rim of the crater then drop steeply down, keeping to the left of a group of tall rocky pinnacles, then swinging right (north) to reach the Hot Springs at the head of the Suam Gorge (see the Uganda Mt Elgon section for more details). This takes about four to five hours there and back from the Lookout Block.

From the Lookout Block, you can also aim south, inside the crater, to reach the col on the southern end of Koitoboss. From the col, you can reach the summit of Koitoboss Peak, the highest point on this side of the mountain, by following a faint path which leads up the southern shoulder of the peak, then along the base of cliffs on its western side, to scramble up a steep, densely vegetated gully to reach the flat top, and a large cairn that marks the summit (4187 metres). It takes about three to four hours there and back from the Lookout Block.

It may be possible to camp nearer (or inside) in the crater, but water supplies here are not always reliable.

Stage 4 After reaching the Hot Springs and/or Koitoboss, retrace your route back down to the roadhead and forest station. From the camping place to the forest station could be done in one long day.

Optional Traverse From the Lookout Block you could attempt a complete traverse of the mountain by circling the crater rim and descending on the Kimilili Route. This is a very demanding trek, involving two or three more days and some good navigation, but it's also spectacular and very satisfying, and worth considering if you're properly equipped and supplied.

From the Lookout Block, follow the directions given earlier to reach Koitoboss Col, and from here aim generally south-west, inside the crater rim, contouring and keeping high to avoid dropping down into the deep valleys to your right (west), but keeping below the crest of the rim to avoid rocky outcrops. There is no path, and the going is hard, through groundsels and low bush. After about three hours, you'll reach a large dome-topped buttress at the north-eastern end of Lower Elgon Peak. Pass to the right of this, then contour right (do not go steeply up) to pass through a col in the crater rim to the west of Lower Elgon Peak. Keep contouring left and then down over a series of flat terraces to reach Lower Elgon Tarn. (From the tarn you can scramble up the gully in the cliffs behind to reach the summit of Lower Elgon Peak.) Camping is possible here.

From the tarn, aim south, keeping to the right of the huge separate buttress standing to the south of the main peak. Cross the southern shoulder of this buttress and con-tinue south down the crest of a broad grassy ridge, crisscrossing in places to pass small rocky outcrops on the crest. You might find traces of a faint path. If not, keep aiming south, and avoid tending too far left, keeping to the right (west) side of the ridge-top, above a valley down to your right. About three hours from Lower Elgon Tarn, you should cut across the remains of a faint track. Follow this downhill for another 30 minutes to reach the abandoned hut (sometimes called Austrian Hut). This is a good place to camp. Water is available from the stream in the valley down to the east.

From here it's 30 km, mainly downhill, along the park track, past Chepkitale Forest Station, to reach Kaberua Forest Station and the village of Kapsakwony. This section could probably be done in a long day, but the condition (and legality) of walking down this route depends on whether this area is incor-porated into the Mt Elgon National Park (see the Future Possibilities section).

Other Routes

The Masaba Route, starting from the village of Masaba (sometimes spelt Masara) on the eastern side of the mountain, is now com-pletely overgrown and not feasible. The Suam Gorge Route, which followed the river along the border between Uganda and Kenya, is also completely disused. Due to its obviously sensitive nature, you should avoid this area, downstream of the Hot Springs.

Future Possibilities

There have been proposals to enlarge Mt Elgon National Park to include the area of forest around the Kimilili Route, and to re-open Chepkitale Forest Station. This will have two likely effects: the track will be improved, making vehicle access and day-walks to Lower Elgon Peak easier; but, in common with the rest of the national park, you will not be allowed to enter without a vehicle, and will only be allowed to walk on the high moorland with an armed ranger.

The Kimilili track may be extended north-eastwards to join the existing national park track near its current roadhead. If this happens, it will be possible to walk in a long day from the Kimilili roadhead up to Lower Elgon Peak, then round the crater rim to Koitoboss, and back down to the national park roadhead, to be picked up or met by a vehicle there.

It is also possible that the Kenyan national park authorities might be influenced by events in the Uganda park and relax the rules to make it easier for wilderness trekking on this side of Mt Elgon. If this does happen, all the routes outlined here will be much more attractive for independent trekkers, and the mountain could become an important trek-king area, with good quality treks to easily rival some of those on the major peaks of Mt Kenya, Kilimanjaro and the Rwenzoris.

THE CHERANGANI HILLS

The Cheranganis are in the north of Kenya, about 300 km from Nairobi. Although usually referred to as 'Hills' there are several summits here above 3000 metres, and the highest peak, Nakugen or Kamalagon, is at 3370 metres, which makes the Cheranganis the fourth-highest range in Kenya.

Unlike the other major mountains of Kenya, the Cheranganis are not volcanic in origin. They were created by localised uplift and the erosion of the surrounding landscape. Steep escarpment walls surround the range on three sides, separating the fertile farmland and forest on the high ground from the semi-desert scrubland at their base.

The Cheranganis also differ from most of the other large mountain ranges in Kenya in that they are populated. The people are rural, growing crops and keeping sheep and cattle. The lower areas on the southern and eastern parts of the range are quite densely inhabited, with farms and extended villages. The best trekking is in the higher northern areas, but even here there are small scattered villages; the whole range is crisscrossed by a network of paths and tracks, which makes it ideal trekking country.

Maps

The northern section of the Cheranganis is covered by Survey of Kenya 1:50,000 map sheets 75/2 (Sigor), 76/1 (Chesegon), 75/4 (Cherangani) and 76/3 (Tot), and the whole range is covered by the 1:250,000 sheet NA-36-12 (Kapenguria).

Access

Access is fairly straightforward: the main tarred road north from Kitale towards Lodwar on the west side of Lake Turkana passes along the west side of the range. Public transport runs along this road. There are also several smaller roads which can be used if you've got your own car.

Until about 20 years ago, the Cheranganis were a restricted area, but during the 1970s the region was opened up and several local farm development schemes were introduced. Although access to the higher parts of the range was made considerably easier, the Cheranganis remained rarely visited. Some enterprising walkers did make it this far, and several good car-assisted day-walks have become established as 'regulars'. The number of outside visitors slowly continued to increase, although very little long-distance trekking was done, even though there was enormous potential.

Trekking Routes

Walking conditions are generally not strenu-

Acacia tortilis

ous, and most paths and tracks pass through gently rolling grassland. Weather in the dry season can be pleasant, although conditions can be almost as severe as those on Mt Elgon, so you should be well-equipped, and self-contained, with tent and camping gear. There are some small shops in the larger villages, but you should plan to be fairly self-sufficient in food. Water is generally available, except on the higher ridges.

Unfortunately, further development of the Cheranganis as a walking area was halted during the early 1990s when the region was effectively closed by politically inspired inter-tribal violence. This was still the case in late 1992. However, the area will almost certainly open up again in the future and will remain an excellent area for competent and enterprising trekkers to explore.

There are no set routes, so you'll just have to follow local paths, using your compass and asking directions as you go. Some basic Swahili is almost essential here.

On the northern side of the range a spectacular trek of three to four days is possible round the head of the Weiwei Valley, between Mt Koh and the Sondhang Ridge.

A longer trek of five to six days follows the Sondhang Ridge southwards to reach another peak called Kalelaikelat, and then follows the edge of the huge Tangasia Valley to the village of Sina. From here it drops off the escarpment to cross the Moruny River at Kachemogan and goes through dry bush country to meet the main road north of Chepareria.

Places to Stay

At the foot of the hills are two places for accommodation, where you can also get more route information, hire local guides, and make inquiries about the security situation. These are: *Sirikwa Safaris Guest House*, run by Mrs Barnley, about 25 km north of Kitale on the main road towards Lodwar. You can camp in the garden for a small fee, or stay (with breakfast) in one of the rooms (advance booking sometimes required, contact Let's Go Travel in Nairobi); or the *Marich Pass Field Studies Centre* further north, just past the junction to Sigor, which has a campsite and bandas for hire.

THE LOITA HILLS

Longer walks are feasible in the Loita Hills, to the south-west of Nairobi in Maasailand. This is a fascinating area, with good walking through areas of bush and grassland, and a chance of seeing wildlife and the local Maasai people. Possible routes include a three or four day north-south traverse of the range from the village of Maji Moto down towards Osubuko (or Supugo, and various other spellings), the highest point in the hills at about 2680 metres. There are also several other possibilities in the plains to the west of the hills nearer the Maasai Mara National Reserve. Unfortunately, the Loitas are very difficult to reach without your own car, and you need to be completely self-contained with food and gear when you get there. Guides, usually Maasai morans, are also essential to help find water and to smooth any encounters with other Maasai warriors. By far the easiest way of walking here for several days is to join an organised trek (see the Kenya Trekking Companies section).

THE NORTH

Further afield, in the semi-deserts of northern Kenya, are several remote mountain areas including the Mathews Range (also called the Lengyio or Lenkiyio Range), the Ndoto Mountains and Mt Kulal, to the east of Lake Turkana. Local conditions usually limit walks to a day or two, and reaching these mountains usually takes much longer than the walking itself, although there are some longer possibilities if you've got time, money and full vehicle support. Organised treks, with camels to carry gear and water, are available in the Ndotos area (see the Kenya Trekking Companies section).

Uganda

During the dark days of Idi Amin and the various civil wars that followed his rule, Uganda was essentially off-limits for trekkers and travellers. But now the long 'years of terror' are over and Uganda is once again open to visitors (although fighting continues in the north of the country). The roads and towns are being reconstructed and the people seem to be getting on with rebuilding their lives.

For trekkers, Uganda's main attraction is the Rwenzori Range, the fabled Mountains of the Moon, a true African highland wilderness, which includes the third-highest peak on the continent. And in the far east of the country, on the border with Kenya, is Mt Elgon, another East African giant which has recently been given protected Forest Park status and is now welcoming trekkers.

Facts about the Country

HISTORY
The early history of Uganda up to the end of the 19th century is covered briefly in the Facts about the Region chapter.

The Colonial Period
When the European colonial powers divided up East Africa at the end of the 19th century, the large African kingdoms of Buganda and Bunyoro, plus some other smaller ones, became a British protectorate. Its name was changed to Uganda in the early 1900s after the British government agreed to recognise the *kabakas* (kings) as rulers of the people, and the kings agreed to recognise the authority of the protectorate.

In the 1930s, the railway line from Mombasa to Lake Victoria was extended to Kampala, the capital. Plantations were established and the local people were encouraged to grow cotton and coffee as cash crops, but European settlement was minimal compared with the neighbouring colony in Kenya.

Transition & Independence
Moves towards independence gained ground in the late 1950s, and the colony became independent in 1962. The kabaka became president and head of state, while Milton Obote, who had been active in the nationalist movements of the '50s, became prime minister.

But after this relatively smooth transition, things began to go rapidly downhill. In 1966, Obote ordered his army commander, one General Idi Amin, to attack the palace of the kabaka. The king escaped to the UK and Obote declared himself president. In 1971, when Obote was abroad at a conference, Amin pulled a similar trick and, with the backing of the army, took control of the country. The terrors of the period that followed are well recorded elsewhere. Thousands of Ugandan peasants were killed, merely for being members of the wrong tribe, or even for being Christian (Amin was a Muslim). Educated people in the towns were also seen as a threat and many were murdered openly by army death squads. All Asians living in Uganda, mainly involved in business and commerce, were expelled and their property confiscated. Factories and plantations were nationalised, then mismanaged and virtually destroyed. Hundreds of millions of dollars disappeared into the overseas bank accounts of Amin and his supporters while the country literally fell apart.

Up until this time the Western powers had condemned Amin's actions, while continuing to support his regime by buying coffee and providing luxury goods for the military elite. In 1978, sanctions were finally imposed by the UK and the USA. For Uganda and (more importantly) the army, this made conditions even worse. To create a diversion for his increasingly dissatisfied generals, later the same year Amin ordered an invasion of northern Tanzania, supposedly to punish president Julius Nyerere for assisting Ugandan exiles in the early '70s. The Tanzanian army later repulsed the Ugandan forces and went on to 'liberate' Kampala. Meanwhile, Amin escaped to Libya.

If anything, the period that followed was even more anarchic than the Amin years. Ugandan and Tanzanian soldiers turned into bandits and highwaymen. Death and chaos were still very much the order of the day. Two new presidents were appointed but with little authority.

Elections were finally held in 1980 and Milton Obote came to power for the second time, but tribal mass killings and the murder of suspected opponents continued. In fact, more people were killed during Obote's rule than during Amin's. Meanwhile, a guerrilla group called the National Resistance Army (NRA), under the leadership of Yoweri Museveni, was established in western Uganda. This rebel army grew but, in 1985, before it was in a position to take control, Obote was deposed in a coup led by Tito Okello, an officer from Obote's own troops, again with the backing of the army.

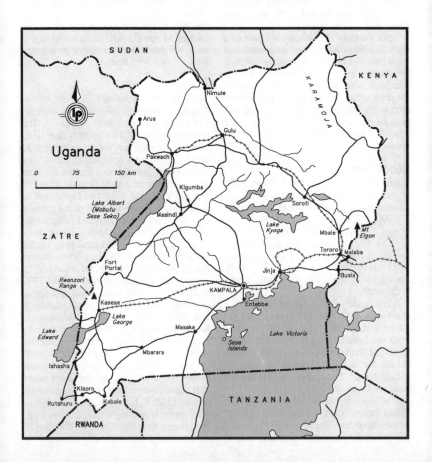

Modern Times

Peace talks between the Okello government and the NRA rebels failed, and this set the stage for civil war and yet another period of terror and suffering for the Ugandan people. In 1986, after gradually pushing across the country, the NRA finally took Kampala and the forces of Okello were chased across the border into Sudan.

The NRA became the National Resistance Movement (NRM) and has since remained a popular government. Controls are strict, but the army remains disciplined, and the country is definitely returning towards something near normal with increasing momentum and confidence.

Since the early 1990s many of Kampala's main buildings have been renovated and roads from the capital to the east and west of the country have been completely rebuilt. Financial controls have been lifted, factories are once again making goods and there is food in the shops. Several Asian and European people, who left or were expelled after Amin's takeover, have returned to the country.

GEOGRAPHY

Uganda measures about 500 km from north to south, and 450 km from east to west, at its widest points, with an area of around 236,000 sq km, less than half the size of Kenya. Uganda is on the western edge of the African High Plateau and much of the country is flat, featureless plain, averaging 1500 metres above sea level in the south, sloping very gradually to about 1000 metres in the north.

It is a country dominated by lakes: in the south is Lake Victoria, and in the west Lake Albert (called Lake Mobutu on the Zaire side) and Lake Edward (once, briefly, Lake Idi Amin). In the centre of the country, linked to Lake Victoria by the Nile, are the tentacles of Lake Kyoga. The land is well-watered and good for farming.

The western branch of the Great Rift Valley forms Uganda's natural and political western boundary. The Rwenzori Mountains rise above the plains on the eastern side of

Baobab tree *(Adansonia digitata)*

the Rift in the south-west corner of the country. Mount Elgon, Uganda's other major peak, is right on the other side of the country on the border with Kenya.

CLIMATE

Like the other countries of East Africa, Uganda's climate is influenced by altitude, and is tropical rather than equatorial. The dominant feature of the climate pattern is the band of rain which moves across the region, creating two wet seasons and two dry seasons each year. The dry seasons are from the end of May until early October, when it's dry and cool, and from late November to early March. In the far north of the country the movement of the rain-band creates only one rainy season, from April to September.

In the southern and central parts of the country, maximum daytime temperatures during the cool, dry season are around 25°C. In the warm dry they can rise to about 27°C or 28°C. Above the plains, on the mountains, generally the higher you go, the colder it gets. And in common with all African equatorial mountains, although the daily maximum temperatures vary only slightly throughout the year, there are great differences between day and night. On the lower slopes of Mt Elgon or the Rwenzoris, maximum daytime temperatures are usually around 15-20°C, falling to 10-15°C in moorland zones, where night temperatures often drop to near freezing. Above 4000 metres on the Rwenzoris, maximum daytime temperatures are around 5°C and always below freezing at night. Daytime temperatures on the high slopes of Elgon are similar and frosts at night are not uncommon.

ECONOMY

Uganda's economy is predominantly agricultural. The main export is, and always has been, coffee. Other cash crops include cotton and tea. Development of any other crops or industry has been hindered by the political events since independence. Most people are farmers working a small plot for their own needs or for local trading, or employed on large plantations. *Matoke* (green bananas) is the staple food crop.

POPULATION & PEOPLE

Uganda's population was estimated at around 17 million in 1991, growing at a rate of around 3% per year, which puts the country high in the league of population growth-rates. Around Lake Victoria, and in the west and south of the country, the people are of Bantu origin (including the predominant Buganda and the Bakonjo people of the Rwenzori). Also in the west are groups of pre-Bantu Pygmy people. North of Lake Kyoga, and in the north-east of the country, the people belong to the Nilotic group (including the Lango, Acholi and Karamajong).

RELIGION

Most people are Christians, while the remainder, to a greater or lesser degree, follow traditional beliefs. There are also small groups of Muslims.

LANGUAGE

All the main groups have their own languages and dialects. English is used as a common language and very widely spoken throughout the country. Swahili is used only in the east, although many people can speak a few words wherever you go.

Facts for the Trekker

VISAS & CUSTOMS

Visas are required by citizens of all countries, except those from some Commonwealth countries (apart from the UK) and some European countries.

At Kampala airport, some officials are hot on vaccination certificates: make sure yours are in order, otherwise you'll be sent to the very suspect medical room for a jab on the spot.

There are no restrictions on the amount of hard currency you can carry in or out, but you are not allowed to import or export more than USh 5000. Currency declaration forms are no longer used, although there's always a possibility of them being reintroduced.

As always, entry regulations are liable to change, so check the latest requirements with your nearest embassy, high commission or tourist office.

MONEY

The unit of currency is the Ugandan shilling (USh). Cents (there used to be 100 of them in a shilling) are no longer used. Money can now be changed in private foreign exchange (forex) bureaus, which have sprung up all over Kampala and in several smaller towns, and revolutionised moneychanging. These bureaus buy and sell money freely, with the minimum of hassle, and offer a better rate than the banks. And it's all completely legal. Many banks also have forex desks (make sure you go to the right desk).

Inflation used to be very high in Uganda but with the freeing of currency regulations it has stabilised slightly. The rates quoted here, which were correct at the end of 1992, are likely to be off the mark by the time you read this, but they should be near enough to give you an idea.

US$1 = USh 1200
UK£1 = USh 2200

When converting prices quoted in this book in USh, use the rates here; the actual cost in hard currency is unlikely to have changed much. Note that rooms in large hotels, national park entrance fees and some organised safaris have to be paid for in US dollars or another hard currency, and shillings are not accepted.

The only problem with Ugandan currency is that bank-note production has not kept pace with the rate of inflation. While you're getting over 1000 shillings for your dollar, the largest notes available are usually for only USh 500, (and often USh 200 or 100 is all the banks have) so you'll need a small rucksack to carry your money! This might change, as new notes of appropriate denominations have been promised.

WHEN TO GO

The best time for trekking on the mountains of Uganda is during the dry seasons, from the end of May until September, when it's dry and cool, and from late November to early March, when it's warmer (see the Climate section for more details). At the end of the dry season haze and smoke from burning old crops can reduce visibility.

Having said that, the Rwenzoris are notoriously wet, even in the dry season, when it can (and does) rain at any time, or snow and hail at higher altitudes (although after rain the air is clear and you may get better views).

Mount Elgon also has an unpredictable weather pattern, as the local climate is influenced by air movements over Lake Victoria, and it can rain at any time, although generally you can count on there being more in the wet season! Hail and snow are not uncommon at any time of year.

HOLIDAYS

As well as Christmas Day, Boxing Day, New Year's Day, and Easter Friday and Monday, public holidays include:

26 January	NRM Government Day
1 May	Labour Day
9 October	Independence Day

GUIDEBOOKS & MAPS

There is no single guidebook which covers just Uganda. For independent travel around the country, your best option is Lonely Planet's *East Africa – a travel survival kit*, which has a good chapter on Uganda and also covers several other countries in the region.

For general travel around the country, there is no good map of Uganda available. In Nairobi you can buy maps of East Africa, which cover Uganda, along with Kenya, Tanzania and parts of other countries, but these only show main features and are no use if you leave the main routes, or go trekking.

Most parts of the country are also covered by the Uganda Survey Department maps, originally drawn by the British Directorate of Overseas Surveys. These maps may be available from the Map Sales Office in the Department of Land Surveys & Mapping, near the post office in Entebbe (off the road towards the airport), although stocks are unreliable.

For the mountains and trekking areas covered in this chapter, some large-scale maps and detailed guidebooks are available (see the individual trekking sections).

TREKKING COMPANIES

The tourist business in Uganda is very small, and there are only a few companies in Kampala doing anything in the way of organised safaris or all-inclusive treks. If you've got your own gear, and plenty of time, you can make all your own arrangements anyway.

But if you're short of time and want to avoid hassles you can join an organised trek. The following companies have been recommended:

Hot Ice
> Spear House, Jinja Rd, PO Box 151, Kampala (☎ 267441, ☎ & fax 242733). This is an experienced company doing very good quality treks on the Rwenzoris, including technical ascents of the peaks if required, providing staff, equipment and food, and making all necessary arrangements. Treks are designed to suit your own requirements and costs start at around US$100 per day per

person for a group of four. Hot Ice also organise luxury and standard wildlife safaris in some of Uganda's other national parks, which can be combined with a Rwenzori trek, and can make general bookings and reservations.

Spear Touring Safaris
Spear House, Jinja Rd, Kampala (☎ 259950, fax 234903). This company offers an eight-day trip which includes four days trekking in the Rwenzoris, transport from Kampala, food, equipment, and B&B accommodation for around US$600 per person for a group of four. They also do wildlife safaris, but I've never heard of anybody going with them so the quality is unknown.

Other specialist trekking and climbing outfits doing Rwenzori trips are based in Nairobi (see Trekking Companies, in the Kenya chapter).

ACCOMMODATION IN KAMPALA

If you arrive by air, or come overland from Nairobi, you'll probably spend a night or two in Kampala, arranging return transport or stocking up on supplies in between treks.

The city centre is quite small. Security is generally not a problem in Kampala on main streets during the day, but there's obviously a lot of poverty in the city, so it's best not to wander around at night.

For accommodation, there's something for most budgets, although nothing like the choice you get in Nairobi. At the top of town, and the top of the price range, is the recently refurbished *Sheraton Hotel*, with most of the features you'd expect, and prices too, with singles/doubles from US$166/185 including breakfast. If you feel the need for a splurge (after 10 days' bog-bashing in the Rwenzoris, maybe), the Sheraton does special weekend deals with doubles at US$140 including breakfast, for two nights.

Near the Sheraton, at the bottom of Sezibwa Rd, is the *Fairway Hotel*, now privately owned again, and rapidly improving, with singles/doubles for US$40/60 including breakfast. In the Muyenga part of town are the *Reste Corner Hotel*, the *Diplomate Hotel* and the *Penine Hotel*. The former has an excellent restaurant, the latter two have

good good views over the city. All are reasonable at around $40/60 for singles/ doubles.

Outside the city centre, the *Lion Hotel* and the *Rena Hotel*, on Namirembe Rd, are small and basic but clean and safe, with doubles for around US$25, which is a lot for what you get, although over the last year or so, more hotels in this range have been opened and competition is forcing prices down.

For cheaper accommodation, back in the centre near the railway station, the *Tourist Motel* has basic doubles for USh 9000. The cheapest place in town is the *YMCA* at the far end of Buganda Rd, about two km outside the city centre. For USh 2000 you can sleep on the floor, and might even find a mattress if you get there early. This place is a school so you have to be up before 8 am, but you can hang around or eat in the snack-bar during the day. Camping in the grounds is allowed, but it still costs USh 2000 and the staff don't recommend it.

For more details on places to stay in or near the trekking areas are given in the relevant sections.

Getting There & Away

You can travel between Uganda and the neighbouring East African countries of Kenya, Tanzania and Malawi by air or overland. How you travel depends on how much time you've got, and the amount of travelling, as opposed to trekking, you want to do. In this section it's presumed that you want to take a fairly direct route between the trekking areas in the different countries.

TO/FROM KENYA
Air
There are international flights between Kampala (Entebbe) and Nairobi, usually about five or six flights a week in each direction. The one-way fare is about US$100.

Road

The main border crossing between the two countries is at Malaba, north of Lake Victoria. Malaba is linked to Kampala and Nairobi by good sealed roads. There's an overnight bus between Kampala and Nairobi, operated by the Akamba Bus Company. The office is in De Winton Rd, and the fare is USh 15,000 one way (see the Kenya Getting There & Away section).

In Kampala, public transport to the border leaves from the bus and matatu station. It may be easier to do the journey in stages via Jinja and Tororo, although if you've no need to go into Tororo, you can get off at the junction by the petrol station about three km south of the town and continue straight on for the border (another 10 km). Going from the border towards Kampala you may have to do the same. Fares between Kampala and the border or Tororo are about USh 4000.

You can walk across the border – it's only a few hundred metres between the two border posts.

On the Kenya side there are regular buses and matatus between the border and Bungoma, Eldoret and Nairobi (see the Kenya chapter for details).

Formalities at the Malaba (Uganda/Kenya) border are straightforward for both countries (for more details, see the Kenya chapter).

Train

There is a line between Kampala and Tororo, but the trains are very slow and unreliable, so you're better off using road transport. Although a rusty track crosses the border there are no international services and you'll still have to walk between the two countries. Trains on the Kenyan side, between Malaba and Nairobi, are good and worth using (see the Kenya chapter).

TO/FROM TANZANIA
Air

International flights between Kampala (Entebbe) and Dar es Salaam go about three times a week in each direction, and cost around US$200. In Tanzania there are regular flights (at least once per day) between Dar and Kilimanjaro International Airport (KIA) which is in northern Tanzania and nearer the main trekking areas. There are no direct flights at present between Kampala and KIA. However, for travelling quickly between Uganda and northern Tanzania you're much better off flying between Kampala and Nairobi, and going by road between Nairobi and Arusha or Moshi (see the Tanzania Getting There & Away section).

Road

The easiest way to get between the trekking areas of Uganda and those in Tanzania by road is through Kenya, via Nairobi (see the Kenya Getting There & Away section).

Boat

The Lake Victoria ferry service has been reintroduced (see Getting There & Away in the Tanzania chapter for details).

TO/FROM MALAWI
Air

Flights between Kampala and Lilongwe go about twice a week and cost about US$400 one way. They usually go via Nairobi and/or Dar. Some even go via Gaberone and Harare).

Road

Uganda and Malawi do not share a common border, so the easiest way to travel overland between these two countries is through Kenya and Tanzania (see the Getting There & Away and Getting Around sections of the Kenya and Tanzania chapters).

Getting Around

You can travel to, or between, the trekking areas in Uganda by road or rail. There are no internal flights of use to trekkers, although you can charter a five-seater plane from Entebbe to Dasese for $620 (details from Hot Ice in Kampala).

ROAD

Most roads in Uganda are in very bad condition, although the main routes through the country, from Kampala to Malaba and Mbale, and from Kampala, via Mbarara, to Kasese and Fort Portal, have recently been sealed and are in excellent condition.

Bus & Minibus

On all the main routes there are buses, which tend to be rather slow, and minibuses, which are faster. Travellers have written to say that the speed of the minibuses verges on the supersonic. It seems better to go in a kronky old bucket, as the new minibuses go too fast and kill people. In Kampala they all leave from the main bus station. It can be hard to find the right bus or minibus, but just ask around and you'll soon be shown to the transport you want. In other towns there's either a small bus station, or vehicles leave from the market.

Most vehicles leave when full (really full), but others seem to keep to some kind of a departure timetable and leave half-empty, picking up people along the way. Minibus fares are very reasonable: about USh 5000 between Kampala and Mbarara, and USh 8000 between Kampala and Kasese. Between Kampala and Tororo or Malaba is about USh 4000. Buses are around half this price.

Taxi

Taxis in Kampala are often indistinguishable from private cars (usually because they are private cars, moonlighting). A trip across town will cost between USh 1000 and USh 2000, and from town to the airport at Entebbe (about 30 km) USh 30,000. If you're flying into Kampala and the bank is closed, taxi drivers will take you into town for US$25 cash.

In Kampala and several other towns you'll see bicycle taxis (or *boda-bodas*), where the passenger sits on a large cushion on the rack behind the saddle. This is the nearest Africa gets to a rickshaw! Short rides (eg from the Saad Hotel in Kasese to the railway station – the only one I've had) are about USh 300. Heavy rucksacks cost extra.

Car Rental

Saloon cars cost around $90 per day, 4WD around $120. Hot Ice (see Trekking Companies) can assist if you need to hire a car.

Hitching

There are very few private cars on the road in Uganda, but if you've got time it's possible to travel this way. There are a lot of expatriate aid workers, usually driving between Nairobi and Kampala, who may stop. Otherwise your lift will probably be in a truck, where you'll be expected to pay about the same as the bus fare anyway.

TRAIN

From Kampala, the main railway lines go east to Malaba and west to Kasese. Unless you're particularly interested in train travel, or have a couple of days to spare, these services are worth avoiding. There is no 1st class, and many 2nd-class coaches are without windows and lights. Conditions in 3rd class are even worse. Derailments and breakdowns are common (allow for at least two per trip). The Kampala-Kasese journey is advertised at about 15 hours, but it often takes twice as long. If you still want to try it, the fare between Kampala and Kasese is USh 3300 in 2nd class and 2250 in 3rd class. Between Kampala and Malaba costs USh

2000/1400. The line may close completely in 1993.

The Rwenzori Mountains

The Rwenzoris, often called The Mountains of the Moon, lie on the Uganda-Zaire border and mark the frontier between the high savanna plains of East Africa and the low dense forests of the west. Unlike the other major mountains in this region, the Rwenzoris are not volcanic in origin; they were formed by uplift associated with the formation of the western branch of the Great Rift Valley, which runs just to the west of the range.

And unlike the other major mountains, which rise as single peaks, the Rwenzoris are a true mountain range covering a wide area. There are six main massifs, each with several peaks, most with glaciers and coverings of permanent snow. The highest point in the Rwenzoris is Margherita Peak on Mt Stanley. At 5109 metres (16,763 feet), this is the third-highest point in Africa. Many of the other peaks are above, or just under, 5000 metres. Perhaps not surprisingly, one of the Rwenzoris' other names is 'The Alps of Africa'.

Although the local Bakonjo people had been hunting in the Rwenzoris' forested foothills for centuries, the early European explorers knew nothing of the range, as it was usually hidden by mist and clouds of rain. It is this almost constant rain that creates the snow and ice on the main peaks, and feeds the streams and rivers lower down which eventually become headwaters of the White Nile.

The explorer Henry Stanley was probably the first European to see the Rwenzoris, when he explored the region around Lake Victoria in the 1870s. On a return expedition in 1888, Stanley named the range Mt Gordon Bennet, after the owner of the New York Times who funded his trip, but fortunately the name never stuck. It wasn't until 1906, after all the other great East African mountains had been explored and climbed, that Prince Luigi di Savoia, better known as the Duke of Abruzzi, led a huge expedition into

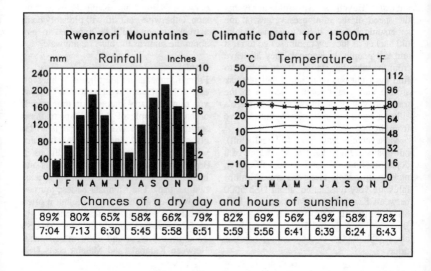

Rwenzori Mountains — Climatic Data for 1500m

Chances of a dry day and hours of sunshine

89%	80%	65%	58%	66%	79%	82%	69%	56%	49%	58%	78%
7:04	7:13	6:30	5:45	5:58	6:51	5:59	5:56	6:41	6:39	6:24	6:43

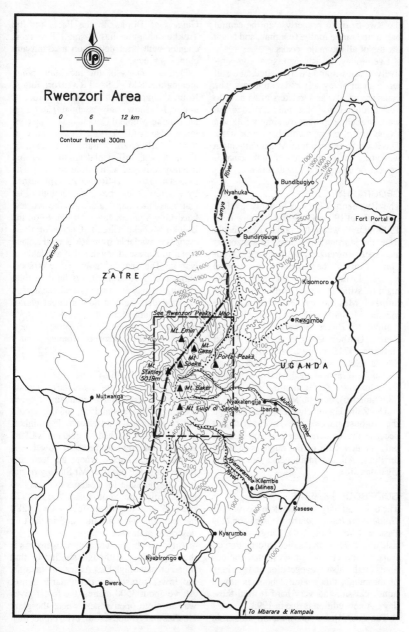

the Rwenzoris to properly map the central part of the range for the first time, and reach the top of all the major peaks.

Even today, the Rwenzoris are comparatively unknown and rarely visited, and still retain an air of mystery and remoteness. The paths are narrow and trekkers often have to push through dense bush and bamboo forest, wade though deep bogs, or simply follow a vague line of cairns across bare rock slabs. The Rwenzoris are a true African mountain wilderness and a trek here, although demanding, can be a very satisfying experience.

GEOGRAPHY

The Rwenzori Range is roughly oval in shape, about 100 km long and 40 km wide at 1500 metres, where the range rises steeply from the surrounding plains. (Rwenzori is also spelt Ruwenzori, but both are corruptions of one of the mountains' many local names.) In the centre of the range are the main massifs. These are (with their highest points): Mt Stanley (Margherita, 5109 metres), Mt Speke (Vittorio Emanuele, 4890 metres), Mt Baker (Edward, 4843 metres), Emin (Umberto, 4798 metres), Gessi (Iolanda, 4715 metres) and Mt Luigi di Savoia (Sella, 4627 metres). Each massif also has several other peaks; the most notable are Alexandra (5091 metres) and Albert (5087 metres), both on Mt Stanley.

The Zaire-Uganda border passes through the highest part of the Rwenzoris, but because the western side is much steeper, only about a fifth of the range is in Zaire territory. All the main peaks are on the Ugandan side.

GUIDEBOOKS & MAPS

The best, and only, guidebook to the range is *Guide to the Ruwenzori* by H Osmaston & D Pasteur (West Col, UK). Originally published in 1972, with detailed information on walking and climbing routes, plus copious notes on the history, vegetation and geology of the range, this beautiful book is now a minor classic, and very hard to find these days. A new edition is due in 1993.

The *East Africa International Mountain Guide* (see Books, in the Facts for the Trekker chapter) has a small Rwenzori chapter with brief details on trekking and climbing routes.

Detailed maps of the mountain range include the 'RMS/USAid Rwenzori Tourist Routes' map, which is the most recent, although it shows only essential features on the Bujuku-Mubuku Circuit and has no contours. Also available is the Uganda Surveys 'Central Rwenzori' map, at a scale of 1:25,000, with sufficient detail for a trek and recently re-issued with colour shading. The easiest map to use is 'Ruwenzori', published by Andrew Wielochowski, although older editions of this map do not show the two new huts (Guy Yeoman and John Matte) on the Bujuku-Mubuku Circuit. Copies of these maps are available from RMS or the Saad Hotel in Kasese. They are also available in Nairobi. The Uganda Surveys 1:50,000 sheet number 65/2 (Margherita) is hard to find, although it may also be re-issued. It has been reported that there is now a direct photographic enlargement of the 1:50,000 65/2 published by Uganda Lands & Survey Department, entitled 'Ruwenzori Mountains' at a scale of 1:25,000.

TREKKING INFORMATION

To get to the summit of any of the three main peaks involves technical mountaineering, or crossing steep snow and ice, and this should not be attempted by trekkers. The highest point normally reached by trekkers is Elena Hut (4540 metres), at the snout (lower end) of the Elena Glacier, where the technical routes up to the peaks of Mt Stanley begin. It is also possible for trekkers to cross two major cols, the Scott-Elliot Pass (4370 metres) and the Freshfield Pass (4280 metres), and these are included in the trek described in this section.

An important feature of the Rwenzoris is the vegetation. Although similar to that found on other high East African mountains, the lower forests are particularly dense. Above about 3500 metres, the forest gives way to more open zones, where the giant lobelias and groundsels are even bigger than on the other major East African mountains. The soil in the Rwenzoris is very thin, and easily eroded when the fragile vegetation cover is disturbed. This has been a problem on the upper slopes, where trekkers trying to avoid boggy sections have gradually increased the width of the paths.

But the main feature of the Rwenzoris is the weather. The range is notoriously wet: rain and mist, even in the dry season, are not uncommon. Apart from the highest sections of the route, thick mud is very much the order of the day, and many trekkers do the entire route in rubber boots (wellies or gumboots). I've seen people in fishing waders, and even in toe-to-thigh leggings made out of wet-suit material. On the steep slopes, where you'd expect the water to run off, the path can still be a thick morass, and the only thing likely to be flowing downhill is you! One writer has pointed out that Mt Kenya's infamous Vertical Bog is like a gently sloping damp patch compared with some parts of the Rwenzoris.

The nearest town to the Rwenzori Range is Kasese, about 300 km directly west of Kampala (almost 500 km by road).

Route Standard & Days Required
On many maps of the Rwenzoris, dotted lines indicate several routes from the foothills up onto the higher peaks. In reality, all but two of these routes are completely overgrown and very rarely used.

On the eastern side of the mountains, the two main routes that do exist follow the Bujuku and Mubuku rivers. These can be combined to make a very satisfying circular trek, following the two main valleys, crossing two major cols, and passing through the very heart of the range. This trek is described in detail here. Other trekking possibilities are outlined at the end of the section.

The Bujuku-Mubuku Circuit can be very tough. The paths are often boggy, and you may have to wade through knee-deep mud on several occasions. In the forest, the vegetation is dense and you'll also have to clamber over fallen branches and exposed roots. On the boglands, you often have to leap from tussock to tussock, in an attempt

(often vain) to keep out of the mud. This is not a route for the faint-hearted. But for many trekkers, the tough conditions, combined with the wierd vegetation and spectacular views of the main massifs and their glaciers, occasionally glimpsed through the cloud, are all part of the attraction. The Rwenzori range is a real African mountain wilderness, but, if you want your wilderness easy, this is not the place to be.

The Bujuku-Mubuku Circuit takes a minimum of six days, although seven is more common, and extra nights can be spent at higher huts, if you're going to sidetrack to any of the other valleys and passes in the main peak area.

Although the range is not as high as Kili or Mt Kenya, acclimatization is stll important. The gradual ascent forced by the position of huts and the route itself should help, but if you do feel bad effects from the altitude, the advice is the same as anywhere else: go down (see Acute Mountain Sickness, in the Health & First Aid chapter).

Guides & Porters
At present (1992) you can trek in the Rwenzoris without using guides and porters, although only very experienced trekkers should consider this, and even then it is unwise to trek without at least one other companion.

Most trekkers take local guides and porters. Guides are highly recommended as the paths are not always clear, and misty conditions often make route-finding difficult. Porters are optional but make the trekking much easier.

Guides and porters can be arranged through Rwenzori Mountaineering Services (RMS), a local cooperative founded in 1987, and supported by the American development organisation USAid. Money raised by the cooperative goes into projects in the local community. So far, a school and a dispensary have been built. The RMS also control the huts on the Bujuku-Mubuku Circuit.

The RMS headquarters is at Nyakalengija, near Ibanda, at the start of the route, and they also have an office in Kasese, at 33 Alexandra Street, a few blocks up from the Saad Hotel. Guides and porters can be reserved in advance by writing to RMS at PO Box 33, Kasese, but in practice this doesn't speed up the process very much. If you arrive in Kasese in the afternoon, you can still arrange a trek to start the next day.

RMS fees are:

Service fee	USh 20,000 per trekker
(this includes use of huts)	
Guide	USh 2100 per day
Porter	USh 4100 per day
Food	USh 1400 per guide/ porter per day
Equipment for guide/porters (obligatory):	
Blanket & coat	USh 5000 per guide/ porter per trip
Cooking pot	USh 2000 per pot
Panga for guide	USh 3000
Sacks for porter	USh 700 each
Matches	USh 800 per packet
Transport, Kasese-Ibanda	USh 1000 per trekker, each way

This system of fees may appear complicated, but it's actually very efficient: all costs are swiftly added up in the RMS office, you pay a single price and everything is taken care of.

Normally, for the seven-day circuit, two porters are required for each trekker; one for your kit and another for your food. Two trekkers hiring one guide and four porters pay about USh 90,000 each. In 1992 this was about US$90. Even if the fees go up (with inflation), the final cost in dollars will be about the same. Add US$10 for the national park entrance fees, and you're looking at about US$100 a person for a six-day Rwenzori trek, or slightly less if there's a larger group and, of course, more if you stay for extra days.

Note that a day is calculated to be the stage between two huts. If you combine two stages, your guides and porters get double for that day. They also get double wages if it snows, which is fair enough, as a lot of these guys go barefoot. (This might not be an actual rule, but it seems to be a tradition that's stuck since the Duke of Abruzzi's time.) The porters' maximum load is 12 kg, to which they add their own bags.

The RMS employ 60 guides and over 400 porters, which means most of them only work once or twice a season (the rest of the time they cultivate their small-holdings). This is why they have to be provided with blankets, coats, pangas and cooking pots every time. At the end of the trek the blankets and coats belong to the porters and guides, but the pots and panga technically belong to you, although it has become customary to give them away as an extra tip.

Crowned crane

Top: View across the massif from the summit of Chambe Peak, Mulanje (DE)
Bottom: Sombani Hut, Mulanje Massif, Malawi (DE)

Top: Trackless rolling grassland, north side of Nyika Plateau, Malawi (DE)
Bottom: Livingstonia Route: View from eastern escarpment, Nyika Plateau (DE)

Without exception, the RMS guides and porters are completely trustworthy, hard-working, and amongst the nicest people you could meet anywhere in Africa. I have never heard any complaints, either from them or about them. A tip at the end of the trek is usually appropriate and this should normally be equivalent to pay for an extra one or two days.

Park Fees & Regulations

Most of the range and all of the trek described in this section are inside the newly created Rwenzori Mountains National Park (RMNP). The RMNP headquarters are in Nyakalengija. At present, entrance fees for non-citizens are US$10 per person per entry (not per day), although this may change. There are no park regulations concerning trekkers, although laws restricting open fires may soon be introduced.

(The RMNP should not be confused with the old Ruwenzori National Park, still shown on some maps, between lakes Edward and George, which has now reverted to its original name of Queen Elizabeth II National Park.)

Trek Administration Although the Rwenzoris are relatively seldom-visited, it is still possible to find some of the huts very crowded if your visit coincides with a large group. You can avoid this by checking the situation with RMS, and delaying your start if necessary until the route is 'clear'. However, this plan falls down slightly if a group decides to spend more than one night at any of the huts.

The official line at RMS is that they keep a tight control of numbers entering the park, and if any of the huts are likely to be full, they will prevent more people from going up. This plan is hard to implement, however, as RMS take bookings at both their Ibanda and Kasese offices, and don't always communicate efficiently between the two.

If the number of trekkers increases any further, this problem will have to be tackled more seriously. One of the stumbling blocks at present (1992) is that RMS and the RMNP

do not always agree on how trekking and trekkers' facilities in the Rwenzoris should be administered.

Naturally, RMS officials resent the new park administrators 'taking over', but it may have some advantages. It has been suggested that some local businessmen had a more than healthy interest in the organisation's finances.

There has also been some disagreement between RMS and their USAid backers on one side, and some conservationist bodies on the other, about the future siting of huts, the building of boardwalks across some of the bogs, provisions for porters and guides, and even about the number of trekkers that should be allowed into the mountains at any one time.

It is likely that RMS and the RMNP will establish their respective responsibilities and, hopefully, will work together for the benefit of the mountain environment and the local people who depend on it. Trekkers should be prepared for some changes in the way Rwenzori trekking is organised.

Supplies

To provide for a trek in the Rwenzoris, you can buy enough in Kasese, which has a few shops with reasonable stocks and a good market, although you get a lot more choice in Kampala. In Kasese market you can also buy rubber boots. Nyakalengija has a small shop, but don't rely on it for anything more than biscuits and soft drinks. There is nothing inside the park.

PLACES TO STAY
Kasese

Top of the range is the *Hotel Margherita*, about five km outside town, with clean, self-contained singles/doubles for US$25/35. Breakfast is an extra USh 3000. (A taxi between town and the hotel costs USh 2000, and the hotel has a car which will pick up and drop off guests.)

Most trekkers stay at the *Saad Hotel* in the centre of town. It's basic, although these days you get water and electricity most of the time. Self-contained rooms (double or single) cost USh 6000, and an extra bed costs another USh 1000. There's a good-value restaurant downstairs and the hotel will store extra gear for you while you're trekking. The manager and his staff are very friendly.

If you're counting every shilling, there are some real cheapie lodging houses in the area between the Saad and the market, with beds for around USh 3000.

Nyakalengija

Nyakalengija, near Ibanda, is at the end of the dirt road, and the start of the main trekking route into the Rwenzoris. There's a bunkhouse near the RMS office where a bed costs USh 2000 and a basic evening meal USh 750. About one km further up the track, the *Rwenzori Safari Hotel* is being built by the manager of the Saad Hotel. It will be a simple resthouse, built specifically for trekkers, and should be finished by 1993. Camping is available at the Safari Hotel or the RMS bunkhouse.

On the Mountains

The main trekking route through the Rwenzoris has huts built along it, spaced a day's walk apart. Some huts are new and in good condition, others are old and dilapidated. Each hut (sometimes called 'tourist camps') has another hut nearby for the use of guides and porters. Rock shelters are no longer used on this route.

There are no facilities at any of the huts, apart from wooden sleeping platforms and maybe a couple of old tables: you need sleeping bags, mats and cooking equipment. One of the most popular huts (Bujuku) is also one of the smallest, and it can get crowded if a couple of groups turn up at the same time. Although a tent is not essential, if you've got one, you might as well take it in case any of the huts are busy.

GETTING THERE & AWAY

The easiest way to get to Kasese (the town nearest the Rwenzoris) from Kampala is by road.

Road

Buses and minibuses run between Kampala and Kasese every day. Direct buses leave early in the morning; later in the day you may have to do the journey in stages. The usual route is via Masaka and Mbarara, as the road is in very good condition. If the Kampala to Fort Portal road is repaired (it is currently in very bad condition), this will be a quicker way. The direct bus between Kampala and Kasese costs about USh 5000, minibuses about USh 8000.

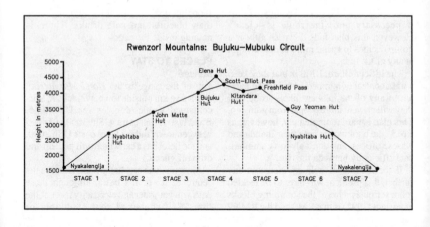

Rwenzori Mountains: Bujuku–Mubuku Circuit

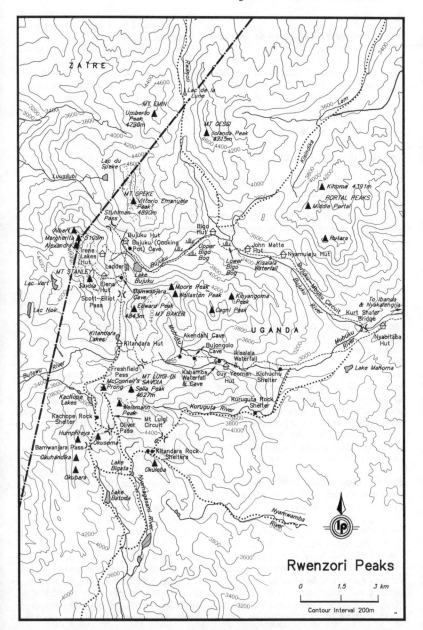

Rwenzori Peaks

0   1.5   3 km

Contour Interval 200m

Train

The train between Kampala and Kasese runs about three times a week in each direction, supposedly overnight but sometimes taking more than two days. Fares are cheap (USh 3300 in 2nd class) but the track and locos are in very bad condition: derailments are common, but not usually serious as the train goes so slowly. This journey is for train buffs only (see Getting Around).

THE BUJUKU-MUBUKU CIRCUIT
Access

This trek starts at the small village of Nyakalengija, a few km up the dirt road from the slightly larger village of Ibanda. Nyakalengija is in fact a 'suburb' of Ibanda and the two names seem to be used interchangeably.

To reach Nyakalengija from Kasese, take the sealed main road, from the roundabout between the Saad Hotel and the station, towards Fort Portal. After about 12 km, a dirt road branches off on the left. Ibanda and the RMS headquarters are signposted. Buses and minibuses run between Kasese and Fort Portal, and can drop you at this junction. From there you'll have to walk, or you may be lucky and get a lift with a tractor or pick-up. From the junction to Nyakalengija is another 12 km. If you've arranged a trek through RMS, they have a van which goes at least once each day between Kasese and Nyakalengija, and you can get a ride on this.

Before starting your trek, you have to pay park fees, or any outstanding RMS fees not finalised in Kasese.

Stage 1: Nyakalengija to Nyabitaba Hut

(10 km, 4-5 hours, 1000 metres ascent)
From the Park and RMS headquarters continue up the track, round a pond and over a brick bridge, and through a grassy area near the school. This is where the new *Rwenzori Safari Lodge* will be when it's finished.

Continue past huts and through fields, and through patches of bamboo and high 'elephant grass' (there are several forks and junctions, but the main path is usually the most well-trodden) to enter the forest reserve, marked by a sign, about one hour from Nyakalengija.

The path continues through the forest with the large Mubuku River on your right. You cross a couple of smaller streams flowing into the main river. The bush is dense: it'll rip your legs if you're wearing shorts, and anything tied to the outside of your rucksack.

About 1½ hours from the start of the forest reserve the bush thins slightly and the path climbs steeply up a ridge with forested valleys on either side. Follow this ridge for another 1½ to two hours, to reach Nyabitaba Hut (2650 metres).

Nyabitaba is in good condition, with sleeping platforms for about 20 people. There's a toilet and water from a tap about 50 metres further up the path towards a more basic hut used as a shelter by porters.

Across the valley from the hut (mist permitting), you can see the steep walls of Rutara, the nearest of the Portal Peaks. (In this route description, every time I mention the view that can be seen from each col, peak or valley bottom, it always presumes that the weather is clear. Most often it isn't, but it gets a bit repetitive putting 'mist permitting' every time!)

Stage 2: Nyabitaba Hut to John Matte Hut

(7 km, 5-6 hours, 700 metres ascent)
From Nyabitaba Hut continue along the path to a fork. Take the path to the right, and drop to the new Kurt Shafer Bridge, just below the confluence of the Bujuku and Mubuku rivers, (half an hour from the hut).

Before this large suspension bridge was built, crossing the rivers here was a risky enterprise. Previous bridges were smaller and got washed away in floods. Kurt Shafer was director of the USAid programme in Uganda, who provided finance for the bridge and other facilities in the park.

From the bridge continue steeply through mud and dense vegetation, and over rocks and roots. After an hour, you reach the base of some large mossy cliffs on your right, while down to the left the valley side drops steeply to the river. After another two hours you reach Nyamuleju Hut, which is now in very bad condition and not normally used. If you do stay here there's a place for one tent and a rock shelter nearby.

From Nyamuleju Hut, continue along the path. Down to the left is Kisalala Waterfall. The vegetation thins out, groundsels appear for the first time, and you enter the giant heather zone. The path drops to the river, passing another rock shelter (called Magania) on the right. The path climbs away from the river, up through heather to reach John Matte Hut (3350 metres), about one hour from Nyamuleju.

John Matte Hut is new and in good condition. From the veranda you get great views down the Bujuku Valley, with Rutara and the other Portal Peaks on the left and the steep sides of Kinyangoma on the right.

Stage 3: John Matte Hut to Bujuku Hut
(6 km, 5-6 hours, 630 metres ascent)
From the hut, drop down to the river from behind the porters' shelter, and follow the path, keeping the river on your left. Fifteen minutes from the hut the path crosses the river on a rocky ford. Upstream, to the west, you can see the bulk of the east wall of Mt Speke.

The path skirts the left-hand (south) edge of the Lower Bigo Bog to reach Bigo Hut, about one hour from John Matte Hut. This hut is small, basic and not used very much. There is plenty of room for camping though, and it's in a pleasant open setting, with good views of the surrounding peaks. Nearby is a cave for porters.

The path turns south-west, passing through dense vegetation again, keeping south of the river as the Bujuku Valley narrows. Up to the right is Mt Speke, although the summit, Vittorio Emanuele Peak, is obscured by lower peaks.

One to 1½ hours from Bigo Hut, you'll reach the edge of the Upper Bigo Bog. This used to be a major obstacle, involving hours of painfully slow progress across mud and tussocks. Now a line of wooden boards has been laid across the bog, turning it into a 15-minute stroll. (The laying of boardwalks

like this has created a great deal of controversy between conservationists and 'developers', and the boards may be replaced or even removed. (See Trek Administration, earlier in this chapter.)

At the other end of the bog, the path is steeper but over slightly easier ground, as it crosses and re-crosses the stream for almost two hours until reaching the edge of Lake Bujuku. When the lake is low, the water flowing from it runs underground and you can walk along the dry stony stream bed. Keep the lake to your left. Up to your left you may be able to see the summit peaks of Mt Stanley. On your right is a large rock shelter; this is Bujuku Cave (marked on some maps as Cooking Pot Cave). Continue up the valley for 20 minutes to reach Bujuku Hut (3977 metres).

Bujuku Hut is one of the oldest huts on the Bujuku-Mubuku Circuit. It is also the smallest and, being near the main peaks of Speke, Baker and Stanley, it is also one of the most popular. There's room for ten comfortably, but be prepared for a squeeze if a group arrives.

Margherita, the summit of Stanley, cannot be seen from Bujuku Hut. For the best chance of a view, return to Lake Bujuku in the late evening or early morning.

Sidetrack 1: Stuhlman Pass
(2 hours, 180 metres ascent)
If you've got the time and energy for an afternoon stroll, you can walk from Bujuku Hut up to the Stuhlman Pass (4160 metres), which is the main col between mounts Stanley and Speke, to the north-west of the hut.

From the hut, follow the path that goes uphill, into the valley leading up to the col. Near the top, a path forks off right. Keep left. (Right is the path to the technical route up Mt Speke.) The path is clear and it takes about an hour to get from the hut up to the pass. This is the watershed of the Rwenzoris, running north-south through the range but all streams to the east and west eventually flow into Lake Albert. In this way, all the water running off the Rwenzori eventually empties into the Nile.

The watershed is also the traditional boundary between Uganda and Zaire, although the actual border is a straight line from Margherita Peak, the summit of Mt Stanley, to a point between the summits of mounts Emin and Gessi, passing about one km to the west of the watershed.

Views from the pass are worth the walk up. Looking back over the hut, the dark walls of Mt Baker, and its summit covering of snow, can be seen on the other side of the valley. Up to the right are the flanks of Mt Stanley, while to the left are the peaks of Mt Speke.

Sidetrack 2: Stuhlman Pass & Lac du Speke

(4-5 hours, 270 metres ascent)

If you spend two nights at Bujuku Hut, you can walk to Lac du Speke on the day in between. Like many of the features on the west side of the Rwenzoris, it has a French name, as Zaire is a former Belgian colony.

The first part of the route, up to the Stuhlman Pass is as described in Sidetrack 1. From the pass, you need to tend right, below the west side of Mt Speke, gaining height slightly to avoid passing below the lake. Allow about 1½ hours from the pass to the lake, and then another two to get back to the hut. A guide is recommended for this route, which should not be attempted in bad weather.

Stage 4: Bujuku Hut to Kitandara Hut

(4 km, 5-6 hours, 390 metres ascent, plus 340 metres descent)

From the hut follow the path downhill to Bujuku (Cooking Pot) Cave, then aim south, across the boggy valley floor, to start going up the valley side, with the main peaks of Mt Stanley on your right. If it's clear you'll be able to see Margherita and the surrounding glaciers on the summit. After an hour of steep uphill climbing through groundsels, the path enters a gully with a steel ladder leading up to level ground and a fork in the paths. The right fork leads up to Elena Hut and the snout

of the Elena Glacier (see the Elena Hut side-track description).

Keep straight on and continue up as the groundsels thin out and it gets rockier, to reach the Scott-Elliot Pass (4370 metres), the main col between mounts Stanley and Baker, 2½ to three hours from Bujuku Hut. Just before the pass, there's a fork where the path down from Elena Hut comes in from the right. Keep left here. Up to the left, on top of a rock buttress, is a large pole, used as a marker when deep snow hides the path.

Cross the col and continue downhill, passing another large marker pole. Up to the right, the main glaciers are visible, with Elena Hut at their base. Straight ahead, down in the valley bottom, you can see the Kitandara Lakes with Mt Luigi di Savoia behind them. Continue, mainly downhill, to reach a viewpoint overlooking the upper Kitandara Lake. Pass to the left of the lake, to reach the porters' hut, then down for another five minutes to reach Kitandara Hut (4027 metres) and the lower lake, about two hours from the Scott-Elliot Pass.

Kitandara Hut is in reasonable condition, although the broken windows make it draughty. There's space for about 15 people to sleep comfortably on the triple-level platforms (25 at a push). The setting is one of the best in the Rwenzori, right next to the lake, with great views back up the valley to the main peaks.

Sidetrack: Elena Hut

(2-3 hours, 170 metres ascent from Stage 4 path)

On the route from Bujuku to Kitandara, you can branch off at the fork in the path, just past the steel ladder (described in Stage 4), and go up to Elena Hut and the snout of the Elena Glacier. The hut is small but in good condition, and is normally used by climbers doing the technical routes on Mt Stanley, who stay here to get an early start for the peaks. You can sidetrack up here for lunch, before descending to the Scott-Elliot Pass and rejoining the main route.

From the fork, the path goes steeply up, winding and zig-zagging, past occasional cairns. After an hour, you pass Bamwanjara Rock Shelter on your left. Continue up, with the cliffs on your left. The vegetation thins out and you cross lichen-covered rocks. Twenty minutes from the rock shelter the path changes direction sharply, turning back on itself. The cliffs are now on your right. After 50 metres you reach some marker posts and more cairns. The path coming up from the Scott-Elliot Pass joins from the left. Continue across bare rock, which is slippery, especially after rain. There is no path and only occasional cairns, so care should be taken. Head for the snout of the glacier, due west. You reach Elena Hut (4540 metres) about 1½ to two hours from the fork above the ladder.

Elena Hut is a wild place to stay, far above the vegetation line, perched on bare rock, with spectacular views up to the huge white bulk of the glacier looming overhead, and down into the Kitandara Valley.

From Elena Hut, retrace the route to the point where the path coming up from Scott-Elliot Pass forks right (about 20 minutes from the hut). Take this path, steeply down over scree, slabs and boulders, to meet the main Bujuku-Kitandara path about one hour from Elena Hut. Turn right, and go up for a few metres to reach the crest of the Scott-Elliot Pass. From here resume Stage 4.

Elena Hut

If you want to extend your trek and stay at Elena your gear needs to be up to scratch, as it gets very cold here. There's no firewood, and water has to be melted from snow or collected from pools, although some of these are not very clean. It's better to bring some clean water with you from Bujuku. Porters do not normally stay at Elena Hut as it's too cold and there's not enough room in the hut. They will carry stuff up here, then return to Bujuku, coming up to collect you again the next day (or after however long you want to stay). Guides will stay at Elena but should be provided with extra blankets and paid a bonus. If you do want to stay at Elena Hut make sure your guide knows this before you leave Nyakalengija.

Stage 5: Kitandara Hut to Guy Yeoman Hut

(5 km, 5-6 hours, 250 metres ascent, plus 830 metres descent)

From Kitandara, the path climbs very steeply over boulders and through dense groundsels. As you get higher, you can see eastwards into the Butawu Valley, with its river flowing down towards Zaire. On the right side of this valley, the southern shoulder of Mt Stanley leads up to Luigi di Savoia Peak, with the tongue of the Savoia Glacier to its right. Even higher up this path, the Edward Glacier on the top of Mt Baker also comes into view.

An hour from Kitandara, the path reaches more level ground. Looking back now towards Mt Stanley you can see the Elena Glacier and the tiny dot of Elena Hut below its snout. Even the ridge that extends east from Margherita can be seen although the peak itself is obscured by Savoia. From this point, the tilted block formation of the whole range is clearly evident. It plays games with your perspective and even makes the horizon appear to slope.

Where the path levels out, there's a fork. (To the left leads up to the summit of Mt Baker, another route for mountaineers.) Keep straight on, through undulating moorland. To the right are the peaks of Sella and Weismann on Mt Luigi di Savoia (called 'Rigi' by local guides), with the rock pillar of McConnell's Prong on the western end of the ridge.

After half an hour the path crosses the Freshfield Pass (4280 metres), the main col between mounts Baker and Luigi di Savoia. You get your last views of Mt Stanley, and a whole new vista opens up in front. This is the Mubuku Valley, crossed by hills of jagged slanting strata, with Lake Mahoma at its end, and the distant plains just visible beyond.

From the pass, go steeply down through mud and boulders to cross a stream after about an hour. From here, slog through bog and tussocks, gradually downhill. After half an hour, up a small valley to the left, you can see Moore Glacier, with the Moore and Wollaston Peaks to its right. The Mubuku River flows in from the left in the valley down below, as you follow a muddy ledge to reach the large Akendahi Cave. Sound from the river below echoes off the back wall of the cave as if water is flowing behind it. Continue for 15 minutes more to reach another large cave called Bujongolo (two to three hours from the Freshfield Pass). This was where the Duke of Abruzzi's expedition camped during the 1906 expedition. Carved on the wall of the cave are several European and African names and some very old dates. Some guides point out the names of their older relatives who carried gear on this original Rwenzori trek.

From Bujongolo the path enters giant heather. Through a gap you can see a long grassy clearing on the valley floor below, with the river meandering through it, and the green roof of Guy Yeoman Hut just visible at its end. Continue down, beside the Mubuku River, crossing briefly to its north bank, then crossing back again. About an hour from Bujongolo, you cross a small stream flowing into the river from the right. Up to the right is the picturesque Kabamba Waterfall, flowing down from a cliff and cascading off a large boulder. You enter a long grassy clearing and half an hour from the waterfall reach Guy Yeoman Hut (3540m).

Guy Yeoman Hut is new and in good condition, with room for about 20 people. From the hut veranda, you can look straight across the valley to Cagni Peak. At the far end of the valley, the snow- and ice-covered main peaks of Mt Baker can also be seen.

Stage 6: Guy Yeoman Hut to Nyabitaba Hut

(6 km, 4-5 hours, 800 metres descent)
From the hut, the path continues down the Mubuku Valley, through dense vegetation. Down to the left you can see the Ikisalala Waterfall. Just over half an hour from the hut, cross to the north side of the Mubuku River (take great care if the river is in flood), and shortly after that start descending very steeply beside a stream bed of bare rock, which you cross and re-cross several times. This section requires a fair bit of concentration: one slip in the wrong place and you

could go a long way down. Take extra care in the wet. (When the river is in flood, the section is virtually impossible. Some maps show a 'new route' around this tricky section, but it is rarely used and is very overgrown.) The last part of the path down goes below overhanging cliffs and involves some easy scrambling. At the foot of this steep section is Kichuchu Rock Shelter, two to three hours from Guy Yeoman Hut. There's room for a couple of tents here, but the rock shelter does not provide much protection for porters.

From Kichuchu, cross the stream again, then pass through thick vegetation and thicker bog for about an hour to reach the main Mubuku River, which you cross on a wide rocky ford to its south bank. (Again, take great care if the river is in flood. Somebody got swept away here furing 1992, and drowned.) There are more flowers and birds here, after the relatively barren sections further up. You may even see monkeys or, more likely, the ends of chewed bamboo.

The path follows a narrow ridge, with steep drops to the Mubuku River to the left, through bogs, crossing and re-crossing a small stream. After an hour the path becomes drier and the path in from Lake Mahoma joins from the right. Fifteen minutes further and the path from the Kurt Shafer Bridge joins from the left. Another five minutes further down the valley is Nyabitaba Hut (see Stage 1).

You can stay here or continue down to Nyakalengija. If you do these two stages in one, guides and porters should be paid for two days.

Stage 7: Nyabitaba Hut to Nyakalengija

(10 km, 2-3 hours, 1000 metres descent)
Retracing the route of Stage 1, drop down the steep ridge to meet the Mubuku River, leave the forest reserve, and pass through the fields to reach the park and RMS headquarters at Nyakalengija.

OTHER ROUTES

The Bujuku-Mubuku Circuit is the only trekking route in the Rwenzoris that is relatively easy to use. Although conditions are hard, with steep gradients, deep bogs and dense vegetation, the paths can generally be followed without the need for any real trailblazing or bush-cutting. But beyond this circuit, any other routes that you may see marked on maps or mentioned in older guidebooks are now very difficult or even impossible to use. It is very important to realise that these paths are not just overgrown – they simply do not exist at all.

If you lust for adventure and want to attempt one of the other routes, you have to cut your own path for some of the way. This requires a team of porters, hired specially for path-cutting, plus another team to carry their blankets and food, plus a team to carry your own gear. Even with good cutters and porters you could expect to cover only a few km a day in this way, and if you are not properly equipped and supplied, the chances of getting seriously, even fatally, lost are high.

On the Rwenzoris' higher slopes, the vegetation is not so dense, but the going is still very hard. You can explore some short distances, but at these heights you stand a good chance of wandering across cliffs, ridges, even glaciers, and needing specialised mountaineering knowledge and equipment. Obviously, for anything off the main route, a very experienced guide is also essential. You might have to wait a day or two at the RMS headquarters while a guide who knows the particular area you want to visit is summoned.

When deciding on a route, you must plan to spend each night at a large rock shelter for the porters, even if you have a tent. (In fact, a tent is essential. Western trekkers are not as hardy as Bakonjo porters!)

If all this hasn't put you off, there is one last point to remember. Bushwhacking expeditions in the far southern end of the range are not recommended. There are small groups of separatist Rwenzururu rebels based in this region, which is not recommended for visitors.

The following route is a feasible proposition, if you really want to experience Rwenzori wilderness at its wildest.

Mt Luigi Circuit

This route branches off the usual Bujuku-Mubuku Circuit at Kitandara Hut and rejoins the route at Kichuchu Shelter in between Guy Yeoman and Nyabitaba huts, circling the western, southern and eastern sides of the Mt Luigi di Savoia massif.

This is not a route to be taken at all lightly. There is no set path, the vegetation is very dense, and the going is not just hard, it's exhausting. This route takes at least four long days, although you'll probably want to stop for a rest day about halfway. This is added onto the five or six days it takes you to do the rest of the usual circuit. You must be absolutely sure that your guide knows this area, and the position of the rock shelters. Two people will need at least 10 porters for the whole trek, although there will be difficulties finding big enough rock shelters. The best thing is to arrange to be re-supplied at Kitandara by some extra porters coming up the Mubuku Valley. In this way you can do the Mt Luigi Circuit with just seven or eight porters and a guide.

This is a brief description of the route. Each day takes seven to nine hours of walking to cover four to five km.

Stage 1: Kitandara Hut to Kachope Rock Shelter From Kitandara Hut, go south alongside the southern lake and the Butawu stream for a short distance, then steeply up and down across ridges on the west side of the mountain for several hours. From a viewpoint you can see the lower Kachope Lakes, as you go up to the higher lake and walk along its northern and eastern shore. The going is hard, across piles of rocks with dense vegetation. Between the rocks are deep holes, some of them big enough to fall into. There is no rock shelter by the lake so continue uphill, south from the lake for about an hour, to reach the large shelter and a place to camp.

Stage 2: Kachope to Kitandara Rock Shelter (Kitandara Rock Shelter lies directly to the north of Okuleba Peak, not to be confused with the hut of the same name that you left yesterday.) From the Kachope Rock Shelter, continue southwards to pass between the peaks of Humphreys and Okusoma at the Bamwunjara Pass (4450 metres). (Another way goes east, over the Oliver Pass, but this is a technical mountaineering route.) There are good views from the pass: north to the Kitandara Valley, south down to Lake Batoda. Continue downhill, tending east round the southern slope of Mt Okusoma to reach Lake Bigata, where there is a very small rock shelter. From here you aim north-east, over the northern shoulder of Mt Okuleba to reach the Kitandara Rock Shelter and a place to camp.

Stage 3: Kitandara to Kuruguta Rock Shelter From Kitandara Rock Shelter continue north-east, uphill to pass a small lake. Continue up, over very loose ground, to go through a col at about 4400 metres, across a bog, and descend very steeply down, avoiding crevasses, into the densely vegetated Kuruguta Valley. Go eastwards down the valley, where a lot of cutting is needed, to reach Kuruguta Shelter, and a space for camping. (This stage is probably the hardest, and you might consider staying here two nights, to rest and soak up the atmosphere.)

Stage 4: Kuruguta to Kichuchu Rock Shelter Continue east down the valley (the easiest thing to do is actually walk in the stream) to pass the other Kuruguta Shelter, then tend left as the valley swings north. The vegetation gets increasingly dense, with the porters having to do a lot of strenuous panga-wielding, until you reach Kichuchu Shelter. It takes about six hours to cover the two km from Kuruguta.

You are now back on the main path. You can camp here, although the cave for the porters isn't very big, or continue downhill to reach Nyabitaba Hut after another two hours.

Smugglers' Paths

The only other routes in the Rwenzoris that might be possible to follow are the smugglers' paths that are still occasionally used. At certain times, there's a lot of illicit trade in coffee, millet, even gold, going across the mountains between Zaire and Uganda. Ask your guide for more information, although you'll need to use a certain amount of diplomacy here.

Future Possibilities

The Rwenzori Mountains became a national park in 1991, and the new administration plans to try and reduce some of the pressure on the main circuit route by opening up new trekking routes (or reopening old ones) from the lower slopes up to the central peaks area. Some of these may have been opened by the time you get there, so make inquiries at the park headquarters. Even if the routes have been opened, it's unlikely that new huts will be built, so you'll need to be self-contained and either provide more tents for your porters, or plan your trip to spend each night by a rock shelter.

The new routes that are planned include the following:

North From Bundibugiyo and the villages of Nyahuka and Bundimbuga, using the ridge to the east of the Lamya River, crossing between Mt Gessi and the Portal Peaks to meet the main circuit at Bigo Hut.

East From Rwagimba, following the Rwimi Valley westwards to meet the route from Bundibugiyo just north of Portal Peaks. Another route south from this, passing to the east of Portal Peaks to reach the Mubuku River opposite Nyabitaba Hut.

South From the Kilembe Mines, near Kasese, going up the Nyamwamba Valley to meet the the Mt Luigi Circuit route at Kitandara Rock Shelter, and then continuing via Bamwunjara Pass to Kitandara Hut on the main route.

There are also very long-term plans for routes from Kyarumba up the ridge to the west of the Nyamagasani River, and from Bwera, via the area around Ruata Peak, to go past Lake Batoda and through the Bamwunjara Pass to reach Kitandara Hut.

How long it will take to cut and establish any of these routes is difficult to say. However, the national park should be congratulated for producing these plans and encouraged to fulfil at least some of them.

Zaire Route

There is another trekking route on the Zaire side of the Rwenzoris, starting from Mutwanga and leading through the Virunga National Park to Moraine Hut on the west side of Mt Stanley. There are no regularly used paths linking this route to the Bujuku-Mubuku Circuit, and a traverse is not possible anyway, due to border restrictions. For descriptions of this route (which may be very dated) have a look at *Guide to the Ruwenzori* and the *East Africa International Mountain Guide* (see the Rwenzori Guidebooks & Maps section).

Mt Elgon

Mount Elgon is the second-highest mountain in Uganda, in the far east of the country, straddling the border with Kenya. It is also the fifth-highest mountain massif in the region, with excellent trekking potential, although it is frequently overlooked by visitors to East Africa. For many years, during Uganda's 'bad times', the mountain was completely off-limits to tourists. Even after the country's general reconciliation, Elgon remained difficult to reach from Uganda or Kenya, due to its sensitive border position.

Like many of the other major East African mountains, Mount Elgon is volcanic in origin. It has a very broad base, which leads geologists to believe that at one time Elgon may have been higher than Kilimanjaro or Mt Kenya. At the top of the mountain is a large crater, surrounded by a ring of several separate peaks. You can easily trek to the highest part of the mountain and descend onto the crater floor, or bag a few of the peaks without technical climbing.

The mountain's title is a corruption of its local name, Oldoinyo Ilgoon, meaning 'Breast Mountain' in the Maasai language. The people who lived in caves on the forested eastern slopes of the mountain until middle of this century were called Elgony or Il-Kony (there are several spelling variations), and were distantly related to the Maasai. On the western side of the mountain the people are Bagusu (or Gusi), of Bantu origin. They named the two highest peaks that they could see Wagagai and Bamasaba, meaning Father and Mother. Bamasaba appears highest from this view and the name seems to have been transferred to the whole mountain. The explorer Henry Stanley referred to a mountain called Masaba which he saw when travelling through this area in 1878, to the north of Lake Victoria. The geographer C W Hobley, writing in 1897 after a complete circumnavigation of Mt Elgon, called it Masawa.

Today, the mountain is commonly called Elgon on both the Kenyan and Ugandan sides. Wagagai is the highest peak, at 4321 metres (14,172 feet) although, rather confusingly, there are two peaks with this name. Bamasaba is generally called Jackson's Summit after one F Jackson, a colonial official and later governor of the Uganda Protectorate, who was probably the first European to reach the crater rim, in 1890.

Through the 1970s and 1980s, the Uganda side of Mt Elgon was very seldom (if ever) visited by tourists. Several rebel groups were active in the area, there was a lot of poaching, and the whole Uganda-Kenya border zone was notorious 'bandit country'. Due to the general anarchy, and a complete breakdown of local government, many people moved into the supposedly protected areas of forest reserve on Elgon's western slopes and cleared the vegetation for planting crops.

The civil war ended in 1986 and by the early 1990s Uganda was receiving a great deal of overseas aid money for development and conservation schemes. One of these included a project on Mt Elgon and in 1992 the forest reserve was turned into a forest park, giving it similar status to a full national park and considerably more protection. The Ugandan Government's Department of

Environment Protection is currently re-establishing the boundary of the park to prevent further encroachment (while still allowing the local people to harvest wood and bamboo at a sustainable level), and encouraging visitors to come for hiking and trekking on the mountain. The new park authorities realise that the presence of visitors is just one way that the park can provide revenue and employment for local people, thereby greatly increasing its chances of survival in an area where the already high demand for cultivation land is increasing.

This is good news for the local people and for visiting trekkers. Although the Kenyan side of Mt Elgon is difficult to reach, and has no provisions for independent trekkers, the Ugandan side really seems to have got its act together. The Ugandan Government should be congratulated for strongly supporting this new project.

Although the mountain's full potential cannot be realised by trekkers (who are not allowed to cross the border into Kenyan territory), the Uganda side of Mt Elgon is one of the great undiscovered secrets of East Africa, offering high quality wilderness trekking in a remote and seldom-visited area.

GEOGRAPHY

The Mt Elgon massif is roughly circular in shape, slightly elongated north to south, measuring about 110 km by 90 km where the main bulk of the mountain rises from the surrounding plains. The base of the mountain is actually broader than Kilimanjaro's, and Elgon is described as 'encompassing the largest surface area of any extinct volcano in the world'.

Although Mt Elgon may have been higher than Kilimanjaro and Mt Kenya at one time, it has since been eroded to its present broad dome. At the top of the dome are the remains of a crater, which has collapsed to form a caldera, now a large basin some five km across, with a group of peaks in a ring around its rim.

The crater rim has several low points, with 'cols' or passes between the peaks, and is broken completely in one place by the Suam Gorge. The crater is a large catchment for the Suam River which flows down the gorge, forming the border between Kenya and Uganda at this point.

The northern, eastern and southern sides of Mt Elgon slope gradually down to the plains, but the western side of the mountain is steeper. The highest peak on the whole massif is Wagagai, at 4321 metres (14,172 feet), on the western rim of the crater and easily reached by the main route on this side. Just to the north of this is Jackson's Peak (4160 metres), and to the south-east lies another peak called Wagagai (4298 metres) which seems to be the result of an early cartographic error. In an attempt to avoid confusion the smaller peak is called Little Wagagai in this book.

Other major peaks on Mt Elgon include Mubiyi, Cepkwango, Kapkwammesawe and Kabiyagut, which together form a long ridge, mainly above 4000 metres, on the north side of the crater rim. There is also Koitoboss (4187 metres), an impressive, steep-sided peak on the eastern (Kenyan) side, and Lower Elgon Peak (4300 metres), sometimes called Sudek, on the south-eastern side, which is split by the Kenya-Uganda border.

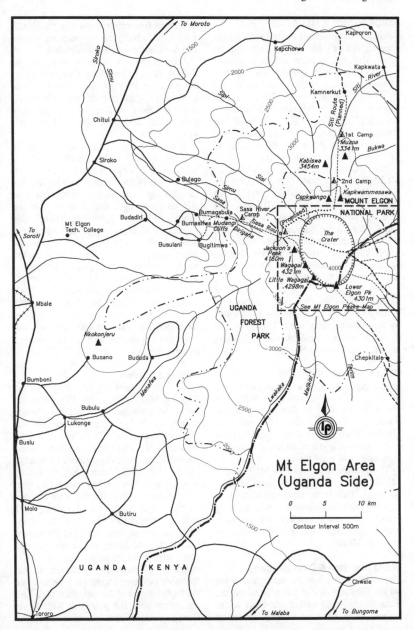

Mt Elgon Area
(Uganda Side)

0   5   10 km

Contour Interval 500m

GUIDEBOOKS & MAPS

There are no guidebooks specifically on the Uganda side of Mt Elgon, although the Forest Park headquarters will be producing a small information booklet during 1993. *Mountain Walking in Kenya* and *Mountains of Kenya* (see the Kenya Guidebooks & Maps section) both cover the crater area, and several of the main peaks, which will be particularly useful if trekkers are allowed access to the Kenyan side of the mountain in future (see Future Possibilities).

The trekking routes on the Uganda side of Mt Elgon, as described in this section, are covered by the Uganda Survey 1:50,000 map sheets 54/4 (Budadiri), 55/3 (Elgony), and 55/1 (Kaproron). (The Elgony sheet is numbered 74/3 by the Survey of Kenya.) The whole mountain is also covered by an old 1:250,000 tourist map with additional information and altitude tinting, although this may be hard to find these days.

The main peaks and crater, plus the Kenyan side of the mountain, are shown in detail on the 'Mount Elgon' map published by Andrew Wielochowski. This map also shows the roads around the whole Mt Elgon area. It is available in Nairobi.

TREKKING INFORMATION

Mount Elgon is a spectacular mountain area, which receives very few visitors. While it is not quite as wild or demanding as the Rwenzoris, it's a close second for trekkers in Uganda, in terms of wilderness and scenery, with less mud, and a much better chance of clear skies and good views.

The nearest large town to Mt Elgon is Mbale, about 250 km by road east of Kampala. This is the third-largest town in Uganda, with shops, banks, hotels and a big market. The new Forest Park Headquarters may be built here (or in Budadiri, about 30 km from Mbale).

Route Standard & Days Required

The main approach to the crater and peaks on the Ugandan side of the mountain is the Sasa Route (also called the Sasa River Route), which has been recently opened up by the new forest park authorities. This is still a seldom-visited area, so paths are narrow and faint, and nonexistent in places.

Some parts of the ascent are steep, but the daily distances are not long. One particularly steep section, through mud and dense bush, gives you a small taste of Rwenzori conditions, but the rest of the route is generally good going underfoot through forest and open moorland.

The trek described takes a minimum of four days (three nights), although a very worthwhile sidetrack to the Hot Springs on the far side of the crater floor adds another day. Fit and experienced trekkers can also add another long sidetrack to include the summit of Lower Elgon Peak. There's also the option to do a complete traverse of the massif by descending another newly established route down to Kamnerkut, on the northern side of the mountain, which adds at least one extra day, bringing the total length of the trek up to six or seven days.

Although altitude should not be a big problem if you ascend sensibly, you will feel the effects if you are not acclimatized, so an extra day can also be spent on the ascent to prevent this.

Guides & Porters

Guides and porters can be arranged at the Wagagai Hotel in Budadiri. The guides are either park rangers or freelancers, while porters are local villagers. It is possible that the park authorities will introduce licences for approved guides and porters in the future. Current daily wages are: guides USh 5000, porters USh 4500. You pay half the money in advance, so they can buy food for the trek, and the other half after the trek. A tip for good service might be an extra day's pay for a four- to five-day trek. Guides are not obligatory but strongly recommended. Porters are also useful, and hiring them means you put some money into the local economy.

Some park rangers may have tents, but freelance guides and porters use the caves on the higher slopes of the mountain. New huts are being built for guides at Sasa River Camp, and on the northern route to

Kamnerkut. Rangers will be stationed at the huts permanently and be in radio contact with the park headquarters. They will also have first-aid kits and assist where possible in emergencies. Trekkers cannot use these huts, although they can camp nearby. Separate shelters may be built for porters.

Supplies

In Mbale you can buy a good range of foods in tins and packets, mainly imported from Kenya, and there is also a good market for fruit and veg. In Budadiri there is also a market selling vegetables and a few small shops with basic tinned foods. Buy what you can locally as it all helps the local economy.

Warning

Mount Elgon is a big, wild mountain. Even the few established routes are sometimes hard to follow, especially in the rain and thick mists that are not uncommon on the higher slopes. Guides are recommended, but

may not be familiar with every part of the mountain, so you should still know how to use your compass, have good gear and at least one day's extra food, especially if you're going off the established routes and sidetracks. If you leave your tent and go out for a day walk, take adequate spare clothing and rain gear. If there's a group of you and you're splitting, whistles are useful in case of emergency. This might sound a bit over the top, but Mt Elgon is exhilarating precisely because it can be serious, and you can only enjoy it fully if you're properly equipped.

PLACES TO STAY
Mbale

Top of the range, on the outskirts of town in what used to be called the European Quarters, is the *Mount Elgon Hotel*, with self-contained doubles for US$35 including breakfast, pleasant gardens and a reasonable restaurant. In the town centre, round the

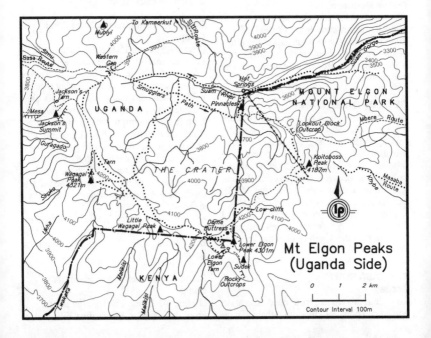

Mt Elgon Peaks
(Uganda Side)

0   1   2 km

Contour Interval 100m

clock tower, are a couple of tatty, dirty, local hotels with doubles for around USh 4500. Nearby is *St Andrew's Hostel*, basic but clean and safe, and the best value for budget travellers, with doubles at USh 3500 and singles (better condition but only one bed) at USh 4000. It's cheaper to take a double even if you're on your own! The cheapest place in town is *St Austin's Catholic Church Hostel*, up the hill from the market, with singles at USh 2300 (no doubles) and a 10 pm curfew.

Budadiri

Budadiri is a large village near the start of the main trekking route up Mt Elgon. The *Wagagai Hotel* is the only hotel in the village and the place to arrange guides and porters. The new Forest Park Headquarters may be built here.

Rooms are spartan, although being improved gradually, and cost USh 5000 per person. Camping is permitted in the grounds.

On the Mountain

The new Forest Park has long-term plans to build Rwenzori-style huts for trekkers, but these are unlikely to be installed for a few years yet. Until then, trekkers must camp. You need to be fully self-contained with tent and camping equipment.

GETTING THERE & AWAY

Buses and minibuses run regularly between Kampala and Mbale every day, generally leaving in the morning. Buses take most of the day, but minibuses are quicker. The minibus fare is about USh 5000. There is a railway line between Kampala and Tororo, and minibuses between Tororo and Mbale, but the trains are very slow and unreliable.

Mbale can also be very easily reached from Kenya, by crossing the border at Malaba (see the Uganda Getting There & Away section).

THE SASA ROUTE
Access

To reach this route, you need to get to Budadiri, about 30 km from Mbale. There

are a few matatus each day between Mbale and Budadiri. The fare is about USh 2000.

If you're driving or hitching, leave Mbale on the main road towards Soroti, turn right after six km (signposted Siroko). Continue for five km, to reach a dirt road on the right, marked by several signposts including the technical College and Masaba Secondary School. Nearby are some small shops. Continue up the dirt road, past the Technical College on the left, then through several villages to reach Budadiri.

The Sasa Route can be reached from the villages of Bumasifwa (three km from Budadiri) or Bugitimwa (about seven km from Budadiri). From the far end of Budadiri Village, which straggles along the road for about three km, just past Masaba Secondary School, the road forks. Go left to Bumasifwa. For Bugitimwa, keep straight on to Busulani (some matatus go this far) then go steeply uphill, past the church and primary school to your left, over a small bridge to reach Bugitimwa market.

Stage 1A: Bugitimwa to Sasa River Camp

(6 km, 4-5 hours, 1500 metres ascent)
From the market, take the track which leads steeply uphill, with small huts on both sides. The track turns into a path, passing through fields. There are many paths in this area, making this section hard to follow. Generally keep high. You might be able to ask directions to the forest. Local people will probably guess where you're going. Even if you're not taking a guide up to the top, one is certainly useful for this section. Continue for two hours, gaining height all the time, to reach the forest park boundary, marked by a signpost.

About 10 minutes before the boundary, you meet the path coming up from Bumasifwa. Route description continued below.

Stage 1B: Bumasifwa to Sasa River Camp

(10 km, 4-5 hours, 1500 metres ascent)
From the centre of Bumasifwa Village con-

tinue up the dirt road for four km to reach the smaller settlement of Bumagabula. Some matatus go all the way here, but only if the road is dry. From Bumagabula, follow the main path that leads up towards the forest. This route is not as steep as the approach from Bugitimwa, but it's slightly longer, so it takes about the same time. There the path forks in several places. If in doubt, there will be people around who can show you the way to the forest. A guide is useful for this section. After about two hours, the path from Bugitimwa joins from the right, by a tree and a large stone. Ten minutes later you'll reach the forest park boundary, marked by a signpost.

As you leave the cultivated area and enter the forest park, the path gets even steeper. After 20 minutes you'll reach Mudangi Cliffs, some sheer rock slabs where you have to go up two precarious wooden ladders. It may feel a bit wobbly, but when you see a young boy come down the ladder in bare feet with a huge bundle of bamboo on his head, you'll feel you shouldn't make such a big deal of it...

Above Mudangi, the path is not so steep and enters the forest proper. At a fork, after about 45 minutes, keep left. The forest begins to thin out and you enter the bamboo zone. Continue, gaining height all the time, to reach the Sasa River, about two hours from Mudangi. Cross the stream and go up the far bank to reach Sasa River Camp (2850 metres). This is an area of flat grass in the bamboo, good for camping, and with a very basic bamboo shelter nearby. The new park intends to build a rangers' patrol hut here during 1993 and, sometime after that, a hut for trekkers.

Stage 2: Sasa River Camp to Jackson's Caves

(10 km, 5½-6½ hours, 1210 metres ascent)
Fill your water bottle here, as this is the last reliable source before the tarn (pool) by Jackson's Caves. From Sasa River Camp, continue up the path through the bamboo. At a fork, reached after ten minutes, keep left. After half an hour cross a small stream and

enter dense bush. The path is steep and boggy, crossing roots and boulders.

About 2½ to three hours from Sasa River, you come out of the bush and into heathland. The site of the old Sasa Hut is down to your right, but it's completely rotted away now. After another half an hour, there's a large grey outcrop on your left with a small 'hunters' cave' (slight overhang) at its base. This provides the last bit of shelter until Jackson's Caves.

Continue through the moorland. Soon after the hunters' cave, the path tops a small rise and you can see the domed peak of Jackson's Summit on the skyline. To its left are the more angular peaks of Mubiyi. Wagagai is hidden from view.

About 1½ to two hours from the hunters' cave you reach a fork. (It is possible to camp near here on a small hillock to the left of the path.) Keep right at this fork.

(The left path leads to the low point in the crater rim, between Jackson's Summit and Mubiyi, which is called Uganda Pass or the Western Gap. This path goes into the crater itself, aiming towards the east side of the crater and Kenya. During Uganda's various civil wars, when trade with Kenya came to a virtual standstill, this route was used by local people smuggling coffee into Kenya and coming back with maize or other things they couldn't buy in Uganda. It is still sometimes called the Smugglers' Path.)

From the fork where you kept right, continue up as the heath gives way to grassy moorland. Cross a few small streams and keep aiming directly for the peak of Jackson's Summit, to reach Jackson's Tarn on your left, about one hour from the fork. Keeping the tarn to your left, go round its eastern side, then tend right and up again to see Jackson's Caves, a series of overhangs below cliffs, on your right (4060 metres). There's room for a couple of tents here, or down by the tarn, and the overhang provides shelter for guides and porters. The water from the tarn is clean. Keep it that way. Take water from the pool, but don't put anything in it. Don't wash here with soap or detergent. Ensure your guides and porters do the same.

After you've put your tent up, if you've still got a few hours of daylight left, the weather is clear, and you're feeling OK, it's worth continuing up the path for another hour or so, to the crest of the main crater rim, from where you can see down into the crater and across to several of the surrounding peaks. This is useful for acclimatization and orientation. Follow the first part of the Stage 3 description.

Alternatively, go up to the summit of Jackson's Summit, as described in the next sidetrack.

Sidetrack: Jackson's Tarn to Jackson's Summit

(1 hour, 100 metres ascent)
The dome of Jackson's Summit is clearly visible from the tarn. Take a faint path due south, aiming directly for the summit. Continue, rising gently, for 45 minutes, to reach the base of a steep section of angular boulders. Scramble up these for five minutes to reach Jackson's Summit (4160 metres). A small cairn marks the highest point.

(On a nearby rock, when I was there, were some coins and even bank notes held down by stones. My guide laughed when I asked about offerings to Mother Masaba, but left the money where it was.)

Return to the caves by the same route.

Stage 3: Jackson's Caves to Wagagai Summit & return

(4 km, 2-3 hours, 260 metres ascent plus 4 km, 2 hours, 260 metres descent)
With your back to the caves, turn right up the path, heading roughly east, uphill, on a faint path through the grass. Jackson's Summit is to your right (south) obscured at first, but then coming into view.

(You can combine Jackson's Summit with this stage to Wagagai by tending right (north-east) at the base of the steep section down from Jackson's Summit, and continuing (with steep cliffs dropping down on your right) to meet the path coming up from the caves to the crater rim.)

Half an hour from the caves, the path curves round the head of a small hanging

valley which drops away to the right, then goes up the next ridge diagonally (left to right) to reach its crest, about one hour from the caves. This is the crater rim, and your first chance to see down into the crater itself.

The crater is about five km across, surrounded by a circular rim, with several peaks rising above the rim. Directly opposite your viewpoint, due west, you can see a large gap in the crater wall. This is the Suam Gorge, where all the water collected in the huge bowl of the crater flows out towards the east. The River Suam, which flows down the gorge, forms the Uganda-Kenya border. To the right (south) of the gorge, a ridge of minor peaks rises towards the prominent rock tower of Koitoboss (4187 metres). Further round (south-west), the next major peak is Lower Elgon (4301 metres), with a distinct dome-topped buttress on its left (northern) end. Due south from your viewpoint, at the end of the ridge, is the flat-topped peak of Wagagai, looking deceptively close.

Continue along the crest of the broad ridge, following a small path that runs due south, between the crater on your left (east) and the head of the Guragado Valley on your right (west), aiming straight for Wagagai. After half an hour, you reach a fork. Keep right (left drops down into the crater), to cross a large area of flat bare rock. Down to the left, in the crater, is a small tarn.

From here, the path gets steeper as it goes up through groundsels and over rocks towards the main summit. You reach the summit of Wagagai (4321 metres) about an hour from the flat rock. A large cairn marks the top.

From the summit, to the north and east, you can see the whole expanse of the crater, with its ring of peaks, while to the south and west the broad valleys on the outer slopes of the crater drop away towards the forest and the farmland far below.

Return to Jackson's Caves by the same route.

Alternative Campsite

Just a few metres down from the summit of Wagagai, there's a small flat patch of rock where a couple of tents can be pitched for grandstand views of sunrise over the crater (freestanding only, as guys and pegs are unusable here). This is an excellent site but you need to be completely self-contained and well kitted out. Winds up here can be very strong, and there's a good chance of snow or hail. After rain, water collects in small pools on the summit, but this is not reliable so you might have to bring it from Jackson's Tarn, or be prepared to walk back there. Guides and porters, if you have them, will sleep at Jackson's Caves anyway.

Next morning, return to Jackson's Caves by the same route, or take the Extra Sidetrack outlined at the end of this trek description (Wagagai Peak to Lower Elgon Peak & Tarn).

Sidetrack: Jackson's Caves to Hot Springs & return

(11 km, 4-5 hours plus 11 km, 4-5 hours)
This sidetrack is a good day-walk from Jackson's Caves, taking you through the gap between Mubiyi and Jackson's Summit, and then across the floor of the crater to the Hot Springs at the head of the Suam Gorge. It's advisable to do this walk after you've been up to Wagagai and back, as the views from the crater rim will help your orientation on the crater floor. Alternatively, as the crater floor is lower, it can help you acclimatize for the stage to Wagagai. Whichever way you do it, it's easiest to base yourself at Jackson's Tarn for at least three nights, doing the walks on the days in between.

From Jackson's Tarn, follow the path back down towards Sasa River for half an hour to the fork where the path from the crater comes in from the right. This is the 'Smugglers' Path'. Take this path and follow it back up the valley, past a large cave, aiming east towards the col in the crater rim, called Uganda Pass or the Western Gap, reached after about an hour.

(It's also possible to reach the Western Gap direct from Jackson's Tarn by following the path up towards Wagagai to reach the viewpoint on the rim described in Stage 3, and then dropping down in a north-easterly

direction to the Gap. This involves some tricky route-finding and steep scrambling over cliffs, some of which are quite large, and could be very dangerous in the mist.)

From the Western Gap, the path is fairly clear as it drops gradually and crosses two tributaries of the Suam River, then continues to head south-east, keeping about 700 metres south of the river. About 1½ to two hours from the Western Gap you reach a junction of two paths. Keep straight on, aiming towards a group of large pinnacles and rock towers on the valley side to the south of the gorge entrance. Below these pinnacles, tend left (north), keeping to fairly level ground. Ignore the main path which leads steeply uphill to the right (south) of the pinnacles (this continues into Kenyan territory), and keep aiming north to cross the stream again onto the north bank about 2½ to 3½ hours from the Western Gap. At the base of the steep valley-side are several small pools of hot water. These are the Hot Springs. Don't expect steaming geysers here. Even the depth of the water seems to alter; sometimes they're deep enough to bathe in, but at other times they're no more than warm puddles. Don't get too excited. The walk across the crater floor is much more interesting.

Note that the paths described here may get increasingly faint, as there's no need for Ugandans to smuggle coffee into Kenya any more. Also be careful after rain, as the Suam River can rise very quickly and become too fast to cross safely.

After a dip in the springs, return to Jackson's Caves by the same route.

Stage 4: Jackson's Caves to Sasa River Camp

(10 km, 3-4 hours, 1210 metres descent)
If you camped on Wagagai Summit, retrace the route back down to Jackson's Tarn (one to two hours). If you camped at Jackson's Caves return to the tarn, then retrace the route of Stage 2, passing the hunters' cave after one to 1½ hours and reaching Sasa River Camp after another two to 2½ hours.

Stage 5: Sasa River Camp to Bugitimwa or Bumasifwa

(3-4 hours, 1500 metres descent)

From Sasa River Camp, cross the river and retrace the route of Stage 1. After half an hour, keep left at a fork. Ten minutes further a path comes in from the left. You'll reach the top of the ladders about 1½ hours from Sasa River. Go down the ladders and the last steep bit to leave the forest park and enter the fields. Ten minutes from the forest park boundary, by a tree and a large stone, the path divides. Go left to Bugitimwa, straight on to Bumasifwa, both reached after another 1½ to two hours.

(Stages 4 and 5 can be combined into one long day.)

Sidetrack: Wagagai Peak to Lower Elgon Peak & Tarn

(14 km, 7-10 hours)

Lower Elgon Peak lies to the south-east of Wagagai, about a fifth of the way round the crater rim. The walk between these two peaks is spectacular, but long and hard, requiring good navigation. It goes through low bush and tussock grass for much of the way, although you do run across faint poachers' paths and game trails. Do not attempt it if you're not fit, well-acclimatized and competent with map and compass. You cross into Kenyan territory briefly near Lower Elgon Peak, but this is unlikely to be a problem.

It takes 3½ to five hours each way to do this sidetrack. From Jackson's Caves, a pre-dawn start is essential. Time can be saved if you camp on the summit of Wagagai the night before, although this depends on water availability. However, because it's an out and back route, if you do start running out of time you can easily turn back at any point.

In between Wagagai and Lower Elgon Peak are three other peaks. The middle of these is Little Wagagai. From the summit of (Big) Wagagai and from the crater floor, these separate peaks cannot be easily distinguished. Little Wagagai and the peak to its east appear to be one long peak when seen from the north.

From Wagagai summit, drop down by a series of rocky ledges, to the ridge that extends roughly south-east from the summit. Follow this to its end, then descend steeply again, down the side of a rock buttress. With great care, keep aiming east and then south east, contouring round the inner wall of the crater. You might cut across a faint path that leads from the small pool to the north of Big Wagagai towards a low point on the crater rim to the east of Little Wagagai. Keep contouring where possible north of Little Wagagai and the peak to its east, to reach a col between that peak and Lower Elgon Peak. Cross through this col onto the south (outside) of the crater rim (and into Kenyan territory). Tend left and keep contouring, dropping gradually over a series of flat rocky ledges to reach Lower Elgon Tarn.

From the tarn, you can see a steep gully to the left of the highest cliffs directly to your north-east. Scramble up this gully to the flat top of the peak, then turn left (north-west) to reach a large cairn marking the summit (4301 metres).

Return to Wagagai and Jackson's Caves by the same route.

FUTURE POSSIBILITIES
The Siti Route

The new forest park authorities have plans to establish another trekking route on the northern side of the mountain which will link in with the Sasa Route to make an excellent traverse of the Mt Elgon massif. With sidetracks, this could involve at least a week of top-quality highland wilderness trekking.

The route is planned to start from the village of Kamnerkut, reached by a track which branches off the road round the north side of the mountain, between Kapchorwa and Kaproron.

The route follows a ridge, keeping to the east side of the Siti River, up a valley between the peaks of Kabiswa (also called Piswa) and Muzoa. The first hut/campsite will be where the path crosses the river, at around 2800 metres, the second will be further up, at around 3500 metres. From there the route will cross a col between the peaks of Chepwango and Kapkwammesawe, to the east of Mubiyi, to enter the crater, following a broad ridge between two tributaries of the Suam River, to meet the main Smugglers' Path that goes between the Western Gap (Uganda Pass) and the Hot Springs.

This new route can also be done in reverse, as a descent route from the crater after you've come up the Sasa Route. If you do the traverse this way, you can also get more information on directions and conditions from the park headquarters at the Wagagai Hotel in Budadiri.

The Crater Circuit

There's a chance that the new forest park authorities may persuade the Kenyan national park, on the eastern side of the mountain, to allow trekkers into Kenyan territory for short periods (even though a full Uganda-Kenya traverse is unlikely to be permitted).

If this does happen it will make a three-quarter circuit (or even a full circuit) of the crater rim a viable option. From Wagagai you could continue to Lower Elgon Peak, as described in the Sasa Route sidetrack, then continue round the inside of the rim to Koitoboss Col and Koitoboss Peak, and from there to the Lookout Block and the Hot Springs, as outlined in the Kenya Mt Elgon section. From the Hot Springs you can complete the three-quarter circuit by following the Smugglers' Path roughly westwards across the crater, back to the Western Gap, as described in the sidetrack in this section. This circuit could also be done the opposite

way, but the direction outlined here (anti-clockwise) would probably be easier.

The circuit would take three days, and would be a serious undertaking. You would have to be well-kitted, as strong winds, sleet and hail around the crater are not uncommon, and you would be completely self-contained with good camping gear and three days' worth of food (plus an extra day for emergencies). You would have to know how to use a map and compass, because much of the route does not follow paths at all and would rely on good cross-country navigation. Water is available with certainty at only two points, and these would make obvious places for overnight camps.

From the campsite by Jackson's Pool, you would allow one day to go via Wagagai to Lower Elgon Peak, where you could camp near the tarn. On the next day you could reach Koitoboss Col by following faint paths or simply making your own way through tussock grass and low bush round the inner edge of the crater, and then circle round to camp by the Hot Springs (with an optional sidetrack up to the summit of Koitoboss if you had the time and energy). On the last day you'd return to Jackson's Pool in about four to five hours by the Smugglers Path, or go the harder (longer) way via the northern ridge and the peaks of Kapkwammesawe, Chepwango and Mubiyi.

This complete walk around the crater rim has been recorded only once in recent years, done by two hardy stalwarts from the Mountain Club of Kenya. As access continues to improve on the Uganda side of the mountain, the route may soon be successfully followed by lesser mortals.

Malawi

The tourist brochures bill Malawi as 'the warm heart of Africa' and, for once, the hype is true; Malawi really is one of the most beautiful countries in the East African region and (although I hate to generalise) the Malawians do seem to be among the friendliest people you could meet anywhere.

For most visitors, the country's main attraction is Lake Malawi, one of the Great Rift Valley lakes, stretching some 500 km

down the eastern border. The name Malawi is thought to have come from the local word *maravi*, which means reflected light, or haze. Most of Malawi's high-profile wildlife reserves are near the lake, and there's a also number of large hotels and 'resorts' built along the southern shore.

The main attractions for trekkers are the highland wilderness areas of the Mulanje Massif and the Nyika Plateau. There are no snow-capped peaks in Malawi, but there are high mountains, with deep valleys, sheer escarpments and dramatic peaks, and some of the most enjoyable hill-walking routes in Africa.

Facts about the Country

HISTORY
The pre-colonial history of Malawi is linked to the history of East Africa as a whole, which is covered in more detail in the Facts about the Region chapter.

The Slave Trade
In the early 19th century, Swahili and Arab slave-traders were beginning to move inland from the coast, and many settled in the area around the north of Lake Malawi, founding several towns, including Karonga and Nkhotakota. The slave traders had considerable influence in the area: today, large boats on the lake are still built in the Arab dhow design, and many of the people in the northern lake-shore regions are Muslim.

The horrors of the slave trade were witnessed by the Scottish missionary-explorer David Livingstone, who became the first European to travel in the area in the mid-19th century. His descriptions later inspired more missionaries to come to Malawi with the intention of halting the slave trade and spreading Christianity among the local people.

The Colonial Period

The early missionaries were followed by pioneer traders, and behind them came the first settlers from Europe. By 1878, the African Lakes Company, later to become the Mandala Trading Company, had built a trading centre in Blantyre. By 1883 it even had its own bank. Settlers continued to arrive and at the end of 1889 the area to the west of the lake and south into the Shire Highlands was declared a British Protectorate, called Nyasaland. In 1891 the borders were officially defined and Blantyre became the centre of the colonial government. But it wasn't all a smooth ride; in the mid and late 1890s there were several confrontations between the colonial forces and local chiefs engaged in the slave trade, which was still flourishing at that time.

More opposition to the colonial government came in the early 1900s from John Chilembwe, a local priest who had studied at mission colleges in Britain and America. He protested about forced labour schemes used in the new plantations that were being established by the settlers, but he was largely ignored. At the outbreak of WWI, Chilembwe continued to speak out against the forced conscription of African men into the colonial army. He organised several attacks on plantations and government buildings around the country, but his rebellion was short-lived and swiftly crushed.

Transition & Independence

After WWI, the British began to introduce ways for the African population to become involved in the administration of the country. Things happened slowly, however, and it wasn't until the 1950s that Africans were actually allowed to enter the government.

In 1953, Nyasaland was joined to the Federation of Northern and Southern Rhodesia (today's Zambia and Zimbabwe), but the federation was opposed by the newly formed anti-colonial Nyasaland African Congress Party. The leading figure of this independence movement was Dr Hastings Banda, who had studied and worked in Britain and

David Livingstone

The Missionaries

The first missionaries who came to Malawi suffered terribly from malaria and other illnesses, and were forced to return to the coast. But Livingstone's death, in 1873, rekindled missionary zeal in Britain, and support for missions in this part of Africa. In 1875, a group of missionaries from The Free Church of Scotland arrived at Lake Malawi and built a new mission at Cape Maclear, which they named Livingstonia, after the great man himself. Their early mission sites on the lake shore were also malarial, so in 1894 the Livingstonia Mission was moved to an area of high ground in between the eastern escarpment of the Nyika Plateau and Lake Malawi. This site was successful; the mission flourished and is still there today.

Meanwhile, in 1876, another group of missionaries from the Established Church of Scotland built a mission in the Shire Highlands which they called Blantyre, after Livingstone's birthplace. Blantyre is now Malawi's commercial capital and the mission is still an important centre with a church, hospital and school.

Ghana, before he returned to Malawi in 1958.

By the end of the 1950s the British Empire was on the wane, and in the early '60s several African countries became independent of the old mother country. In 1963 Nyasaland left the federation and in 1964 became the independent country of Malawi. Banda was the first prime minister, and became president two years later. The party changed its name to the National Congress Party (NCP), and Malawi became a one-party state.

President Banda continued to consolidate his position in the government and in 1971 he was declared President for Life. By 1977 he was also Minister for Foreign Affairs, Commander in Chief of the Armed Forces, Chancellor of the University, and Chairman of the NCP (still the only legal party in the country).

Modern Times

President Banda continues to rule Malawi in his unique, rather unconventional style. Relations with South Africa have always been good, much to the chagrin of other countries in the region, especially the so-called frontline states. Most of Malawi's exports and imports go through South Africa, and a large number of Malawian men go there to work in the mines.

At one time, President Banda openly criticised other African leaders whose policies he regarded as impractical, but relations with the neighbouring countries of Tanzania, Zambia and Zimbabwe have improved in recent years, and Malawi has moved into a position as mediator between South Africa and the frontline states.

In Malawi, opposition or criticism of any kind has not been tolerated, and President Banda has strongly resisted calls for a multi-party political system similar to those being introduced in other African countries.

His Excellency...

It is usual to show great respect for the president in public places. His full title is His Excellency the Life President, Ngwazi Dr Hastings Kamuzu Banda. The polite form of reference is simply 'His Excellency'.

GEOGRAPHY

Malawi is a small country, long and narrow, wedged between Zambia, Tanzania and Mozambique, with no direct access to the sea. The country is roughly 900 km long, and between 80 km and 150 km wide, with an area of about 120,000 sq km. The country's most obvious geographical feature is Lake Malawi, the third-largest lake in Africa, covering almost a fifth of Malawi's total area.

The Great Rift Valley passes through Malawi, and the lake lies in a trough formed by the valley. The lake shore is sandy in many places, with natural beaches, particularly in the southern part of the lake, where several hotels and resorts have been built.

Beyond the beaches, a narrow strip of low ground runs along the west side of the lake, then the land rises steeply in a series of escarpments to a high rolling plain that covers much of the northern part of the country. Here the population is light and scattered. In the south and centre of the country the land is lower, densely populated and intensively cultivated, with farms and plantations.

Malawi's main highland areas are the Nyika and Viphya plateaus in the north, and the Mulanje Massif in the south. There are also several isolated hills and small mountains dotting the country. The largest is Zomba Plateau, near the town of the same name.

With the vast majority of the population living in rural areas, Malawi has very few urban centres. There are four cities: Lilongwe, the administrative capital, in the centre of the country; Blantyre, the commercial capital with its sister city, Limbe, in the south; Zomba, the political capital, between Lilongwe and Blantyre; and Mzuzu, the main town in the north. There are a few other small towns, mainly along the lake shore. Fewer than a million people live in towns and cities; the rest of the population live in scattered villages and individual homesteads.

CLIMATE

Malawi has a single wet season, from mid-October to April, and a dry season from May to October. During the wet season, daytime temperatures are warm, and conditions humid in low areas. The dry season is cooler, with July being the coolest month. During September, at the end of the dry season, it can become hot and humid at midday, especially in low areas.

Daily temperatures in the lower areas do not fluctuate much, averaging about 26°C in January and 21°C in July. On the highland areas, daytime temperatures in July are usually between 10°C and 15°C, while in September they get up to 20°C and above. Night-time temperatures on the highlands are low, sometimes dropping below freezing on clear nights in July.

ECONOMY
Malawi's economy is dominated by agriculture. About 85% of the people are subsistence farmers or plantation workers. The main exports are tea, tobacco and sugar, usually grown on large plantations, but also on smaller farms cultivated by a single family. Most people cultivate their own plot of land, to provide food for their needs. Any surplus is sold in markets or to the government-run agricultural cooperatives. Maize and rice are staple food crops. Until recently Malawi was self-sufficient in food crops, but some food now has to be imported.

POPULATION & PEOPLE
Malawi's population in 1991 was estimated at around nine million, including almost half a million refugees from Mozambique. The population is growing by about 4% a year, one of the fastest rates in Africa. All the African people are of Bantu origin: the main groups are Chewa in the central region, Yao in the south and Tumbuka in the north.

Because there is no industry in Malawi, vast numbers of young men go to South Africa to work there, mainly in mining.

There are small populations of Asian and European people, living mainly in the cities, and involved in commerce, plantations, aid and development, or the diplomatic service.

RELIGION
Most people in Malawi are Christian, usually members of one of the protestant churches

originally founded by the missionaries who came to Malawi in the late 19th century. There are large groups of Muslims in the north.

LANGUAGE
All the main groups in Malawi have their own language or dialect. The Chewa are the dominant group; their language, called Chichewa, is the national language and widely used throughout the country as a lingua franca. English is the official language and is very widely spoken, particularly in the main towns.

Facts for the Trekker

VISAS & CUSTOMS
Visas are required by citizens of most countries, except those from Commonwealth countries, the USA and some countries in Western Europe. There are no restrictions on the amount of hard currency you can bring in or out, but you are not allowed to import or export Malawian currency. Currency declaration forms are no longer used. All entry regulations are liable to change, so contact your nearest Malawi embassy, high commission or tourist office for up-to-date information.

Malawi immigration and customs officials are always polite and friendly, but they play strictly by the rules. If everything is in order you'll have no problems.

Note: It is illegal for women to wear trousers in Malawi, except for sporting purposes, or if decreed by their religion. This rule was introduced because women tourists in short trousers caused offence and embarrassment, so now it's knee-length skirts only. This rule does not apply on the lake shore or when trekking in the mountains. Some women travellers have tried to show their opposition to this 'oppresive' rule, by wearing shorts or trousers in public, and found that local women were shocked and offended. Breaking this rule helps nobody and proves nothing.

Men don't get away unscathed either: long hair (defined as falling in bulk to the collar) is banned, and beards must be tidy. These rules are strictly enforced.

MONEY

The unit of currency is the Malawi kwacha (MK), divided into 100 tambala. Most large towns have banks, and there is sometimes a demand for hard currency on the black market, where rates are about 15% more than the banks. Inflation is high in Malawi, so the exchange rates given here will probably be out of date by the time you read this, but they should give you an idea. Prices quoted in kwacha in this chapter should be converted at these rates; the actual cost in hard currency is unlikely to change very much.

US$1 = MK 4
UK£1 = MK 7

Air tickets and rooms in large hotels usually have to be paid for in hard currency, but most other things are payable in kwacha.

WHEN TO GO

The best time for trekking in Malawi is during the dry season from April to September; it's cooler in the first months (July is the coolest time), then increasingly warm towards September (see the Climate section). On Mulanje during the early months of the dry season, it can become very misty, sometimes for up to five days at a time, making route-finding difficult and conditions potentially dangerous. This mist is called a *chiperone* (pronounced 'chiperoni').

On the mountains and in the national parks, August is a busy period, mainly because the weather is good, and also because this is school holiday time. The more popular huts on Mulanje are likely to be full, especially at weekends, although if you're trekking in the remoter parts of this massif, and on the Nyika Plateau, you're unlikely to see many other people.

In the month before the rains, the views

from both Mulanje and Nyika can sometimes be obscured by haze and smoke from grass burning on the lower plains.

In recent years, the weather patterns in Malawi have become less predictable. The rain has been arriving later, and the chiperones seem to be occurring less frequently. On the high mountain areas, though, you should always be prepared for rain and thick, wet mist, even in the dry season.

TOURIST INFORMATION

In Blantyre, the tourist office is on the main street (in Hardele House, opposite the British Council) and can provide you with straightforward information on hotels, public transport, shops, hospitals and so on.

In Lilongwe, the National Parks & Wildlife Office, in the city centre, has information on treks and trekking areas. It's open from 8 am to noon and from 1 to 4 pm.

USEFUL ORGANISATIONS

The Mountain Club of Malawi is a disparate organisation mainly for Malawians and foreign residents. Occasional club nights and walking meets are arranged, but they don't normally cater for tourists. However, visitors are welcome to join club activities, especially members of other walking and climbing organisations, although it is not always possible to help with transport, equipment and so on. A newsletter is produced every two months and is available from the Tourist Office in Blantyre, or direct from the club, PO Box 240, Blantyre.

The Wildlife Society of Malawi is an active conservation organisation, formerly called the National Fauna Preservation Society. They publish several field guides to different parts of Malawi, and have close links with the Department of National Parks and Wildlife. Contact the society direct for more information and a list of publications: PO Box 1429, Blantyre (☎ 643428).

HOLIDAYS

Aside from Christmas Day, Boxing Day, New Year's Day, and Easter Friday and Monday, public holidays include:

3 March	Martyrs' Day
14 May	Kamuzu Day
6 July	Republic Day
17 October	Mother's Day
21 December	National Tree Planting Day

GUIDEBOOKS & MAPS

The bookshops in the main towns are well stocked with locally produced general guidebooks, field guides and histories. These include:

Visitors' Guide to Malawi by Martine Maurel (Southern Book Publishers, Johannesburg), which covers the whole country, and is aimed mainly at car drivers. Also available in South Africa.

Blantyre and the Southern Region of Malawi, published by Central Africana Ltd, PO Box 631, Blantyre, a general visitors' guide to the towns, parks, hotels and places of interest. Companion volumes are *Lilongwe and the Central Region* and *Mzuzu and the North*.

Malawi Wildlife, Parks and Reserves by Judy Carter (Macmillan/Central Bookshops) is a beautiful book, with concise and useful information, and good coverage of the mountain areas, although its large size makes it difficult to carry around.

Malawi's National Parks and Game Reserves and *Day Outings from Blantyre*, useful booklets, both published by the Wildlife Society of Malawi.

A Guide to Malawi's National Parks and Wildlife by G D Hayes.

There are also several specific smaller guides devoted to aspects such as the fish of Malawi, the orchids, snakes, trees and so on.

Maps of Malawi, suitable for general travelling, are not widely available outside the country, but you can easily buy them in bookshops in Malawi. For more detail, government survey maps are available from the Department of Surveys Public Map Office in Blantyre, on the corner of Victoria Ave and Independence Drive, or in Lilongwe, just off the roundabout near the Sports Club. The staff are helpful, there are no formalities, and maps cost about MK 10. Maps of popular areas, such as Mulanje, occasionally go out of stock.

Maps and guidebooks on individual trekking areas are covered in the relevant sections.

TREKKING COMPANIES

The Mulanje Massif and the Nyika Plateau are ideal for independent trekking, but they receive few visitors so there are no specialised trekking operators in Malawi. But a few of the safari companies also arrange treks and walks. Malawi's safari scene is much smaller than Kenya's and Tanzania's, so you can't just go into an office and expect to join a trip next day. Most companies only have one or two departures a month, and prefer to take bookings in advance. Contact the companies direct for more information. If you're in Malawi and fancy joining a trip, it's always worth giving them a ring to see what they've got going.

(There are no area codes in Malawi. The international code for Malawi, if you're phoning from abroad, is 265.)

Safari companies that have been recommended include:

Central African Wilderness Safaris, (PO Box 489, Lilongwe, ☎ 723527, fax 723548.)

Land and Lake Safaris, (PO Box 30239, Lilongwe 3, ☎ 723459, fax 734356.) These companies both organise safaris to all parts of Malawi, including the Nyika Plateau, the Mulanje Massif, Liwonde National Park and the lake, with optional extensions to the Luangwa Valley in Zambia. They both also do special tailor-made walking safaris which spend more time in the mountain areas and less time in the parks.

TRAVEL AGENTS

In Lilongwe, the Central African Wilderness Safaris Travel Shop is an advisory service and booking agency, and can help you with internal and international flight reservations, accommodation bookings for the national parks, short safaris and car hire (PO Box 489) (☎ 723527).

A general travel agent in Blantyre is Soche Tours and Travel, in the Mount Soche Hotel (☎ 620777).

ACCOMMODATION IN LILONGWE

If you are flying into Malawi, you'll arrive at Lilongwe first (unless you taking a connecting flight to Blantyre), and you'll probably pass through here in between the mountain areas. There's not a huge choice of hotels in Lilongwe, but the list here will given you an idea of what's available.

Lilongwe became the capital of Malawi in 1975. It is a small city, divided into two sections: the new part has the government offices; the old town has the bus station, the market, the shops, and most of the hotels.

Top of the range in the old city is the *Lilongwe Hotel*, right on the main street, with restaurants, bar, swimming pool and singles/doubles at MK 350/450 including breakfast. Even smarter is the *Capital Hotel* in the new city; it's a full international-class hotel, used by businesspeople and diplomats, with all facilities and rooms at MK 480/610 including breakfast. Best value in the mid-range price bracket is the *Golden Peacock*, a small hotel in the old city, within walking distance of the bus station and market, where double self- contained rooms are MK 120. Down the scale is the *Council Resthouse*, right next to the bus station; fairly basic doubles cost KM 50. You can camp at the *Lilongwe Golf & Sports Club*, on a safe site with toilets and showers, for MK 12 per person. More details about places to stay in or near the trekking areas are given in the relevant sections.

Getting There & Away

You can travel between Malawi and the other countries covered in this book using air, road or rail transport. The method you use will depend on the time you've got available and the amount of travelling (as opposed to trekking) you want to do. In this chapter it's presumed you want to take a fairly direct route between the trekking areas in the various countries.

TO/FROM TANZANIA
Air
International fights between Lilongwe and Dar es Salaam go twice a week, and cost around US$200 one-way. Kilimanjaro International Airport (KIA) is much nearer

Tanzania's main trekking areas so, if you're going to fly from Lilongwe, you might as well go all the way to KIA, which means taking one of the daily Dar-KIA flights. But it's probably easier to fly Lilongwe-Nairobi and travel between Nairobi and Arusha by road (see the Tanzania Getting Around and Getting There & Away sections).

Road
The only land crossing between Malawi and Tanzania is at Kaporo, in the far north of Malawi.

Bus On the Malawi side, there's a bus most days between Karonga, the first/last town, and the border. It leaves Karonga in the afternoon and gets to Kaporo Village in the evening. The main customs and immigration post is here, but it's still about another 10 km to the actual border, where there's a small guard post. The bus arrives here long after 6 pm, when the border is closed, which means waiting all night for it to open. There's no hotel, but most local people seem to sleep in the nearby primary school. There's also a patch of grass outside the school, where you could pitch a tent.

Next morning, you need to check through the guard post and walk across the bridge to the Tanzanian customs and immigration on the other side. The Tanzanian border officials here used to have a reputation for being the toughest in East Africa, but as Tanzania's entry and exit regulations have been relaxed, so the guys at Kaporo have mellowed a bit too.

From here there's no public transport, so you'll have to walk about seven km to the junction with the Kyela-Mbeya road. From here you can find a bus or a lift to Mbeya, where you can pick up a bus or train to Dar es Salaam (see the Tanzania Getting Around section).

There is supposed to be a direct bus service between Mzuzu and Dar, but days and times are vague, so inquire at the bus station in Mzuzu.

Hitching A new road is being built between Karonga and Mbeya, so you might find a lift in either direction with one of the construction workers. When the road is finished it is likely that public transport links between these two towns will improve.

If you're coming into Malawi from Tanzania, see the Tanzania Getting There & Away section for more details.

TO/FROM KENYA
Air
Flights between Lilongwe and Nairobi go four times a week, and a one-way flight costs between US$200 and US$300.

Road
Malawi and Kenya do not share a common border, so all road journeys between these two countries have to go through Tanzania. For details see the Getting Around and Getting There & Away sections in the Kenya and Tanzania chapters.

TO/FROM UGANDA
Air
Flights between Lilongwe and Kampala go about twice a week and cost about US$400 one way. (See Uganda chapter for more details).

Road
Malawi and Uganda do not share a common border, so the easiest way to travel overland between these two countries is through Tanzania and Kenya. For details see the the Getting There & Away and Getting Around sections in the Kenya and Tanzania chapters.

Getting Around

You can travel around Malawi by air, road, rail and boat. Of all the countries described in this book, and possibly of all the countries in Africa, Malawi has one of the best public road and air transport systems. It's a real joy to use, and makes travelling between the trekking areas fairly hassle-free.

AIR
Air Malawi's internal flights are reasonably priced and reliable. There are at least two flights a day between Lilongwe and Blantyre, for MK 200 one way, and three flights a week between Lilongwe and Mzuzu for MK 180. Other flights are unlikely to be useful for trekkers. Internal flights can be paid for in kwacha.

To/From the Airport
From the city centre to the airport by taxi, in Blantyre or Lilongwe, costs MK 35 to MK 50 (rates are negotiable).

The large hotels in each city run shuttle buses to meet the main flights. Non-residents have to pay, but it's usually cheaper than a taxi.

ROAD
Most of the main roads in Malawi are tarred. Secondary roads are usually graded, and normally in fairly good condition. Other routes are not so good, and after heavy rain they are often impassable, sometimes for weeks.

The main route through Malawi runs from the north of the country down to Mzuzu, then through the centre of the country to Lilongwe, and onto Blantyre in the south; it's good quality tar all the way.

Bus
Buses are operated by a private company called Stagecoach, and come in several different types: Coachline, a luxury service that runs non-stop between Blantyre and Lilongwe every day (MK 50) and Lilongwe and Mzuzu three times a week each way (MK 70), with air-conditioning, free papers and in-flight food, steward service and top-quality drivers; Express, fast comfortable buses with limited stops and no standing allowed, running between the main towns (Blantyre-Lilongwe MK 28, Lilongwe-Mzuzu KM 38); Inter-city, similar to express buses, but with more stops (Mzuzu-Lilongwe MK 20); there are also local services which cover the quieter routes and tend to be slow and crowded, but are often the only pubic transport available.

For luxury and express buses you can buy tickets in advance and have a reserved seat. The day before is usually sufficient for express buses, but on the Coachline bus a week's notice is sometimes required, particularly for Friday and Sunday services. In some areas, mainly in the south, private minibuses also operate between the towns and villages, costing about the same as a local bus.

All towns have a main bus station where long-distance and inter-city buses arrive and leave. Blantyre has two bus stations – one in the centre of town, another just outside the centre at Chilika, near the railway station and the Government Resthouse. In Lilongwe, the Coachline bus goes to/from the depot near the supermarkets on Kamuzu Procession Rd, and the Capital Hotel in the new city, not from the main bus station. In Blantyre this bus goes to/from the Mount Soche Hotel and not the main bus stations.

Taxi

Taxis operate in the main towns only. You can find them outside bus stations, airports or large hotels. There are no meters, so rates are negotiable, particularly on airport runs. Check the price at the start of the journey. Short journeys around town start at MK 10.

Car

For trekking in Malawi you're unlikely to need a car, as all areas can easily be reached by public transport. A car can be useful, though, if time is short, or you want to combine trekking with some game-viewing or general travelling around Malawi.

There are several car-hire companies in Blantyre and Lilongwe, and a few in Mzuzu. Some companies have offices in more than one city and you can do pick-up-drop-off deals. It's also possible to hire a car with a driver, usually for only a slight extra charge, which is useful if you're short of time and want to be dropped off at the start of your trek.

Rates for a small car start at MK 50 per day, plus around 70 tambala per km and another MK 20 a day for insurance. Larger cars are around MK 80 a day, plus 80 tambala per km and MK 25 for insurance.

Recommended companies include:

Avis, PO Box 460, Blantyre, (☎ 624533). Avis has offices at Lilongwe and Blantyre airports, and reservations can be made in advance at any Avis office in the world, although their rates tend to be higher than those of local companies.
SS Rent-a-car, PO Box 997, Kamuzu Procession Rd, Lilongwe (☎ 721179); PO Box 2282, Glyn Jones Rd, Blantyre (☎ 636836)
Car Hire Limited, PO Box 51059, Haile Selassie Rd, Blantyre (☎ 623792); PO Box 695, off Chilambula Rd, Lilongwe (☎ 723812).

These companies also have offices at Lilongwe and Blantyre airports and in some of the large hotels.

Hitching

On the main routes, especially between Mzuzu, Lilongwe, Zomba, Blantyre and the southern lake shore, hitching free lifts is fairly easy. But once you get off the main routes, it becomes very hard. The only cars you're likely to see are government vehicles (with MG number plates) on official business, although sometimes these do stop. Check whether a payment is expected.

TRAIN

The main railway line goes between Blantyre and Lilongwe, via Salima on the lake shore, which isn't very useful if you're trying to get to the trekking areas. Trains are very slow and crowded, and only 3rd class is cheaper than the bus.

BOAT

There are two passenger boats on Lake Malawi, steaming up and down between Monkey Bay in the south and Chilumba or Kaporo in the north, and stopping at about 10 lakeside towns on the way. Local people use the boats as a cheap method of public transport, but many visitors take a cruise just for the experience. For trekkers it can be an interesting way to do part of the journey between Mulanje in the south, to Nyika in the north. The whole trip, from one end of the lake to the other, takes about three days and each boat does one round trip per week.

The *Mtendere* has 2nd- and 3rd-class decks only, and the larger *Ilala* also has a 1st-class deck and cabins. Prices are reasonable in 1st class, very good value in 2nd and ridiculously cheap in 3rd. Reservations are usually required for the 1st-class cabins. For other classes on either boat, you just turn up. On the *Ilala* you can buy food in the restaurant. When boats dock at lakeside towns or villages, local people come out in canoes and sell fruit, dried fish and other food.

The Mulanje Massif

The Mulanje Massif rises steeply and suddenly, with sheer cliffs over 1000 metres high, from an undulating plain in the extreme south of Malawi. It is often misty in this region and Mulanje's high peaks sometimes jut out above the cloud. Appropriately, one of the massif's local names is 'The Island in the Sky'. The stunning scenery, plus easy access, clearly marked paths and a series of well-maintained huts make Mulanje one of the finest trekking areas in Africa.

Mulanje is sometimes called a plateau, implying that it's flat on the top. It isn't. The massif is composed of several separate plateaus and broad river basins, all separated by a series of rocky peaks and ridges. The highest peak on Mulanje is Sapitwa, at just over 3000 metres (9840 ft), the highest point in Malawi and all of Central Africa. There are several other peaks on the massif above 2500 metres, and you can reach most of the summits without technical climbing (although sections of steep scrambling are sometimes involved). If you prefer a less demanding trek, Mulanje's basins and valleys provide fine open walking through undisturbed country, while the peaks themselves create a dramatic backdrop.

Mulanje has been popular with walkers for many years: at the end of the last century, soldiers based at a nearby fort explored much of the area, and in the 1920s, tea-planters

Reedbuck

working in the plains around Mulanje established an Indian style 'hill-station' on the south-western corner of the massif.

Before the Europeans arrived in Malawi it seems that Mulanje was not inhabited by large numbers of people. Although several archaeological sites have been discovered, research indicates that conditions on the massif were not conducive to settlement. The plains around the Mulanje Massif are still used mainly for tea plantations and farmland. The region is densely populated, with great pressure on the land. The massif has been gazetted as a forest reserve, but pine plantations have been established on some of the upper plateaus. However, the artificial plantations cover only a small part of the massif and you can enjoy most of your trekking through untampered natural surroundings.

The Department of Forestry, the Ministry of Natural Resources, and the government of Malawi should be congratulated for maintaining the paths and huts on the Mulanje Massif. By preserving this place of beauty and ecological importance in its natural state, its benefits can be enjoyed both by visitors and by the people of Malawi.

GEOGRAPHY

The Mulanje Massif is roughly square-shaped, measuring about 30 km west to east and 25 km north to south, with an area of at least 600 sq km. On its north-east corner is the outlier, Mchese Mountain (also spelt Michese), separated from the main massif by the Fort Lister Gap.

Mulanje's most obvious features are the steep, almost vertical, cliffs of bare rock which surround the massif, rising abruptly from the flat plain, many over 1000 metres high. The cliffs are dissected by vegetated valleys, where rivers drop in spectacular waterfalls. Most of the paths up onto the top of the massif follow these valleys.

GUIDEBOOKS & MAPS

The only guidebook to the area is the *Guide to the Mulanje Massif*, by Frank Eastwood (Lorton Communications, South Africa), with information on ascent routes and main peaks, but nothing on the routes between the huts. It also includes a large section on Mulanje's rock-climbing routes, and information on geology and wildlife.

The Mulanje Massif is covered by the government survey 1:50,000 map sheet number 1535 D3 (Mulanje), which shows most paths, and all the huts, except Minunu Hut, which is at approximate grid reference 826377. The 1:30,000 'Tourist Map of Mulanje' covers a similar area, overprinted with extra information for walkers, although this version is sometimes out of stock.

The Forestry Department produces a small leaflet with information for visitors; this also contains a map of the Mulanje area.

TREKKING INFORMATION

Although the Mulanje Massif is small compared with the giants of Mt Kenya and Kilimanjaro, it is still a serious mountain, and not to be taken lightly. The main problem for trekkers is unpredictable weather, and you should be prepared for bad conditions at any time of the year (see Warnings).

The nearest large town to the Mulanje Massif is Blantyre. Nearer the massif, on its south-western side, is the small town of Mulanje.

Each hut has a log book, where you write details of your destination, intended route and expected arrival time. The hut caretaker will make sure you do! Be as clear as possible. If you do have an accident, a rescue will be arranged from Likabula Forest Station, so you would need to send a message for help there. The alarm can be raised at Chambe Forest Station, Lujeri Estate and Phalombe Police Station, all of which are linked by telephone to Likabula. Full details of rescue procedures are posted at the Forest Station and each hut.

Acclimatization on Mulanje is not usually a problem, unless you've flown in virtually from sea level and start trying to do Sapitwa on your second day. But even then, you'll only feel slightly out of breath and be forced to go slower. Altitude sickness of any sort is unlikely.

The massif is criss-crossed with firebreaks, some of which are followed by paths. Most firebreaks are composed of three parallel cut-lines about 50 metres apart, but as these can become overgrown and re-cut you should be prepared for 'extra' or 'missing' firebreaks in the route descriptions. Some footpath junctions are signposted, but you shouldn't rely on this, as signs may be destroyed by fire or simply go missing.

The pine plantations on Mulanje were first established by the colonial government in the early 1950s, mainly around Chambe and, to a lesser extent, Sombani. The sides of the massif are too steep for a road, so all the timber is sawn by hand and then carried down on a cable-way (called the 'skyline') or on the heads of forest labourers. As you're going up the Chambe Plateau Path you'll see these guys, sometimes running down, with huge planks of wood balanced on their heads.

The plantations provide employment for local people and wood for the whole of southern Malawi. A bad side effect, apart from plantations being ugly, is the tendency of pine trees to spread slowly across the natural grassland as seeds are blown by the wind. These artificial trees disturb the established balance. The Wildlife Society of Malawi recommends pulling up any young pine trees that you see growing outside the plantation areas.

Another problem on the massif is poaching, usually for small animals like hare or klipspringer, using wire snares. Some of the snares might be set by hut caretakers. You can't blame them – their salaries are very low and they can't afford to buy meat. Even so, if you see a snare, break it. If you feel guilty about depriving the caretaker, explain what you've done and give him some extra money 'to pass on to the hunter'.

Route Standard & Days Required

There are at least 10 routes from the plains up onto the higher parts of Mulanje. Some of these are steep, and the rest are even steeper. Many are also badly overgrown or particularly slippery, and the only way up is to haul yourself from tree to tree. This leaves only five or six ascent routes that you might consider using. Of these, three start at Likabula Forest Station, where all trekkers have to register and pay for huts or camping. Unless you've got your own transport, Likabula is the easiest place to start, so the two routes described in this section both begin here. Once you're on top of the massif, there's a whole network of paths linking the various huts and peaks, and many different permutations are possible. The main routes are described in detail, and other trekking possibilities are outlined, later in this section. Briefly, the main routes are:

A Mulanje Traverse This is only one of many ways of traversing Mulanje. It's a good one though, crossing the heart of the massif, passing through plantation, natural forest and open grassland, with plenty of opportunities for sidetracking, to bag a few peaks and ridges or explore small valleys. The first section of the route, up onto the top of the massif, is steep but steps have been cut for much of the way, which makes things easier. The main paths between the huts are all clear and generally in good condition, mainly undulating with a few short steep sections. Routes from the huts up to the peaks vary: some are clear, although still strenuous, others are overgrown and in bad condition, making route-finding difficult. A trek on this route takes five days and four nights, although you can add an extra stop about halfway through for a rest day.

Chambe-Lichenya Loop This is a shorter trek, which keeps to the western side of the massif, passing through two of Mulanje's largest basins, with some spectacular views from the edge of the western escarpment, and the chance to bag two impressive peaks. Conditions are as described for the Mulanje Traverse. A trek on this route takes three days and two nights.

The number of days given for each route is the usual amount. It normally takes about three to six hours to walk between one hut and the next, which means you can walk in the morning, dump your kit, then go out to explore a nearby peak or valley in the afternoon. You can spend two or more nights at one hut if you want, and go out in a different direction each day, or just sit in the sun and take it easy. Similarly, if you're feeling fit, you can do either of these treks in a day less, although because of the way the huts are spaced, it normally means combining two stages into one, rather than doing an extra bit on each day.

Guides & Porters

Most trekkers on Mulanje do not use guides and porters, but they are available if you need them. Guides are not essential as the routes between huts are generally clear (although some of the routes up to the peaks are not). As on any mountain, porters make the trekking easier, especially for the first day's steep walk from Likabula.

Forest rangers from the Likabula Forest Station, workers from the CCAP (Church of Central Africa Presbyterian) Mission, or men from the nearby village can be hired as porters. Most speak good English, and are generally honest and hard-working. They will stay with you while you're trekking, or go ahead with the bags and wait at the hut, whatever you prefer. Porters also act as guides, if required, although not all of them know the lesser-used routes up to the peaks.

The Forestry Department has set rates for porters between the various points on the massif, and these are generally between MK 3 and MK 5, plus MK 5 per night. Mission rates are about the same. Tips should be about half the set daily fee (an extra MK 2 to MK 3) per day, if the service has been good.

Some Forestry porters are a bit pushy when it comes to tips, whereas the mission and village boys seem to be friendlier. On the other hand, the Forestry porters know the massif better, and would be able to help in case of emergency, whereas freelancers from the village might not be so reliable. It's up to you, but if you do take someone from the village, pay them the same rates. The people around here are desperate for work, and will try to undercut the Forestry rates, but it's not fair to take advantage.

Whoever you take, the total fee for the whole trip should be agreed before departure and paid at the end of the trip. The maximum weight carried is 18 kg. Food must also be provided for the porter, or an extra MK 3 per day paid, in advance, to cover this. If money is provided instead of food, make sure your porter brings everything he needs, and tell him that no other food can be provided. Even if you do this, you'll still feel guilty when you stop for lunch, while the porters sit and watch you, so take a few extra packets of biscuits for them.

Porters can usually be arranged within an hour, especially the villagers, although the Forestry guys need chivying a bit. If you want to leave straight away, your porter will carry your load to Chambe Hut, then return to his house to collect his food and blanket, and then return to the hut in time for the next morning's departure. An extra day's fee is payable for this but it saves a lot of hanging around.

Fees & Regulations

The Mulanje Massif is gazetted as a forest reserve and all visitors must register at Likabula Forest Station before going up onto the massif. No charge is made to enter the forest reserve, but you must pay your hut or camping fees here.

Camping is permitted only near huts, and nowhere else on the massif. Open fires, even by the huts, are not allowed. This is especially important during the latter part of the dry season, from August to October, when there is a serious fire risk. Also forbidden is the picking or collecting of plants and animals.

Supplies

There are no shops on the massif, and only a very small local store at Likabula. Mulanje town has a small supermarket, with enough to provide for a trek, and a market selling fruit and veg. For the best choice of food, Blantyre and Limbe have large, well-stocked supermarkets.

Warnings

If you're on Mulanje in the wet season, or after periods of heavy rain at any time of year, beware of streams becoming suddenly swollen and impassable. Do not try to cross them. Wait until the flood subsides, sometimes after a few hours, or adjust your route to cross in safety further upstream.

Even during dry periods, it's not uncommon to get rain, cold winds and thick mists which can occur very suddenly. It is easy to get lost. Even on the main paths you can miss a junction, or mistake a firebreak for a path. This isn't so much of a problem as long as you've got some warm, waterproof gear. If you haven't, you risk suffering from severe exposure. It's not unknown for trekkers to get lost and die up here. In conditions of poor visibility you should keep to the main paths, and take extra care. Don't follow any firebreaks, unless a main path goes down it, and don't attempt any peaks.

PLACES TO STAY
Blantyre

Blantyre doesn't have a huge choice of places to stay, although you can usually find something to suit your budget.

Top of the range is the *Mount Soche Hotel*, large and rather impersonal, with good facilities and self-contained singles/doubles for MK 275/550 including breakfast. Cheaper and better value is *Ryall's Hotel*, a medium-sized country-style hotel in the city centre, with a bar, restaurant, swimming pool and rooms overlooking a quiet garden for MK 270/420.

Cheaper accommodation can be found at the *Grace Bandawe Conference Centre*, a small, friendly church hostel about two km from the city centre, with self-contained singles/doubles for MK 35/70 including breakfast, or the nearby *CCAP Mission Resthouse* (behind Phoenix School) where a bed in the (clean) dormitory costs MK 25. At the *Council Resthouse*, near the railway station, a (not so clean) double costs MK 17. Camping is allowed at the *Blantyre Sports Club*, near the city centre, for MK 15 per person, which includes temporary club membership.

Mulanje Town

Just downhill from the bus station is the *Mulanje Motel*, which has been recently built, and has clean rooms at MK 40/50 and good-value food in the restaurant. Camping is possible at *Mulanje Club*, on the outskirts of town.

Likabula

At the Forest Station, there's the very good *Forestry Resthouse*, spotlessly clean, with a fully equipped kitchen, comfortable lounge and several twin bedrooms. It used to be one of the best bargains in the country when it cost MK 9 a night, but somebody got wise, and the charge is now MK 54 a double (no singles). You can camp in the grounds of the forest station for MK 1 per night. The *Likabula CCAP Mission Guest House*, next to the forest station, has self-contained chalets for MK 20 per person, or you can sleep in the dormitory for MK 6. Meals are available. There are usually school or church groups staying at the mission.

On Mulanje Massif

On Mulanje Massif are seven Department of Forestry forest huts, equipped with sleeping platforms (no mattresses), benches, tables, and open fires with plenty of wood available.

You provide your own food, cooking gear, candles, sleeping bag and stove (although you can cook on the fire). Each hut has a caretaker who chops wood, lights fires and brings water, for which a small tip should be paid. The huts are (from west to east): Chambe (with room for 16 people); Lichenya (20); Thuchila (pronounced 'Chuchila') (16); Chinzama (12); Minunu (also spelt Mununu or Mnunu) (4); Madzeka (12); and Sombani (8).

Reservations and payments for huts can be made at Likabula Forest Station on arrival, or in advance by writing to the Forest Officer, PO Box 50, Mulanje. The huts cost MK 2.50 per person per night, although this may rise to a realistic price in the near future. Space is usually available, but some huts may be full at weekends and during holidays. If any hut is full on a particular night, you can normally adjust your trek and go to another. As the Forestry Department's reservation system does not require a deposit, some local residents reserve space and then don't turn up. It's worth checking the reservation book to see if this has happened. The staff at the forest station are friendly and will help you get sorted out.

The Mountain Club of Malawi has a small storeroom locker attached to each hut; the locker contains lamps, beds and cooking equipment, but these are reserved for use by club members only.

Some old maps may show other huts, but these have fallen into disuse. The only other place to stay on the massif is the *CCAP Cottage*, on the Lichenya Plateau, run by Likabula CCAP Mission. This is similar to the forestry huts, but there are utensils in the kitchen, and mattresses and blankets in the bedrooms. For this extra luxury you pay MK 5 per night. You can reserve and pay for the cottage at the mission.

There is a small shelter at Chisepo, at the start off the route up Sapitwa Peak, but this is normally only used in emergencies.

Camping is permitted outside the huts (MK 1 per person), but not allowed anywhere else on the massif. You can use the hut for cooking and eating in.

GETTING THERE & AWAY

Blantyre can be reached by air and road (see the Getting Around section for details). Mulanje is linked to Blantyre by a tarred road. There are regular local buses and minibuses, and two express buses each day, between Blantyre and Mulanje town. The journey takes around two hours. It's also possible to hitch along this road, but free lifts are not frequent, so it's probably quicker to get the bus.

From Mulanje town, you have to get to Likabula Forest Station (also spelt Likhabula and Likhubula), about 12 km from Mulanje town (see Access, in the Mulanje Traverse section). Likabula is at the foot of two of the main paths up the massif. Even if you're taking another route, you have to go to the Forest Station to register and make reservations for the mountain huts. This is also the best place to arrange guides and porters, if you want them.

A MULANJE TRAVERSE

This route is one of many traverses that can be made across the Mulanje Massif. It begins at Likabula and ends at Lujeri, on the southern side of the massif; both are easy to reach

with or without your own transport. The route described here can be done in five days and four nights, but there are several variations which can shorten or extend this period.

Access

This route starts at Likabula Forest Station, about 12 km from the centre of Mulanje town. The dirt road to Likabula turns off the main tarred Blantyre-Mulanje road about two km before the centre of the town, signposted to Likabula Pool and Phalombe. There is one bus a day from Blantyre to Phalombe, leaving in the early morning, and going through Likabula. If you're coming from Blantyre on any other bus, or hitching, ask to be dropped at the Likabula junction. From there, either wait for the irregular minibus which runs between Mulanje and Phalombe (via Likabula), try hitching, or start walking (10 km, two to three hours). It's a pleasant walk through tea estates, with good views of the south-west face of Mulanje beyond the tea on your right.

Alternatively, the Reverend Matalulu at Likabula CCAP Mission can pick you up from Mulanje town bus station and take you to Likabula in his car for MK 30. The service is for visitors to the mission, but it seems to be OK even if you're not staying there. If you phone Reverend Matalulu from Blantyre and tell him what time your bus leaves, he'll be there to meet it at Mulanje bus station. The mission phone number is 465262.

At Likabula Forest Station, allow at least an hour to make your hut booking, pay your fees and arrange porters.

Stage 1: Likabula Forest Station to Chambe Hut

(7 km, 2-4 hours, 1000 metres ascent)
From the forest station follow the signposted Chambe Plateau Path up through the compound. After ten minutes you'll reach a junction. Fork left to Chambe Plateau. (The right track, signposted 'Chapaluka Path, Bottom Skyline Station', also leads to Chambe Hut but this route is longer, and in bad condition, so not often used.) The path climbs very steeply, up steps in places, par-

allel to the 'skyline'. After 1½ to three hours (depending on your rate of ascent) the path nears the edge of the Chambe Plateau and aims towards the top skyline station (150 metres to the right). Take a small steep path up to the left for 100 metres to reach a track on level ground. There's a shelter here, sometimes used by people preparing tea and food for the forest workers. Go straight across the track and follow a path down through pine forest to cross a stream on a log bridge. (If the water is high, go upstream about 200 metres – there's a larger bridge.) When you reach another track, turn right and continue through pine plantation. Ignore the tracks forking off left. The Chapaluka Path joins from the right. Half an hour from the tea-shelter, you reach a junction by a bridge. Turn right, cross the bridge, and then turn immediately left. Keep on the track, turning right onto a footpath to reach Chambe Forest Station, one hour from the top skyline station.

Follow the track through the compound, then down to the right to reach Chambe Hut, standing apart from the other buildings, overlooking an area of short grass next to a stream. There are good views of the south-east face of Chambe Peak from the hut veranda.

Sidetrack: Chambe Hut to Chambe Peak Summit

(3-4 hours, 700 metres ascent plus 2-3 hours descent)
From the hut, follow the track back towards the forestry compound. Cross an area of open ground, and go down a grassy bank to meet another track. Turn right and follow this track, across two wooden bridges. Fifteen minutes from the compound, take a path on the right up through plantation and tend right in front of a huge grey rock wall (the eastern end of the south-west face of Chambe), to reach a large boulder on the left. Scramble up this, with the help of steps cut in a log, and then up bare rock to reach easier ground. To the right is a small stream in a narrow wooded gully; this is the last water point.

About one hour from the hut, the path

reaches a col. Turn left here and go up the crest of the ridge, following cairns, and avoiding false trails which contour off to the right. The path levels, dips slightly, then climbs again to reach a small cliff (five metres high) at the top of a bare rock slope. Turn right along the base of the cliff, then go up again to reach a large cairn on a broad level part of the ridge at the foot of the main face (two to 2½ hours from the hut).

You might be happy with reaching this point, which offers excellent views over the Chambe Basin to the escarpment edge and the plains far below. The next stage of the route requires some steep scrambling – which can be intimidating – and should definitely be avoided after rain.

From the cairn, a grassy slope is visible on the lower right side of the main face. To the right of this is a thin strip of bare rock. The path follows this strip to reach the foot of a shallow gully running down a steep cliff. The route goes straight up the gully. This is the most difficult section of the route and great care should be taken. Near the top of the gully, you reach a steep cliff, sloping down left to right. Keep right here, out of the gully, and follow cairns over to the right side of the ridge. Continue upwards, just to the right of the crest of the ridge, towards the apparent summit (the highest point visible). The path crosses boulders, then bare flat rock, to reach the foot of a bulging cliff with a bouldery gully at its right side. Scramble up this gully and continue following cairns, keeping to the right of the ridge. Aim first towards the apparent summit, visible ahead, then towards the foot of a high (25-metre) rounded buttress at the left (north-east) end of the summit ridge. At the foot of the buttress turn left and up, then tend right, keeping the main cliff to your right.

Where the cliff becomes less steep, turn right to scramble up several grooves in the rock to reach the ridge crest. Turn left (south-west) to follow the ridge across easier ground to the summit (2557 metres), marked by a large concrete-and-metal beacon which is not visible until you're almost on it (three to four hours from the hut).

The views from the summit of Chambe Peak in clear weather are superb; you can see most of Mulanje's main peaks, and much of the western side of the massif. Long stretches of the escarpment that surrounds the massif can also be seen, and below this the plains stretch out towards the Zomba Plateau in the north and the mountains of Mozambique in the south. It is often possible to see the waters of Lake Chilwa, to the north-east, and on very clear days Lake Malombe, at the southern tip of Lake Malawi, can also be spotted.

To get back to Chambe Hut retrace the route. Go slowly on the way down; it's easy to go off route, and just as easy to slip and fall on some of the steeper sections. Allow two to three hours for the total descent.

Stage 2: Chambe Hut to Thuchila Hut
(12 km, 4-5 hours)

The path towards Thuchila starts at Chambe Forest Station, passes about 50 metres to the south-west of Chambe Hut, and leads uphill, through pine plantation, following a wide firebreak. After 10 minutes, fork left as the path climbs steeply up through boulders. At a second fork, after another 10 minutes, take the right path through plantation and indigenous woodland before rejoining the firebreak. The path tends up and left across bare rock, then drops to cross a stream. Follow the path up to a small col and then along the left side of a steep valley. Drop to a large col, where the Chambe Basin is joined to the main massif, and contour round the side of a small hill, passing through woodland to reach a junction (about one to 1½ hours from the hut).

From the junction, keep straight on, up a steep path. (The path to the right leads to Lichenya Hut.) To the left are fine views down into the Thuchila Valley. The path reaches its highest point and begins to drop through the grassland of the Thuchila Plateau. About two hours from the hut, you reach Chisepo Junction. The path on the right leads up to the summit of Sapitwa Peak (see Sidetrack, in this stage).

Keep straight on, following the clear path, across several streams (some with large pools) to meet a firebreak, and tend left round the head of a large valley. Continue down the side of the valley to cross more streams and rivers, either by wooden bridges or by paddling. These are all the headwaters of the Thuchila River. At a fork, the right path leads to forestry workers' houses; keep straight on for 200 metres to a crossroads and turn right to Thuchila Hut.

If you sidetracked up Sapitwa, you'll probably be pleased to spend the night here. If you didn't, you could carry on to Chinzama Hut.

Sidetrack: Chisepo Junction to Sapitwa Peak Summit

(3-5 hours, 800 metres ascent plus 2-4 hours, descent)

The summit of Sapitwa is the highest point on the massif, at 3001 metres. You can walk to the top, but it's a toughie, and the upper section involves some scrambling and tricky walking amongst large boulders and dense vegetation.

If you're feeling fit, you could divert from the route between Chambe and Thuchila huts and go up to Sapitwa summit and back. Large rucksacks could be hidden in the bushes and collected again afterwards. Alternatively, spend two nights at either Chambe or Thuchila Hut and do Sapitwa on the day in between. But as Chisepo Junction, the start of the route, is about halfway between the two huts, this doesn't save much time. It's still going to be a long day. If you're doing Sapitwa from either Chambe or Thuchila, add another four to five hours onto the times for doing the peak itself. If you do run out of time, the small metal-roofed Chisepo Shelter, near the junction, provides some basic protection.

From the junction, pass the shelter and cross a stream. Turn left and follow the broad ridge that aims roughly towards the summit. The route is clearly shown, for most of the way, by red marks painted on the rocks, so step-by-step directions are unnecessary. The paint spoils the image of untouched wilderness, but it stops a lot of people from getting lost – and there are a few marks missing, just

to keep you on your toes! As you get near the summit you can see the top, but the route winds tortuously through an area of huge boulders and dense vegetation.

The views from the top, when you do finally make it, are worth the slog. On a clear day, you get a panoramic vista of the whole plateau, the other nearby peaks, the edge of the escarpment and the plains far below.

Stage 3: Thuchila Hut to Sombani Hut, via Chinzama Hut

(12 km, 4-5 hours)

From Thuchila Hut, retrace to the main path and turn right to reach a bridge and junction. Turn right (straight on leads to Tinyade), and follow the path as it climbs over bare rock and through bush to reach a col and junction. Take the left path (the right path leads to Minunu Hut) and drop down into a valley, keeping left to contour round the valley side. Cross several firebreaks, but avoid dropping towards the valley bottom until the hut is visible on the opposite side of the valley. At a clear junction, about two hours from Thuchila Hut, turn right to drop down into the valley, cross two streams and climb steeply up to reach Chinzama Hut, after another 10 minutes.

From Chinzama Hut aim eastwards until the path climbs a small rise with a firebreak on the left and a narrow path forking off to the right. A signpost points back to Chinzama Hut. Take the narrow path as it heads right and climbs up the valley side, through grass and bush and across patches of rocks, to reach a small col. Cross into the next valley, and drop through rolling grassland, crossed by several firebreaks, to reach a junction. Take the left path (the right path leads to Madzeka Hut) and go through grassland to cross a wooden bridge and some small streams (no water during the dry season). The firebreak swings left; take the narrow path straight on, through woodland and plantation, to cross another small stream and reach a fork. The left path leads outside the plantation; the right path climbs through the trees to reach Sombani Hut, about two hours from Chinzama Hut.

Sidetrack: Sombani Hut to Namasile Peak Summit

(2½-3 hours, 600 metres ascent plus 1½-2½ hours descent)

Namasile Peak is the large mountain that dominates the view across the Sombani River valley, directly opposite Sombani Hut. From the hut, the south-east face of Namasile is clearly visible, appearing almost vertical. The path to the summit, steep and strenuous in places but not technically difficult, spirals round the north side of the mountain and approaches the summit from the west (the 'back' of the mountain when viewed from Sombani Hut).

From the hut aim north down a clear path to cross the stream in the valley bottom on a wooden bridge. On the opposite bank is a fork. Keep straight on (right leads towards the Fort Lister Gap), up a firebreak to its end. To the right is a small pool (sometimes dry). Head left, for 50 metres, to reach a large sloping rock slab on the right side of the path. Go up the slab and follow the path, marked by cairns but indistinct in places, aiming towards a low point in the ridge ahead. To the left is a small stream in a valley. The path tends towards this stream, and crosses it between two groups of waterfalls, about half an hour from the hut. This is the last reliable water point.

After crossing the stream, pass to the right of a very large boulder, and then aim west-north-west up towards a low point on the ridge (actually a false ridge), immediately to the right of the main cliffs of the mountain. A very large undercut boulder lies at the centre of this apparent low point. Pass to the left of this to reach the top of the false ridge. Now aim for a low point in the next ridge directly to the right of the main cliffs. You'll reach the foot of the main cliffs about 1½ to two hours from the hut.

Continue up through grass and bush, keeping the base of the main cliffs on your immediate left, to enter a broad gully, covered with vegetation, separating the main cliffs of Namasile from a separate minor peak lying to the north. Go up the broad gully towards a small col but, before reaching the col, head steeply left and up towards the main summit. The summit beacon is visible at the highest point.

You'll think you're nearly there, but now comes the hard bit! The path crosses bare rock and enters an area of large boulders and dense vegetation. The path is cairned, but care should be taken not to get lost on this section. Beyond the boulders the summit beacon is again visible, although the path does not aim directly for it, but zigzags up over boulders and grassy slopes below the beacon to curve round the summit area and approach it from the north-east. Scramble over large rocks to reach the summit beacon (2687 metres), about three hours from the hut.

Views from the summit of Namasile Peak, over the north-eastern side of the Mulanje Massif, are excellent: across the Ruo and Madzeka basins and the upper part of the Sombani River valley. To the north-east the escarpment drops to the Fort Lister Gap, with the separate peak of Mchese beyond.

Return to Sombani Hut by the same route. Take care on the way down; it's easy to miss cairns and go off route. Allow 1½ to 2½ hours for the total descent.

Stage 4: Sombani Hut to Madzeka Hut

(9 km, 3-4 hours)

From Sombani Hut retrace the previous day's route back to the junction. Keep straight on (right goes to Chinzama and Thuchila), then drop steeply to cross a stream in a narrow valley by a 'danger' sign. The path climbs out of the valley then passes through undulating grassland, across a wooden bridge in bad condition, to cross two small cols separated by a swampy basin. The path drops towards the valley, following a firebreak.

About two hours from Sombani Hut you'll reach a fork, marked by a stone pole, where the firebreak aims straight on. Take the left path. Ten minutes further, a path to the left goes towards Nayawani. Keep straight on, down the clear path, across several small plank bridges, to reach Madzeka Hut after another hour.

Sidetrack 1: Madzeka Hut to Nayawani North Peak Summit

(1½-2 hours, 440 metres ascent plus 1-1½ hours, descent)

There are no major peaks that can be easily reached from Madzeka Hut, but Nayawani North is a pleasant little summit. This stroll can be turned into a longer circular walk, taking in the dramatic northern ridge of the mountain (see Sidetrack 2).

From Madzeka Hut, cross the stream that runs past the hut and follow the firebreak (zigzagging steeply in the final section) to a col between the peaks of Nayawani North and South. (From the col the path drops to reach Nayawani Shelf, a rounded terrace covered in a small circular area of natural woodland, on the north-east slope of Nayawani South.)

From the col, turn left (north) to follow a firebreak. Cross a section of steep rock slabs (slippery after rain, avoidable by scrambling up through the boggy tussock grass to the side) to reach the summit of Nayawani North Peak (2285 metres), which offers an excellent panoramic view of the south-eastern part of the Mulanje Massif.

Descend by the same route.

Sidetrack 2: Nayawani Ridge Circuit

(8 km, 3½-5 hours, 440 metres ascent)

This is an excellent route, with fine views from the ridge, but it follows firebreaks for much of the way, and these are steep and rocky, or overgrown and indistinct, in places, and can be quite strenuous, especially if you've already done a long walk to reach Madzeka Hut.

From Madzeka Hut follow the description given already to reach the summit of Nayawani North after 1½ to two hours. Continue to follow the firebreak along the crest of the ridge, which is steep and narrow in places. There are excellent views down into the Muloza Valley on the right (east) and to the Madzeka Basin on the left (west).

About two to 2½ hours from the hut, the path/firebreak descends to a distinct col, crossed at right angles by a firebreak running down into the valleys on either side. Turn left (west), to follow the right side of the valley, down towards the floor of the Madzeka Basin. The going is tough when the grass is high. Keep right, to avoid losing too much altitude, then meet another firebreak that contours along the side of the main ridge. Turn right onto this firebreak and follow it up the valley (north, then north-west), crossing several other firebreaks, to reach a large stream that flows along a wide (10- to 15-metre) strip of exposed rock down the centre of the Madzeka Basin, about 45 minutes to one hour from the col.

Cross the stream (which may be impassable after heavy rain) and follow the firebreak uphill until it meets the main path running from Sombani and Chinzama to Madzeka Hut. Turn left onto this path and follow it down the valley to reach Madzeka Hut, about 1½ to two hours after crossing the large stream.

Stage 5: Madzeka Hut to Lujeri Estate

(9 km, 3-5 hours, 1100 metres descent)

From Madzeka Hut follow the path that heads south-west, across a stream, and down into the large Ndiza Valley (also called the Little Ruo Valley). You'll pass through dense woodland in steep-sided tributary valleys, and over open grassland on the dividing spurs. The path crosses bare rock slabs on the edge of the escarpment and then begins to drop very steeply down almost vertical cliffs. Ladders and staircases have been positioned on the steepest sections. To the left (east) of the path the Ndiza (Little Ruo) River plunges off the escarpment in a spectacular waterfall. Far below, the smooth green fields of the Lujeri tea plantations can be seen.

Continue going down. Your progress will probably be slow: the path is very steep in places, and some of the ladders are rotten, but the views are spectacular. (Great care should be taken when descending in wet conditions.) Three to four hours from Madzeka Hut, the path finally begins to level out and enter conifer plantation, then the outskirts of Nadonetsa, a scattered village. To get through the village, follow the path, fork right, and cross a small stream. A path joins from the right; keep left at the next junction, enter small fields of tea, pass down the village main street, fork right and cross a small bridge. A path joins from the right. Continue straight on, pass more huts, fork right, and pass some large white huts on the right, to cross the (Big) Ruo River on a large steel and concrete footbridge. (There's a fair chance of getting lost here; if in doubt ask for directions to the big bridge).

From the bridge, the path runs parallel and to the right (west) of the river and then heads right, through tea, to meet a dirt road. Turn left onto this, keeping straight on at all junctions to reach Office Number Three, a collection of low white buildings on the left side of the road, about half an hour from the large bridge.

Leaving the Mulanje Massif
From Office Number Three it's still 13 km to the main road that goes back to Mulanje town and Blantyre. You may be lucky and find somebody in the office with a car or a tractor who can help you with a lift. If you're out of luck, you'll have to start walking. From the office, follow the dirt road through the tea plantation, aiming generally south, away from the massif. At a junction after three km turn sharp right towards the large buildings of the tea factory, then right again, keeping the factory on the left, over a large river bridge, to turn left at a junction, and follow this road for about nine km to reach the main tarred road. It'll take you three to four hours to do this walk, depending on the state of your knees after the descent from Madzeka.

When you reach the main road, Mulanje town and Blantyre are to the right (west). Wait here for a bus (several each day) or try hitching.

THE CHAMBE-LICHENYA LOOP
This is a short route, good if you want to get a taste of Mulanje but haven't got time for a complete traverse of the whole massif. It starts and finishes at Likabula Forest Station, so access and exit before and after the trek

are no problem. The route can be done in either direction.

Access
Details on how to reach Likabula Forest Station are given in the Mulanje Traverse section.

Stage 1: Likabula Forest Station to Chambe Hut
(7 km, 2-4 hours, 1000 metres ascent)
This section of the route is the same as Stage 1 of the Mulanje Traverse.

Sidetrack: Chambe Hut to Chambe Peak Summit
This route is also described in the Mulanje Traverse section.

Stage 2: Chambe Hut to Lichenya Hut
(9 km, 3-4 hours)
The path towards Lichenya starts at Chambe Forest Station, passes about 50 metres to the south-west of Chambe Hut, and leads uphill, through pine plantation, following a wide firebreak. After 10 minutes, fork left as the path climbs steeply up through boulders. At a second fork after another 10 minutes, take the right path through plantation and indigenous woodland before rejoining the firebreak.

The path heads up and left across bare rock, then drops to cross a stream. Follow the path up to a small col and then along the left side of a steep valley. Drop to a large col, where the Chambe Basin is joined to the main massif, and contour round the side of a small hill, passing through woodland to reach a junction (about one to 1½ hours from Chambe Hut).

Turn right at this junction (straight on leads to Thuchila), and descend through natural forest. The path levels out and crosses several small streams, the headwaters of the Likabula River. Down to the right is the Likabula Valley, while up to the left are North Peak and West Peak, outliers of Sapitwa.

About 1½ hours from the junction, you'll enter a confusing section, where several firebreaks meet and cross the path. Keep straight on. After a few minutes, the firebreak goes straight on and the path forks off right at a small cairn. Ten minutes later another firebreak comes in from the right. Turn left here, and you'll almost immediately reach another junction. Ignore the path on the right, which goes back towards Likabula and the CCAP (Lichenya) Cottage, and keep straight on down into the Lichenya Basin. Continue for half an hour to reach Lichenya Hut.

Alternative Hut – CCAP Cottage Instead of staying at Lichenya Hut you can stay at the nearby CCAP Cottage, reached after another hour. From Lichenya Hut follow the path in a south-westerly direction, going straight on at a junction five minutes from the hut. Continue on the path as it follows wide firebreaks to reach a crossroads, where you turn right to reach the CCAP Cottage.

Sidetracks from Lichenya Hut

On the wall of the hut are some large maps of the surrounding area, marked with suggested routes, suitable for an afternoon's stroll. This includes the 'jungle path' along the Lichenya River, and an area of natural forest where blue monkeys have been spotted. You can also go past the old airstrip to the top of the frighteningly steep Boma Path that goes down to Mulanje town, for good views over the escarpment. It's also possible to go up to Chilemba Peak from Lichenya Hut (see Stage 3 description) instead of sidetracking off Stage 3.

Stage 3: Lichenya Hut to Likabula, via Chilemba Col

(15 km, 5-6 hours, 360 metres ascent, plus 1400 metres descent)
From Lichenya Hut you can retrace some of the previous day's route, before dropping down the Lichenya Path to Likabula, but it's more interesting to go via Chilemba Col, from where you can sidetrack to the summit of Chilemba Peak for some vertigo-inducing views off the top of Lichenya's west face.

From Lichenya Hut follow the path in a south-westerly direction, going straight on at

a junction five minutes from the hut. Continue on the path as it follows wide firebreaks to reach a crossroads. Straight on goes nowhere, left goes to the disused airstrip. Go right to reach the CCAP Cottage, one hour from Lichenya Hut.

From the CCAP Cottage, two parallel firebreaks lead up towards an obvious col in the ridge, north-east of the cottage. Follow the left-hand firebreak to start with, then cross over to the one on the right when the left gets steep. The col is half an hour from the cottage. Chilemba Peak lies to the left of the col (see Sidetrack, in this Stage).

From the col, drop to a junction. Go left (right goes back towards Lichenya Hut and the Chambe-Thuchila path), downhill through forest and across sections of bare rock. About one hour from the col you reach another junction; keep straight on, downhill to cross a stream and get on a good-quality path which has actually been paved in some places. The going is steep but easy now, with the path crossing streams and gullies on well- built bridges and causeways. About 1½ hours from the col the path crosses a wide riverbed of flat rock, then continues down to enter light forest. Firebreaks come in from the left. (If you're coming up this route, it's important not to follow these firebreaks, as they go directly to the foot of the main cliffs of Lichenya. Keep left, on the main path, and keep the cliffs some 800 metres away on your right shoulder.)

Continue down on the wide path through the forest, keeping right at the main fork, to reach the Likabula River. Before this main fork, smaller paths branch off on the right to the river.

Wade through the river, or jump from rock to rock, and go up the far bank to reach the dirt track between the Mulanje-Phalombe road and the forest station. Turn right then left to reach the forest station.

Sidetrack: Chilemba Col to Chilemba Peak

(1-1½ hours, 150 metres ascent, plus 1 hour descent)
From the left (west) firebreak, on the crest of the col, a faint path leads up the ridge towards

the summit. The path is indistinct in places; keep to the crest of the broad ridge if you lose it. Towards the top, the going gets less steep. Pass through boulders and grass to reach a minor summit, marked by a tall cairn. Drop down to cross a small saddle then scramble up over bare rock to the main summit, marked by a concrete beacon and another tall cairn.

From the summit, to the north you can look across the Likabula River and see the Chambe Basin looking like, well, a basin full of trees. Beyond this is the main south-east face of Chambe Peak. To the left of the Chambe escarpment you can see the flat-topped dome of Chiradzulu Mountain on the horizon. In the other direction you can look back over the Lichenya Plateau, to the sharp edge of the escarpment, and the hazy mountains of Mozambique in the distance.

Retrace the route back to Chilemba Col.

OTHER ROUTES
Ascent
There are several ascent routes from the plains up to the top of the Mulanje Massif, and many paths linking the huts and peaks, giving you an almost endless set of combinations.

Likulezi Mission to Thuchila Hut This is a recommended ascent route, on the north side of the massif. A guide is useful, as the route is not always clear. This route can also be used as a descent after, say, a two-or three-day trip taking in Chambe Hut and Chambe Peak, Sapitwa Peak and Thuchila Hut. From Likulezi (the area is also called Tinyade) you can catch the daily bus that leaves Phalombe around midday, back to Likabula, Mulanje town or Blantyre.

Descent
Sombani Hut to Nambiya Estate This path is a possible descent route in the Fort Lister Gap, on the north-east side of the massif. When you reach the dirt road that passes through the gap, turn left to reach Phalombe Village, from where you can catch the bus.

Boma Path If you're feeling brave, another descent route is the incredibly steep Boma Path from the Lichenya Plateau down to Mulanje town. If you go up from Likabula, coming down this way means you can still do a circuit and be back in Mulanje town without having to worry about transport. This path is very, very steep and precipitous, overgrown in places, slippery in dry conditions, impassable after rain – it's only for the experienced. If that hasn't put you off, from Lichenya Hut, follow the path that aims in a southerly direction, forking left and then right at two junctions. At the plateau edge, an old signpost marks the start of the route down. There are some patches of red paint marking the way, but you'll probably have to bush-bash in some places as you lurch from tree to tree. Below the woodland you enter a grassy area and a maze of woodcutters' paths. Keep going down to the edge of the forest reserve. Paths lead to the tea factory, visible on the right side of Mulanje town, or straight to Mulanje town itself. As you get lower, you'll find plenty of people about, so you can ask directions.

The Nyika Plateau

The Nyika Plateau is in the north of Malawi, overlapping the border with Zambia, and completely different to the Mulanje Massif, Malawi's other major mountain area, in both size and character. Although called a plateau, the Nyika is by no means flat: it consists mainly of rolling grassy hills, split by forested valleys, and surrounded by steep escarpments and several peaks, making it an excellent area for trekking.

This wide expanse of open wilderness has probably existed in its current form for many centuries, and a small population of hunter-gatherers is believed to have inhabited the Nyika more than 3000 years ago. Ancient rock paintings have been found at Fingira Cave, at the southern end of the plateau. For the peoples living on the plains below Nyika, the plateau was a place to hunt and smelt iron, but it was never settled in a big way.

The first Europeans to see the Nyika were Scottish missionaries, inspired by the explorer David Livingstone, who reached this area in 1894. The mission station they built, between the Nyika's eastern edge and Lake Malawi, was named Livingstonia, and is still a thriving centre today.

Scientists and naturalists who visited the Nyika in the early 20th century recognised the biological importance of the plateau. In 1933, measures were taken to protect the juniper forests on the southern part of the plateau from bushfires and, in 1948, this section was made into a forest reserve, and pine plantations were established around Chelinda. In 1965 the whole of the upper plateau was made a national park, and in 1976 this area was extended further to include the lower slopes of the plateau, which are an important water catchment area. This most recent boundary extension included several small settlements, and the people living here were relocated to areas outside the park.

The wild, open nature of the Nyika Plateau attracts visitors who come to view the birds and animals, study the flowers, walk across the hills and valleys, or simply sit in the sun and absorb the magnificent scenery.

GEOGRAPHY

The Nyika Plateau is roughly oval in shape, about 80 km long and almost 50 km across, at its widest points, covering some 3000 sq km, plus the area in Zambian territory. Most of the plateau top is at about 2000 metres, but there are several peaks on its edge which rise above this height, and overlook the steep escarpments that surround the plateau on its western, northern and eastern sides. The highest point on Nyika is Nganda Peak (2607 metres, 8553 feet), which overlooks the northern section of the plateau, and from where you can see into the plains of Zambia in one direction and the distant mountains of Tanzania in the other, as well as the waters of Lake Malawi shining in the distance.

FLORA & FAUNA

Above 1800 metres, most of the Nyika is covered in rolling hills of montane grassland. The land below this altitude, in valleys and on the escarpment edges, is covered in light open woodland called *Brachystegia*, and in between the two vegetation zones you can often see areas of large protea bushes. Other areas are covered in dense evergreen forest, which are thought to be remnants of the extensive evergreen forests that once grew all over Malawi, as well as southern Tanzania, northern Zambia, and Mozambique.

This range of vegetation attracts a varied selection of wildlife, and a major feature of a trek on the Nyika is the number of birds and animals you are likely to see. Most common are the large roan antelope and the smaller reedbuck which move about through the grassland in herds. You'll also see zebra, warthog and eland (although, because they are a favourite target for poachers, these are very shy). Walking quietly, and crossing hilltops slowly, you might also see klipspringer, jackal, duiker and hartebeest (antelope). You might even catch a glimpse of hyaena and leopard, but you'll be more likely to see their footprints and droppings. In the woodland areas, you may see blue monkey and, if you go off the escarpment, down into the lower forest areas, you might even see the signs of

Common duiker

elephant and buffalo. (Because of the wild-life, all trekkers on the Nyika have to be accompanied by a park ranger, or scout, who also acts as a guide. See Guides & Porters.)

More than 250 species of bird have been recorded on Nyika. The best time is November and December, which is not so good for walking, but at other times of the year you'll still see plenty, including the large Denhams's bustard, stalking around in the grassland, as well as wattled crane and red-winged francolin, and sunbirds and weavers in the bush areas.

Nyika is also famous for its wildflowers. Again, the best time is during the rains, but conditions are also good in August and September, when the grassland is covered in colour and small outcrops turn into veritable rock-gardens. Over 120 species of orchid alone grow on the plateau.

GUIDEBOOKS & MAPS

The national park produces a small booklet with good background information on the wildlife and vegetation found on the Nyika. There are also leaflets and displays in the excellent information centre at Chelinda Camp. For more detail, see one of the guide-books to all the national parks, mentioned in the Malawi Guidebooks & Maps section.

The entire Nyika Plateau is covered by the government survey 1:250,000 map sheet 2, but many of the park tracks are not shown, and the scale is too limiting for trekkers. The National Park produces a simple map which shows the tracks and main peaks but has no topographical detail. The plateau is covered by twelve 1:50,000 maps: 1033 B1 – B4, 1033 D1 – D4, 1034 A1 and A3, 1034 C1 and C3. These have excellent topographical detail, but do not show all the park tracks. Chelinda Camp area is covered by 1033 D2.

TREKKING INFORMATION

Nyika may not have the high drama of the snow-capped massifs further north but, without a doubt, it is a uniquely beautiful place, quite unlike any other trekking area described in this book.

The largest town near Nyika is Mzuzu, about 400 km north of Lilongwe.

Route Standard & Days Required

A series of trekking routes (called Wilder-ness Trails) have been set by the national park authorities, varying in length from one day to over a week. These trails are not waymarked, and often do not even follow a path or track. On some sections you simply find your own way through forest, or across open grassland, using a compass, a sense of direction, and the local knowledge of your guide. There are many variations to each trail, particularly the longer ones, and the actual route you take may depend on the time of year, where you're likely to see wildlife, the skill of the guide, or just how you're feeling on the day.

Some of the wilderness trails are out-and-back routes, others start and finish at different points. The best areas for trekking are the escarpments on the plateau edge, so most of the trails are in these areas, and you need to allow at least another day at either end of the trail to walk from, and back to, Chelinda Camp. If you have a car, these first stages can usually be covered by vehicle. Park vehicles are not available for hire, although you may be able to arrange a ride if a vehicle is making an official journey.

But you don't have to keep to these wil-derness trails. They are provided only as suggestions by the park authorities. Basi-cally, you can go anywhere you like for as long as you like. All you need is a guide to go with you, and enough equipment and food to keep going. In this section, several other trekking possibilities are outlined. The routes mentioned briefly here are described in more detail later in this section.

For all trekking on the Nyika, you must provide all the equipment and food you need. Guides have their own sleeping bags, tent and cooking pots, and food. Campsites are not fixed, although in practice the better sites are used more frequently. No facilities of any kind exist at the sites.

On all the routes described in this section, the landscape is undulating, but there are no long (ie all day) ascents and descents as on the larger mountains of Kenya and Tanzania. Consequently, total height gains/losses are very small and not indicated in the descriptions.

Nyika Highlights Route This is not an official wilderness trail, like the ones set by the park, as it follows paths and tracks for much of the way, rather than going through open country. The title is not official either; I've given it this name because it takes in many of Nyika's main attractions. The daily distances are quite long, but there are no major gradients to contend with.

On the sections of the routes which follow park tracks and pass through areas of short grass, the going is easy, but in some areas the grass is long and tussocky, which can be very tiring. Some of the park tracks are drivable, but are very rarely used by vehicles, so you're unlikely to be disturbed. This circular route takes four days, although you could do it in three. The route can be done in either direction.

Livingstonia Route This route follows tracks and paths for its entire length, and drops dramatically down the wooded escarpment on the eastern edge of the plateau, to leave the park and reach Livingstonia. Daily distances are not long, and most of the route is downhill.

The route takes three days, with the possibility of a fourth if you can't find a lift out of Livingstonia. If you're short of time, and feeling fit, the first two stages can be done in one day, but it's long and hard. This route cannot be done in reverse.

Guides & Porters

All trekkers have to be accompanied by a park ranger, called a scout, who will act as guide. Other scouts are available for hire as porters if you need them. Scouts cost MK 10 per day, although this fee may rise soon. If you're booking chalets (see Places to Stay) in advance, scouts can also be arranged then. Alternatively, they can be hired at Chelinda with a day's notice. The park authorities are

trying to promote more trekking on the Nyika, as it's a useful way of providing extra patrols and keeping a check on poaching. It has been known for scouts to see groups of poachers while guiding trekkers and go off to give chase. This is unlikely, but don't complain if it happens, as it's part of the deal.

All the scouts speak English, and are generally very pleasant, knowledgeable about the birds and wildlife, and good company on a long trek. They receive no extra money from the park for this work, so a tip (of around MK 5 per day) at the end of your trek is appropriate if the service has been good.

If your trek finishes outside the park (eg at Uledi or Livingstonia), you must pay for your scout's public transport back to Chelinda, and for any accommodation if he stays out another night.

Even though you've got a guide it's still important to be familiar with the route, conditions, likely times and so on, as the scouts are very fit, and their ideas about daily distances may be different to yours! Let your scout know how long you want to walk for each day, and whether you are 'strong' or 'not so strong'.

Park Fees & Regulations

The Nyika Plateau is a national park and fees are payable: entrance fees for non-citizens are MK 3 per person per day, and MK 7 for a car. These may rise in 1993.

You are not allowed to enter the park unless you are in a vehicle. Once in the park, however, you can leave your car, at your own risk, to walk short distances to visit viewpoints, areas of forest, or other places of interest. For longer walks, all visitors must be accompanied by a scout.

Some of the park tracks are for management use only and not open to public vehicles. However, it is OK to walk on them.

Supplies

There is a small shop at Chelinda Camp, but the stock is limited to maize flour, biscuits, tea and tinned fish, although (in true Malawian style) they stock about three different types of beer. The best place for supplies is

Mzuzu, which has a couple of large super-markets and a very good market for fruit and vegetables.

Warning

During dry periods, sectors of the park are burnt to prevent larger fires later in the season. Before setting off on a trek, enquire at the park office about whether burning is taking place; if it is, avoid the area.

PLACES TO STAY
Mzuzu

The *Mzuzu Hotel*, on the outskirts of the town, is the smartest place, with a golf course, restaurant, bar and coffee shop, and singles/doubles for MK 300/450 including breakfast. The *Government Resthouse*, about one km out of town on the right side of the Nkhata Bay road, has simple but clean rooms for MK 50 a double, and allows camping (MK 10). Further along the road, then down a track on the left (signposted), the *Mtwalo Municipal Resthouse* has basic but accept-able rooms for MK 35 a double, and camping for MK 9. There are several cheap lodging houses in the centre of the old part of town, including the *Jambo Resthouse* with basic rooms for MK 25 and a spartan dormitory (MK 3). On the road towards Rumphi, five km from the town centre, the *Kaka Hotel* has good accommodation, with doubles for about MK 60.

Rumphi

Rumphi has a couple of resthouses near the bus station with doubles for around MK 30. The new *Simphawaka Resthouse*, about 1½ km outside town, is the same standard but quieter.

On the Nyika Plateau

In the Nyika National Park, the main accom-modation centre is *Chelinda Camp*. This is also the park headquarters, with offices, workers' houses, a shop and a petrol pump. For visitors there are fully contained chalets, with their own bathroom, kitchen and dining area, costing MK 31/62 for singles/doubles, or bedrooms in blocks of four, with a shared

bathroom and common room, for MK 15/27. All have fireplaces, firewood, electricity and hot water. A fully-equipped central kitchen and lounge area is open to all visitors. The campsite, about two km north of the park office, costs MK 6 per night. The youth hostel is mainly for school groups but can be used if the chalets and bedrooms are full (MK 14 per person). Near the Juniper Forest (in the southern part of the park, about 30 km from Chelinda by winding park track, via the New Cheilinda Bridge, or about 40 km by te old Chelinda Bridge) is a small cabin with one room containing four beds and basic furniture (MK 14 per person). A caretaker lives nearby.

All bookings for accommodation in the Nyika National Park (recommended at weekends and during holidays) should be made at the central booking office, Depart-ment of National Parks and Wildlife, PO Box 30131, Lilongwe 3 (☎ 730853). Visitors can call in at the office (signposted) near the junction of Kenyatta Rd and Kamuzu Pro-cession Rd.

Accommodation is also available at the *Zambian Resthouse*, in Zambian territory, to the left of the track from Thazima Gate to Chelinda, about 45 km from the gate. There are no border formalities. The resthouse is well maintained, with bedrooms, a lounge, and a well-equipped kitchen. A caretaker is on duty all the time, and a notice board has good information on short walking routes in the area. To stay here costs US$25 or MK 70 per person, or you can camp for US$15 or MK 45. You also have to pay Zambian national park fees, which are US$5 per person, plus US$10 for camping and another US$10 for a car. If these fees don't put you off, you can stay at the resthouse without booking, or reserve space by contacting Robin Pope Safaris, PO Box 320154, Lusaka, Zambia, (telex 40313 ZAHL ZA), or Mr William Gondwe, Private Bag 6, Rumphi. Include a reply address or telex number and allow one month for postal replies.

GETTING THERE & AWAY

Mzuzu is about 400 km north of Lilongwe

by tarred road. The new road through Viphya is faster than the road along the lake shore. Mzuzu is linked to Lilongwe by bus (see Getting Around), and hitching is possible.

From Mzuzu, you need to get to the park headquarters at Chelinda Camp, roughly in the centre of the Nyika Plateau, which has cabins, a campsite, and an information centre. This is also where you arrange your guide.

Bus

If you're on public transport, there's a bus three times a week in each direction between Mzuzu and Chitipa, going through the park, via Thazima and Kaperekezi gates. Ask the driver to drop you at the Zambian Resthouse junction, from where you can walk the 12 km to Chelinda (see Stage 1 of the Nyika Highlights Route), although it's not certain that the park rangers will allow this. It's also possible that the bus route may include a diversion up to Chelinda, and if this is true, then the access problems that have always prevented independent trekkers from reaching Nyika will finally be solved.

If you miss this bus, other buses run regularly between Mzuzu and Rumphi, and from Rumphi there's a bus most days for Katumbi, passing Nyika Junction, from where it's an eight-km walk to Thazima Gate. You can wait at the gate for a lift to Chelinda (this is the method used by park staff and their families). If you get stuck, the rangers at the gate will let you camp there. Some vehicles come through the park, going towards Nthalire and Chitipa, which means they turn left at the Zambian Resthouse junction. You might be able to get a lift to here and walk the rest of the way to Chelinda.

It is also possible to reach Chelinda from the north, from Chitipa via Nthalire and Kaperekezi Gate and Zambian Resthouse junction, from where you follow the directions given earlier.

You cannot reach Chelinda by road from Livingstonia or any other town on the east side of the plateau, despite this being indicated on some maps and even in some guidebooks. There is no road and, as far as anybody can tell, there never was.

Car

If you're driving, from Mzuzu take the tarred road north towards Karonga. After 50 km turn left and follow the minor road for 10 km to reach the small town of Rumphi, at the end of the tar road. Pass through the town and continue on the dirt road for about 60 km, passing several small settlements and junctions with minor tracks, to reach Nyika Junction, where a large track branches off on the right, signposted to Nyika National Park. From this junction follow the track for eight km to reach Thazima Gate (pronounced Tazima, and often spelt this way). All entrance fees must be paid at the gate. Inside the park the dirt road/track is in reasonable condition but the 56 km from the gate to Chelinda Camp can take about two hours to drive, so vehicles are advised not to leave Thazima Gate for Chelinda Camp after 3.30 pm. Petrol is not available between Rumphi and Chelinda, and supplies at Chelinda are not reliable. During the dry season, you can reach Chelinda in a saloon car (although hire companies don't usually allow it) and travel on most of the park tracks.

THE WILDERNESS TRAILS

An outline of each trail is included here. Due to the nature of the trails on Nyika (see Route Standard & Days Required), detailed route descriptions are not possible. They are also unnecessary, as you will be accompanied at all times by a scout. The number of days required are counted from, and back to, the trail head, usually a point on one of the park tracks towards the outer edge of the park. If you're walking from Chelinda Camp to the trail head, and back again after the trek, add at least one extra day either side. The park has numbered each trail.

Trail 1: Mwanda Peak

(1 day)

On the south-western edge of the park, Mwanda Mountain sits astride the Malawi-Zambia border. The route starts on the main

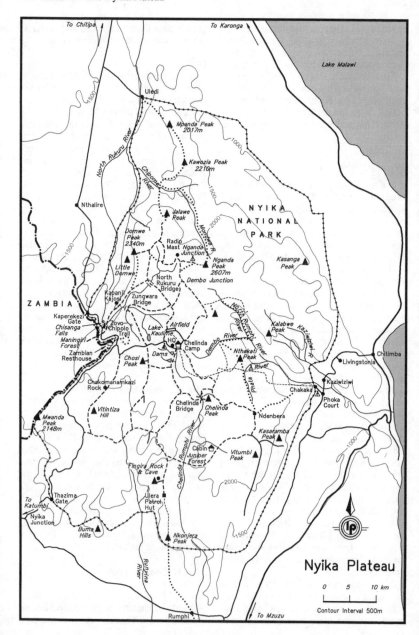

Nyika Plateau

0   5   10 km

Contour Interval 500m

track between Chelinda Camp and Thazima Gate, right next to a signpost marking the boundary of the park. The route crosses grassland then follows the northern ridge of the mountain to reach the summit (2148 metres). The faint trail along the ridge is crossed by several clear trails used by local villagers and poachers crossing between Zambia and Malawi. From the summit you get some good views to the south over towards Vwaza Marsh and northwards to the Viphama Hills in Zambia. You return by the same route. Allow six to eight hours for the round trip.

Trail 2: Nthakati Peak

(2-3 days)

Nthakati Peak (2501 metres) is one of the highest peaks in the park, overlooking the eastern edge of the Nyika Plateau. The trail starts on the park track between Chelinda and Kasaramba peaks and follows the edge of the escarpment to camp beside the Phata River below Nthakati Peak. On the second day you go up Nthakati Peak. From there you either head back towards the Chelinda-Kasaramba track, or continue north-west down to the Dembo Valley, camping another night there, before heading back to Chelinda.

Trail 3: Nkonjera Peak

(1-3 days)

Nkonjera is a large, flat-topped mountain on the southern boundary of the park (also spelt Nkhonjera and Nkonjela). The route starts at the end of the park track that heads directly south from Chelinda, where another track branches off right to Fingira Rock. From here, you pass the Ulera Patrol Hut and continue to the summit (2208 metres), which takes about five to six hours. You can do this in one day, with an early start, although it's better to take two days, camping on the mountain. You can make it into a good three-day trip by diverting off to Fingira Rock, a large cone-shaped rock rising some 60 metres above the surrounding woodland. At its base is a shallow cave containing some very old, very faint, paintings, presumed to be pre-Bantu.

Trail 4: Fishing Trail

As the name implies, this trail is not designed for trekkers. It follows the upper stretches of the North Rumphi River for a fairly short distance, and does not take in any peaks. It can be added on to Trail 2, as the Dembo River flows into the North Rumphi.

Trail 5: Jalawe Peak & Nganda Peak

(4-5 days)

This is a long trek in the northern part of the park, mainly through wooded hills below the main plateau. The route starts near Jalawe Peak, at the end of the most northerly track in the park, and descends to the Chipome Valley, the first night's camp. A second day is spent exploring the valley, returning to the same camp, although you can keep going if you prefer. On the third and fourth days you follow the Chipome and the Lower Mondwe rivers upstream, back up towards the plateau, to reach the summit of Nganda Peak, the highest point on the Nyika, on the last day.

Trail 6: Jalawe, Kawozia and Mpanda Peaks

(5-6 days)

This route is the most strenuous but most rewarding of all the wilderness trails on Nyika and should be attempted only by fit and experienced trekkers. It is only possible in the dry season as it involves crossing several rivers which are too deep to ford during the rains. The route starts near Jalawe Peak, in the northern part of the park, then drops into the Chipome Valley, where you camp for one or two nights, before rising to the summit of Kawozia Peak (2210 metres). From here you follow a spectacular broad ridge, dropping to camp beside one of the small streams that flow off either side, to reach the twin summits of Mpanda Peak (2017 metres). This mountain offers one of the most impressive views in Malawi. From here you can see east to Lake Malawi, north to the mountains of Tanzania and west to Zambia, while the broad mass of the Nyika Plateau lies to the south. Near Mpanda are the ruins of Bleak House, originally built as an outstation by the missionaries of

Livingstonia in the early 1900s. From Mpanda, most trekkers drop to the small village of Uledi, just outside the northernmost corner of the park, and return to Chelinda or Thazima by road via Nthalire. You could walk back the same way but this, of course, would double the length of the trek.

THE NYIKA HIGHLIGHTS ROUTE

This is not a wilderness trail, like the ones set by the park, as it follows paths and tracks for much of the way, rather than cutting through open country. But a trek on this route takes in some of the main attractions and features of the Nyika, including Kaulime Lake, the Zovo-Chipolo Forest, Chisanga Falls, Domwe Peak, the western escarpment and Nganda Peak, the highest point on the plateau. This trek starts and finishes at Chelinda Camp. It can be done in four days, but it could be cut to three by combining Stages 2 and 3 to make a very long middle day, but the other stages are quite long anyway.

Stage 1: Chelinda Camp to Chisanga Falls

(29 km, 7-8 hours)
From Chelinda Camp, follow tracks uphill to the left of the main plantation to reach Lake Kaulime after 1½ hours. This is the only natural lake on the plateau and is the subject of many local stories and beliefs. In the days before Nyika was a park, local people came here to pray for rain, or throw in white beads as a sign of respect for their ancestors. If you listen hard you're supposed to be able to hear the sound of doves calling, or women pounding maize. The lake was thought to be bottomless, and on a misty day it does have a certain air of mystery about it, but it's actually not that deep: you can often see roan antelope wading through it, eating reed shoots.

From Kaulime, follow the track towards Thazima Gate. After an hour or so, as the track curves round to the left, there's a short-cut path on the right, which drops down into a valley and then up the other side, cutting off a big loop in the track. Local people carrying maize and other goods between Chelinda and the villages in Zambia use this path. You meet the track again and, after about 1 km, reach a junction, about three hours from Chelinda. This is the Zambian Resthouse junction (see Places to Stay).

Turn right, following the track towards Kaperekezi Gate. This road was improved by a regiment of the British Army in the mid 1970s; a stone plinth near the junction has the faint picture of an ant on it, a symbol of the regiment's hard work. Ten minutes from the junction on the right, a small path leads to the Zovo-Chipolo Forest, where a small circular trail has been established to show examples of the three main types of vegetation on the plateau: montane grassland, evergreen forest and bog. A booklet about the trail is available from the national parks office in Lilongwe, and sometimes from Thazima Gate or the park headquarters at Chelinda. The word 'zovo' means 'elephant' in the Tumbuka language. One was killed in the forest by a man called Chipolo. Before the lower slopes of the plateau were heavily populated, elephants were more common in these patches of woodland. (It takes about half an hour to walk round the trail.)

The park track here is the border between Malawi and Zambia. Almost straight across the track from the path that leads to Zovo-Chipolo, another path leads to the Zambian Resthouse. Follow this, through Zambia (!), past the resthouse to meet the track again, and follow it for about an hour (your scout will know shortcuts across loops in the main track) until you reach a path on the right going down to Chisanga Falls. From here you get excellent views northwards down the North Rukuru Valley, running along the foot of the western escarpment. Domwe Peak is visible in the distance.

You descend quickly from the grassland, on a clear path, through protea bush and into woodland, leading to the top of the falls. On the right, next to the river, are a few places where you can pitch a tent. It's another 20 minutes down the path to a couple of small viewpoints overlooking the falls.

Stage 2: Chisanga Falls to Domwe Peak

(17 km, 6-7 hours)
From Chisanga Falls, go back upstream, to

meet the new management track, which you follow north. A new bridge is planned across the river here; if it hasn't been built yet, you'll have to wade, or your guide may know of one of the log bridges built by local honey-gatherers. Follow the management track through an area called Zungwara, the name of a village that used to be here, to reach a big rock that forms a natural viewpoint on the edge of the escarpment, 2½ hours from the falls. The rock is called Kapanji Kajosi, meaning 'cave of smoke'. Local people used to live in a cave below the rock, but now it's used only by poachers. From here, you get some spectacular views down into the North Rukuru Valley, and across to the hills of Zambia, and along the escarpment edge to the summit of Domwe Peak.

Follow the track for another hour, then branch off left to follow a faint path that used to be the park boundary before the 1976 extension. You cross two streams, and pass Little Domwe to your left, to reach the summit of Domwe Peak, 2½ hours from Kapanji Kajosi. This is the highest point on the western escarpment (2340 metres).

The best place to camp is in the valley to the north of Domwe Peak near an old scout patrol post. It's hard to find, so check that your scout knows where it is before you leave.

Stage 3: Domwe Peak to Lower Mondwe Stream

(17 km, 5-6 hours, plus 2-3 hours for Nganda Peak)

From Domwe Peak, follow the track in an easterly direction. The radio mast by Nganda Junction can be seen on the horizon. You can cut off a big loop in the track by crossing one of the North Rukuru headwaters. When you meet the track again, continue towards the radio mast. Near the mast (about three hours from Domwe), before going straight for Nganda, you can find a place to camp and go up the peak without carrying your gear, (although it may be misty, in which case pitch camp anyway and go up next morning). There's a place to camp down on the right, just before you reach the junction, but the

water isn't very clean. It's better to continue, past the mast and along the track towards Nganda Peak. Down on the left are some patches of woodland, next to the source of the Lower Mondwe Stream, where you can pitch a tent. Some patches are a bit boggy, but they get drier as you go downstream.

From your campsite, regain the track which runs along the ridge between the radio mast and Nganda Peak. The track turns into a path by two wooden posts, and from there it's about 45 minutes to the summit. Nganda Peak is the highest point on the Nyika Plateau. From the summit, the whole rolling expanse of the plateau spreads away towards the south, and to the north-east you can often see the glistening waters of Lake Malawi. (Allow two to three hours to go up and back.)

Sidetrack: Jalawe Peak

Instead of going straight from Domwe Peak to Nganda, you can follow tracks to Jalawe Peak, which overlooks the steep escarpment of the Chipome Valley, separating the main part of the plateau from its northerly outliers.

When you reach the Jalawe Roadhead, about two hours' walk from Domwe, follow the path that drops down to cross a flat area of grass before rising again up the side of Jalawe Peak. Beyond the highest point of the peak the path continues a short distance to a rocky outcrop (climbed with the help of a wooden staircase) overlooking the Chipome Valley. In the valley bottom, some 1000 metres down the almost sheer sides of the escarpment, elephants can sometimes be seen amongst the trees or alongside the river. (Binoculars are useful here.) Beyond the valley, the land rises steeply again to the peak of Kawozia, and beyond to the twin peaks of Mpanda, the northernmost summit in the park. From Jalawe Peak retrace to the track and continue to Nganda Junction, another three hours.

This sidetrack adds five hours to Stage 3, so if you're going to include it, save the ascent of Nganda Peak until the morning of Stage 4.

From Jalawe it's also possible to descend into the Chipome Valley and follow the

Mondwe River, or elephant trails around the base of the escarpment to the foot of Nganda Peak, and go up to the summit from there. This is a tough walk, though, taking about five to seven hours, and you have to be determined – once you've started this one, there are no short cuts!

Stage 4: Lower Mondwe River to Chelinda Camp

(25 km, 8-10 hours, via Nganda Peak;
20 km, 6-7 hours, direct)
If you're doing Nganda this morning, follow the directions at the end of Stage 3. Alternatively, if you're going straight back to Chelinda, from your campsite retrace to the ridge and then cut across the top of the North Rumphi Valley to meet the track aiming south. Follow this all the way back to the airfield on the north side of the Chelinda plantation, (five to six hours from the campsite). Your guide should know a short cut, across the runway and through the plantation back to Chelinda Camp (another hour).

THE LIVINGSTONIA ROUTE

This route is not a wilderness trail, as it follows tracks and paths all the way. But it goes through some of the most beautiful areas of grassland on the Nyika and drops dramatically down the wooded escarpment on the eastern edge of the plateau. The trek goes from Chelinda Camp to the mission town of Livingstonia, via the villages of Chakaka and Phoka Court, and takes three days, with the possibility of a fourth if you can't find a lift from Livingstonia down to the main Karonga-Mzuzu road that runs beside the lake. If you're short of time, and feeling fit, the first two stages can be done in one day, but it's long and hard.

Only half of the trek is inside the park boundary; the second section passes through villages and fields, but this provides an interesting contrast to the untouched landscape of the park.

If you do this route you have to pay your guide and porters extra to cover the costs of transport and accommodation on their way back to the park. Even if they decide to keep

the money and walk back, it's fair enough: going back up onto the plateau is one hell of a trek! (See the Guides & Porters section.)

This route cannot be done in reverse, unless you go out and back the same way. Apart from it being very tough the other way, you are not allowed to enter the park on foot unless accompanied by a game scout. And this can only be arranged at Chelinda.

Stage 1: Chelinda Camp to Phata Stream

(18 km, 6-7 hours)
From Chelinda Camp, go to the east side of the Chelinda River and follow the track eastward, then south towards Chelinda Peak. There's a shortcut footpath that keeps nearer the river. To your right you can see the Chelinda dams. You meet the main track, follow it briefly, then take another path on its north side. About four hours from Chelinda you cross the track to Nthakati Peak a few times, then drop to cross a tributary of the Phata Stream, (pronounced Pata) reached after another 1½ hours. From there, go up and over a rise, then down to reach the main Phata Stream, crossed by a very basic log bridge. There's a good place for camping next to the river, with the main peak of Nthakati to the north-west overlooking the site.

Stage 2: Phata Stream to Chakaka

(12 km, 5-6 hours)
From Phata Stream, follow the path up the east side of the valley for about 1½ hours to reach the crest of a large broad ridge. For the first time on this trek you can see the edge of the escarpment, with Livingstonia on top of its own small plateau in the middle distance, and beyond that the blue haze of Lake Malawi. The path runs along the crest of the ridge, roughly south-east, following the line of the park boundary before the 1976 expansion.

Turn off the main ridge onto the secondary ridge. Far below in the valley you can see a patchwork of fields, stopping at the edge of the forest which marks the park boundary today. Continue following the ridge down, through forest, bush and long grass, as the ridge turns to a narrow spur with the steep Mpondo and Thithi valleys on either side. You leave the park, and pass huts and small fields. This is the outskirts of Chakaka Village. There are many paths, and your guide will probably have to ask directions. Continue down, still quite steeply, to finally reach a bridge near the junction of the Mpondo and Thithi rivers. On the other side of the bridge is a small coffee-drying compound. The manager is friendly and will let you camp here. Your guide will probably sleep in one of the caretakers' huts.

Stage 3: Chakaka to Livingstonia
(16 km, 5-6 hours)

Follow the small dirt road which leaves the coffee compound and goes down the valley. To your left is the large North Rumphi River. Keep going for about two to three hours to reach the main dirt road between Livingstonia and Rumphi, at a small village called Phoka Court.

This road used to be the main road through the north of Malawi between Mzuzu and Karonga. It's not used much now, as there's a new main road on the other side of Livingstonia, nearer the lake. Phoka is the name of the people in this area, and there was a local 'chief's court' here in colonial times. Today there's a small resthouse, a market and a few shops. A bus from Rumphi arrives in Phoka Court most afternoons, 'sleeps' there, and returns to Rumphi early next morning. The road is steep, so in bad weather the bus doesn't always arrive. After taking you to Livingstonia, your guide will come back here to catch the bus to Rumphi on his way back to Chelinda by road.

From Phoka Court, follow the main dirt road uphill, across the Kaziwiziwi River, and past the old road to the coal mine to reach some steep switchbacks. (The mine is now linked to the new main road.)

Alternative Route It is possible to leave the Chakaka-Phoka Court track about halfway down, drop to cross the river, then go up the ridge on the other side through fields and groups of huts, to come down by the Kaziwiziwi River and then meet the main dirt road to the north of Phoka Court at the foot of the switchback. (This is a shorter route, which avoids some of the dirt road section, but it takes about the same time, as you have an extra ridge to cross.)

The road starts to switchback up some steep ridges, but your guide will know some short cuts. These are even steeper, but not as long. To reach Livingstonia you drop to cross a large stream, then there's one final slog up a steep escarpment to reach the edge of the town near the secondary school. Follow the neat dirt road past the school and the church to reach the Stone House, a museum and small guesthouse. You can buy tea here, and this is where you'll pay off your guide.

Places to Stay in Linvingstonia There are two places to stay: the *Stone House*, built in 1903 and used by Dr Laws, the leading missionary, for 25 years, where comfortable bedrooms, complete with Victorian furniture, cost KM 22 per person; and the *Resthouse*, where things are a little more spartan, for MK 12. Meals are available at both places, or you can use the kitchen in the resthouse to prepare your own food. Camping is allowed at the resthouse garden for MK 6 per person. From the garden you can see down to Lake Malawi, and the beautiful curved spit of land on the north side of the bay that appears in the picture in the church window.

Stage 4: Livingstonia to Chitimba
(20 km, 4-5 hours)

From the crossroads near the resthouse at the end of the main street, continue downhill on a narrow track, then turn right to meet a larger dirt road that comes from the other side of the town. Then you just keep going down and down and down. This is the notorious Livingstonia Escarpment road. The road goes round some pretty sharp bends, and the last 20 are real hairpins. You know there are 20, because each one is numbered. From Livingstonia town, down to the start of

Livingstonia

The history of Livingstonia is described briefly in the introductory section of this chapter. It's a fascinating place; like a small Scottish town teleported into the heart of Africa, complete with red-brick shops, post office, church and clock tower.

It's well worth spending a couple of hours wandering around the town. As well as the museum, there's a secondary school, with a facade just like any other Victorian English grammar school, and the church built in Scottish style, with a beautiful stained- glass window of David Livingstone and his two companions Juma and Guze (sometimes spelt Suzi), with his sextant and medicine chest, and Lake Malawi in the background. Other places of interest include the David Gordon Memorial Hospital, once the biggest hospital in Central Africa, a huge bell on a pedestal that is now a memorial to the Laws family, and the stone cairn that marks the place where Dr Laws and Uriah Chirwa camped in 1894 when they reached this area and decided to build the mission. There's a post office, where you can also make phone calls, a few shops selling basics, a market, on the road between the clock tower and the resthouse, and a mobile bank that comes on the first and third Mondays of every month. There's even the Khondowe Craft Shop selling carvings and clothing made by local people. (Khondowe was the original name of this area, before it was changed to Livingstonia.) Outside the Stone House you might notice some huge letters almost hidden by the grass, designed to be read by anyone who happened to be flying over Livingstonia in a small plane. They read *Ephesians 2-14*.

You can also visit the Manchewe Falls, about five km from the town. This is a spectacular waterfall, about 50 metres high, with a cave behind it where local people used to hide from slave traders. Swimming is possible, too. There are several paths leading to the falls, and several young boys hanging around the Resthouse who will show you the way for a few kwacha. Allow an hour going down and 1½ hours back up. Alternatively, if you're walking to Chitimba, you can go via the falls on the way down. ■

the steep section, there are some short cuts through the fields: the easiest thing to do is ask one of the local boys to show you the way, and pay him a small fee. Paths cut across some of the lower bends too, but many of these are so steep they're hardly any quicker than the road and a lot harder on the legs. From the bottom of the escarpment it's less than a km to Chitimba Village and the junction with the main tarred Karonga-Mzuzu road.

If you can't face the walk down the escarpment, there's no bus, but you might be lucky and find a lift going down to Chitimba. The local shopkeeper goes down to get supplies about once a week or, if it's not his usual day, he'll take you for a negotiable fee (around MK 40).

At Chitimba, you can stay at *Chafika & Sons Resthouse* in basic rooms with mosquito nets (essential) for MK 5, or camp round the back for slightly less. Meals are also basic, but filling. If you want to keep on the move, the bus stop is right outside. There are three buses a day from Karonga to

Mzuzu, via Rumphi, or you can try your luck hitching.

OTHER ROUTES

Due to the nature of the trekking on Nyika, there's an almost endless selection of routes that you can plan yourself, using the map, the knowledge of the game scouts, and a sense of adventure. The warden of the national park, Mr Hector Banda, and his staff, are keen to promote trekking in the park and will be happy to give you help and advice. The information centre may also give you some more ideas. Below are a few more routes that have been suggested by Mr Banda, the scouts, and some other trekkers.

Chakomanamkazi Rock to Fingira Rock

This route traverses the lower wooded hills of the south- western part of the park. Starting from Chakomanamkazi Rock, to the south of the Zambian Resthouse, follow the new track south-westerly, then aim south to Vitintiza Hill and follow the Runyina River southwards, camping on its eastern bank, before crossing a major ridge and tributary of the Runyina to reach the huge rocky cone of Fingira Rock. Allow three days for this section. To reach Chakomanamkazi from Chelinda, take the park tracks via Lake Kaulime and the Zambian Resthouse junction, as described in the Nyika Highlights Route (one day), or cut straight across from Kaulime, via Chosi Peak (one long day). From Fingira back to Chelinda by park track is almost 30 km, another long day.

Fingira Rock to Thazima Gate

Starting from Fingira Rock, you can follow the last section of the route described in the previous paragraph in reverse to reach the Runyina River, then continue westwards to meet the main park track just north of Thazima Gate. Allow one to two days.

Nkonjera Peak to Rumphi Town

If you do Wilderness Trail 3 (Nkonjera Peak), described earlier, after reaching Nkonjera Peak, instead of going back north towards Chelinda, you can continue heading south from the summit and follow old hunters' paths to Rumphi town. This is another day's walk, and it takes you outside the park boundary. This route cannot legally be done in reverse, as you are not allowed to walk into the park without a game scout.

Chelinda Camp to Juniper Forest

From Chelinda Camp follow the Chelinda River southwards, keeping to the valley sides to avoid boggy sections. You meet the park track which crosses the Chelinda River by Chelinda Bridge, below a small mountain called, strangely enough, Chelinda Peak. It's worth going up to the top: this is one of the few peaks in the centre of the plateau with exposed rock at its summit. From there you can continue down to the Juniper Forest, where it's possible to stay in the cabin (see Places to Stay). Allow one long day for this, or two shorter days.

Other Trekking Areas

The Mulanje Massif and the Nyika Plateau are the only mountain wilderness areas in Malawi with good long-distance trekking opportunities.

Malawi also has several excellent smaller mountains which can be covered in a day, although they are beyond the scope of this book. These include mounts Soche, Michiru and Ndirande, the 'Three Peaks of Blantyre', and Dedza and Dzalanyama mountains, between Blantyre and Lilongwe, near the border with Mozambique. Walks in these areas are covered in some of the visitors' guides mentioned in the Malawi Guidebooks & Maps section. It is also possible to walk in the low hills of the Nankumba Peninsula, near the beaches of Cape Maclear, an ideal place to rest up for a few days in between long treks on Mulanje or Nyika.

Other areas where longer treks and walks are possible are outlined here:

THE ZOMBA PLATEAU

The Zomba Plateau rises steeply, like a small version of Mulanje, with sheer escarpments rising over 1000 metres above the plain. This plateau cannot be called wilderness, in the same way as Mulanje and Nyika, but it does have several narrow ridges along the edge of the escarpment, with dramatic views over the plains below, plus a network of paths and tracks in the centre of the plateau through silent pine forests or patches of indigenous woodland, passing waterfalls and small lakes. You could easily pass three or four days doing some fairly easy hiking here, between more strenuous treks on Mulanje and Nyika.

As well as being smaller, Zomba differs from Mulanje in other ways: Mulanje is made up of several separate basins, whereas Zomba is composed of only two, divided by the Domasi Valley; you can't go up Mulanje by car (which keeps it remote and untouched), but Zomba has roads to the top, and much of the southern

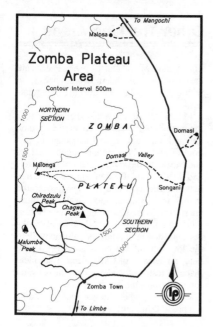

On the southern part of the plateau, the walking routes follow paths and tracks. Some visitors drive around the plateau, but you're unlikely to see more than a few cars, especially on weekdays. All the track junctions on Zomba are numbered. These numbers are indicated on signboards at each junction, and are referred to in this section by the prefix J.

Guidebooks & Maps

A small pamphlet called *Zomba Mountain, A Walkers' Guide* may be available for sale in the reception of the Ku Chawe Inn (see Places to Stay). This was written in 1975, and much has changed since then, but it contains many route descriptions, plus some useful background information.

The Zomba Plateau is covered by the government survey 1:50,000 map sheet 1535/A4 (Zomba), which shows most of the paths and tracks on the plateau, although some new tracks have been constructed since the map was published.

Supplies

Zomba town has several supermarkets and a big well-stocked market. There is no shop or market on the plateau. Drinks, snacks and meals are available at the hotel. Local children sell fruit, vegetables, breadcakes, and some other basic foods, on the roadside between the hotel and the campsite.

Places to Stay

Zomba Town There are a few places to choose from in Zomba town, including the *Government Hostel*, which is actually quite a smart hotel near the State House (parliament building), the *Ndindeya Two Resthouse*, nearer the town centre, with simple but clean rooms and friendly staff, and the cheap *Government Resthouse* by the bus station with basic rooms and camping allowed.

On the Zomba Plateau On the plateau, at the end of the 'Up' road, is the *Ku Chawe Inn*, a good hotel with singles/doubles at MK 250/350, as well as a restaurant and bar.

section of the plateau has been planted with pines. Zomba also has a hotel, a campsite and several picnic places to cater for visitors (mainly local residents who come up at the weekend), plus a permanent population of forestry workers. Several large houses, set in private grounds, have also been built along the south-eastern edge of the plateau.

You can walk on Zomba at any time, but the best weather is during dry period from May to October. After the rains, in May and June, the wild undergrowth is difficult to pass through and paths can be indistinct. As the grass and bushes dry out, and the risk of fire becomes more serious, firebreaks on the plateau are cleared, and the paths, which often follow the firebreaks, are easier to find.

The Zomba Plateau is a forest reserve. A lot of the southern part of the plateau has been planted with pine, but the northern part (north of the Domasi Valley) has been set aside as a wilderness area. There are no tracks or paths in this area and visitors are not encouraged to walk here.

There's also a very nice campsite on the plateau, about one km from the hotel, with water, fireplaces, toilets, showers (sometimes hot), and a guard during the day, for MK 5.

Access

At the foot of the southern slopes of the Zomba Plateau is the large town of Zomba, linked to both Blantyre and Lilongwe by good tarred roads. From Zomba town a tarred road leads through the outskirts, past the State House and then steeply up the escarpment to the top of the plateau (about 10 km). After the last junction, the road is one-way only, and called the 'Up' road. The 'Down' road descends further to the east.

There is no public transport from Zomba town up to the plateau. You can walk up the Up road, which has excellent views (often missed by drivers, who have to concentrate on the narrow turns), or you can try hitching.

The best way is to walk up the Potato Path, which goes straight up the escarpment.

The Potato Path

This is a footpath linking the Domasi Valley to Zomba town, running straight over the southern half of the Zomba Plateau. The Domasi Valley has fertile soil and a reliable water supply ideal for growing vegetables, which the local people carry to the big market in Zomba town along this path, making it well worn and easy to follow.

The start of the path is signposted at a sharp left-hand bend on the Up road about two km from Zomba town. The path climbs steeply, through woodland, crossing a forestry track and the Down road, to reach the top of the plateau near the hotel. Allow two to three hours for the ascent.

Routes on the Plateau

Once you've reached the top of the plateau, you can base yourself at the hotel or the campsite for a couple of nights and explore the area on the days in between. Basically, you can go where you like anywhere south of the Domasi Valley. There's a maze of paths and tracks, but with a compass and a

map, you're unlikely to get hopelessly lost. For help with orientation, there's even a model of the plateau in the hut by the hotel.

Williams Falls & Ngondola Village From the hotel or campsite follow park tracks to the crossroads at junction three (J 3), over a bridge, past a track on the left to the trout farm, past a track on the right (J 4) towards Mandala Falls, and past a track on the left (J 5) to the forestry houses. The small but picturesque Williams Falls are down to your left after about an hour. The track curves round to the right, but take the path straight on, over the stream. This is the Potato Path again. You'll probably see local people walking along it.

Follow the path up through plantation to meet a track at a junction (J 21). The path follows the track again until a left curve, where the path goes straight on, over a small bridge, and meets another track. Turn left onto this track and follow it until, at a right bend, the path forks off left and up over a small hill to rejoin the track on the other side. This track meets the Outer Circular Drive (OCD) at a junction (J 10) near several small huts. This is Ngondola Village. (Allow about three hours from the campsite.)

At the junction avoid the small path leading straight on between the huts. Turn right onto the OCD, then fork immediately left to follow a track down through trees to the edge of the Domasi Valley. Here you get a good view of the northern half of the Zomba Plateau (also called the Malosa Plateau). The rolling open grassland of the north contrasts sharply with the pine forests of the south, showing how the whole plateau would have appeared before the plantations were established.

From Ngondola Village you can retrace to the hotel and campsite or make your own way back by other paths and tracks. The following description is only one of many ways.

From J 10 continue east on the OCD. A track from Ngondola Village joins from the left. Turn right off the OCD onto a minor track, dropping down through plantation, to

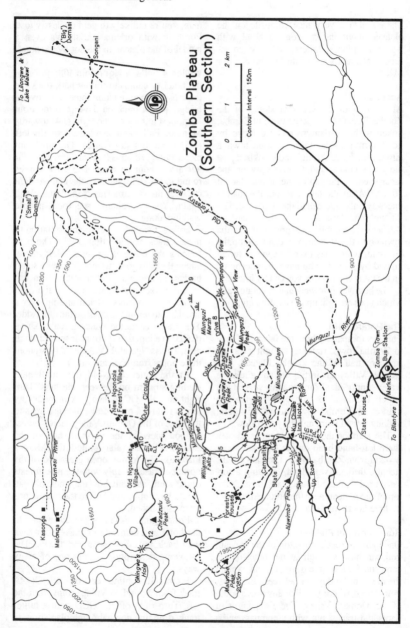

Zomba Plateau (Southern Section)

Contour Interval 150m

0   1   2 km

meet another track at a junction (not numbered). Turn left onto this track (effectively straight on) and continue downhill to J 20 where a track joins from the right. Keep straight on, crossing a small bridge. A track joins from the left, but this is not obvious. Keep straight on, crossing the main Mlunguzi River, to meet the OCD again (J 6). Turn right, and follow the OCD past the track on the left that goes up to the summit of Chagwa Peak (an interesting diversion, with excellent views from the top, which takes an extra one to 1½ hours), to reach the Williams Falls on the right. From here retrace the route described earlier from the falls back to the campsite and hotel.

The Zomba Plateau Circuit The Zomba Plateau south of the Domasi Valley takes the form of a large basin, surrounded by a rim of higher peaks and ridges. This basin is the catchment area for the Mlunguzi River, which begins as a marsh on the eastern side of the plateau then flows in an arc across its centre, finally leaving the basin at the lowest point in the rim to drop down the Mlunguzi Gorge to Zomba town.

This route follows the outer rim of the basin, using a combination of paths and tracks, and passing many of Zomba's highlights including the summit of Malumbe Peak (the highest point on Zomba), Chingwe's Hole, Queen's View and the Mlunguzi Dam.

Start near the hut that has the model of the plateau. Fork immediately left, towards State Lodge, and follow the tarred road up to Skyline View (a viewpoint and site of the cableway which used to link the plantations on the plateau with the sawmill outside Zomba town). From Skyline View the ridge up towards Nawimbe Peak, with a firetower near the summit, can be clearly seen. Aim towards this, along a track, passing between huts, to follow a firebreak along the ridge crest. Another firebreak runs to the right of the one on the ridge. Take the firebreak which is easiest to follow, to reach the firetower and the beacon on the summit of Nawimbe Peak. From the firetower you get

an excellent view to the north-east over the whole Zomba plateau, and to the south down to Zomba town and the surrounding plains, with the Mulanje Massif often visible in the distance.

From Nawimbe summit, follow the firebreak along the ridge crest, which can be rocky and overgrown in places, to reach the radio masts on the summit of Malumbe Peak (2085 metres).

From the summit of Malumbe a track leads down the north-western side of the ridge to meet the OCD at J 13. (Just before this junction a footpath on the left cuts off a large loop in the track.) Follow the OCD, turning left onto a small track (J 12), to reach Chingwe's Hole, about three to four hours from the campsite.

Local legend tells that Chingwe's Hole is bottomless, and was once used as a burial chamber. In more recent times, rock falls have reduced the hole to no more than 20 metres deep, and the trees that grow around the rim make it look even less impressive. Far more dramatic is the view along the escarpment from a point on the edge less than a minute's walk from Chingwe's Hole. Have a look at that instead!

From Chingwe's Hole you leave the dramatic outer edge of the Zomba Plateau and follow the OCD along a low ridge that separates the northern rim of the Mlunguzi basin from the Domasi Valley.

Keep on the track, past J 11 to reach J 10, where the Potato Path crosses the OCD.

Continue on the OCD, past several minor tracks on the left and right, to reach J 9, where a track turns off left towards Songani. Keep on the OCD, and take the next track on the left to reach Emperor's View. A track runs along the top of the escarpment (keeping the edge to the left) to reach Queen's View.

From Queen's View (named after Queen Elizabeth, wife of King George VI, who visited Zomba in 1957) and Emperor's View (after Emperor Haile Selassie of Ethiopia, here in 1964) you can get excellent views over Zomba town and the plains on the south- eastern side of the plateau (two to three hours from Chingwe's Hole).

From Queen's View follow the track that runs along the escarpment edge, then tends right, away from the edge and into woodland. A track joins from the right, and another branches off to the left (leading to the summit of Mlunguzi Peak). Keep straight on, to reach Chagwa Dam on your right. As the track curves right to cross the dam wall, take the path straight on into a grassy area, heading right and down to cross a stream and enter woodland. A path joins from the right. Continue through bush and woodland, steeply down to meet a track. Turn right onto the track and follow it over a bridge. As the track curves to the right, the path forks off to the left and continues to drop down through woodland to meet another track. Cross straight over this to reach Mlunguzi Dam on the right side of the path. The path crosses the concrete dam wall and joins a track leading steeply up the bank away from the dam. Turn left at the first junction and then right at the second to meet the Down road.

Turn right onto the Down road (ie heading up), and follow it, past a track on the right to Mandala Falls, to fork left at the next junction, past the school on the left to reach the campsite (two to three hours from Queen's View).

Leaving the Plateau There are several ways off the plateau. You can retrace the Potato Path, or follow the Down road, where you might get a lift with a tourist car or logging truck.

Alternatively, from J 9 on the OCD, you can follow the track towards Songani, and follow old logging tracks and paths all the way down (steeply) to Songani Village (about 15 km from the OCD) on the main tarred road about 15 km north-east of Zomba town. From here you can get public transport

or hitch back to Zomba town. It may also be possible to branch off right on the way down, to follow some of the old forest tracks that run (more gradually) down the eastern escarpment straight to the northern end of Zomba town.

It is also possible to drop off the northern escarpment into the Domasi Valley. This is the northern section of the Potato Path. From Ngondola Village the path aims downhill and divides in several places, leading either to Malonga, the small settlement at the head of the valley, or to any of the others spread along on the valley floor. A large path leads eastwards along the valley floor, and meets a track running close to the river, which reaches the small village of Domasi. The track continues down to Songani Village on the main tarred road about 15 km north-east of Zomba town. (Do not confuse 'small' Domasi with 'big' Domasi, a larger village on the east side of the main road.)

MANGOCHI MOUNTAIN

One other interesting area for walkers is Mangochi Mountain, at the southern end of Lake Malawi. This is a hilly, tree-covered area, which is protected as a forest reserve. There are the ruins of an old colonial fort here, and elephants from the nearby Liwonde National Park sometimes migrate up into the forested hills during the rainy season. Walking trips into the forest reserve, for two or three days, can be arranged at the Palm Beach Leisure Resort, which is on the lake shore to the north of Mangochi town. This is a fairly smart place with chalets, bungalows and a campsite, set on a beautiful beach surrounded by (not surprisingly) a grove of palm trees. You can get more information from a travel agent in Blantyre or Lilongwe.

Index

Keep in touch!

We love hearing from you and think you'd like to hear from us.

The Lonely Planet Newsletter covers the when, where, how and what of travel. (AND it's free!)

When...*is the right time to see reindeer in Finland?*
Where...*can you hear the best palm-wine music in Ghana?*
How...*do you get from Asunción to Areguá by steam train?*
What...*should you leave behind to avoid hassles with customs in Iran?*

To join our mailing list just contact us at any of our offices. (details below)

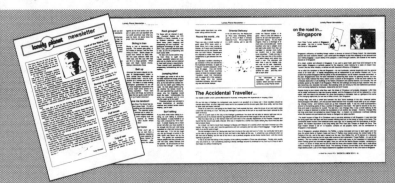

Every issue includes:

- *a letter from Lonely Planet founders Tony and Maureen Wheeler*
- *travel diary from a Lonely Planet author - find out what it's really like out on the road*
- *feature article on an important and topical travel issue*
- *a selection of recent letters from our readers*
- *the latest travel news from all over the world*
- *details on Lonely Planet's new and forthcoming releases*

Also available Lonely Planet T-shirts. 100% heavy weight cotton (S, M, L, XL)

LONELY PLANET PUBLICATIONS
Australia: PO Box 617, Hawthorn, 3122, Victoria (tel: 03-819 1877)
USA: Embarcadero West, 155 Filbert Street, Suite 251, Oakland, CA 94607 (tel: 510-893 8555)
UK: Devonshire House, 12 Barley Mow Passage, Chiswick, London W4 4PH (tel: 081-742 3161)

Guides to Africa

Africa on a shoestring
From Marrakesh to Kampala, Mozambique to Mauritania, Johannesburg to Cairo – this guidebook has all the facts on travelling in Africa. Comprehensive information on more than 50 countries.

Central Africa - a travel survival kit
This guide tells where to go to meet gorillas in the jungle, how to catch a steamer down the Congo...even the best beer to wash down grilled boa constrictor! Covers Cameroun, Central African Republic, Chad, The Congo, Equatorial Guinea, Gabon, São Tomé & Principe, and Zaïre.

East Africa - a travel survival kit
Detailed information on Kenya, Uganda, Rwanda, Burundi, eastern Zaïre and Tanzania. The latest edition includes a 32-page full-colour Safari Guide.

Egypt & the Sudan - a travel survival kit
This guide takes you into and beyond the spectacular and mysterious pyramids, temples, tombs, monasteries, mosques and bustling main streets of Egypt and the Sudan.

Kenya - a travel survival kit
This superb guide features a 32-page 'Safari Guide' with colour photographs, illustrations and information on East Africa's famous wildlife.

Morocco, Algeria & Tunisia - a travel survival kit
Reap the rewards of getting off the beaten track with this practical guide.

South Africa, Lesotho & Swaziland - a travel survival kit
Travel to southern Africa and you'll be surprised by its cultural diversity and incredible beauty. There's no better place to see Africa's amazing wildlife. All the essential travel details are included in this guide as well as information about wildlife reserves.

West Africa - a travel survival kit
All the necessary information for independent travel in Benin, Burkino Faso, Cape Verde, Côte d'Ivoire, The Gambia, Ghana, Guinea, Guinea-Bissau, Liberia, Mali, Mauritania, Niger, Nigeria, Senegal, Sierra Leone and Togo.

Zimbabwe, Botswana & Namibia - a travel survival kit
Exotic wildlife, breathtaking scenery and fascinating people...this comprehensive guide shows a wilder, older side of Africa for the adventurous traveller. Includes a 32-page colour Safari Guide.

Also available:
Swahili phrasebook, **Arabic (Egyptian)** phrasebook & **Arabic (Moroccan)** phrasebook

Lonely Planet Guidebooks

Lonely Planet guidebooks cover every accessible part of Asia as well as Australia, the Pacific, South America, Africa, the Middle East, Europe and parts of North America. There are five series: *travel survival kits*, covering a country for a range of budgets; *shoestring guides* with compact information for low-budget travel in a major region; *walking guides*; *city guides* and *phrasebooks*.

Australia & the Pacific
Australia
Bushwalking in Australia
Islands of Australia's Great Barrier Reef
Fiji
Melbourne city guide
Micronesia
New Caledonia
New Zealand
Tramping in New Zealand
Papua New Guinea
Bushwalking in Papua New Guinea
Papua New Guinea phrasebook
Rarotonga & the Cook Islands
Samoa
Solomon Islands
Sydney city guide
Tahiti & French Polynesia
Tonga
Vanuatu
Victoria

South-East Asia
Bali & Lombok
Bangkok city guide
Myanmar (Burma)
Burmese phrasebook
Cambodia
Indonesia
Indonesia phrasebook
Malaysia, Singapore & Brunei
Philippines
Pilipino phrasebook
Singapore city guide
South-East Asia on a shoestring
Thailand
Thai phrasebook
Vietnam, Laos & Cambodia
Vietnamese phrasebook

North-East Asia
China
Mandarin Chinese phrasebook
Hong Kong, Macau & Canton
Japan
Japanese phrasebook
Korea
Korean phrasebook
Mongolia
North-East Asia on a shoestring
Seoul city guide
Taiwan
Tibet
Tibet phrasebook
Tokyo city guide

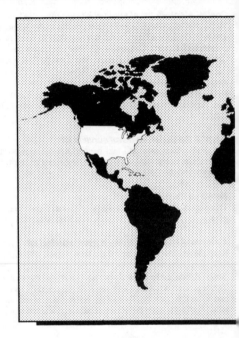

West Asia
Trekking in Turkey
Turkey
Turkish phrasebook
West Asia on a shoestring

Middle East
Arab Gulf States
Egypt & the Sudan
Egyptian Arabic phrasebook
Iran
Israel
Jordan & Syria
Yemen

Indian Ocean
Madagascar & Comoros
Maldives & Islands of the East Indian Ocean
Mauritius, Réunion & Seychelles

Mail Order

Lonely Planet guidebooks are distributed worldwide. They are also available by mail order from Lonely Planet, so if you have difficulty finding a title please write to us. US and Canadian residents should write to Embarcadero West, 155 Filbert St, Suite 251, Oakland CA 94607, USA; European residents should write to Devonshire House, 12 Barley Mow Passage, Chiswick, London W4 4PH; and residents of other countries to PO Box 617, Hawthorn, Victoria 3122, Australia.

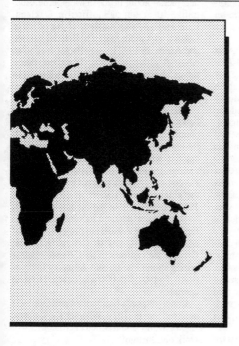

Indian Subcontinent
Bangladesh
India
Hindi/Urdu phrasebook
Trekking in the Indian Himalaya
Karakoram Highway
Kashmir, Ladakh & Zanskar
Nepal
Trekking in the Nepal Himalaya
Nepal phrasebook
Pakistan
Sri Lanka
Sri Lanka phrasebook

Africa
Africa on a shoestring
Central Africa
East Africa
Trekking in East Africa
Kenya
Swahili phrasebook
Morocco, Algeria & Tunisia
Moroccan Arabic phrasebook
South Africa, Lesotho & Swaziland
Zimbabwe, Botswana & Namibia
West Africa

Central America
Baja California
Central America on a shoestring
Costa Rica
La Ruta Maya
Mexico

North America
Alaska
Canada
Hawaii

South America
Argentina, Uruguay & Paraguay
Bolivia
Brazil
Brazilian phrasebook
Chile & Easter Island
Colombia
Ecuador & the Galápagos Islands
Latin American Spanish phrasebook
Peru
Quechua phrasebook
South America on a shoestring
Trekking in the Patagonian Andes

Europe
Dublin city guide
Eastern Europe on a shoestring
Eastern Europe phrasebook
Finland
Iceland, Greenland & the Faroe Islands
Mediterranean Europe on a shoestring
Mediterranean Europe phrasebook
Poland
Scandinavian & Baltic Europe on a shoestring
Scandinavian Europe phrasebook
Trekking in Spain
Trekking in Greece
USSR
Russian phrasebook
Western Europe on a shoestring
Western Europe phrasebook

The Lonely Planet Story

Lonely Planet published its first book in 1973 in response to the numerous 'How did you do it?' questions Maureen and Tony Wheeler were asked after driving, bussing, hitching, sailing and railing their way from England to Australia.

Written at a kitchen table and hand collated, trimmed and stapled, *Across Asia on the Cheap* became an instant local bestseller, inspiring thoughts of another book.

Eighteen months in South-East Asia resulted in their second guide, *South-East Asia on a shoestring*, which they put together in a backstreet Chinese hotel in Singapore in 1975. The 'yellow bible' as it quickly became known to backpackers around the world, soon became *the* guide to the region. It has sold well over half a million copies and is now in its 7th edition, still retaining its familiar yellow cover.

Today there are over 120 Lonely Planet titles in print – books that have that same adventurous approach to travel as those early guides; books that 'assume you know how to get your luggage off the carousel' as one reviewer put it.

Although Lonely Planet initially specialised in guides to Asia, they now cover most regions of the world, including the Pacific, South America, Africa, the Middle East and Europe. The list of *walking guides* and *phrasebooks* (for 'unusual' languages such as Quechua, Swahili, Nepalese and Egyptian Arabic) is also growing rapidly.

The emphasis continues to be on travel for independent travellers. Tony and Maureen still travel for several months of each year and play an active part in the writing, updating and quality control of Lonely Planet's guides.

They have been joined by over 50 authors, 54 staff – mainly editors, cartographers, & designers – at our office in Melbourne, Australia, 10 at our US office in Oakland, California and another three at our office in London to handle sales for Britain, Europe and Africa. In 1992 Lonely Planet opened an editorial office in Paris. Travellers themselves also make a valuable contribution to the guides through the feedback we receive in thousands of letters each year.

The people at Lonely Planet strongly believe that travellers can make a positive contribution to the countries they visit, both through their appreciation of the countries' culture, wildlife and natural features, and through the money they spend. In addition, the company makes a direct contribution to the countries and regions it covers. Since 1986 a percentage of the income from each book has been donated to ventures such as famine relief in Africa; aid projects in India; agricultural projects in Central America; Greenpeace's efforts to halt French nuclear testing in the Pacific and Amnesty International. In 1992 $85,000 was donated to such causes.

Lonely Planet's basic travel philosophy is summed up in Tony Wheeler's comment, 'Don't worry about whether your trip will work out. Just go!'